The **Rough Guide** to

Rome

written and researched by

Martin Dunford

with additional contributions by

Jeffrey Kennedy and Norm Roberson

**ROUGH
GUIDES**

NEW YORK • LONDON • DELHI

www.roughguides.com

△ Piazza San Pietro

Introduction to
Rome

Rome is arguably the most fascinating city in the world, an ancient and beguiling place packed with the relics of well over two thousand years of inhabitation. You could spend a month here and still only scratch the surface. Yet it is so much more than an open-air museum: its culture, its food, its people, make up a modern, vibrant city that would be worthy of a visit irrespective of its history. As a historic place, it is special enough, but as a contemporary European capital, it is utterly unique.

Perfectly placed between Italy's North and South, and heartily despised by both, Rome is perhaps the ideal capital for a country only fully united in 1870 and possessing no shortage of great rival cities. Once the seat of the most powerful empire in history, and still the home of the papacy within the Vatican city state, Rome is seen as a place somewhat apart from the rest of the country, spending money made elsewhere on the bloated government machine. Romans, the thinking seems to go, are a lazy lot, not to be trusted and living very nicely off the fat of the rest of the land. Even the locals find it hard to disagree with this analysis: in a city with under three million people, there are 600,000 office workers, compared to an industrial workforce of one sixth of that.

For the traveller, all of this is much less evident than the sheer weight of history that the city supports. Beginning with the city's celebrated classical features, most visibly the Colosseum, and the Forum and Palatine Hill, Rome boasts an almost uninterrupted sequence of spectacular monuments – from early Christian basilicas, Romanesque churches, Renaissance palaces, right up to the fountains and churches of the Baroque period, which perhaps more

than any other era has determined the look of the city today. There is then the modern epoch, with the ponderous Neoclassical architecture of the post-Unification period to the self-publicizing edifices of the Mussolini years. All these various eras crowd in on one other to an almost overwhelming degree: there are medieval churches atop ancient basilicas above Roman palaces;

houses and apartment blocks incorporate fragments of eroded Roman columns, carvings and inscriptions; roads and piazzas follow the lines of ancient amphitheatres and stadiums.

All of which means Rome is not an easy place to absorb on one visit, and you need to take things slowly, even if you have only a few days here. Most of the sights can be approached from a variety of directions, and part of the city's allure is stumbling across things by accident, gradually piecing together the whole, rather than marching around to a timetable on a predetermined route. In any case, it's hard to get anywhere very fast. Despite regular pledges to ban motor vehicles from the city centre, the congestion can be awful. On foot, it's easy to lose a sense of direction winding about in the twisting old streets but you're so likely to come upon something interesting it hardly makes any difference.

Rome doesn't have the nightlife of, say, Paris or London, or even of its Italian counterparts to the north – culturally it's rather provincial – and its food, while delicious, is earthy rather than haute cuisine. But its atmosphere is like no other city – a monumental, busy capital and yet an appealingly relaxed place, with a centre that has yet to be taken over by chainstores and big multinational hotels. Above all, there has perhaps never been a

Ancient Rome

Everyone who visits Rome wants to see the sites of the ancient city, and these are easy enough to find – they literally litter the city centre. There is however, one concentrated sector that could keep you busy for a couple of days on its own: the Forum, the heart of the city during the Republic, and the adjacent Palatine Hill, where the ultra-rich lived – and where the city was legendarily founded by Romulus and Remus. These two areas are surrounded by the columns and plinths of other fora built during Imperial times that are under continuous excavation, as well as the iconic bulk of the Colosseum, and some recently opened Roman houses up on the Celian Hill. Just beyond, the Baths of Caracalla and Domus Aurea both give a perfect impression of the gargantuan building tendencies of the late Empire and its despots, while back in the city centre the giant dome of the Pantheon demonstrates the ingenuity of its architects. A short trip outside the city, the ruins of Ostia, Rome's former port, are also strikingly well preserved. Once you have seen what's left of the monuments and buildings of the Romans, take some time to visit the city's amazing classical museums – the two main branches of the Museo Nazionale Romano, the Palazzo Altemps and Palazzo Massimo, plus the Capitoline Museums and its branch at Centrale Montemartini. Together they house the most awesomely complete collection of Roman sculpture, frescoes and other relics that you'll find anywhere – all unmissable.

So much to see, so little time

As you'll see from our "32 things not to miss" (p.x), you can't see everything on a first visit to Rome. The best thing is to enjoy the city: take in the attractions that interest you most at an easy pace, and look forward to the next time you're here when you can see what you missed. The following suggested itineraries give you an idea of what's possible in a day. They're mainly designed around the key sights and include suggestions for where and when to have lunch. But don't be afraid to skip the galleries and monuments and just wander!

Three days
- Galleria Doria Pamphilj; Pantheon; centro storico (lunch); Piazza Navona; Palazzo Altemps.
- Forum; Colosseum; Palatine (picnic lunch); Capitoline Museums; Jewish Ghetto; Campo de' Fiori.
- St Peter's; Borgo (lunch); Vatican Museums.

Six days
As above plus...
- Galleria Barberini; Fontana di Trevi; Piazza di Spagna (lunch); Piazza del Popolo; Castel Sant' Angelo.
- Via del Corso; Via Veneto; Pincio Gardens; Galleria Borghese; Villa Borghese (picnic lunch); Villa Giulia.
- Domus Aurea; Monti (lunch); Santa Maria Maggiore; Palazzo Massimo.

Nine days
As above plus...
- Villa Farnesina/ Galleria Corsini; Trastevere (lunch); Janiculum Hill.
- Aventine Hill; Baths of Caracalla; Testaccio (lunch); Centrale Montemartini.
- San Clemente; San Giovanni in Laterano (lunch); Aurelian Wall; Via Appia Antica.

better time to visit the city, whose notoriously crumbling infrastructure is looking and functioning better than it has done for some time – the result of the feverish activity that took place in the last months of the twentieth

century to have the city centre looking its best for the Church's millennium jubilee. Museums, churches and other buildings that have been "in restoration" as long as anyone can remember have reopened, and some of the city's historic collections have been rehoused, making it easier to get the most out of Rome.

Orientation

Rome's city centre is divided neatly into distinct blocks. The warren of streets that makes up the centro storico occupies the hook of land on the left bank of the River Tiber, bordered to the east by Via del Corso and to the north and south by water. From here Rome's central core spreads east: across Via del Corso to the major shopping streets and alleys around the Spanish Steps down to the main artery of Via Nazionale; to the major sites of the ancient city to the south; and to the huge expanse of the Villa Borghese park to the north. The left bank of the river is oddly distanced from the main hum of this part of the city, home to the Vatican and Saint Peter's, and, to the south of these, Trastevere – even in ancient times a distinct entity from the city proper and the focus of a good part of the city centre's nightlife.

To see most of this, you'd be mad to risk your blood pressure in any kind of vehicle, and really the best way to get around the city centre and

Baroque Rome

If any one period can be said to define Rome, it's the Baroque, an era of flamboyance and drama in art and architecture that grew out of the Catholic Church's need to re-establish itself during the Counter-Reformation. There are Baroque churches, fountains and sculptures all over Rome, but two artists in particular define the period: Gianlorenzo Bernini and Francesco Borromini, whose works compete for space and attention throughout the city. Bernini was responsible for the Fontana dei Quattro Fiumi in Piazza Navona (pictured below), the church of Sant'Andrea del Quirinale, and the colonnades of St Peter's Square, among other things; but arguably his best sculptural work is in the Galleria Borghese, or in various churches, such as his statue of St Theresa in Santa Maria della Vittoria. Borromini, his great rival at the time, built the churches of San Carlo alle Quattro Fontane and Sant'Ivo, both buildings intricately squeezed into small sites – Borromini's trademark. The two highlights of the Baroque period, though, are probably the flamboyant main salone of the Palazzo Barberini, by Pietro da Cortona, and the church of the Gesú, whose decorative flourishes, on a vast scale, typify the style and the times.

▽ Roman mosaic

points east to Termini is to walk. The same goes for the ancient sites, and probably the Vatican and Trastevere, too – although for these last two you might want to jump on a bus going across the river. Keep public transport for the longer hops, down to Testaccio, EUR or the catacombs and, of course, for trips out of the city – to the excavations at Ostia and Tivoli, or one of the nearby beaches.

When to visit

Rome is a year-round city, and you can really visit at any **time of year**. Some times, however, are better than others. If you can, you should avoid visiting Rome in July and August, when the weather is hot and sticky, and those Romans that don't

make their living exclusively from the tourist industry have left town; many businesses are closed, and in those places that are open most of the patrons will be fellow tourists. The weather is more comfortable in May, June and September, when most days will be warm but not unbearably so, and less humid, though you'll still find the city busy during these times; April, outside Easter, and October, are quieter and the weather can still be clement – making this in many ways the ideal time to come. The winter months can be nice, with many of the city's more popular sights pleasantly

△ Window with shutters, Tridente

uncrowded: the weather can be rainy but the temperatures are usually mild. Whenever you visit, you'd be well advised to book your accommodation in advance.

What to wear is almost as important as when to come. Sturdy, comfortable shoes are essential – you're going to be doing a lot of walking – and, if you're here during the summer, you should wear loose, cool clothes, and a sunhat. Bear in mind that some sights – the catacombs, the Domus Aurea, even some churches – can be unlit and cold, even when it's warm outside, so dress in layers; bear in mind also that even on the hottest days you are required to cover up to enter many churches. Be frugal with your possessions when sightseeing, and only take out as much money, or jewellery, as you can bear to lose; pickpockets can be rife during the high season.

Average monthly temperatures and rainfall

	Jan	Feb	Mar	Apr	May	Jun	Jul	Aug	Sep	Oct	Nov	Dec
max. temp. (°C)	12	13	15	18	23	23	30	30	27	22	16	13
min. temp. (°C)	3	4	5	8	11	15	17	18	15	11	7	4
max. temp. (°F)	53	55	59	65	73	81	87	87	80	71	61	55
min. temp. (°F)	37	38	41	46	52	58	63	64	59	51	44	39
rainfall (inches)	4	4	3	3	2	1	1	1	3	4	5	4
rainfall (mm)	103	98	68	65	48	34	23	33	68	94	130	111

things not to miss

It's not possible to see everything that Rome has to offer in one trip — and we don't suggest you try. What follows is a selective taste of the city's highlights, from outstanding museums and ancient sites to Roman food and shopping. They're arranged in five colour-coded categories to help you find the very best things to see, do, eat and experience. All highlights have a page reference to take you straight into the guide, where you can find out more.

01 The Forum Page **73** • The heart of the ancient world is almost unrecognisable now, but is no less evocative for all that.

03 Fontana di Trevi Page 67 • Squeezed into the narrow streets of the city centre, this is Rome's flashiest and largest fountain. It's fantastic, especially if you manage to stumble upon it by accident.

02 Football Page 249 • Rome-Lazio derbies at the Stadio Olimpico are extreme, passionate affairs: not to be missed if you're lucky enough to be here at the right time, and can get hold of a ticket.

04 Palazzo Massimo Page 108 • Branch of the Museo Nazionale Romano, with an unsurpassed collection of Roman busts and other sculpture, jewellery and coins, and wall paintings.

06 Domus Aurea Page 116 • The underground remains of Nero's vast pleasure palace are now open to the public.

05 Via dei Coronari Page 47 • Rome's antiques row, lined with shops selling everything from heavy Renaissance chests and furniture to Italian designer cool from the 1960s.

07 **Via Condotti** Page **60** • If you can afford it, it's worth knowing that this and the streets around are the best places to shop for designer togs.

08 **Campo de' Fiori** Page **53** • Held each morning, the market here is one of Rome's oldest, while in the evening the square's bars and restaurants form one of the city centre's main nightlife hubs.

09 **Santa Maria Maggiore** Page **119** • One of the most important and impressive of Rome's patriarchal basilicas.

10 **Palazzo Altemps** Page **48** • The centro storico branch of the Museo Nazionale Romano, focusing on Roman sculpture.

11 **Trastevere** Page **139** • Wandering through the streets and tiny piazzas of Trastevere is what a visit to Rome is all about.

12 Pasta Page **206** • The basis of the Roman diet, and of some typical Roman dishes such as *Cacio e Pepe* and *Amatriciana*.

13 Villa Borghese Page **127** • The city centre's largest open space has plenty to do – a couple of superb galleries, a zoo, balloon rides – but also lots of quiet spaces to snooze if you just need to chill out.

15 Piazza Navona Page **43** • If Rome has a centre, this is probably it. Sitting drinking a coffee here and watching the world go by is the quintessential Roman experience.

14 Tivoli Page **172** • Worth the hour or so's journey to see both the ruins of Hadrian's retirement villa just outside, and the gardens-cum-waterpark of the Renaissance Villa d'Este.

16 Sistine Chapel Page **164** • Michelangelo's frescoes look better than ever following their restoration.

17 **Anzio**
Page **184**
• The best
beaches – and
nicest town –
within easy reach
of the city
if you're yearning
for the sea.

18 **Galleria Borghese**
Page **129** • A fantastic collection
of Bernini sculptures together with a
fine collection of Renaissance paintings,
in a beautifully restored seventeenth-
century villa.

19 **San Giovanni in Laterano**
Page **121** • Rome's cathedral, and the
home of the Roman Catholic Church until it was
replaced by the Vatican.

20 **Coffee** Page **203** • Even if
you don't normally drink coffee
you should do so in Rome – it's a way of
life, and tastes better, too!

21 **The Pantheon** Page **39** • By far
the most intact of Rome's – perhaps
the world's – ancient Roman monuments.

22 Capitoline Museums
Page **34** • Two amazing museums in one, sited at the heart of the ancient Roman Republic – one displaying Roman sculpture, the other Roman sculpture and Italian paintings.

23 Ice cream Page **203** • The best way to finish off an evening out in Rome.

24 Colosseum Page **82** • The most-photographed of Rome's monuments, but deservedly so. The completeness and ingenuity of this forerunner of all arenas do not disappoint.

25 Spanish Steps Page **62** • Everyone hangs out here at some point during their trip.

26 Raphael Stanze Page **161** • The frescoes here, most of them completed by Raphael to a commission by Julius II, come close to rivalling the Sistine Chapel as the Vatican Museums' main attraction.

27 **St Peter's** Page **182** • It's not the most beautiful church you'll ever visit, but it overwhelms with its grandeur and significance.

29 **Pizza** Page **206** • There's nothing quite like Roman pizza – thin, crispy, and utterly delicious.

31 **Keats-Shelley House** Page **62** • Artist's garret that was occupied by Keats when he died, and which has been lovingly preserved as a shrine to the poet and his Romantic chums.

28 **Janiculum Hill** Page **146** • A peaceful escape from the city centre, over which it enjoys unrivalled views.

30 **San Clemente** Page **124** • The epitome of Rome – an ancient temple under an ancient basilica topped by an ancient church.

32 **Galleria Doria Pamphilj** Page **38** • Perhaps the best and most intimately displayed of Rome's private art collections.

Contents

Using this Rough Guide

We've tried to make this Rough Guide a good read and easy to use. The book is divided into eight main sections, and you should be able to find whatever you want in one of them.

Colour section

The front **colour section** offers a quick tour of Rome. The **introduction** aims to give you a feel for the city, with suggestions of when to go and how to plan your visit. Next, the author rounds up his favourite aspects of the city in the **things not to miss** section – whether it's a special gallery, an amazing ancient site, or the best in Roman food. Right after this comes a full contents list.

Basics

The Basics section covers all the **pre-departure** nitty-gritty to help you plan your trip. This is where to find out which airlines fly to Rome, what paperwork you'll need, what to do about money and insurance, security and public transport – in fact, just about every piece of **general practical information** you might need.

The City

This is the heart of the Rough Guide, divided into user-friendly chapters, each of which covers a specific area. Every chapter starts with an **introduction** that helps you to decide where to go, followed by an extensive tour of the sights.

Listings

Listings contains all the consumer information needed to make the most of your stay in Rome, with chapters on **accommodation** for all budgets, places to **eat and drink**, **nightlife** and **culture** spots, **shopping** and **sports** and outdoor activities.

Contexts

Read Contexts to get a deeper understanding of what makes Rome tick. We include a brief **history**, selected **writing** on Rome, plus a detailed further reading section reviewing dozens of **books** relating to the city.

Language

The **language** section offers useful guidance for speaking Italian and pulls together all the vocabulary you might need on your trip, including a comprehensive **menu reader**.

small print + Index

Apart from a full index, which includes maps as well as places, this section covers publishing information, credits and acknowledgements, and also has our contact details in case you want to send us updates, corrections or suggestions for improving the book.

Colour maps

The back colour section contains **maps** of the city, with sights and attractions clearly marked, and a plan of the metro system to help you find your way around.

Map and chapter list

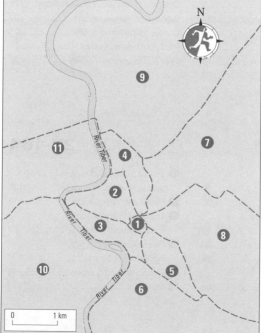

Contents

Colour section

Basics

The City

Listings

185–259

Contexts

261–289

Language

291–298

small print + Index

307–320

Colour maps at back of book

1. Rome and around
2. Rome
3. Centro storico
4. East central Rome

5. North central Rome
6. Vatican City
7. Trastevere and Testaccio
8. Trains and metro

Basics

Basics

Getting there

The quickest and easiest way to get to Rome is to fly direct to one of its two airports: Fiumicino (Leonardo da Vinci) and Ciampino (see "Arrival", p.15). There are direct flights from most European capitals, with the flight time from London around two and a half hours. There are also a number of non-stop flights from North America, though your choices widen considerably if you fly via a European gateway city or connect from Milan.

Booking flights online

Many airlines and travel websites offer you the opportunity to **book tickets online**, cutting out the costs of agents and middle-men. Good deals can often be found through discount or auction sites, as well as through the airlines' own websites – bear in mind that tickets are usually non-refundable and non-changeable. Students and those under 26 may be able to find even cheaper flights through specialist agents such as Council Travel or STA Travel (see below).

Online booking agents

Ⓦ **www.cheapflights.co.uk**,
Ⓦ **www.cheapflights.com** Flight deals, travel agents, plus links to other travel sites.
Ⓦ **www.cheaptickets.com** US discount flight specialists, also has deals on hotels and car hire.
Ⓦ **www.expedia.co.uk**, Ⓦ **www.expedia.com** Discount air fares, all-airline search engine and daily deals.
Ⓦ **www.hotwire.com** US website with lots of last-minute deals, savings of up to forty percent on regular published fares.
Ⓦ **www.lastminute.com** UK site that offers good last-minute holiday package and flight-only deals.
Ⓦ **www.opodo.com** Pan-European site funded by the major European airlines that efficiently tracks down the cheapest and most convenient scheduled flight, and also offers accommodation, car rental and other services.
Ⓦ **www.skyauction.com** US site that auctions tickets and travel packages using a "second bid" scheme. The best strategy is to bid the maximum you're willing to pay, since if you win you'll pay just enough to beat the runner-up regardless of your maximum bid.

Ⓦ **www.travelocity.co.uk**,
Ⓦ **www.travelocity.com** Good web fares and deals on car rental, accommodation and lodging.
Ⓦ **www.travelshop.com.au** Australian website offering discounted flights, packages, insurance, online bookings.

From the UK and Ireland

Most travellers from the UK and Ireland will choose a direct flight to Rome as there's a wide range of routes and airlines available. Rail travel provides a more leisurely alternative, whereas coach journeys are likely to appeal only when the flights or trains are fully booked.

By air

British Airways operates the most services from the UK to Rome, flying to Fiumicino from London (Gatwick and Heathrow), Birmingham and Manchester. The Italian national carrier, Alitalia, also flies from Heathrow. From Ireland, Aer Lingus and Alitalia fly direct from Dublin but flying via the UK offers a wider choice of airlines and fares. Among the budget carriers, Ryanair flies to Ciampino from Stansted and Glasgow Prestwick; easyJet flies there from Stansted and East Midlands; Globespan offers low-cost flights to Fiumicino from Glasgow Prestwick and Edinburgh. Really, the best place to start is with the **low-cost airlines**: with them, you can occasionally pay as little as a few pounds each way, plus tax, and you can often find flights for £50–60 return or less. However, during the summer (mid-June–August), you'll be lucky to get a flight for much less than £100 return, even with the low-cost carriers, and with the full-service airlines you'll pay up to around £150; April–May and September–October you'll pay less; and in between November and March bargains abound, even on the full-service airlines. Bear in mind that prices will always be higher for prime weekend flight times and of course cheaper for the graveyard early-morning and late-night slots.

Airlines in the UK and Ireland

Aer Lingus UK ☎0845/9737 747, Republic of Ireland ☎0818/365 000, ⊛www.aerlingus.ie.
Alitalia UK ☎0870/5448 259, Republic of Ireland ☎01/677 5171, ⊛www.alitalia.it.
British Airways UK ☎0845/77 333 77, Republic of Ireland ☎1800/626 747, ⊛www.britishairways.com.
easyJet UK ☎0870/600 0000, ⊛www.easyjet.com.
Globespan UK ☎0131/4412700, ⊛www.flyglobespan.com
Ryanair UK ☎0870/156 9569, Republic of Ireland ☎01/609 7800, ⊛www.ryanair.com.

Flight and travel agents in the UK and Ireland

Co-op Travel Care Belfast ☎028/9047 1717, ⊛www.travelcareonline.com.
Flightbookers UK ☎0870/010 7000, ⊛www.ebookers.com.
Go Holidays Dublin ☎01/874 4126, ⊛www.goholidays.ie.
Joe Walsh Tours Dublin ☎01/676 0991, ⊛www.joewalshtours.ie.
Lee Travel Cork ☎021/277 111, ⊛www.leetravel.ie.
Premier Travel Derry ☎028/7126 3333, ⊛www.premiertravel.uk.com.
STA Travel UK ☎0870/1600 599, ⊛www.statravel.co.uk.
Trailfinders UK ☎020/7628 7628, ⊛www.trailfinders.com.
usit NOW Dublin ☎01/602 1600, ⊛www.usitnow.ie.

By rail

Travelling **by train** to Rome is no less expensive than flying, but it can be an enjoyable and relaxing way of getting to the city if you want to visit other parts of Italy, or even Europe, on the way. A return ticket from London to Rome, using Eurostar and the super-fast TGV through France, costs anything from £99 to well over £200, depending on how long you

go for, and whether you spend a Saturday night away, and the journey takes 18–20 hours. Advance booking is essential, and discounts (for under-26s) and special offers are legion. The Eurostar passenger train (☎0870/160 6600, ⊛www.eurostar.com) goes from Waterloo International in London to Paris (2hr 40min) and Brussels (2hr 20min) via Ashford in Kent. The cheapest return ticket to Paris costs around £80, though restrictions apply. You can get through-ticketing to Rome – including the tube journey to Waterloo International – through Rail Europe (☎09705 848848, ⊛www.raileurope.co.uk), or from most travel agents or mainline train stations in the UK; add-on prices for a return ticket from Edinburgh, Glasgow, Manchester and Birmingham range from £15 to £30. Note that InterRail (⊛www.interrail.com) and Eurail (⊛www.eurail.com) passes give discounts on the Eurostar service.

By bus

It's difficult to see why anyone would want to travel to Rome by **bus**, unless they had a phobia of flying – and of trains. National Express Eurolines (UK ☎0870/514 3219, Ireland ☎01/836 6111, ⊛www.eurolines.co.uk) do, however, have occasional bargain offers, but generally you'll pay around £80 for a return ticket on a journey that takes a gruelling 24 hours or more. Eurolines has a frequent service from Dublin, Cork, Limerick and Belfast to London.

Organized tours

Don't be put off by the idea of taking a **package**: it can save time and stress and can work out cheaper, depending on the time of year and where you decide to stay, although you should bear in mind that most websites offering cheap flights give plenty of hotel and other options too. There is a plethora of operators selling short-break deals to Rome, some of them – like Martin Randall (see below) – specialists offering small-group tours focusing on art or the archeological sights, and often giving access to places that aren't otherwise open. For an ordinary city break, you can reckon on spending upwards of £350 per person for three nights in a three-star hotel between April and October, including flights, though special offers can sometimes cut prices drastically, especially for late bookings. Specialist tours tend to cost up to £1000 for a week.

Tour operators in the UK and Ireland

ACE Study Tours ☎01223/835 055, ⓦwww.study-tours.org.
Citalia ☎020/8686 5533, ⓦwww.citalia.co.uk.
Eurobreak ☎020/8780 7700, ⓦwww.eurobreak.com.
Exclusive Italy ☎01892/619650, ⓦwww.exclusivedestinations.co.uk.
Italian Connection ☎020/7520 0470, ⓦwww.italian-connection.co.uk.
Magic of Italy ☎020/8939 5453, ⓦwww.magictravelgroup.co.uk.
Martin Randall Travel ☎020/8742 3355, ⓦwww.martinrandall.com.

From the US and Canada

From the US and Canada there are a number of **direct** flights to Rome (all arriving at Fiumicino). However, there are more flights available to Milan so it may be more convenient to transfer there (or complete the journey by train). Alitalia and Delta Airlines have the most direct routes, with daily flights to Rome from New York (and to Milan from New York, Miami, Chicago and Boston). American Airlines has a direct route from Chicago to Rome, Continental flies from New York (Newark) to Rome and Milan, and Air Canada and Alitalia fly to Rome direct from Toronto. Also, many European carriers fly to Rome from their capitals, and have connections to all the major US and Canadian cities – British Airways, Air France, KLM and Lufthansa are likely to have the best deals and the most frequent connections. You could also consider picking up a cheap flight to one of the big European gateways, such as London, Paris, or Amsterdam, and flying the rest of the way to Rome with one of the European low-cost carriers (see above).

As direct scheduled **fares** don't vary as much as you might think, you'll more often than not be basing your choice on flight timings, routes, ticket restrictions, and even the airline's reputation for comfort and service. It's a long flight between North America and Rome, around nine hours from New York, Boston and the eastern Canadian cities, twelve hours from Chicago, and fifteen hours from Los Angeles, so it's as well to be fairly comfortable and to arrive at a reasonably sociable hour. The cheapest round-trip fares you'll find start at around $500 from the East Coast in low season, rising to about $1000 during the summer; add another $250 or so for flights from LA, Miami and Chicago, and note that these prices usually mean a change somewhere, either in North America or at one of the big European gateways. For direct flights, you can reckon on paying $1200–1500 in high season, $500–750 in low season. From Canada, expect to pay high-season fares of Can$1000–1500, not flying direct, around Can$2000 flying direct.

Airlines

Air Canada ☎1-888/247-2262, ⓦwww.aircanada.ca.
Air France US ☎1-800/237-2747, Canada ☎1-800/667-2747, ⓦwww.airfrance.com.
Alitalia US ☎1-800/223-5730, Canada ☎1-800/361-8336, ⓦwww.alitalia.com.
American Airlines ☎1-800/433-7300, ⓦwww.aa.com.
British Airways ☎1-800/247-9297, ⓦwww.ba.com.
Continental Airlines ☎1-800/231-0856, ⓦwww.continental.com.
Delta Air Lines ☎1-800/241-4141, ⓦwww.delta.com.
KLM ☎1-800/447-4747, ⓦwww.klm.com.
Lufthansa US ☎1-800/645-3880, Canada ☎1 800/563-5954, ⓦwww.lufthansa-usa.com
Northwest Airlines ☎1-800/447-4747, ⓦwww.nwa.com.

Flight and travel agents in North America

Airtech ☎1-877/247-8324 or 212/219-7000, ⓦwww.airtech.com.
Council Travel ☎1-800/226-8624, ⓦwww.counciltravel.com.
Skylink US ☎1-800/247-6659 or 212/573-8980, Canada ☎1-800/759-5465, ⓦwww.skylinkus.com.
STA Travel ☎1-800/777-0112 or 781-4040, ⓦwww.sta-travel.com.
Student Flights ☎1-800/255-8000 or 480/951-1177, ⓦwww.isecard.com.

TFI Tours International ☎1-800/745-8000 or 212/736-1140, ⊛www.lowestairprice.com.
Travac ☎1-800/872-8800, ⊛www.thetravelsite.com.
Travelers Advantage ☎1-877/259-2691, ⊛www.travelersadvantage.com.
Travel Cuts Canada ☎1-800/667-2887, US ☎1-866/246-9762, ⊛www.travelcuts.com.

Packages and organized tours

As well as the online booking agents (see p.9), which can combine deals on flights, accommodation and car hire, there are dozens of companies operating fully **inclusive tours** to Rome; these range from full-blown luxury escorted affairs to small groups sticking to specialized itineraries. Prices vary widely, so check what you are getting for your money (many don't include the cost of the air fare). You can expect to pay from around $1500 for a week in a three-star hotel in Rome, including air fares. At the more rarefied end of things, with one of the small, cultural specialists, or luxury operators, costs can be around $2000-plus for a week, sometimes not including air fares.

Tour operators in North America

Abercrombie & Kent ☎1-800/323-7308 or 630/954-2944, ⊛www.abercrombiekent.com.
Central Holidays ☎1-800/935-5000, ⊛www.centralholidays.com.
Cross Culture ☎1-800/491-1148 or 413/256-6363, ⊛www.crosscultureinc.com.
Europe Through the Back Door ☎425/771-8303, ⊛www.ricksteves.com.
New Frontiers ☎1-800/366-6387, ⊛www.newfrontiers.com.

From Australia and New Zealand

There are **no direct flights** to Italy from Australia or New Zealand, but plenty of airlines fly to Rome via an Asian or European city. Alitalia flies in conjunction with other carriers (from Auckland via Sydney and Bangkok/Singapore to Rome or Milan); British Airways to Rome from Auckland via Singapore/Bangkok or LA; Qantas to Rome from Auckland, Christchurch or Wellington via Sydney or Melbourne; JAL to Rome from Auckland (with inclusive overnight stop in Tokyo/Osaka); Malaysia

and Thai to Rome from Auckland via Kuala Lumpur and Bangkok respectively. **Round-trip fares** to Rome and Milan from the main cities in **Australia** cost A$1500–2000 in low season, and A$1700–2500 in high season. You are likely to get most flexibility by travelling with Alitalia, Thai, British Airways or Qantas, which offer a range of discounted Italian tour packages and air passes, although you can generally find cheaper offers with carriers like Taiwan's China Airlines or Indonesia's Garuda. **Round-trip fares** to Rome from **New Zealand** cost NZ$2000–2500 in low season to NZ$2200–2800 during high season. As always, you're best off searching the discount agents and online sites for the best fares before checking the airlines direct.

Airlines

Alitalia Australia ☎02/9262 3925, ⊛www.alitalia.com
British Airways Australia ☎02/8904 8800, New Zealand ☎0800/274 847, ⊛www.britishairways.com.
Cathay Pacific Australia ☎13 17 47, New Zealand ☎09/379 0861 or 0508/800 454, ⊛www.cathaypacific.com.
China Airlines Australia ☎ 02/9313 4571, ⊛www.china-airlines.com.
Garuda Australia ☎02/9334 9970, New Zealand ☎09/366 1862, ⊛www.garuda-indonesia.com.
Japan Airlines Australia ☎02/9272 1111, New Zealand ☎09/379 9906, ⊛www.japanair.com.
KLM Australia ☎1300/303 747, New Zealand ☎09/309 1782, ⊛www.klm.com.
Lufthansa Australia ☎1300/655 727, New Zealand ☎09/303 1529, ⊛www.lufthansa.com.
Malaysia Airlines Australia ☎13 26 27, New Zealand ☎09/373 2741, ⊛www.mas.com.my.
Qantas Australia ☎13 13 13, New Zealand ☎09/661 901, ⊛www.qantas.com.au.
Singapore Airlines Australia ☎13 10 11, New Zealand ☎09/303 2129, ⊛www.singaporeair.com.
Thai Airways Australia ☎1300/651 960, New Zealand ☎09/377 3886, ⊛www.thaiair.com.

Flight and travel agents

Budget Travel New Zealand ☎09/366 0061 or 0800/808 040, ⊛www.budgettravel.co.nz.
Destinations Unlimited New Zealand ☎09/414 1680, ⊛www.etravelnz.com.

Flight Centres Australia ☏13 31 33 or 02/9235 3522, New Zealand ☏09/358 4310, ⊛www.flightcentre.com.au.
STA Travel Australia ☏1300/733 035, ⊛www.statravel.com.au, New Zealand ☏0508/782 872, ⊛www.statravel.co.nz.
Trailfinders Australia ☏02/9247 7666, ⊛www.trailfinders.com.au.
Travel.com Australia ☏1300/130 482 or 02/9249 5444, ⊛www.travel.com.au, New Zealand ☏09/359 3860, ⊛www.travel.co.nz.

Tour operators in Australia and New Zealand

Abercrombie and Kent Australia ☏03/9536 1800 or 1300/851 800, New Zealand ☏0800/441 638, ⊛www.abercrombiekent.com.au.
CIT Australia ☏02/9267 1255, ⊛www.cittravel.com.au.
Explore Holidays Australia ☏02/9857 6200 or 1300/731 000, ⊛www.exploreholidays.com.au.

Red tape and visas

British, Irish and other EU citizens can enter Italy and stay as long as they like on production of a valid passport. Citizens of the United States, Canada, Australia and New Zealand need only a valid passport, too, but are limited to stays of three months. All other nationals should consult the relevant embassy about visa requirements.

Italian embassies and consulates abroad

Australia 12 Grey St, Deakin, Canberra, ACT 2600 ☏02/6273 3333, ⊛www.ambitalia.org.au. Consulates in Melbourne ☏03/9867 5744 and Sydney ☏02/9392 7900.
Canada 275 Slater St, Ottawa, ON, K1P 5H9 ☏613/232-2401, ⊛www.italyincanada.com. Consulates in Montréal ☏514/849-8351 and Toronto ☏416/977-1566.
Ireland 63–65 Northumberland Rd, 6365 Dublin 4 ☏01/660 1744.

New Zealand 34–38 Grant Rd, PO Box 463, Thorndon, Wellington ☏04/473 5339, ⊛www.italy-embassy.org.nz.
UK 14 Three King's Yard, London W1Y 2EH ☏020/7312 2200, ⊛www.embitaly.org.uk. Consulates in Edinburgh ☏0131/226 3695 and Manchester ☏0161/236 9024.
USA 3000 Whitehaven St NW, Washington DC 20008 ☏202/612-4400, ⊛www.italyemb.org. Consulates in Chicago ☏312/467-1550, New York ☏212/737-9100 and San Francisco ☏415/292-9210.

Insurance and health

Even though EU health care privileges apply in Italy, you'd do well to take out an insurance policy before travelling to cover against theft, loss, illness or injury. Before paying for a new policy, however, it's worth checking whether you are already covered: some all-risks home insurance policies may cover your possessions when overseas, and many private medical schemes include cover when abroad.

If you're not already covered, you might want to contact a specialist travel insurance company, or consider the travel insurance deal we offer (see box below). A typical policy usually provides cover for the loss of baggage, tickets and – up to a certain limit – cash or cheques, as well as cancellation or curtailment of your journey. Many policies can be chopped and changed to exclude coverage you don't need – for example, sickness and accident benefits. If you do take medical coverage, ascertain whether benefits will be paid as treatment proceeds or only after your return home, and whether there is a 24-hour medical emergency number. When securing baggage cover, make sure that the per-article limit – typically under £500 – will cover your most valuable possession. If you need to make a claim, you should keep receipts for medicines and medical treatment, and in the event you have anything stolen, you must obtain an official statement from the police.

Health

EU citizens can take advantage of Italy's **health services** under the same terms as Rome's residents, but you'll need form E111, available from any main post office. The Australian Medicare system also has a reciprocal health-care arrangement with Italy. We've listed late-night pharmacies, English-speaking dentists and doctors, and city centre hospitals in the Directory chapter so you should never be at a loss should the worst happen (emergency numbers are listed on p.26). Bear in mind you'll pay through the teeth for a dentist as these are not covered by the *mutua* or health service.

Rough Guides travel insurance

Rough Guides Ltd offers a low-cost travel insurance policy, especially customized for our statistically low-risk readers by a leading British broker, provided by the American International Group (AIG) and registered with the British regulatory body, GISC (the General Insurance Standards Council). There are five main Rough Guides insurance plans: No Frills for the bare minimum for secure travel; Essential, which provides decent all-round cover; Premier for comprehensive cover with a wide range of benefits; Extended Stay for cover lasting four months to a year; and Annual multi-trip, a cost-effective way of getting Premier cover if you travel more than once a year. Premier, Annual Multi-Trip and Extended Stay policies can be supplemented by a "Hazardous Pursuits Extension" if you plan to indulge in sports considered dangerous, such as scuba-diving or trekking. For a policy quote, call the Rough Guide Insurance Line: toll-free in the UK ☎0800/015 09 06 or ☎+44 1392 314 665 from elsewhere. Alternatively, get an online quote at
ⓦwww.roughguides.com/insurance

Ararival

Reaching the centre of Rome is pretty straightforward for air and rail travellers. You'll most likely end up at Termini station – very close to the top attractions and the bulk of accommodation. If arriving by taxi or bus, remember Rome's notorious traffic can add significantly to your journey time.

By air

Rome has **two airports**: Leonardo da Vinci International, better known simply as **Fiumicino**, which handles most scheduled flights, and **Ciampino**, where you'll arrive if you're travelling on a charter or with one of the low-cost European airlines. Both airports are run by Aeroporti di Roma which provides live flight information and timetables in English at ⓦ www.adr.it. Taxis in from either airport cost €40–60, more at night, and take thirty minutes from Fiumicino, around forty-five minutes from Ciampino (remember to agree a price beforehand or check that the meter is running); they're worth considering if you are in a group but otherwise the public transport connections, especially those from Fiumicino, are pretty good. It's worth knowing that taxis going **back to the airport** cost a little more, and that Enjoy Rome (see p.17) runs an airport shuttle bus to Fiumicino (£42 for up to 3 people, €60 for up to 6 people).

Fiumicino Airport

Fiumicino (FCO) is Rome's largest airport and is about 30km southwest of the city. There are three terminals: A is for domestic flights, B for international flights within the EU, and C for all other international flights. Fiumicino is connected to the city centre by direct trains which make the thirty-minute ride to Termini for €8.80; services begin at 6.38am and leave half-hourly until 11.38pm. Alternatively, there are more frequent trains to Trastevere, Ostiense and Tiburtina stations, each on the edge of the city centre, roughly every twenty minutes from 6.27am to 11.27pm; tickets to these stations cost less – €4.70 – and Tiburtina and Ostiense are just a short (€1) metro ride from Termini, making it a cheaper (and not necessarily much slower) journey; or you can catch city bus #175 from Ostiense, or city bus #492 or #649 from Tiburtina, to the centre of town (again €1). These cheaper alternatives do inevitably, however, involve a certain amount more bag-hauling.

Ciampino Airport

The city's second airport, **Ciampino** (CIA) has three terminals: Departures, Arrivals and General Aviation, and is only 15km south east of Rome. However, as it lacks a rail connection, it can take longer to reach the centre than from Fiumicino. If you're travelling with one of the low-cost airlines, easyJet or Ryanair, the best thing to do is to take one of their shuttle buses to Termini (they pull up on Via Marsala), which leave half an hour after each arrival – costs are around €8 single, €12 return. Otherwise COTRAL buses run every half an hour from the airport to the Anagnina metro station, at the end of line A – a thirty-minute journey (€1.30), from where it's a twenty-minute ride into the centre (a further €1). Failing that, you can take a bus from the airport to Ciampino overground train station, a ten-minute journey, and then take a train into Termini, which is a further twenty minutes from there.

By train

Travelling by **train** from most places in Italy, or indeed from other parts of Europe, you will arrive at **Stazione Termini**, centrally placed for all parts of the city and meeting-point of the two metro lines and many city bus routes. There's a **left-luggage** facility here (daily 7am–midnight; €3.10 per piece every 5hr), but bear in mind that they won't accept plastic bags; note that the Enjoy Rome office (see p.17) will also look after its customers' luggage.

Among **other rail stations** in Rome, Tiburtina is a stop for some north–south intercity trains; selected routes around Lazio are handled by the Regionali platforms of Stazione Termini (a further five-minute walk from the regular platforms); and there's also the COTRAL urban train station on Piazzale Flaminio, which runs to La Giustiniana – the so-called Roma-Nord line.

By bus

Arriving by **bus** can leave you in any one of a number of places around the city. The main station is Tiburtina, Rome's second railway terminal after Termini, and connected to the city centre by metro line B or buses #492 or #649; most national and international bus services stop here. Other bus stations, mainly serving the Lazio region, include: Ponte Mammolo (trains from Tivoli and Subiaco); Lepanto (Cerveteri, Civitavecchia, Bracciano area); EUR Fermi (Nettuno, Anzio, southern Lazio coast); Anagnina (Castelli Romani); Saxa Rubra (Viterbo and around). All of these stations are on a metro line, except Saxa Rubra, which is on the Roma-Nord line and connected by trains every fifteen minutes with the station at Piazzale Flaminio, on metro line A.

By road

Coming into the city by **road** can be quite confusing and isn't really advisable unless you're used to driving in Italy and know where you are going to park (see p.20). If you are on the A1 highway coming from the north take the exit "Roma Nord"; from the south, follow exit "Roma Est". Both lead you to the Grande Raccordo Anulare (GRA), which circles the city and is connected with all of the major arteries into the city centre – the Via Cassia from the north, Via Salaria from the northeast, Via Tiburtina or Via Nomentana from the east, Via Appia Nuova and the Pontina from the south, Via Prenestina and Via Casilina or Via Cristoforo Colombo from the southeast, and Via Aurelia from the northwest. From Ciampino, either follow Via Appia Nuova into the centre or join the GRA at junction 23 and follow the signs to the centre. From Fiumicino, just follow the A12 motorway into the city centre; it crosses the river just north of EUR, from where it's a short drive north up Via Cristoforo Colombo to the city walls and, beyond to the Baths of Caracalla.

Information, websites and maps

Information

There are **tourist information booths** on arrival at Fiumicino (daily 8.15am–7pm; ⓣ06.6595.6074), and by platform 2 at Termini Station (daily 8am–9pm; ⓣ06.4890.630), although the long queues that often develop at both of these mean you're usually better off heading straight for the main **tourist office** at Via Parigi 5 (Mon–Sat 9am–7pm; ⓣ06.3600.4399; ⓦwww.romaturismo.it), ten minutes' walk from Termini. They have free maps that should – together with our own – be ample for finding your way around, although the rest of their information can be uneven. There are also **information kiosks** in key locations around the city centre (daily 9am–6pm). They, too, have (sometimes outdated) general information but the staff usually speak English, and they are useful for free maps, directions and up-to-the-minute information (opening times, for example) about nearby sights.

Information kiosk locations

Piazza di Spagna Largo Goldoni ⓣ06.6813.6061
San Giovanni Piazza San Giovanni in Laterno ⓣ06.7720.3535

Via Nazionale Palazzo delle Esposizioni
☎06.4782.4525
Piazza Navona Piazza delle Cinque Lune
☎06.6880.9240
Castel Sant'Angelo Piazza Pia ☎06.6880.9707
Fori Imperiali Piazza del Tempio della Pace
☎06.6992.4307
Trastevere Piazza Sonnino ☎06.5833.3457

You might be better off bypassing the official tourist offices altogether and going to **Enjoy Rome**, Via Marghera 8a (Mon–Fri 8.30am–7pm, Sat 8.30am–2pm; ☎06.445.1843, ℻06.445.0734, ℗www .enjoyrome.com), whose friendly, English-speaking staff run a free room-finding service; they also organize tours (see p.21), have a left-luggage service for those who take them, and run shuttle buses to the airport (see p.15). Their information is often more up to date and reliable than that handed out by the various tourist offices, and they will also advise on where to eat, drink, and party, if you so wish. Finally the city authorities run a **helpline** – ☎ 06.06.06 – which is open Monday to Saturday 4pm–7pm and can answer questions in many different languages on all aspects of the city.

For what's-on information, the city's best source of **listings** is perhaps *Romac'è* (€1, Thursdays), which has a helpful section in English giving information on tours, clubs, restaurants, services and weekly events. The ex-pat bi-weekly, *Wanted in Rome* (€0.75, every other Wednesday), which is entirely in English, is also a useful source of information, especially if you're looking for an apartment or work. If you understand a bit of Italian, there's the daily arts pages of the Rome **newspaper**, *Il Messaggero*, which can be found in most bars for the customers to read, and lists movies, plays and major musical events. The newspaper *La Repubblica* also includes the "*Trova Roma*" section in its Thursday edition, another handy guide to current offerings.

Rome online

℗**www.enjoyrome.com** Helpful site of the helpful Rome tourist organization, with information on accommodation and tours – and links to other popular Rome websites.

℗**www.romeguide.it** The place to go whether you're after a bus or walking tour of the city centre, a guide to a particular monument or gallery, even the chance to go on a "ghost tour" of Rome. Good for up-to-date information on concerts and events too.

℗**www.comune.roma.it** Italian-language website of the Rome city authorities but with information in English, particularly useful material if you're spending longer in the city.

℗**www.capitolium.org** The official website of the Roman forums, with pictorial reconstructions of how the ruins would have looked in their day, as well as how they look now; material on life in ancient Rome; and even a live web view of the forum.

℗**www.catacombe.roma.it** Official site of Rome's Christian catacombs, with visuals, historical descriptions, and explanations of ancient symbols – a good supplement to our own accounts if you're extra keen.

℗**www.vatican.va** Slick, multilingual website of the Holy See, with material – some still under construction – on the Vatican Museums, the institutions of the city state and its online newspaper.

℗**www.venere.it/home/lazio/roma** Good general site for accessing Rome hotels online – if this book fails you.

Maps

You should find the **maps** in this book more than adequate for your needs. If you require something more detailed, then the best choice (though I guess we would say this) is *Rome The Rough Guide Map*, which is waterproof, rip-proof and includes the locations of most of the recommendations in this book. If you want something more detailed then you're probably best off with the 1:10,000 Michelin map, which includes more coverage of the outskirts and suburban neighbourhoods.

City transport and tours

As in most Italian cities, the best way to get around Rome is to walk – you'll see more and will better appreciate the city. Rome wasn't built for motor traffic, and it shows in the congestion, the pollution, and the bad tempers of its drivers. However, it has good public transport on the whole – a largely efficient blend of buses, a few trams and a small two-line metro.

ATAC: buses, trams and metro

ATAC (*Agenzia dei Transporti Autoferro-tranviari del Commune di Roma*) runs the city's bus, tram and metro service. There is a toll-free **enquiries line** (Mon–Fri 8am–6pm; ☎800.431.784) or try their website: ⊛www.atac.roma.it which has tourist info in English, a route planner and links to the individual trambus and metro sites (see below).

Tickets and passes

Flat-fare **tickets** cost €1 each and are good for any number of bus or tram rides and one metro ride within 75 minutes of validating them – you need to punch your ticket before you ride on the metro and as you get on a bus or tram; otherwise you can be fined. Tickets are available from tobacconists, newsstands and ticket machines located in all metro stations and at major bus stops. You can also get a **day pass**, valid on all city transport until midnight of the day purchased, for €3.10, or a **seven-day pass** for €12.40. Finally, it's worth knowing that there are hefty spot fines (around €50) for fare-dodging, and pleading a foreigner's ignorance will get you nowhere. **BIRG tickets** (regional transport passes) for COTRAL and ATAC services, available from machines in the metro, *tabacchi* and newsstands, are well worth buying if you are going out of Rome for the day; prices depend on the number of zones you use and the distance you intend to travel.

Buses and trams

The bus and tram service, "trambus" (⊛www.trambus.com), is on the whole pretty good – cheap, reliable and as quick as the clogged streets allow (see opposite for useful routes). Remember to board through the rear doors and punch your ticket as you enter. There is also a small network of electric minibuses that negotiate the narrow backstreets of the old centre. Around midnight, a network of nightbuses clicks into service, accessing most parts of the city through to about 5am; they normally have conductors so you can buy a ticket on board (but keep spare tickets handy just in case); they are easily identified by the owl symbol above the "bus notturno" schedule.

Metro

Rome's **metro** or "Met.Ro" as it calls itself (⊛www.metroroma.it), runs from 5.30am to 11.30pm, though it's not as useful as you might think, since its two lines – A (red) and

Travellers with disabilities

Only two stops on line A have accessibility for **disabled persons** (Cipro-Musei Vaticani and Valle Aurelia) but bus #591 does the same route and can accommodate those with disabilities. Also, be advised that on line B, Circo Massimo, Colosseo and Cavour do not have accessibility but bus #75 stops at those sights and has new buses that can accommodate those with disabilities (although you may have to wait for a few of the older buses to go by).

Useful bus routes

#23 Piazza Clodio–Piazza Risorgimento–Ponte Vittorio Emanuele II–Ponte Garibaldi–Via Marmorata–Piazzale Ostiense–Basilica di S. Paolo.

#30 Express Piazza Clodio–Piazza Mazzini–Piazza Cavour–Corso Rinascimento–Largo Argentina–Piazza Venezia–Luntotevere Aventino–Via Marmorata–Piramide–Via C.Colombo–EUR.

#40 Termini–Via Nazionale–Piazza Venezia–Largo Argentina–Chiesa Nuova–Piazza Pia.

#64 Termini: Piazza della Repubblica–Via Nazionale–Piazza Venezia–Corso Vittorio Emanuele II–St Peter's.

#110 Open Termini–Quirinale–Colosseo–Bocca della Verità–Piazza Venezia–Piazza Navona–San Pietro–Piazza Cavour–Ara Pacis–Fontana di Trevi–Via Veneto.

#175 Termini–Piazza Barberini–Via del Corso–Piazza Venezia–Teatro di Marcello–Aventino–Stazione Ostiense.

#271 S.Paolo–Via Ostiense–Piramide–Viale Aventino–Circo Massimo–Colosseo–Piazza Venezia–Ponte Sisto–Castel Sant'Angelo–Piazza Risorgimento–Ptavviano–Foro Italico.

#492 Stazione Tiburtina–Termini–Piazza Barberini–Via del Corso–Piazza Venezia–Largo Argentina–Corso del Rinascimento–Piazza Cavour–Piazza Risorgimento.

#590 Same route as metro line A but with accessibility for disabled; runs every 90 minutes.

#660 Largo Colli Albani–Via Appia Nuova–Via Appia Antica.

#714 Termini–Santa Maria Maggiore–San Giovanni in Laterano–Baths of Caracalla–EUR.

#910 Termini–Piazza della Repubblica–Via Piemonte–Via Pinciana (Villa Borghese)–Piazza Euclide–Palazetto dello Sport–Piazza Mancini.

Tourist buses
#110 Open Termini–Quirinale–Colosseo–Bocca della Verità–Piazza Venezia–Piazza Navona–San Pietro–Piazza Cavour–Ara Pacis–Fontana di Trevi–Via Veneto.

Archeobus Termini–Piazza Venezia–Bocca della Verità–Circo Massimo–Terme di Caracalla–Porta San Sebastiano–Parco Appia Antica–Domine Quo Vadis–Catacombe di S. Callisto–Catacombe di S. Sebastiano–Circo di Massenzio–Valle della Carffarella–Ninfeo di Villa dei Quintili–Casal Rotundo–Aquedotti Romani–Villa dei Quintili.

Night buses
#29N Piazzale Ostiense–Lungotevere Aventino–Lungotevere De'Conci Via Crescenzio–Via Barletta–Piazza Marina–Via Belle Arte–Viale Liegi–Viale Regina Margherita–Via dei Marruccini–Via Labicana–Viale Aventino–Piazzale Ostiense.

#40N Same route as metro line B.

#55N Same route as metro line A.

#78N Piazza Clodio–Piazzale Flaminio–Piazza Cavour–Largo di Torre Argentina–Piazza Venezia–Via Nazionale–Termini.

Useful tram routes
#3 Stazione Trastevere–Viale Trastevere–Ponte Sublicio–Via Marmorata–Piramide–Viale Aventino–Circo Massimo–Colosseo–San Giovanni–San Lorenzo–Via Nomentana–Parioli–Villa Borghese.

#8 Largo Argentina–Viale Trastevere–Piazza Mastai–Piazza I.Nievo–Stazione Trastevere.

#19 Porto Maggiore–San Lorenzo–Viale Regina Margherita–Viale Belle Arti–Ottaviano–Piazza Risorgimento.

#30 Piramide–Viale Aventino–Colosseum–San Giovanni–Viale Regina Margherita–Villa Giulia.

B (blue); they're working on line C – are directed more at ferrying commuters out to the suburbs than transporting tourists around the city centre. Nonetheless, there are a few useful city-centre stations: Termini is the hub of both lines, and there are stations at the Colosseum, Piazza Barberini and Piazza di Spagna.

Maps

Metro **maps** are posted up in every station, and we've printed one at the end of this book. If you're going to use the system a lot, especially the buses, it may be worth investing in the excellent detailed **Lozzi transport map**, available from most newsstands, or getting hold of the official **ATAC map** – free from tourist information offices, and from the **ATAC information office** in the centre of Piazza dei Cinquecento – although this can be out of date and somewhat unreliable.

Taxis

The easiest way to get a **taxi** is to find the nearest taxi stand (*fermata dei taxi*) – central ones include Termini, Piazza Venezia, Piazza San Silvestro, Piazza di Spagna and Piazza Barberini. Alternatively, taxis can be radio paged (℡06.3570, ℡06.4994, ℡06.6645, ℡ 06.88.177 or ℡06.5551), but remember that you'll pay for the time it takes to get to you. Only take licensed yellow or white cabs, and make sure the meter is switched on; a card in every official taxi explains – in English – the extra charges for luggage, late-night, Sundays and holidays, and airport journeys. Meters start at €2.33 (more at night and on Sundays), plus a charge of €1.04 per item of luggage; the meter clicks up at the rate of €0.78 every 140m. To give you a rough idea of how much taxis cost, you can reckon on a journey across the centre costing around €8, if the traffic isn't too bad, though on a Sunday this will be a little more – say €10 – and at night close to double this amount.

Car and bike rental – and parking

Car rental is only worthwhile for trips out of the city, and you'd be crazy to bring your own car into the centre of Rome. If you do, bear in mind that non-residents are not allowed to drive in the old centre so you'll need to **park** somewhere just outside. You can park on the street for around €1 an hour (8am–8pm) or there are parking garages in the Villa Borghese (around €1per hour) in front of Stazione Termini (€5 for 2 hours, then €1.50 per hour). There are also car parks next to the terminal metro stations, from where it's easy to get into the city centre. Renting a **bike** or **moped/scooter** can be a more efficient way of nipping around Rome's clogged streets, and there are plenty of places offering this facility. Rates are up to around €10 a day for bikes, about €30 a day for mopeds and €40 a day for scooters.

Bike and scooter rental

Collalti Via del Pellegrino 82 ℡06.6880.108; closed Mon. Does bike rental and repairs.
I Bike Rome Villa Borghese underground parking, Via Veneto ℡06.3225240. Scooter and bike rental from €35 for mopeds, €40 for scooters and €10 a day for bikes.
Rent-a-Scooter Motoservices Via F. Turati 50 ℡06.446.9222. The best deal for scooters and offers a 10 percent discount to Rough Guide readers.
Romarent Vicolo dei Bovari 7a ℡06.689.6555. Scooter and bike rental.
Roma Solutions Corso Vittorio Emanuele II 204 ℡06.446.9222/06.687.6922. Scooter and bike rental.
Treno e Scooter Rent Stazione Termini ℡06.488.2797. Scooter and bike rental – €5.50–9.50 day for bikes, €31–59.50 for moped or scooters – and discounts for those with valid train tickets.

Tours

A number of companies run **organized trips** around the city centre, though these are, for the most part, quite pricey and not really worth the money. Probably the best value, for general orientation and a glance at the main sights, is the ATAC-run **#110 Open** bus tour which uses open-topped red double-deckers with an audio guide. Buses leave regularly from Termini Station between 9am and 8.30pm and cost €13 for a hop-on, hop-off service. ATAC also operates the **Archeobus**, a guided minibus tour calling at fifteen archeological sites including the Catacombs and the Circo di Massenzio (tours leave Temini between 9.45am and 4.45pm; €7.75) – see p.19 for itineraries of ATAC tours (⑩www.trambus.com/servizituristici).

Tour companies

Enjoy Rome Via Marghera 8a; Mon–Fri 8.30am–7pm, Sat 8.30am–2pm; ☏06.445.1843, ℻06.445.0734, ⑩www.enjoyrome.com. Runs inexpensive walking tours of Rome given by native English speakers. Prices start at €20 for three-hour tours of places such as the Vatican, the Catacombs and Appian Way, Trastevere and the Jewish Ghetto and Ancient Rome and the Historic Centre – which they also do at night.

Institute of Design and Culture ☏214/853-5603, ⑩www.urban-iconography.org. US-based organization offering a great range of city courses and tours with a cultural slant led by experts on Rome. They're not cheap but you get what you pay

for; choose from anything from the Etruscans to *Tosca* – even offers cooking classes with visits to the city's markets.

Il Sogno Viale Regina Margherita 192 ☏06.8530.1758, ℻06.8530.1756. Runs a range of tours and is perhaps the best one-stop place to go if you're not sure what you want.

Rome Revealed ☏06.324.741, ⑩www.romerevealed.com. Decent tours run by native English speakers, with prices starting at €25.

Vastours Via Piemonte 32/34 ☏06.481.4309, ℻06.481.8000, ⑩www.vastours.it. Operates a range of themed city centre excursions by coach with English-speaking guides; cost €30–40, more with lunch included. They also run a 'Ciao Roma' trolleybus tour of the city centre, which stops at twelve stops between 8.30am and 6pm daily, and which you can get on and off as you please; tickets cost €18 and ar valid all day.

Opening hours and public holidays

The city's opening hours are becoming more flexible, but Rome still largely follows a traditional Italian routine. Most shops and businesses open Monday to Saturday from around 8am to 1pm, and from about 4pm to 7pm, though many shops close on Saturday afternoons and Monday mornings; a few of the more international businesses follow a nine-to-five schedule.

The other factors to be aware of are **national holidays** and the fact that in **August**, particularly during the weeks either side of *Ferragosto*, most of Rome flees to the coast, and many shops, bars and restaurants close and the only people around are other tourists. On official national holidays everything closes down except bars and restaurants.

Public holidays

January 1 (New Year's Day)
January 6 (Epiphany)
Pasquetta (Easter Monday)
April 25 (Liberation Day)
May 1 (Labour Day)
August 15 (*Ferragosto*; Assumption of the Blessed Virgin Mary)
November 1 (*Ognissanti*; All Souls' Day)
December 8 (*Immaccolata*; Immaculate Conception of the Blessed Virgin Mary)
December 25 (*Natale*; Christmas)
December 26 (*Santo Stefano*; St Stephen's Day)

Sights and museums

It's likely that you'll be spending a fair amount of your time in Rome visiting its dazzling array of museums, galleries, churches and ancient sites. They are not all that the city has to offer, but they are, inevitably, one of the reasons most people visit – and rightly so: nowhere in the world, perhaps, has such a collection of treasures from so many different eras.

Museums and galleries

Most **museums and galleries** are closed on Mondays. **Opening hours** for state-run museums are generally 9am–7pm, Tuesday to Saturday, and 9am–1pm on Sunday. Most other museums roughly follow this pattern, too, although they are more likely to close for a couple of hours in the afternoon, and have shorter opening hours in winter. Many large museums also run late-night openings in summer (till 10pm or later on Tuesday–Saturday, or 8pm on Sunday). There is no museum pass that will get you into all the main attractions in Rome. However, some sights are grouped together to make it easier and cheaper to visit them. For example, Rome's ancient sculpture and other artefacts have been gathered together into the **Museo Nazionale Romano**, which operates on three main sites: Palazzo Massimo, the Terme di Diocleziano, around the corner from Termini, and Palazzo Altemps, in the centro storico. You can buy a ticket from each location that gains entry to all the others for just €9, and it's valid for seven days.

Ancient sites

Again, there's no city-wide pass to get you into all the main **ancient sites**, but the Colosseum and Palatine are visitable on a combined ticket, and you can buy a seven-day ticket that gives entry to the Colosseum, Palatine Hill, Baths of Caracalla, Crypta Balbi and the collections of the Museo Nazionale Romano for €20 – probably the city's best bargain. The **opening times** of ancient sites are more flexible: most sites open every day, often Sunday included, from 9am until late evening – frequently specified as one hour before sunset, and thus changing according to the time of year. In winter, times are drastically cut, if only because of the darker evenings; 4pm is a common closing time.

Churches

Rome is very used to tourists, but the rules for visiting **churches** are much as they are all over the Italy. **Dress** modestly, which usually means no shorts (not even Bermuda-length ones) for men or women and covered shoulders for women, and try to avoid wandering around during a service. We've given **opening hours** throughout the

Chiuso per restauro

You may also find buildings of all kinds **closed for restoration** (*chiuso per restauro*), and it's usually pretty uncertain when they might reopen. The most notable casualties at the time of writing were the Museo Barracco, Ara Pacis and church of Santa Maria della Concezione, but as you might expect it's changing all the time and by the time you read this these may well be open and others closed. If there's something you really want to see, and you don't know when you might be back in Rome, it might be worth trying to persuade a workman or priest/curator to show you around even if there's scaffolding everywhere.

guide, but most major Roman churches – and most of the ones written up in this book – open in the early morning, at around 7am or 8am, and close around noon, opening up again at 4pm and closing at 6pm or 7pm. Some of the less-visited churches will open only for early morning and evening services, and some are closed at all times except Sundays and on religious holidays; if you're determined to take a look, you may have to ask around for the key, or make an appointment with the custodian.

Costs, money and banks

In recent years the economic boom and the introduction of the euro, not to mention the glut of visitors, have conspired to increase prices in Rome, indeed across Italy as a whole, and accommodation costs in particular have soared. Nonetheless, for most basics – eating out, having a drink, public transport – Rome is still a relatively cheap European capital.

Check the individual Listings chapters for further details on costs for Accommodation (p.198) and Eating and Drinking (p.216). You could survive on around €30 per day staying in the cheapest accommodation and eating out occasionally at the more modest restaurants but a daily budget is likely to be €90–120 staying at moderate hotels, seeing a good range of the sights and eating out regularly.

Italy (and the Vatican) replaced the lira with the **euro** (€) on January 1, 2002. There are seven euro notes – in denominations of 500, 200, 100, 50, 20, 10, and 5 euros, each a different colour and size – and eight different coin denominations, including 2 and 1 euros, then 50, 20, 10, 5, 2, and 1 cents. Euro coins feature a common EU design on one face, but different country-specific designs on the other (the rare Vatican euro features the face of Pope John Paul II). At the time of writing the rate of exchange was £1 = €1.50; US$1 = €0.82; Aus$1 = €0.55; NZ$ = €0.48; for the latest rates check: ⓦwww.oanda.com or ⓦwww.xe.com.

Changing money

As ever you'll get the best rate of exchange (cambio) at a **bank**. Banks are open Monday to Friday mornings 8.45am–1.30pm, and for an hour in the afternoon (usually 3–4pm). Outside banking hours, the larger **hotels** will change money or traveller's cheques, or there are plenty of **exchange bureaux** – normally open evenings and weekends.

Carrying money

If you're travelling from the UK it's a good idea to have some euros on you when you arrive; otherwise just use your debit card in the local **ATM machines** (Bancomats). The flat transaction fee is usually quite small – your bank will be able to advise on this. Bancomats accept all major cards, with a minimum withdrawal of €50 and a maximum of €250 per day.

Travellers from elsewhere, or on longer stays, may prefer to use **traveller's cheques**. American Express and the Thomas Cook and Visa alternatives are widely accepted. Buying online in advance usually works out cheapest. Make sure you keep the purchase agreement and a record of cheque serial numbers safe and separate from the cheques themselves. In the event that cheques are lost or stolen, the issuing company will expect you to report the loss forthwith to their office in Italy; most companies claim to replace lost or stolen cheques within 24 hours. It's advisable to buy euro traveller's cheques rather than dollars or pound sterling since you won't have to pay commission when you cash them.

Credit cards are a very handy backup source of funds, and can be used either over the counter or in ATMs, providing you have a PIN number that's designed to work overseas. Remember that all cash advances are treated as loans, with interest accruing daily from the date of withdrawal; there is often a transaction fee on top of this. A compromise between traveller's cheques and plastic is **Visa Travel Money**, a disposable pre-paid debit card with a PIN which works in all ATMs that take Visa cards. The card is available in most countries from branches of Thomas Cook and Citicorp. For more information, check the Visa Travel Money website: ⊛ international.visa.com/ps/products /vtravelmoney.

Post, phones and email

Post

Rome's **main post office** on Piazza San Silvestro is open Monday–Friday 8.30am–6.30pm, Saturday 8.30am–1pm; other post office hours vary, but tend to be something like Monday–Friday 8.30am–2pm, Saturday 8.30am–1pm. Stamps (*francobolli*), are also sold in *tabacchi*, who will often also weigh your letter. The Italian postal system is one of the slowest in Europe so if your letter is urgent make sure you send it *posta prioritaria* which has varying rates according to weight and destination. If you don't want to trust to the Italian post at all, in Rome at least you have a choice: the Vatican postal system is quicker, loses less, and you get the benefit of an exotic Vatican postmark. However, not unreasonably you have to use Vatican stamps and post your items from the Vatican itself. For this there are post offices and boxes in Piazza San Pietro and in the Vatican Museums.

Central post offices

Piazza San Silvestro 12
Via Cavour 277
Via Terme Diocleziano 30 (Termini)
Via Monterone (Piazza Venezia)
Via Arenula (Largo Argentina)
Via Milano 10 (Via Nazionale)

Phones

Public telephones, run by Telecom Italia, come in various forms, usually with clear instructions in English. Coin-operated machines are increasingly hard to find so you will probably have to buy a **telephone card** (*carta* or *scheda telefonica*), available from *tabacchi* and newsstands for €2.50 or €5 or €7.75. Note that the perforated corner of these cards must be torn off before they can be used. If you can't find a phone box, bars will often have a phone you can use – look for the yellow or red phone symbol. The telephone code for Rome is 06; you must dial this before any Roman number, even if you are in Rome. Numbers beginning ☎800 are free, ☎170 will get you through to an English-speaking operator, ☎176 to international directory enquiries. Phone **tariffs** are among the most expensive in Europe, though there is a reduced rate for off-peak calls (weekdays 6.30pm–8am, weekends 1pm Sat–8am Mon for national calls; 10pm–8am Mon–Sat and all day Sun for international calls).

Calling home from Rome

You can call abroad from most public phone boxes with an **international phone card** on sale at main post offices. The two most common phone cards are the *Columbus* card for calls to Western Europe and North America and the standard *Scheda Telefonica Internazionale* for the rest of the world. A slightly cheaper option at peak calling times is the *Europa Card* for calls to Europe, US and Canada only; you don't insert it into the phone but dial a central number and then a PIN code given on the reverse of the card. Alternatively you could consider a **telephone charge card** from your phone company back home. Using a PIN number, you can make calls from most hotel, public and private phones that will be charged to your account. Most major charge cards (eg BT, AT&T, Telstra) are free to obtain but bear in mind that rates aren't necessarily cheaper than calling from a public phone.

You can make **international reversed charge** or **collect calls** (*chiamata con addebito destinatario*) by dialling ☎170 and following the recorded instructions.

International codes

UK and Northern Ireland international access code + 44 + city code.
Republic of Ireland international access code + 353 + city code.

USA and Canada international access code + 1 + area code.
Australia international access code + 61 + city code.
New Zealand international access code + 64 + city code.

Calling Rome from abroad

To call Rome **from abroad**, dial the access code ☎00 from the UK, Ireland and New Zealand, ☎011 from the US and Canada, ☎0011 from Australia, followed by the code for Italy 39, then the local number including the 06 code.

Mobile phones

Mobile phones in Italy work on the GSM European standard. You will hardly see an Italian without his or her *telefonino*, but if you are going to join them make sure you have made the necessary "roaming" arrangements before you leave home. You are also likely to be charged extra for incoming calls when abroad, as the people calling you will be paying the usual rate. If you want to retrieve messages while you're away, you might have to ask your provider for a new access code. For further information about using your phone abroad contact your network or check out @http://www.telecomsadvice.org.uk.

Email and Internet

To access your email and the Internet, check out the **Internet cafés** listed on p.223. Otherwise try one of the following which all offer access for €4–6 an hour.
Museo del Corso Via del Corso 320 ☎06.678.6209; Tues–Fri 10am–8pm, Sat 10am–10pm, Sun 10am–8pm, closed Mon.
Netgate Piazza Firenze 25 ☎06.689.3445; Mon–Sat 10.30am–10.30pm.
Internet Point Via Gaeta 25 ☎06.4782.3862; Mon–Sun 9am–12am.

Crime and personal safety

Rome is a pretty safe city by any standards, but particularly when compared to its counterparts in the US and UK. The main thing is to make sure you're not too obvious a target for petty criminals by taking some common-sense precautions.

Most of the crime you're likely to come across will be **bag-snatching**, where gangs of either Gypsy kids or *scippatori* or "snatchers" operate; *scippatori* work on foot or on scooters, disappearing before you've had time to react; the kids are more likely to crowd you in a group, trying to work their way into your bags or pockets while you're trying to shoo them away. As well as handbags, they whip wallets, tear off visible jewellery and, if they're really adroit, unstrap watches. You can minimize the risk of this happening by being discreet: don't flash anything of value, keep a firm hand on your camera, and carry shoulderbags, as Italian women do, slung across your body. It's also worth being vigilant when withdrawing money from **ATMs**. Be aware of anyone standing too close or trying to distract you during a withdrawal – they may be trying to read your PIN or clone your card using a "skimmer" machine. Contact your bank or credit card provider immediately if you suspect you're a victim of card fraud.

There are not really any **parts of town** you should avoid: the area around Termini is a bit rough and sleazy but more uncomfortable (especially for women on their own) than dangerous. Deserted stretches around Ostiense or Testaccio are probably worth avoiding at night, but again this is just to be on the safe side rather than because of any track record of violent crime in these areas.

Police

If the worst happens, you'll be forced to have some dealings with the **police**, which in Italy is principally divided between the the **Vigili Urbani**, mainly concerned with directing traffic and issuing parking fines; the **Polizia Statale**, the main crime-fighting force; and the **Carabinieri**, with their military-style uniforms and white shoulder belts, who also deal with general crime, public order and drug control. The **Polizia** enjoy a fierce rivalry with the **Carabinieri** and are the ones you'll perhaps have most chance of coming into contact with, since **thefts** should be reported to them. You'll find the address of the **Questura** or police station in the telephone directory and we've included details of the main one in the Directory, p.259.

Emergencies

For help in an **emergency**, call one of the following national emergency telephone numbers:

☎112 for the police (Carabinieri).

☎113 for the police or any emergency service, including ambulance (Soccorso Pubblico di Emergenza).

☎115 for the fire brigade (Vigili del Fuoco).

☎116 for road assistance (Soccorso Stradale).

☎118 for an ambulance (Ambulanza).

The City

The City

Piazza Venezia and the Capitoline Hill

F or many people the modern centre of Rome is **Piazza Venezia**. It's not
so much a square as a road junction, and a busy one at that, but it's a good
central place to start your wanderings, close to both the medieval and
Renaissance centre of Rome and the bulk of the ruins of the ancient
city. Flanked on all sides by imposing buildings, it's a dignified focal point for
the city in spite of the traffic, and a spot you'll find yourself returning to time
and again – by some way the best landmarked open space in Rome, with the
great white bulk of the Vittorio Emanuele Monument marking it out from
almost anywhere in the city. The **Vittoriano**, as it's known, is now open to the
public, and despite being a widely disliked building is one of the best sights in
the city – not only for the views, but for the alternative route it gives to the
Piazza del Campidoglio and the unmissable **Capitoline Museums** on the
Capitoline Hill, the first-settled and most central of Rome's seven hills.

Piazza Venezia

There's not much need to linger on **Piazza Venezia** itself: it's more a place
to catch a bus or pick up a taxi than soak up the atmosphere. A legacy of
nineteenth-century Rome, it looked quite different a couple of hundred years
ago, when it was the domain of the Venetian pope, Paul II, whose Palazzo Venezia
dominated this part of the city, its gardens reaching around on the south side
where the Vittoriano now stands. On the opposite, northern side, the canyon of
Via del Corso, Rome's main street, begins its mile-and-a-half journey to the other
side of the city centre at the Piazza del Popolo. Its entrance here is flanked by the
nineteenth-century Palazzo Bonaparte on the right and the more stately bulk of
the Palazzo Doria Pamphilj on the left (see Chapter 2, The centro storico).

Palazzo Venezia

Forming the western side of the piazza, **Palazzo Venezia**, Via del Plebiscito
118 (Tues–Sun 8.30am–7pm; €4), was the first large Renaissance palace in the
city, built for the Venetian pope, Paul II, in the mid-fifteenth century and for a
long time the embassy of the Venetian Republic. More famously, Mussolini

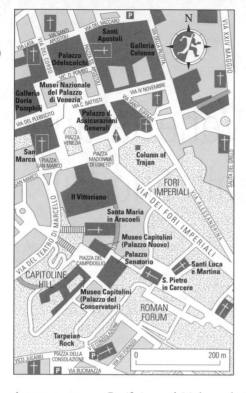

moved in here while in power, occupying the vast Sala del Mappamondo and making his declamatory speeches to the huge crowds below from the small balcony facing on to the piazza proper. In those days the palace lights would be left on to give the impression of constant activity in what was the centre of the Fascist government and war effort; now it's a much more peripheral building, a venue for great temporary exhibitions and home to a **museum** of Renaissance arts and crafts made up of the magpie-ish collection of Paul II. Much of this is closed to the public at present but its collection of **paintings** is open and includes a lot of fifteenth-century devotional works from central and northern Italy.

Among numerous *Crucifixions* and *Madonnas*, look out for an arresting double portrait of two young men by Giorgione; a late-sixteenth century *Deposition of Christ* by Borgianni, in which Christ is viewed from the feet up by way of clever use of perspective (a copy, basically, of Mantegna's painting of the same subject); and Algardi's bust of Innocent X. Otherwise, walk out to the palace's loggia for a view over the palm-filled courtyard **gardens** – some of the prettiest in Rome, though visitable only by appointment.

San Marco

Adjacent to the palace on its southern side, the church of **San Marco** (daily 8.30am–12.30pm & 4–7pm; closed Mon am & Wed pm), accessible from Piazza San Marco, is a tidy basilica, one of the oldest in Rome, having been founded in 336 AD on the spot where the apostle is supposed to have lived while in the city. It was rebuilt in 833 and added to by various Renaissance and eighteenth-century popes, and is a warm, cosy church, restored by Paul II – who added the graceful portico and gilded ceiling – with an apse mosaic dating from the ninth century showing Pope Gregory IV offering his church to Christ, oddly – and inexplicably – above a gracious semicircle of llamas. Back outside, tucked away in the corner, the statue of the busty harridan is **"Madam Lucretia"**, actually an ancient depiction of Isis, who like Pasquino a few hundred metres away is known as one of Rome's talking statues – commenting in a satirical fashion on the affairs of the day.

Rome's talking statues

As the home of the papacy, Rome has always been a political city, and its people have always enjoyed commenting on and arguing about the important issues of the day. They liked to do this more than ever during Renaissance times, when the antics of the Church, in particular the pope and the powerful Roman families who vied to fill the post, were the subject of intense curiosity and scrutiny. A number of **"talking statues"** – usually ancient, unidentified pieces, among them Madam Lucretia outside the basilica of San Marco, Pasquino in the centro storico, and Marforio, now in the courtyard of the Palazzo Nuovo (see p.35) – were a focus for this, hung as they were with witty rhymes and notes commenting on the hubris and foolishness of the movers and shakers of the papal city – a kind of gossip column-cum-parliamentary sketch that would attract people to talk and laugh at their political masters.

Vittorio Emanuele Monument

The rest of the buildings on Piazza Venezia pale into insignificance beside the marble monstrosity rearing up across the street from San Marco – the **Vittorio Emanuele Monument** or Vittoriano (daily 9.30–6.30pm; free), erected at the turn of the nineteenth century as the "Altar of the Nation" to commemorate Italian Unification. Variously likened in the past to a typewriter (because of its shape), and, by American GIs, to a wedding cake (the white marble used will never mellow with age), King Vittorio Emanuele II, who it's in part supposed to honour, probably wouldn't have thought much of it (he was by all accounts a modest man). Indeed, the only person who seems to have benefited from the building is the prime minister at the time, who was a deputy for Brescia, from where (perhaps not entirely coincidentally) the marble was supplied.

The Vittoriano was closed to the public for years, but it's now open, which is just as well as at least that gives it a (kind of) purpose. It's great to clamber up and down the sweeping terraces and flights of steps which before you could only gaze at from the street. There are things to see inside the monument, though perhaps only on a rainy day: a vast and deadly Museo di Risorgimento, a collection of military flags, and a bookshop; and there are regular temporary art and other exhibitions held in the various echoing chambers. But it's the outside of the structure that should command most of your attention, full as it is of the weighty symbolism that was typical of the period. The figures either side of the entrance represent the two seas that flank Italy – the Tyrrhenian (on the right) and the Adriatic (on the left). At the top of the stairs is the Tomb of the Unknown Soldier, flanked by eternal flames and a permanent guard of honour. Above this is an **equestrian statue** (10m x 12m) of Vittorio Emanuele II, one of the world's largest (his moustache alone is 3m long), which sits on a plinth friezed with figures representing the major cities of the Italian Republic. Above here, the huge, sweeping gallery stretches the width of the monument, with figures symbolising the regions of Italy. The whole thing is undeniably impressive, if only for the sheer audaciousness of its conception, and there's a café around the back, from where you can now walk all the way through to Piazza del Campidoglio behind. Wherever you stand, though, the views of the city are the thing, most of all perhaps because it's the one place in Rome from which you can't see the Vittoriano.

△ Vittorio Emanuele Monument

The Capitoline Hill

The real pity about the Vittorio Emanuele Monument is that it obscures views of the **Capitoline Hill** behind – once, in the days of imperial Rome, the spiritual and political centre of the Roman Empire. The name derives from its position as the "caput mundi" or "head of the world", and its influence and importance resonate to this day, not least in language – words such as "capitol" and "capital" originated here, as did the word "money", which comes from the temple to Juno Moneta that once stood on the hill and housed the Roman mint. The Capitoline also played a significant role in medieval and Renaissance times: the flamboyant fourteenth-century dictator, Cola di Rienzo, stood here in triumph in 1347, and was murdered here by an angry mob seven years later – a humble nineteenth-century statue marks the spot where he is said to have died. And Michelangelo gave the hill's **Piazza del Campidoglio** its present form, redesigning it as a symbol of Rome's regeneration after the city was sacked in 1527. These days the Capitoline forms a tight, self-contained group of essential attractions, with the focus on its pair of **museums** and the church of Santa Maria in Aracoeli. The nice thing is that it is much more linked to the rest of the city than it once was, with walkways connecting with the Vittoriano in one direction and down to the Roman Forum in the other.

Santa Maria in Aracoeli

The church of **Santa Maria in Aracoeli** (daily: summer 7am–noon & 4–6.30pm; winter closes 5.30pm) crowns the highest point on the Capitoline Hill, and is built on the site of a temple to Jupiter where, according to legend, the Tiburtine Sibyl foretold the birth of Christ. It is reached by a flight of steps erected by Cola di Rienzo in 1348, the **Aracoeli Staircase**; the climb to the top is steep but the church, one of Rome's most ancient basilicas, is worth it. Inside, in the first chapel on the right, there are some fine, humane frescoes by Pinturicchio recording the life of San Bernardino – realistic tableaux of landscapes and bustling town scenes. The church is also known for its role as keeper of the so-called "**Bambino**", a small statue of the child Christ, carved from the wood of a Gethsemane olive tree, that is said to have healing powers and was traditionally called out to the sickbeds of the ill and dying all over the city, its coach commanding instant right of way through the heavy Rome traffic. The Bambino was stolen in 1994, however, and a copy now stands in its place, in a small chapel to the left of the high altar.

Piazza del Campidoglio

Next door to the Aracoeli Staircase, the **Cordonata** is an elegant, smoothly rising ramp, and as such a much gentler climb. Topped with two Roman statues of Castor and Pollux, it leads to **Piazza del Campidoglio**, one of Rome's most perfectly proportioned squares, designed by Michelangelo in the last years of his life for Pope Paul III, who was determined to hammer Rome back into shape for a visit by the Holy Roman Emperor, Charles V. In fact, Michelangelo died before his plan was completed (the square wasn't finished until the late seventeenth century), but his designs were faithfully executed, balancing the piazza, redesigning the facade of what is now Palazzo dei Conservatori and projecting an identical building across the way, known as Palazzo Nuovo. These buildings, which have recently been completely renovated, are home to the **Capitoline Museums** and feature some of the city's most important ancient sculpture. Both are angled slightly to focus on **Palazzo Senatorio**, Rome's town hall. In the centre of the square Michelangelo placed an equestrian statue of Emperor Marcus Aurelius, which had previously stood unharmed for years outside San Giovanni in Laterano; early Christians had refrained from melting it down because they believed it to be of the Emperor Constantine (the first Roman ruler to acknowledge and follow Christianity). After careful restoration, the original is behind a glass wall in the Palazzo Nuovo, and a copy has taken its place at the centre of the piazza.

The Capitoline Museums

If you see no other museums of **ancient sculpture** in Rome, at least try to see the Capitoline Museums (Tues–Sun 9am–8pm; €7.80, €9 for Centrale Montemartini as well, see Chapter 6; ⓦwww.museicapitolini.org), which are perhaps the most venerable of all the city's collections. They're divided into two parts, one devoted only to sculpture, the other more extensive and more of a mixture, with a gallery of paintings as well. You should see both areas of the museum rather than choosing one. **Tickets** are valid for a day so you can see both parts, and have a break for a stroll around the Roman Forum in between.

Palazzo dei Conservatori

The **Palazzo dei Conservatori** on the right is perhaps the natural place to start, home as it is to the museums' ticket office. It's the larger, more varied collection, with some ancient sculpture but later pieces too; some of the ancient stuff is littered around the **courtyard** you pass through to get in – not least the feet, hand and other fragments of a gigantic statue – believed to be of the Emperor Constantine – that is one of the most popular images of Rome. Inside, the centrepiece of the first floor, the **Hall of the Orazie e Curiaze**, where the curators of the collections used to meet, is appropriately decorated with giant late-sixteenth-century frescoes showing legendary tales from the early days of Rome – *The Discovery of the She-wolf*, at the western end, faces the *Rape of the Sabine Women* at the opposite end. For the moment a giant bronze statue, again of Constantine, or at least its head, hand, and orb, have been relocated here from the courtyard, along with a rippling bronze of Hercules, found near the Circus Maxentius, while presiding over all is a colossal statue of Pope Innocent X. The rooms that follow have more friezes and murals showing events from Roman history, most notably the **Hannibal Room**, covered in wonderfully vivid fifteenth-century paintings recording Rome's wars with Carthage, and so named for a rendering of Hannibal seated impressively on an elephant. The sacred symbol of Rome, the Etruscan bronze **she-wolf** nursing the mythic founders of the city, gets a room to itself; the twins themselves are not Etruscan but were added by Pollaiuolo in the late fifteenth century.

The second-floor picture gallery – the pinacoteca holds **Renaissance painting** from the fourteenth century to the late seventeenth century – well-labelled, with descriptions of each painting in Italian and English. The paintings fill half a dozen rooms or so, and highlights include a couple of portraits by Van Dyck and a penetrating *Portrait of a Crossbowman* by Lorenzo Lotto; a pair of paintings from 1590 by Tintoretto – a *Flagellation* and *Christ Crowned with Thorns*; some nice small-scale work by Annibale Carracci; and a very fine early work by Ludovico Carracci, *Head of a Boy*. There are also several sugary works by Guido Reni, done at the end of his life. In one of two large main galleries, there's a vast picture by Guercino, depicting the *Burial of Santa Petronilla* (an early Roman martyr who was the supposed daughter of St Peter), which used to hang in

St Peter's and arrived here via the Quirinale palace and the Louvre, to hang alongside several other works by the same artist, notably a lovely, contemplative Persian Sibyl and a wonderful picture of Cleopatra cowed before a young and victorious Octavius. In the same room, there are also two paintings by Caravaggio, one a replica of the young *John the Baptist* which hangs in the Palazzo Doria Pamphilj, the other a famous canvas known as the *Fortune-Teller* – an early work that's an adept study in deception.

Palazzo Nuovo

The same ticket gets you into the **Palazzo Nuovo** across the square – also accessible by way of an underground walkway that takes in yet more sculpture, the remains of a Roman temple, and, above all, a terrace which has probably the best, certainly the most close-up, **views** of the Roman Forum just below. The Palazzo Nuovo is the more manageable of the two museums, its first floor concentrating some of the best of the city's **Roman sculpture** into half a dozen or so rooms and a long gallery crammed with elegant statuary. There's the remarkable, controlled statue of the *Dying Gaul*, a Roman copy of a Hellenistic original; a naturalistic *Boy with Goose* – another copy; an original, grappling depiction of *Eros and Psyche*; a *Satyr Resting*, after a piece by Praxiteles, that was the inspiration for Hawthorne's book *The Marble Faun*; and the red marble *Laughing Silenus*, another Roman copy of a Greek original. The main *salone* has two statues of an old and a young centaur facing each other, and a naturalistic *Hunter* holding up a rabbit he has just killed. Walk through from here to the **Sala degli Imperatori**, with its busts of Roman emperors and other famous names, including a young Augustus, a cruel Caracalla, and, the centrepiece, a lifesize portrait of Helena, the mother of Constantine, reclining gracefully. Also, don't miss the *Capitoline Venus*, housed in a room on its own – a coy, delicate piece, again based on a work by Praxiteles. Finally, the **palace courtyard** is dominated by the large Fountain of Marforio, a bearded figure who, like the figure outside the church of San Marco, was known as one of Rome's "talking statues", renowned in Renaissance times for speaking out in satirical verse against the authorities on topical issues of the day (see box p.31).

The Tarpeian Rock and San Pietro in Carcere

After seeing the museums, walk around behind the Palazzo Senatorio for another great view down over the Forum, with the Colosseum in the background. There's a copy of the statue of Romulus and Remus suckling the she-wolf here, while on the right, Via del Monte Tarpeio follows, as its name suggests, the brink of the old Tarpeian Rock, from which traitors would be thrown in ancient times – so called after Tarpeia, who betrayed the city to the Sabines. Steps lead down from here to the little church of San Pietro in Carcere (daily: summer 9am–noon & 2.30–6pm; winter 9am–noon & 2–5pm; donation expected), built above the ancient Mamertine Prison, where spies, vanquished soldiers and other enemies of the Roman state were incarcerated, and where St Peter himself was held. Steps lead down into the murky depths of the jail, where you can see the bars to which he was chained, along with the spring the saint is said to have created to baptize other prisoners. At the top of the staircase, hollowed out of the honeycomb of stone, is an imprint claimed to be of St Peter's head as he tumbled down the stairs (though when the prison was in use, the only access was through a hole in the ceiling). It's an unappealing place even now, and you won't be sorry to leave – through an exit cunningly placed to lead you through the gift shop.

The centro storico

The real heart of Rome is the **centro storico** or "historic centre", which makes up the greater part of the roughly triangular knob of land that bulges into a bend in the Tiber, above **Corso Vittorio Emanuele II** and to the west of **Via del Corso**, Rome's main street. This area, known in ancient Roman times as the Campus Martius, was outside the ancient city centre, a low-lying area that was mostly given over to barracks and sporting arenas, together with several temples, including the **Pantheon**. Later it became the heart of the Renaissance city, and nowadays it's the part of the town that is densest in interest, an unruly knot of narrow streets and alleys that holds some of the best of Rome's classical and Baroque heritage and its most vivacious street- and nightlife. It's here that most people find the Rome they have been looking for – the Rome of small crumbling piazzas, Renaissance churches and fountains, blind alleys and streets humming with scooters and foot-traffic. Whichever direction you wander in there's something to see; indeed it's part of the appeal of the centre of Rome that even the most aimless ambling leads you past some breathlessly beautiful and historic spots.

From Via del Corso to the Pantheon

The eastern boundary of the historic centre, **Via del Corso** is Rome's main thoroughfare, linking Piazza Venezia at its southern end with the Piazza del Popolo to the north. You can follow it all the way up, dipping into the centro storico as and when you feel like it. The streets on this side of the centre focus on the ancient Roman dome of the **Pantheon**, and further north on the offices of the **Italian parliament** and prime minister.

Via del Corso

On its eastern side, **Via del Corso** gives onto the swish shopping thoroughfares that lead up to Piazza di Spagna; and on its western side, onto the web of streets that tangles its way right down to the Tiber. Named after the races that used to take place along here during Renaissance times, the street has had its fair share of famous residents during the years: Goethe lived for two years at no.18, close to the Piazza del Popolo end; the Shelleys – Percy and Mary – lived for several years in the Palazzo Vesporio, at Via del Corso 375 (now a bank), during which time they lost their son William to a fever. More recently, it has become Rome's principal shopping street, home to a mixture of

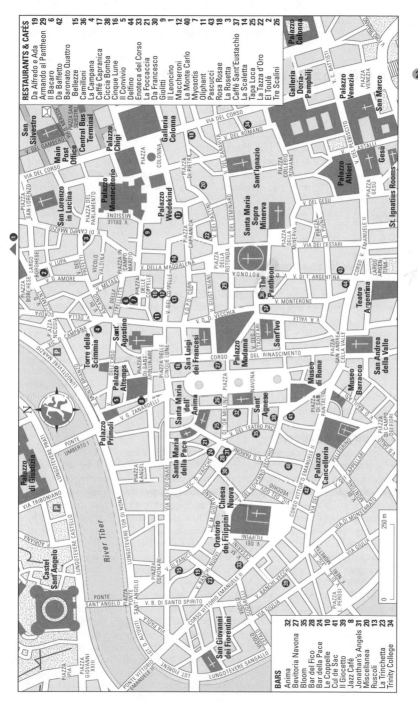

upmarket boutiques and chain stores that make it a busy stretch during the day, full of hurrying pedestrians and crammed buses, but a relatively dead one come the evening.

2 The Palazzo and Galleria Doria Pamphilj

Walking north from Piazza Venezia, the first building on the left of Via del Corso, the **Palazzo Doria Pamphilj**, is among the city's finest Rococo palaces, with a facade added in 1734 to a building that was the product of years of construction and re-modelling dating back to Roman times, when a storehouse stood on this site. The Doria Pamphilj family were (and are) one of Rome's most illustrious, and still own the building and live in part of it. They were also prodigious collectors of art, and inside, through an entrance on Piazza di Collegio Romano, the **Galleria Doria Pamphilj**, Via del Collegio Romano 2, constitutes one of Rome's best late-Renaissance art collections (Mon–Wed & Fri–Sun 10am–5pm; €8, including audio guide in English; private apartments tours every 30min 10.30am–12.30pm; €3.50; Ⓦ www.doriapamphilj.it).

The private apartments

The first part of the gallery is made up of a series of **private apartments**, furnished in the style of the original palace, through which you're guided by way of the gallery's free audio tour, narrated by the urbane Jonathan Pamphilj. On view is the large and elegant reception hall of the original palace, off which there is a room where the Pamphilj pope, Innocent X, used to receive guests, complete with a portrait of the great man. There are also a couple of side salons filled with busts and portraits of the rest of the family; a late – and probably by Rococo standards, rather poky – ballroom, complete with a corner terrace from which the band played; and a private chapel, which astonishingly contains the incorruptible body of St Theodora, swathed in robes, and the relics of St Justin under the altar.

The picture gallery

Beyond here, the **picture gallery** extends around a courtyard, the paintings mounted in the style of the time, crammed in frame-to-frame, floor-to-ceiling. The labelling is better than it once was, with sporadic paintings labelled, and selected others numbered and described on the audio tour, but it's still deliberately old-fashioned, and perhaps all the better for it. Just inside, at the corner of the courtyard, there's a badly cracked bust of Innocent X by **Bernini**, which the sculptor apparently replaced in a week with the more famous version down the hall, in a room off to the left, where Bernini appears to have captured the pope about to erupt into laughter. In the same room, **Velázquez**'s famous painting of the same man is quite different, depicting a rather irritable character regarding the viewer with impatience.

The rest of the collection is just as rich in interest, and there are many paintings and pieces of sculpture worth lingering over. There is perhaps Rome's best concentration of **Dutch** and **Flemish** paintings, including a rare Italian work by Brueghel the Elder, showing a naval battle being fought outside Naples, complete with Vesuvius, Castel Nuovo and other familiar landmarks, along with a highly realistic portrait of two old men, by Quentin Metsys, and a Hans Memling *Deposition*, in the furthest rooms, as well as a further Metsys painting – the fabulously ugly *Moneylenders and their Clients* – in the main gallery. There is also a *St Jerome*, by the Spanish painter Giuseppe Ribera, one of 4 supposed to have painted of the saint; Carracci's bucolic *Flight into E* painted shortly before the artist's death; two paintings by Caravaggio – *M Magdalene* and *John the Baptist*; and *Salome with the head of St John*, by Titia. Spare some time, also, for the marvellous classical statuary, busts, sarcophagi and figurines, displayed in the Aldobrandini room and on the Via del Corso side of the main gallery. All in all, it's a marvellous collection of work, displayed in a wonderfully appropriate setting.

Sant'Ignazio

The next left off Via del Corso after the palace leads into **Piazza di Sant'Ignazio** (daily 7.30am–12.30pm & 4–7.15pm), a lovely little square, laid out like a theatre set and dominated by the facade of the Jesuit church of **Sant'Ignazio**. The saint isn't actually buried here; appropriately, for the founder of the Jesuit order, he's in the main Jesuit church, the Gesù, a little way south. But it's a spacious structure, worth visiting for its marvellous Baroque ceiling by Andrea del Pozzo showing the entry of St Ignatius into paradise, a spectacular work that employs sledgehammer trompe l'oeil effects, notably in the mock cupola painted into the dome of the crossing. Stand on the disc in the centre of the nave, the focal point for the ingenious rendering of perspective: figures in various states of action and repose, conversation and silence, fix you with stares from their classical pediment.

The Pantheon

From Sant'Ignazio, Via del Seminario leads down to **Piazza della Rotonda**, one of the city's most picturesque squares, and perhaps suffering because of it, invariably thronged with sight-weary tourists, hawkers and street musicians, besieging the café tables that fringe the edge. The waters of the fountains in the middle are a soothing influence, an eighteenth-century construction topped by yet another obelisk, but the main focus of interest is of course the **Pantheon** (Mon–Sat 9am–6.30pm, Sun 9am–1pm; free), which forms the square's southern edge, easily the most complete ancient Roman structure in the city and, along with the Colosseum, visually the most impressive. Though originally a temple that formed part of Marcus Agrippa's redesign of the Campus Martius in around 27 BC – hence the inscription – it's since been proved that the building was entirely rebuilt by the emperor **Hadrian** and finished around the year 125 AD. It's a formidable architectural achievement even now, although like the city's other Roman monuments, it would have been much more sumptuous in its day. It was consecrated as a Christian site in 609 AD and dedicated to Santa Maria ai Martiri in allusion to the Christian bones that were found here; a thousand years later, the bronze roof was stripped from the ceiling of the portico by Pope Urban VIII, to be melted down for the baldachino in St Peter's and the cannons of the Castel Sant'Angelo. (Interestingly, some of the "stolen" bronze later found its way back here when, after Unification, the cannons were in turn melted down to provide materials for the tombs of two Italian kings, which are housed in the right and left chapels.)

Inside, you get the best impression of the engineering expertise of Hadrian: the diameter is precisely equal to its height (43m), the hole in the centre of the dome – from which shafts of sunlight descend to illuminate the musty interior – a full 9m across. Most impressively, there are no visible arches or vaults to hold the whole thing up; instead they're sunk into the concrete of the walls of the building. Again, it would have been richly decorated, the coffered ceiling heavily stuccoed and the niches filled with the statues of gods. Now, apart from the sheer size of the place, the main point of interest is the **tomb of Raphael**, between the second and third chapel on the left, with an inscription by the humanist bishop Pietro Bembo: "Living, great Nature feared he might outvie Her works, and dying, fears herself may die." The same kind of sentiments might well have been reserved for the Pantheon itself.

Santa Maria sopra Minerva

There's more artistic splendour on view behind the Pantheon, though Bernini's diminutive **Elephant Statue** doesn't really prepare you for the church of Santa Maria sopra Minerva beyond. The statue is Bernini's most endearing piece of work, if not his most characteristic: a cheery elephant trumpeting under the weight of the obelisk he carries on his back – a reference to Pope Alexander VII's reign and supposed to illustrate the fact that strength should support wisdom. **Santa Maria sopra Minerva** (Mon–Sat 7am–7pm, Sun 8am–7pm) is Rome's only Gothic church, and worth a look just for that, though its soaring lines have since been overburdened by marble and frescoes. Built in the late thirteenth century on the ruins of a temple to Minerva, it is also one of Rome's art-treasure churches, crammed with the tombs and self-indulgences of wealthy Roman families. Of these, the Carafa Chapel, in the south transept, is the best known, holding Filippino Lippi's fresco of *The Assumption*, a bright, effervescent piece of work, below which one painting shows a hopeful Carafa (the religious zealot, Pope Paul IV) being presented to the Virgin Mary by Thomas Aquinas; another depicts Aquinas confounding the heretics in the sight of two beautiful young boys – the future Medici popes Leo X and Clement VII (the equestrian statue of Marcus Aurelius, destined for the Capitoline Hill, is just visible in the background). You should look, too, at the figure of *Christ Bearing the Cross*, on the left-hand side of the main altar, a serene work that Michelangelo completed for the church in 1521.

Sant'Ivo alla Sapienza

A few steps west of the Pantheon, on Corso del Rinascimento, the rather blank facade of the **Palazzo della Sapienza** cradles the church of **Sant'Ivo alla Sapienza** (Sun 10am–1pm) – from the outside at least, one of Rome's most impressive churches, with a playful facade designed by Borromini. Though originally built for the most famous Barberini pope, Urban VIII, the building actually spans the reign of three pontiffs. Each of the two small towers is topped with the weird, blancmange-like groupings that are the symbol of the Chigi family (representing the hills of Monti Paschi), and the central cupola spirals helter-skelter-fashion to its zenith, crowned with flames that are supposed to represent the sting of the Barberini bee, their family symbol. Inside, too, it's very cleverly designed, impressively light and spacious given the small space the church is squeezed into, rising to the tall parabolic cupola.

San Luigi dei Francesi

Just north of Sant'Ivo, there's a constant police presence around the seventeenth-century **Palazzo Madama**, which holds the offices and chamber of the Italian upper house or Senate. Cutting back towards the Pantheon, on to the bottom end of **Via della Scrofa**, the French national church of **San**

Luigi dei Francesi (daily except Thurs afternoon 7.30am–12.30pm & 3.30–7pm) is another church in the vicinity of the Pantheon that is worth a look, mainly for the works by **Caravaggio** that it numbers amongst its collection. In the last chapel on the left are three paintings: the *Calling of St Matthew*, in which Christ points to Matthew, who is illuminated by a shaft of sunlight; Matthew visited by an angel as he writes the Gospel; and the saint's martyrdom. Caravaggio's first public commission, these paintings were actually rejected at first, partly on grounds of indecorum, and it took considerable reworking by the artist before they were finally accepted.

Sant'Agostino

Further north up Via della Scrofa, off to the left, the Renaissance facade of the church of **Sant'Agostino** (daily 7.45am–noon & 4–7.30pm) takes up one side of a drab piazza of the same name. It's not much to look at from the outside, but a handful of art treasures might draw you in: this was the church of Rome's creative community in the sixteenth century and as such drew wealthy patrons and well-connected artists. Just inside the door, the serene statue of the *Madonna del Parto*, by Sansovino, is traditionally invoked during pregnancy, and is accordingly surrounded by photos of newborn babes and their blissful parents. Further into the church, take a look also at Raphael's vibrant fresco of *Isaiah*, on the third pillar on the left, beneath which is another work by Sansovino, a craggy *St Anne, Virgin and Child*. But the biggest crowds gather around the first chapel on the left, where the *Madonna di Loreto*, painted in 1605 by Caravaggio, is a characteristic work of what was at the time almost revolutionary realism, showing two peasants praying at the feet of a sensuous *Mary and Child*, their dirty feet and scruffy clothes contrasting with the pale, delicate feet and skin of Mary.

Torre della Scimmia

Just beyond Sant'Agostino on Via dei Portoghesi, take a look at the **Torre della Scimmia** – literally the "Tower of the Monkey" – which grows almost organically out of a fork in the road above an ivy-covered palazzo. The story goes that in the seventeenth century a pet monkey kidnapped a child and carried it to the top of the tower; the father of the child called upon the Virgin for help and the monkey promptly clambered down, delivering the child to safety. By way of thanks, the man erected a shrine to the Virgin, which you can still see at the top of the tower, accompanied by a glowing lamp that is to this day kept constantly burning.

Piazza di Montecitorio

A couple of minutes' walk from the Torre della Scimmia, **Piazza di Montecitorio** takes its name from the bulky **Palazzo di Montecitorio** on its northern side, home since 1871 to the lower house of the Italian **parliament** – the building itself is a Bernini creation from 1650. The obelisk in the centre of the square was brought to Rome by Augustus and set up in the Campus Martius, where it formed the hand of a giant sundial.

Piazza Colonna

Just beyond, off Via del Corso, the **Piazza Colonna** is flanked on its north side by the late sixteenth-century **Palazzo Chigi**, official residence of the

△ Torre dell' Orologio

prime minister and as such not open to the public. The **Column of Marcus Aurelius**, which gives the square its name, was erected between 180 and 190 AD to commemorate military victories in northern Europe, and, like the column of Trajan which inspired it, is decorated with reliefs depicting scenes from the campaigns. The statue of St Paul on top was added by Sixtus V, made from bronze from the ancient doors of the church of Sant' Agnese fuori le Mura (see Chapter 7). As for the square, it used to be the site of the city's principal coffee-roasters' market, so was always a busy spot, and it still has an elegant backdrop in the **Palazza Wedekind**, home to *Il Tempo* newspaper, whose dozen or so Ionic columns, originally Roman, support a gracious balustraded terrace. Across the way, the **Galleria Alberto Sordi**, a classic Y-shaped nineteenth-century shopping arcade has recently reopened after being closed for years. Renamed after a famous Italian actor (actors used to hang out here seeking work), it's as spruce and sleek as it was in its heyday.

San Lorenzo in Lucina

A little further up Via del Corso, on the left, the wedge-shaped **Largo San Lorenzo** is a surprisingly spacious and relatively peaceful escape from the bustle of the Corso. On its left side, the church of **San Lorenzo in Lucina** (daily 8am–noon & 4–7.30pm) stands out among the largely undistinguished buildings, due to its manifestly ancient campanile and columned portico; the church originally dates from the fifth century but was rebuilt in the twelfth century. Inside, like so many Roman churches, it doesn't look or feel nearly so old – indeed much of it dates from the seventeenth century – but there are several features of interest, not least a section of the griddle on which St Lawrence was roasted (see p.112), in a reliquary in the first chapel on the right – though this is almost impossible to see. A little further down on the same side, the tomb of the French painter **Nicholas Poussin** is a delicate nineteenth-century marble affair by his compatriot Chateaubriand; Poussin spent much of his life in Rome, and died here in 1665. Beyond, take a look also at Bernini's bust of the doctor of Innocent X, Fonseca, in the next chapel but one, and the *Crucifixion* by Guido Reni in the apse.

Piazza Navona and around

The other half of the centro storico focuses on and around **Piazza Navona**, Rome's most famous square – a pedestrianized oval that is as picturesque as any piazza in Italy, and lined with cafés and restaurants and often thronged with tourists, street artists and pigeons. The best time to come is at night, when the inevitably tourist-geared flavour of the place is at its most vibrant, with crowds hanging out around the fountains or clocking the scene while nursing a pricey drink at a table outside one of the bars, or watching the buskers and street artists entertain the throng.

Piazza Navona

Piazza Navona takes its shape from the first-century AD Stadium of Domitian, the principal venue of the athletic events and later chariot races that took place in the Campus Martius (see p.36). Until the mid-fifteenth century the ruins of the arena were still here, overgrown and disused, but the square was given a facelift in the mid-seventeenth century by Pope Innocent X, who built most of the grandiose palaces that surround it and commissioned Borromini to design the facade of the church of **Sant'Agnese in Agone** on the piazza's western side. The story goes that the 13-year-old St Agnes was stripped naked before the crowds in the stadium as punishment for refusing to marry, whereupon she miraculously grew hair to cover herself. She was later martyred by a sword blow to her throat. Nowadays she is the patron saint of young girls; this church, typically squeezed into the tightest of spaces by Borromini, is supposedly built on the spot where it all happened.

Opposite, the **Fontana dei Quattro Fiumi**, one of three that punctuate the square, is a masterpiece of 1651 by Bernini, Borromini's arch-rival. Each figure represents one of what were considered at the time to be the four great rivers of the world – the Nile, Danube, Ganges and Plate – though only the horse, symbolizing the Danube, was actually carved by Bernini himself. It's said that all the figures are shielding their eyes in horror from Borromini's church facade (Bernini was an arrogant man who never had time for the work of the less successful Borromini), but the fountain had actually been completed before the facade was begun. The grand complexity of rock is topped with an Egyptian obelisk, brought here by Pope Innocent X from the Circus of Maxentius.

Bernini also had a hand in the fountain at the southern end of the square, the so-called **Fontana del Moro**, designing the central figure of the Moor in what is another fantastically playful piece of work, surrounded by toothsome dolphins and other marine figures. The fountain at the opposite end of the square, the **Fontana del Nettuno**, is equally fanciful, depicting Neptune struggling with a sea monster, surrounded by other briny creatures in a riot of fishing nets and nymphets, beards and breasts, scales and suckers.

Piazza Pasquino

Just south of Piazza Navona, immediately behind the Palazzo Braschi, it's easy to miss the battered torso of **Pasquino**, even in the small triangular space of **Piazza Pasquino**, in the corner of which it still stands. Pasquino is perhaps the best-known of Rome's "talking statues" of the Middle Ages and Renaissance times, upon which anonymous comments on the affairs of the day would be attached – comments that had a serious as well as a humorous intent (see Chapter 1). Pasquino gave us our word "pasquinade", but nowadays the graffitied comments and photocopied poems that occasionally grace the statue are usually somewhat lacking in wit.

Museo di Roma

Backing on to Piazza Navona, the eighteenth-century Palazzo Braschi is the home of the **Museo di Roma**, Piazza San Pantaleo 10 (Tues–Sun 9am–7pm; €6.20; ⓦ www.museodiroma.commune.roma.it), which has a recently restored permanent collection relating to the history of the city from the Middle Ages to the present day. To be honest, it's a large museum and is only sporadically interesting. Indeed the building – particularly the magnificent **Sala Nobile** where you go in, the main staircase, and one or two of the renovated rooms, not least the exotically painted Sala Cinese and Sala Egiziana – is probably the main event. But there's interest in some of the **paintings**, which show the city during different eras – St Peter's Square before Bernini's colonnade was built, jousting in Piazza Navona and the Cortile Belvedere in the Vatican, big gatherings and processions in the Campidoglio and Piazza del Popolo – and **frescoes** from demolished palaces provide decent enough highlights. There are, too, portraits and busts of the most eminent Roman families, most of whom made pope at one time or another – not only Braschi, but also the Corsini, Chigi, Odelaschi, names which resonate elsewhere around historic parts of the city, and who gaze out of the rooms here with deadly and penetrating self-importance.

Sant'Andrea della Valle

Across the road towards Largo Argentina, the church of **Sant'Andrea della Valle** (Mon–Sat 7.30am–noon & 4.30–7.30pm, Sun 7.30am–12.45pm & 4.30–7.45pm) has the distinction of sporting the city's second-tallest dome (after St Peter's), built by Carlo Maderno. Inside, it's one of the most Baroque of Rome's churches, a high, barn-like building, in which most of your attention is drawn not only to the dome, decorated with paintings of the *Glory of Paradise* by Giovanni Lanfranco, but also to a marvellous set of frescoes in the apse by his contemporary, Domenichino, illustrating the life of St Andrew, and centring on the monumental scene of his crucifixion on the characteristic transverse cross. In a side chapel on the right, you may, if you've been in Rome a while, recognize some good-looking copies of not only Michelangelo's *Pietà* (the original is in St Peter's), but also of his figures of *Leah* and *Rachel*, from the same artist's tomb of his patron, Julius II, in the church of San Pietro in Vincoli (see p.117).

Museo Barracco

Immediately across the road from the Palazzo Braschi, Piazza dei Baullari 1 is the so-called **Piccola Farnesina** palace, built by Antonio Sangallo the Younger. The palace itself actually never had anything to do with the Farnese family, and took the name "little Farnese" because of the lilies on the outside of the building, which were confused with the Farnese heraldic lilies. It is currently being restored, but it normally holds the **Museo Barracco**, a small but fine-quality collection of ancient sculpture that was donated to the city at the turn of the century by one Baron Barracco. There are ancient Egyptian and Hellenistic pieces, including two sphinxes from the reigns of Hapsupset and Rameses II, an austere head of an Egyptian priest and a bust of a young Rameses II and statues and reliefs of the God Bes from various eras. Look out also for ceramics and statuary from the Greek classical period – essentially the fourth and fifth centuries BC – a small but very high-quality collection which includes a lovely, almost complete figurine of Hercules; a larger figure of an athlete copied from an original by Policlitus; a highly realistic bitch washing herself from the fourth century BC; and a complete and very beautiful votive relief dedicated to Apollo. In a small room at the front of the building, there are also later Roman pieces, most notably a small figure of Neptune from the first century BC and an odd, almost Giacometti-like column-sculpture of a very graphically drawn hermaphrodite. Look also at the charming two busts of young Roman boys opposite, which date from the first century AD.

Palazzo della Cancelleria

Further along Corso Vittorio Emanuele II is the grand **Palazzo della Cancelleria**, the seat of the papal government that once ran the city; Bramante is thought to have had a hand in its design, and it is certainly a gorgeous and well-proportioned edifice, which exudes a cool poise quite at odds with the rather grimy nature of its location. You can't get in to see the interior, but you can stroll into the marvellously proportioned, multi-tiered courtyard which is treat enough in itself, although the adjacent church of **San Lorenzo in Damaso** also forms part of the complex and is open regular church hours.

Via del Governo Vecchio and around

Back in the heart of the old city, **Via del Governo Vecchio** leads west from Piazza Pasquino through one of Rome's liveliest quarters. The street was named for the **Palazzo Nardini** at no.39, which was once the seat of the governors of Rome. It's being restored at the moment but normally you can wander in to look at its elegant courtyard. However, this part of Rome is best-known for its **nightlife**, its narrow streets noisy at night, and holding some of the city's most vigorous restaurants and bars.

A little way down on the left, the delightful small square of **Piazza del Orologio** is so called because of the quaint clocktower that is its main feature. The clock is part of the **Oratorio dei Filippini**, designed by Carlo Borromini, which backs onto the Chiesa Nuova (see below) and is part of the same complex: the followers of Filippo Neri (founder of the Chiesa Nuova) attended musical gatherings here as part of their worship, hence the musical term "oratorio". Nowadays it's given over to a library of nineteenth-century literature and hosts temporary exhibitions – take the time to sneak in and rest for five minutes in its elegant orange-tree-shaded courtyard. Just off the square, there's a scatter of antique and bric-a-brac shops, which signal that you're just around the corner from Rome's antiques ghetto, Via dei Coronari (see below).

Chiesa Nuova and around

The **Chiesa Nuova** (daily 8.30am–noon & 4.30–7pm) backs onto Via del Governo Vecchio and is another highly ornate Baroque church – which is strange, because its founder, **St Philip Neri**, didn't want it decorated at all. Neri was an ascetic man, who tended the poor and sick in the streets around here for most of his life, and commissioned this church, on the site on an earlier structure – Santa Maria in Valicella – which had been donated to him and his followers by Gregory XIII, in 1577. Neri died in 1595, after a relatively normal day of saintly tasks – his last words were "Last of all, we must die." He was canonized in 1622, and this large church, as well as being his last resting-place (he lies in the chapel to the left of the apse), is his principal memorial. Inside, its principal features include three paintings by Rubens hung at the high altar, centring on the *Virgin with Angels*, and, perhaps more obviously, Pietro da Cortona's ceiling paintings, showing the *Ascension of the Virgin* in the apse, and, above the nave, the construction of the church and Neri's famous "vision of fire" of 1544, when a globe of fire entered his mouth and dilated his heart – a physical event which apparently affected his health thereafter.

San Giovanni dei Fiorentini

The architect Borromini is buried across the way, in the church of **San Giovanni dei Fiorentini**, set on its own small square, Piazza d'Oro, beyond which is the river. Its eighteenth-century facade is as monumental as any of Rome's churches, but inside is a relatively plain affair, built originally by

Sansovino on the orders of the Medici pope, Leo X, who wanted to see an expression of Florentine pride on his doorstep. The church was finished, in the early 1600s, by Carlo Maderno, who added the dome, beneath which Raggi's flamboyant seventeenth-century altarpiece depicts *The Baptism of Christ*. Look out also for the naive statue of a young John the Baptist, above the doorway to the sacristy, next to which there's a bust of another Florentine pope, Clement XII, carved by Bernini. It's worth knowing, too, that San Giovanni extends a special welcome to pets, and you'll often see churchgoers wandering in with cat baskets and the like.

Via dei Coronari

Cross back over the busy Corso Vittorio Emanuele II and you'll find yourself at the end of narrow **Via dei Coronari**, which leads back through the centro storico to the top end of Piazza Navona. This street, and some of the streets around, are the fulcrum of Rome's **antiques** trade, and, although the prices are as high as you might expect in such a location, there is a huge number of shops (Via dei Coronari consists of virtually nothing else), selling a tremendous variety of stuff, and a browse along here makes for one of the city's absorbing bits of sightseeing.

Santa Maria dell'Anima

A few steps right off Via dei Coronari takes you down Via dell'Anima, where the church of **Santa Maria dell'Anima** (daily 8am–1pm & 4–7.30pm) is another darkly cosy Roman church, crammed into a seemingly impossibly small space. Nowadays it's the German national church in Rome, and a richly decorated affair, almost square in shape, with a protruding main sanctuary flanked by Renaissance tombs. The one on the right, a beautiful, rather sad concoction, is that of the last non-Italian pope before John Paul II, the Dutchman Hadrian VI, who died in 1523, while at the far end, above the altar, there is a dark and glowing *Virgin with Saints* by Giulio Romano.

Santa Maria della Pace

Just off to the left of Via dei Coronari, the church of **Santa Maria della Pace** (Tues–Sat 8.30am–noon & 4–8pm) dates originally from the late fifteenth century but has a façade and portico that were added a couple of hundred years later by Pietro da Cortona. Inside, if you're lucky enough to find the church open, you can see Raphael's frescoes of various sibyls above the Chigi chapel (first on the right), executed in the early sixteenth century. But perhaps the most impressive part of the church is the attached **chiostro del Bramante**, finished in 1504, a beautifully proportioned, two-tiered cloister that is nowadays given over to fairly decent temporary art exhibitions.

Stadium of Domitian

At the far end of Via dei Coronari, just off the north side of Piazza Navona, there are some visible remains of the **Stadium of Domitian**, on which Piazza Navona just behind was based (Sun 10am–12.30pm). You can visit these on a short, half-hour guided tour, in English or Italian, and in doing so you can learn a little more about the stadium and its relationship with present-day Piazza Navona. But to be honest there's not a lot more to see than you can view from the street.

Palazzo Altemps

Just across the street from the north end of Piazza Navona, **Piazza Sant'Apollinare** is the home of the beautifully restored **Palazzo Altemps** (Tues–Sun 9am–7pm; €5, €9 for a combination ticket that includes Palazzo Massimo, Colosseum and Palatine; guided tours in English every hour Sat & Sun, €3.10). Built between 1477 and completed just under a hundred years later, it now houses a branch of the Museo Nazionale Romano, a relatively new – and important – addition to the sights around Piazza Navona, and you'd be well advised to make some time for it, housing as it does the cream of Museo Nazionale's aristocratic collections of Roman statuary. Divided between two storeys of the palace, in rooms which open off its elegant courtyard, most of what is on display derives from the collection of the seventeenth-century Roman cardinal, Ludovico Ludovisi – pieces he either purchased elsewhere to adorn his villa on the Quirinal Hill, or found in the grounds of the villa itself, which occupied the site of a former residence of Julius Caesar.

The ground floor

First up, at the far end of the courtyard's loggia, is a statue of the emperor Antoninus Pius, who ruled from 138 to 161 AD, and, around the corner, a couple of marvellous heads of Zeus and Pluto, a bust of Julia, the daughter of Emperor Augustus, and a grave-looking likeness of the philosopher Demosthenes, from the second century AD. Further rooms hold more statuary. There are two, almost identical statues of *Apollo the Lyrist*, a magnificent statue of Athena taming a serpent, pieced together from fragments found near the church of Santa Maria sopra Minerva, an *Aphrodite* from an original by Praxiteles, and, in the far corner of the courtyard, a shameless *Dionysus* with a satyr and panther, found on the Quirinal Hill.

The first floor

Upstairs you get a slightly better sense of the original sumptuousness of the building – some of the frescoes remain and the north loggia retains its original, late-sixteenth-century decoration, simulating a vine-laden pergola, heavy with fruit, leaves and gambolling putti. Also, the objects on display are if anything even finer. The **Painted Views room**, so called for the bucolic scenes on its walls, has a fine statue of Hermes, restored in the seventeenth century in an oratorical pose according to the fashion of the time; the **Cupboard Room**, next door, named for its fresco of a display of wedding gifts, against a floral background, has a wonderful statue of a warrior at rest, something called the *Ludovisi Ares*, which is perhaps an image of Achilles, restored by Bernini in 1622, and, most engagingly, a charmingly sensitive portrayal of *Orestes and Electra*, from the first century AD by a sculptor called Menelaus – his name is carved at the base of one of the figures.

Beyond are even more treasures, and it is hard to know where to look first. One room retains a frieze telling the story of **Moses** as a cartoon strip, with each scene displayed by nude figures as if on an unfurled tapestry, while in the room itself there is a colossal head of Hera, and – what some consider the highlight of the entire collection – the famous *Ludovisi throne*: an original fifth-century BC Greek work embellished with a delicate relief portraying the birth of **Aphrodite**. She is shown being hauled from the sea, where she was legendarily formed from the genitals of Uranus, while on the other side reliefs show a flute player and a woman sprinkling incense over a flame – rituals associated with the worship of Aphrodite.

Further on, the **Fireplace Salon**, whose huge fireplace is embellished with caryatids and lurking ibex – the symbol of the Altemps family – has the *Suicide of Galatian*, apparently commissioned by Julius Caesar to adorn his Quirinal estate; at the other end if the room, an incredible sarcophagus depicts a battle between the Romans and barbarians in graphic, almost viscerally sculptural detail, while in the small room next door there are some quieter, more erotic pieces – a lovely *Pan and Daphne*, a *Satyr and Nymph*, and the muses *Calliope* and *Urania*. Once you've made it to here, you'll be ready for a quick peek at the **Altemps chapel**, off the opposite end of the fireplace room, and a skim back through your favourite pieces, before leaving what is without question one of Rome's best collections of classical art.

Palazzo Primoli

Around the corner from Palazzo Altemps, at the end of Via Zanardelli, the sixteenth-century **Palazzo Primoli** was the home of a descendant of Napoleon, Joseph Primoli. Newly restored, it houses two minor museums that may command your attention on the way to the Vatican, just across the Tiber from here. The first, the **Museo Mario Praz** (Tues–Sat 9am–7pm; free), on the first floor, was the home of one Mario Praz, an art historian and writer who lived here for twenty or so years until his death in the 1980s, and it is kept pretty much as the elegant and cultured Praz left it. Next door, the second museum, the **Museo Napoleonico** (Tues–Sat 9am–7pm; €2.60), is less interesting if you're anything but an enthusiast for the great Frenchman and in particular his dynasty. Rome was home for the Bonapartes in the 1820s, after Pauline married Camillo Borghese, and Napoleon's mother, Letizia, also lived nearby – and this is a rather weighty assortment of their personal effects. There's a letter from Napoleon himself from his exile in St Helena, a bad portrait of Pauline, a stirring depiction of Napoleon III, portraits of Count Primoli's mother, Carlotta Bonaparte, sketchbook in hand, hung amongst a number of her own quite adept drawings, even a Napoleonic bike. All things considered, though, it takes a pretty gritty determination, or a peculiar fascination with the family, to get through it all.

Campo de' Fiori, the Ghetto and around

T his chapter is really Rome's old centre part two, covering the area which lies between the Corso Vittorio Emanuele II – the main thoroughfare which dissects the historic city core – and the Tiber. It's a very similar neighbourhood, the same cramped, wanderable streets opening out onto small squares flanked by churches, although it's more of a working quarter – less monumental, with more functional buildings and shops, as evidenced by its main focus, **Campo de' Fiori**, whose fruit and veg stalls and rough-and-ready bars form a marked contrast to the pavement artists and sleek cafés of Piazza Navona. Across the river to the west lies the Vatican and to the south Trastevere, both covered in separate chapters. To the east it merges into the gloomy streets and scrabbly Roman ruins of the **Old Jewish Ghetto**, a small but atmospheric neighbourhood that nuzzles up close to the city's giant central synagogue, while just north of here lies the major traffic intersection and ancient Roman site of **Largo di Torre Argentina**.

Largo di Torre Argentina and around

Largo di Torre Argentina is a good-sized square, frantic with traffic circling around the ruins of four (Republican-era) **temples** and the channel of an ancient public lavatory, now home to a thriving colony of cats and sporadically open to the public, although it's more a place to wait for a bus than to linger deliberately. On the far side of the square, the **Teatro Argentina** was in 1816 the venue for the first performance of Rossini's *Barber of Seville*, not a success at all on the night: Rossini was apparently booed into taking refuge in Bernasconi's pastry shop that used to be next door. Built in 1731, it is today one of the city's most important theatres, and has a small museum that can be visited by appointment. It is also thought, incidentally, that it was built over the spot where Caesar was assassinated.

Via del Plebiscito and the Gesù

Via del Plebiscito, a dark, rather gloomy thoroughfare, links Largo Argentina with Piazza Venezia, 500m or so away. Halfway down on the left, flanking the north side of **Piazza del Gesù**, the dark grey decaying bulk of the **Palazzo Altieri** was a monster of a project in its time that – a contemporary pasquinade quipped – looked set to consume Rome by its very size. The Altieri pope, Clement X, had the palace built around the house of an old woman who refused to make way for it: the two spyhole windows that were left can still be seen above the ground-floor windows, three windows to the right of the main entrance. Unfortunately, you can't visit the palace which is now used as offices.

Lording it over the piazza (said, incidentally, to be the windiest in Rome) is the church of the **Gesù** (daily 6am–12.30pm & 4–7.15pm), the first Jesuit church to be built in Rome, a symbol of the Counter-Reformation. High and wide, with a single-aisled nave and short transepts edging out under a huge dome, it was ideal for the large and fervent congregations the movement wanted to draw; indeed, it has since served as the model for Jesuit churches everywhere. The facade is by Giacomo della Porta, the interior the work of Vignola. Today it's still a well-patronized church, notable for its size (the glitzy tomb of the order's founder, St Ignatius, is topped by a huge globe of lapis lazuli – the largest piece in existence) and the staggering richness of its interior, especially the paintings of Baciccio in the dome and the ceiling's ingenious trompe l'oeil, which oozes out of its frame in a tangle of writhing bodies, flowing drapery and stucco angels stuck like limpets.

The Rooms of St Ignatius

Next door to the Gesù church, the **Rooms of St Ignatius** (Mon–Sat 4–6pm, Sun 10am–noon; free, €1 for the useful illustrated guide) occupy part of the first floor of the **Jesuit headquarters**, and are basically the rooms – recently restored – where St Ignatius lived from 1544 until his death in 1556. There are just three simple chambers, where the saint and founder of the Jesuit order studied, worshipped and received visitors. One was his **private chapel**, others hold **artefacts** from his life – his shoes, vest and cloak, the robe he was buried in, his writing desks and original documents, and a bronze bust of the great man based on his death mask. But the true draw here is the **decorative corridor** just outside. Decorated by Andrea Pozzo in 1680, it's a superb exercise in perspective on a small scale, an illusion of a grand hall in what is a relatively small space. Stand on the rose in the centre and the room's architectural fancies, putti, garlands and scallop shells are precise and true; walk up and down and the ceiling beams bend, the figures stretch and the scrollwork buckles – giving the bizarre feeling of a room almost shifting before your eyes. It's a feast of technical trickery and grandiose brushwork – all in weird contrast to the basketball courts that occupy the quadrangle down below.

Crypta Balbi

Cutting back to Largo Argentina, following Via delle Botteghe Oscure, the **Crypta Balbi** on the corner of Via Caetani (Mon & Wed–Sun 9am–7.45pm; €4), is the site of a **Roman theatre**, the remains of which later became incorporated in a number of medieval houses. There's a ground-floor exhibition which takes you through the evolution of the site in painstaking, sometime excruciating, detail, with lots of English explanation, along with bits of pottery, capitals and marble plaques; and hourly tours take you

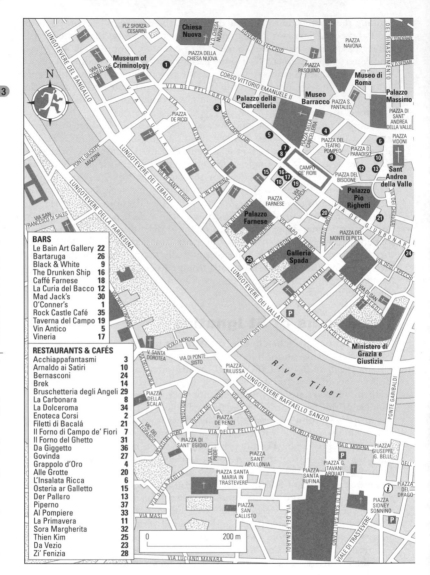

BARS

Le Bain Art Gallery	22
Bartaruga	26
Black & White	9
The Drunken Ship	16
Caffé Farnese	18
La Curia del Bacco	12
Mad Jack's	30
O'Conner's	1
Rock Castle Café	35
Taverna del Campo	19
Vin Antico	5
Vineria	17

RESTAURANTS & CAFÉS

Acchiappafantasmi	3
Arnaldo ai Satiri	10
Bernasconi	24
Brek	14
Bruschetteria degli Angeli	29
La Carbonara	8
La Dolceroma	34
Enoteca Corsi	2
Filetti di Bacalá	21
Il Forno di Campo de' Fiori	7
Il Forno del Ghetto	31
Da Giggetto	36
Govinda	27
Grappolo d'Oro	4
Alle Grotte	20
L'Insalata Ricca	6
Osteria ar Galletto	15
Der Pallaro	13
Piperno	37
Al Pompiere	33
La Primavera	11
Sora Margherita	32
Thien Kim	25
Da Vezio	23
Zi' Fenizia	28

down into the site proper, where you can try to glean what you can from the various arches, latrines, column bases and supporting walls that essenti-ally make up the cellar of the current building. But the real interest is in the close dissection of one city block over two thousand years – a dissection that could presumably be equally well applied to almost any city corner in Rome.

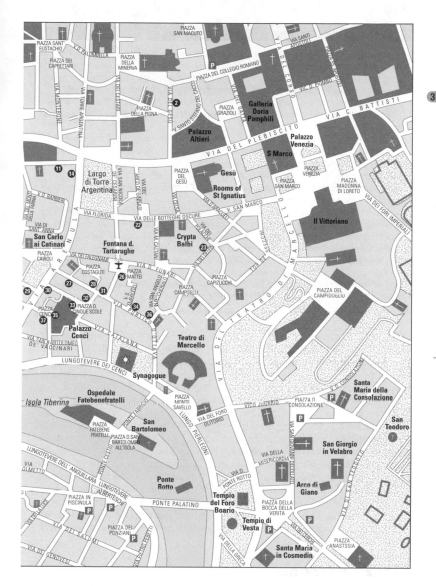

Campo de' Fiori and around

From Largo Argentina you can either push on down Corso Vittorio Emanuele II or cut left along Via Arenula towards the Tiber and right at Piazza Cairoli into the network of streets that centres on **Piazza Campo de' Fiori**, in many ways Rome's most appealing square. Home to a lively fruit and vegetable **market** (Mon–Sat 8am–1pm), it's flanked by restaurants and cafés,

Aldo Moro

A little way up Via Caetani on the left, close to the corner of Via dei Funari is a memorial to the former Italian prime minister **Aldo Moro**, whose dead body was left in the boot of a car here on the morning of May 9, 1978, 54 days after his **kidnap** by the *Brigate Rosse* or Red Brigades. It was a carefully chosen spot, not only for the impudence it showed on the part of the terrorists, in that it was right in the centre of Rome, but also for its position midway between the headquarters of the Communist and Christian Democrat parties.

A plaque (and sometimes a wreath) marks the spot, and tells part of the story of how Moro, a reform-minded Christian Democrat, was the first right-wing politician to attempt to build an alliance with the then popular Italian Communists. Whether it was really left-wing terrorists who kidnapped him, or whether it was darker, right-wing forces allied to the establishment, or perhaps a combination of the two, there's no doubt that Moro's attempt to alleviate the Right's postwar monopoly of power found very little favour with others in power at the time – though that didn't make his death any less of a shock. Given the *"Mani pulite"* years, that have followed, during which corruption in both politics and business was supposed to have been exposed and to some extent ended, and the minuscule change and the political cynicism that has resurfaced in the 1990s, it's a tragedy which must still carry a lot of resonance for Romans. The prime minister who took over after Moro's death was after all none other than the recently tried (and acquitted) elder statesman of Italian politics, Giulio Andreotti.

and is busy pretty much all day. No one really knows how the square came by its name, which means "field of flowers", but one theory holds that it was derived from the Roman Campus Martius which used to cover most of this part of town; another claims it is after Flora, the mistress of Pompey, whose theatre used to stand on what is now the northeast corner of the square – a huge complex by all accounts, which stretched right over to Largo Argentina. You can still see the foundations in the basement of the *Da Pancrazio* restaurant, on the tiny Piazza del Biscione, and the semicircular Via de' Grotta Pinta retains the rounded shape of the theatre. Later, Campo de' Fiori was an important point on papal processions between the Vatican and the major basilicas of Rome (notably San Giovanni in Laterano) and a site of public executions. The most notorious killing here is commemorated by the statue of **Giordano Bruno** in the middle of the square. Bruno was a late-sixteenth-century freethinker who followed the teachings of Copernicus and was denounced to the Inquisition; his trial lasted for years under a succession of different popes, and finally, when he refused to renounce his philosophical beliefs, he was burned at the stake.

Piazza Farnese

Just south of Campo de' Fiori, **Piazza Farnese** is a quite different square, with great fountains spurting out of carved lilies – the Farnese emblem – into marble tubs brought from the Baths of Caracalla, and the sober bulk of the **Palazzo Farnese** itself, begun in 1514 by Antonio di Sangallo the Younger and finished off after the architect's death by Michelangelo, who added the top tier of windows and cornice. The building now houses the French Embassy and is closed to the public, which is a pity, since it holds what has been called the greatest of all Baroque ceiling paintings, Annibale **Carracci**'s *Loves of the Gods*, finished in 1603. However, even from the outside it's a tremendously elegant and powerful building; indeed, of all the fabulous locations that Rome's embassies enjoy, this has to be the best. To get in, you need special permission from the French authorities – and you must have a good reason for doing so. If you can't face the bureaucracy, or just don't have the time, peek into the building at night when the first floor is sometimes lit up enough for parts of the ceiling to be seen from the outside.

Galleria Spada

Make do instead with the **Palazzo Spada**, a couple of blocks east down Via Capo di Ferro, and the **Galleria Spada** (Tues–Sun 8.30am–7.30pm; €5.50) inside – walk right through the courtyard to the back of the building. Although its four rooms, decorated in the manner of a Roman noble family, aren't spectacularly interesting unless you're a connoisseur of seventeenth- and eighteenth-century Italian painting, it does have one or two items of interest. Best are two portraits of Cardinal Bernadino Spada by Reni and Guercino, alongside works by Italian-influenced Dutch artists (Van Scorel, Van Honthorst), and, among bits and pieces of Roman statuary, a seated philosopher. The building itself is great: its facade is frilled with stucco adornments, and, left off the small courtyard, there's a crafty **trompe l'oeil** by Borromini – a tunnel whose actual length is multiplied about four times through the architect's tricks with perspective – though to see this you have to wait for one of the guided tours (held every hour, on the half-hour).

Via Giulia

Behind the Farnese and Spada palaces, **Via Giulia**, which runs parallel to the Tiber, was built by Julius II to connect Ponte Sisto with the Vatican. The street was conceived as the centre of papal Rome, and Julius commissioned Bramante to line it with imposing palaces. Bramante didn't get very far with the plan, as Julius was soon succeeded by Leo X, but the street became a popular residence for wealthier Roman families, and is still packed full with stylish palazzi and antique shops and as such makes for a nice wander, with features such as the playful **Fontana del Mascherone** to tickle your interest along the way. Just beyond the fountain, behind the high wall of the Palazzo Farnese, the arch across the street is the remnant of a Renaissance plan to connect the Farnese palace with the Villa Farnesina across the river, while further along still, the **Palazzo Falconieri**, recognizable by the quizzical falcons crowning each end of the building, now the home of the Hungarian Academy, was largely the work of Borromini, who enlarged it in 1646–49.

On the corner of Via Gonfalone, the **Museo Criminologico** (Tues & Thurs 9am–1pm & 2.30–6.30pm, Wed, Fri & Sat 9am–1pm; €2; ⓦ www.museocriminologico.it) provides a small but intriguing look at crime in general and the criminal underworld of Italy in particular. There are some gruesome early instruments of torture – manacles, lashes, head braces – a display on the unfortunate Beatrice Cenci (see p.56) and a selection of guillotines and nooses and various articles worn by the condemned, although inevitably the most interesting stuff – if you can read Italian – is that most pertinent to the world of **Italian crime**: the Mafia, the *Brigate Rosse*, Italian prison life. All in all a perfect antidote to the more effete Renaissance splendours of Via Giulia and around.

Continue to the end of Via Giulia for the church of **San Giovanni dei Fiorentini** (covered on p.46).

The Jewish Ghetto

By way of contrast, cross over to the far side of Via Arenula and you're in what was once the city's **Jewish Ghetto**, a crumbling area of narrow, switchback streets and alleys, easy to lose your way in, and with a lingering sense of age. There was a Jewish population in Rome as far back as the second century BC, and with the accruing of Middle Eastern colonies, their numbers eventually swelled to around 40,000. Revolts in the colonies led to a small tax on Jews and a special census, but they were never an especially persecuted group, and were only effectively ghettoized here in the mid-sixteenth century when Pope Paul IV issued a series of punitive laws that forced them into what was then one of Rome's most squalid districts: a wall was built around the area and all Jews, in a chilling omen of things to come, were made to wear yellow caps and shawls when they left the district. Later, after Unification, the ghetto was opened up. However, by the late 1930s, Jews were again being victimised – barred from certain professions and prohibited from marrying non-Jews under Mussolini's racial legislation. The subsequent Nazi occupation brought inevitable deportations but the majority of Rome's Jewish population survived, and currently numbers 16,000 (around half Italy's total). This is nowadays, however, spread all over the city, and a handful of kosher restaurants, butchers and the like are pretty much all that remains to mark this out from any other quarter of the city.

Via Portico d'Ottavia and around

The main artery of the Jewish area is **Via Portico d'Ottavia**, which leads down to the **Portico d'Ottavia**, a not terribly well-preserved second-century BC gate, rebuilt by Augustus and dedicated to his sister in 23 BC, that was the entranceway to the adjacent **Teatro di Marcello**. This has served many purposes over the years: begun by Julius Caesar, finished by Augustus, it was pillaged in the fourth century and not properly restored until the Middle Ages, after which it became a formidable fortified palace for a succession of different rulers, including the Orsini family. The theatre has been recently restored and provides a grand backdrop for classical concerts in the summer.

Palazzo Cenci and Piazza Mattei

Retracing your steps slightly, off **Piazza delle Cinque Scuole**, a gloomy arch leads past one side of the **Palazzo Cenci**, which huddles into the dark streets here, a reminder of the untimely death of one **Beatrice Cenci**, who was executed, with her stepmother, on the Ponte Sant'Angelo in 1599 for the murder of her incestuous father – a story immortalized in verse by Shelley and in paint by an unknown artist whose portrait of the unfortunate Beatrice still hangs in the Palazzo Barberini. On a more lighthearted note, crossing to the other side of Via del Portico d'Ottavia, follow your nose to **Piazza Mattei**, whose **Fontana delle Tartarughe**, or "turtle fountain", is a delightful late-sixteenth-century creation, perhaps restored by Bernini, who apparently added the tortoises.

Santa Maria in Campitelli

Via dei Funari leads east out of Piazza Mattei towards Piazza Campitelli, where **Santa Maria in Campitelli** is a heavy, ornate church built by Carlo Reinaldi in 1667 to house an ancient image of *The Virgin* that had been deemed to have miraculous powers following respite from a plague. Everything in the church focuses on this small framed image, encased as it is in an incredibly ornate golden altarpiece which fills the entire space between the clustered columns of the transept. There's not much else to see in the church, although the paintings, including a dramatic *Virgin with Saints* by Luca Giordano, in the second chapel on the right, represent the Baroque at its most rampant.

The Synagogue

The Ghetto's principal Jewish sight is the huge **Synagogue** by the river (Mon–Thurs 9am–4.30pm, Fri 9am–1.30pm, Sun 9am–noon; closed Sat & Jewish holidays; €6), built in 1904 and very much dominating all around with its bulk – not to mention the carabinieri who stand guard 24 hours a day outside, ever since a PLO attack on the building in 1982 killed a 2-year-old girl and injured many others. The only way to see the building is on one of the short guided tours it runs regularly in English, afterwards taking in the small two-room **museum**. The interior of the building is impressive, rising to a high, rainbow-hued dome, and the tours are excellent, giving good background on the building and Rome's Jewish community in general.

Isola Tiberina

Almost opposite the synagogue, the **Ponte Fabricio** crosses the Tiber to **Isola Tiberina**. Built in 62 BC, it's the only classical bridge to remain intact without help from the restorers (the Ponte Cestio, on the other side of the island, was partially rebuilt in the last century). As for the **island**, it's a calm respite from the city centre proper, its originally tenth-century church of San Bartolomeo worth a peep, especially if you're into **modern sculpture** – Padre Martini, a well-known local sculptor, used to live on the island, and the church holds some wonderful examples of his elegant, semi-abstract religious pieces. Beyond the island, you can see the remains of **Ponte Rotto** (Broken Bridge) on the river, all that remains of the first stone bridge to span the Tiber. Built between 179 and 142 BC, it collapsed at the end of the sixteenth century.

Piazza Bocca della Verità

East of the Ponte Fabricio, the broad main drag of Via di Teatro di Marcello leads down to **Piazza Bocca della Verità**, past two of the city's better-preserved Roman temples – the **Temple of Portunus** and the **Temple of Hercules Victor**, the latter long known as the temple of Vesta because, like all vestal temples, it is circular. Both date from the end of the second century BC, and although you can't get inside, they're actually fine examples of republican-era places of worship; and the Temple of Hercules Victor is, for what it's worth, the oldest surviving marble structure in Rome.

Santa Maria in Cosmedin

More interesting is the church of **Santa Maria in Cosmedin** (daily 9am–noon & 3–5pm), on the far side of the square   a typically Roman

△ Campo de' Fiori

medieval basilica with a huge marble altar and a colourful and ingenious Cosmati-work floor – one of the city's finest. Outside in the portico, and giving the square its name, is the **Bocca della Verità** (Mouth of Truth), an ancient Roman drain cover in the shape of an enormous face that in medieval times would apparently swallow the hand of anyone who hadn't told the truth. It was particularly popular with husbands anxious to test the faithfulness of their wives; now it is one of the city's biggest tour-bus attractions.

San Giorgio in Velabro

On the northern side, Piazza Bocca della Verità peters out peacefully at the stolid **Arch of Janus**, perhaps Rome's most weathered triumphal arch, beyond which the campanile of the church of **San Giorgio in Velabro** (daily 10am–12.30pm & 4–6.30pm) is a stunted echo of that of Santa Maria across the way. Inside, recently opened after a major restoration, is one of the city's barest and most beautiful ancient basilicas; only the late-twelfth-century fresco in the apse, the work of Pietro Cavallini, lightens the melancholy mood. Cavallini's fresco shows Christ and the Virgin, and various saints, including St George on the left, to whom the church is dedicated – and whose cranial bones lie in the reliquary under the high altar canopy, placed here in 749 AD, shortly after the original basilica was built.

San Teodoro

A few steps away from here, a little way down Via San Teodoro on the right, the round church of **San Teodoro** is open only sporadically, and in any case on the inside its ancient feel has been somewhat smoothed over by the paint and plaster of later years. St Theodore was martyred on this spot in the fourth century AD, and the church dates originally from the sixth century. If you can get in, you'll be lucky enough to see the apse mosaics, which are contemporary with the original church, showing Christ with saints, including a bearded Theodore, next to St Peter on the right.

Tridente

T he northern part of Rome's city centre is sometimes known as **Tridente** due to the trident shape of the roads leading down from the apex of Piazza del Popolo – Via del Corso in the centre, Via di Ripetta on the left and Via del Babuino on the right. The area around **Piazza di Spagna** especially is travellers' Rome, historically the **artistic quarter** of the capital, for which eighteenth- and nineteenth-century Grand Tourists would make in search of the colourful, exotic city. This part of the city has also always had an artistic feel: Keats and Giorgio de Chirico are just two of those who used to live on Piazza di Spagna; Goethe had lodgings along Via del Corso; and places such as *Caffè Greco* and *Babington's Tea Rooms* were the meeting-places of a local artistic and expat community for close on a couple of centuries. Today these institutions have given ground to more latter-day traps for the tourist dollar: American Express and McDonald's have settled into the area, while **Via Condotti** and around is these days strictly international designer territory, with some of Rome's fanciest stores; and the local residents are more likely to be investment bankers than artists or poets. But the air of a Rome being discovered, even colonized, by foreigners persists, even if most of them hanging out on the **Spanish Steps** are mostly flying-visit teenagers.

Piazza di Spagna and around

At the southern end of Via del Babuino, **Piazza di Spagna** further underlines the area's international credentials, taking its name from the Spanish Embassy which has stood here since the seventeenth century (though oddly enough part of the square was also once known as Piazza di Francia for the French church of Trinità dei Monti at the top of the Spanish Steps). It's a long, thin straggle of a square, almost entirely enclosed by buildings and centring on the distinctive, boat-shaped **Fontana della Barcaccia**, the last work of Bernini's father. It apparently commemorates the great flood of Christmas Day 1598, when a barge from the Tiber was washed up on the slopes of Pincio Hill close by. The square itself is fringed by high-end clothes and jewellery shops and is normally thronged with tourists, but for all that it's one of the city's most appealing open spaces, and retains a fair degree of charm. The large **Colonna dell' Immacolata** at the southern end commemorates Pius IX's official announcement, in 1854, of the dogma of the Immaculate Conception, while close by hackles were raised when McDonald's unveiled plans to open a branch on the square in the early 1980s. Their presence here is proof that the American

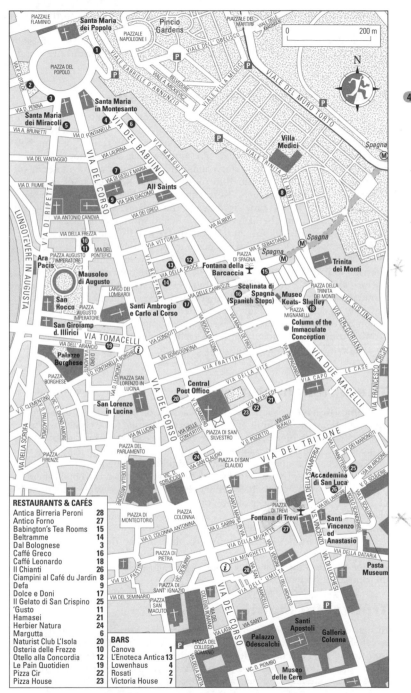

RESTAURANTS & CAFÉS

Antica Birreria Peroni	28
Antico Forno	27
Babington's Tea Rooms	15
Beltramme	14
Dal Bolognese	3
Caffé Greco	16
Caffé Leonardo	18
Il Chianti	26
Ciampini al Café du Jardin	8
Defa	9
Dolce e Doni	17
Il Gelato di San Crispino	25
'Gusto	11
Hamasei	21
Herbier Natura	24
Margutta	6
Naturist Club L'Isola	20
Osteria delle Frezze	10
Otello alla Concordia	12
Le Pain Quotidien	19
Pizza Cir	22
Pizza House	23

BARS

Canova	1
L'Enoteca Antica	13
Lowenhaus	4
Rosati	2
Victoria House	7

multinational won what turned out to be quite a battle. But it's to the city's credit that this is one of the most discreet examples you'll encounter, tucked into one end of the piazza, with thematically appropriate interior decor. Not surprisingly, you can now find branches of McDonald's all over the city – and most of them look much the same as they do anywhere else.

Keats-Shelley Memorial House

Facing directly onto the square, opposite the Barcaccia fountain at Piazza di Spagna 26, the house where the poet John Keats died in 1821 now serves as the **Keats-Shelley Memorial House** (Mon–Fri 9am–1pm & 3–6pm, Sat 11am–2pm & 3–6pm, Sun closed; €3; ⓦwww.keats-shelley-house.org), an archive of English-language literary and historical works and a museum of manuscripts and literary mementoes relating to the Keats circle of the early nineteenth century – namely Keats himself, Shelley and Mary Shelley, and Byron (who at one time lived across the square). Among many bits of manuscript, letters and the like, there's an ancient silver scallop shell reliquary containing locks of Milton's and Elizabeth Barrett Browning's hair – once owned by Pope Pius V, while Keats's death mask, stored in the room where he died, captures a resigned grimace. Keats didn't really enjoy his time in Rome, referring to it as his "posthumous life": he came here only under pressure from doctors and friends when it was arguably already too late. He was also tormented by his love for Fanny Brawne, and he spent months in pain before he finally died, at the age of just 25, confined to the house with his artist friend Joseph Severn, to whom he remarked that he could already feel "the flowers growing over him". Incidentally, if you really want to get into the Romantic poet experience, there's a flat on the third floor available to rent through the UK-based Landmark Trust (☎01628 825925, ⓦwww.landmarktrust.org.uk).

The Spanish Steps

The **Spanish Steps** sweep down in a cascade of balustrades and balconies beside the house, the hangout of young hopefuls waiting to be chosen as artists' models during the nineteenth century; and nowadays the scene is not much changed, a venue for international posing and fast pick-ups late into the summer nights. The steps, like the square, could in fact just as easily be known as the "French Steps" because it was largely a French initiative to build them – previously the French church of Trinità dei Monti was accessible only by way of a rough path up the steep slope. After a few decades of haggling over the plans, the steps were finally laid in 1725, and now form one of the city's most distinctive attractions, built to a design, by one Francisco de Sanctis, that is deliberately showy, perfect for strollers to glide up and down while chatting and looking each other up and down. The steps also contain a religious message, the three flights and three landings an allusion to the Holy Trinity, and the church at the top.

Trinità dei Monti

At the top of the Spanish Steps is the **Trinità dei Monti** (daily 10am–noon & 4–6pm), a largely sixteenth-century church designed by Carlo Maderno and paid for by the French king. Its rose-coloured Baroque facade overlooks the rest of Rome from its hilltop site, and it's worth clambering up just for the views. But while here you may as well pop your head around the door for a

△ Hanging out on the Spanish Steps

couple of faded works by Daniele da Volterra, notably a soft flowing fresco of *The Assumption* in the third chapel on the right, which includes a portrait of his teacher Michelangelo, and a poorly lit *Deposition* across the nave. Poussin considered the latter, which was probably painted from a series of cartoons by Michelangelo, as the world's third-greatest painting (Raphael's *Transfiguration* was, he thought, the best).

Via Sistina

From the church you can either continue left along past the Villa Medici, to the Pincio terrace and the gardens of the Villa Borghese, or head south along **Via Sistina** to Piazza Barberini. Via Sistina was the first of Pope Sixtus V's planning improvements to sixteenth-century Rome, a dead straight street designed to connect Santa Maria Maggiore to Trinità dei Monti, which it still does (kind of), under a variety of names, and in the other direction to Piazza del Popolo, which it never quite managed. Nowadays it's the quickest way of getting to the Via Veneto and Quirinale areas from the Spanish Steps.

Villa Medici

Walking in the opposite direction from the top of the Spanish Steps, you reach the sixteenth-century **Villa Medici**. Perhaps the most interesting thing about it is that it was where Galileo was imprisoned in the 1630s by the Vatican's Holy Office when he claimed – heretically for the times – that the earth was not the centre of the universe but instead revolved around the sun. He was forced to recant his theory and say seven penitential psalms a week for his trouble. Nowadays the villa is home to the French Academy and its interior and sumptuous gardens can usually be visited only on selected days, when they host concerts and art shows. Occasionally, they throw open their doors to the curious public; check the newspapers or usual listings sources to find out when, or the Academy's website – ⓦ www.villamedici.it.

The Pincio Gardens

Further along, on the edge of the Villa Borghese, the terrace and gardens of the **Pincio**, laid out by Valadier in the early nineteenth century and fringed with dilapidated busts of classical and Italian heroes, give fine views over the roofs, domes and TV antennae of central Rome, right across to St Peter's and the Janiculum Hill. The **view** is the main event here, but the benches provide some pleasant shade to take some weight off, and the nineteenth-century **water clock** at the back is a quirky attraction.

Via del Babuino

Leading south from Piazza del Popolo, **Via del Babuino** and the narrow **Via Margutta,** where Fellini once lived, set the tone for the area, which in the 1960s was the core of a thriving art community and home to the city's best galleries and a fair number of its artists, until high rents forced out all but the most successful. Now the neighbourhood supports a prosperous trade in antiques and designer fashions. On the right, a little way down Via del Babuino, the church of **All Saints** is the official English church of Rome, its solid steeple and brick construction, erected in the late nineteenth century, serving as a further reminder of the English connections in this part of town. It's often shut, but if you do manage to get inside you'll be rewarded with an apse mosaic by the Pre-Raphaelite artist Edward Burne-Jones and tiles to a design by William Morris – truly a stronghold of English artists and craftspeople.

Piazza del Popolo and around

At the far end of Via del Babuino, the oval-shaped expanse of **Piazza del Popolo** is a dignified meeting of roads laid out in 1538 by Pope Paul III (Alessandro Farnese) to make an impressive entrance to the city; it owes its present symmetry to Valadier, who added the central fountain in 1814. The monumental **Porta del Popolo** went up in 1655, the work of Bernini, whose patron Alexander VII's Chigi family symbol – the heap of hills surmounted by a star – can clearly be seen above the main gateway.

During summer, the steps around the obelisk and fountain, and the cafés on either side of the square, are popular hangouts. But the square's real attraction is the unbroken view it gives all the way back down Via del Corso, between the perfectly paired churches of **Santa Maria dei Miracoli** and **Santa Maria in Montesanto**, to the central columns of the Vittorio Emanuele Monument. If you get to choose your first view of the centre of Rome, make it this one.

Santa Maria del Popolo

On the far side of the piazza, hard against the city walls, the church of **Santa Maria del Popolo** (Mon–Sat 7am–noon & 4–7pm, Sun 8am–1.30pm & 4.30–7.30pm) holds some of the best **Renaissance art** of any Roman church. The church was originally erected here in 1099 over the burial place of Nero, in order to sanctify what was believed to be an evil place (the emperor's ghost had appeared here several times), but took its present form in the fifteenth century. Inside there are frescoes by Pinturicchio in the first chapel of the south aisle, including a lovely *Adoration of Christ*, full of tiny details receding into the distance. Pinturicchio also did some work in the Bramante-designed apse, which in turn boasts two fine tombs by Andrea Sansovino. The **Chigi chapel**, the second from the entrance in the northern aisle, was designed by **Raphael** for Agostino Chigi in 1516 – though most of the work was actually undertaken by other artists and not finished until the seventeenth century. Michelangelo's protégé, Sebastiano del Piombo, was responsible for the altarpiece, and two of the sculptures in the corner niches, of Daniel and Habakkuk, are by Bernini. But it's two pictures by **Caravaggio** that attract the most attention, in the left-hand chapel of the north transept. These are typically dramatic works – one, the *Conversion of St Paul*, showing Paul and horse bathed in a beatific radiance, the other, the *Crucifixion of St Peter*, showing Peter as an aged but strong figure, dominated by the muscly figures hoisting him up. Like the same artist's paintings in the churches of San Luigi dei Francesi and Sant'Agostino (Chapter 2), both works were considered extremely risqué in their time, their heavy chiaroscuro and deliberate realism too much for the Church authorities; one contemporary critic referred to the *Conversion of St Paul*, a painting dominated by the exquisitely lit horse's hindquarters, as "an accident in a blacksmith's shop".

Casa di Goethe

A short way down Via del Corso from Piazza del Popolo, at no. 18, the **Casa di Goethe** (Tues–Sun 10am–6pm; €3; ⓦ www.casadigoethe.it) is worth a quick look if you're passing. There seem to be houses all over Italy that Goethe stayed in, but he did spend over two years in this one, and wrote much of his classic travelogue *Italian Journey* here. It's been sensitively restored and houses period furniture and prints and drawings relating to the great German writer.

Mausoleum of Augustus

Leading from Piazza del Popolo to Piazza del Augusto Imperatore, **Via di Ripetta** was laid out by Pope Leo X to provide a straight route out of the city centre from the old river port area here. **Piazza del Augusto Imperatore** is an odd square of largely Mussolini-era buildings surrounding the massive **Mausoleum of Augustus** (guided tours Sat & Sun 11am; €5.20), the burial place of the emperor and his family – these days not much more than a peaceful ring of cypresses, circled by paths, flowering shrubs and the debris of tramps. Augustus died in 14 AD, giving way to his son Tiberius, who ruled mostly from his notoriously decadent court in Capri until 37 AD, when Caligula took over and effectively signalled the end of the Augustan age, and the order, prosperity and expansion that defined it. As Augustus himself had it, according to Suetonius: "I found Rome built simply out of bricks: I left her clad in marble."

The mausoleum has been transformed into many buildings over the years, not least a fortress, like Hadrian's mausoleum across the river, and only recently has been opened to the public, albeit by guided tour only. If you can time your visit with a tour, it is worth going inside, although the passageways and central crypt, where the ashes of the members of the Augustan dynasty were kept, don't add much to the picture you get from the outside.

Ara Pacis Augustae

On the far side of the square, the **Ara Pacis Augustae** or "Altar of Augustan Peace" was at the time of writing not open to the public owing to its being renovated and enclosed in a purpose-built structure designed by the New York-based architect Richard Meier. It is, however, a more substantially recognizable Roman remain than the mausoleum, a sculpted marble block built in 13 BC to celebrate Augustus's victory over Spain and Gaul and the peace it heralded. Much of this had been dug up piecemeal over the years, but the bulk of it was found during the middle half of the last century. It was no easy task to put it back together: excavation involved digging down to a depth of 10m and freezing the water table, after which many other parts had to be retrieved from museums the world over, or plaster copies made. But it's a superb example of imperial Roman sculpture and holds on its fragmented frieze the likenesses of many familiar names, most shown in the victory procession itself, which is best preserved on the eastern side. The first part is almost completely gone, but the shape of Augustus is a little more complete, as are the figures that follow – first Tiberius, then the priests with their skull-cap headgear, then Agrippa. The women are, respectively, Augustus's wife Livia, daughter Julia, and niece Antonia, the latter caught simply and realistically turning to her husband. Around their feet run various children clutching the togas of the elders, the last of whom is said to be the young Claudius.

Fontana di Trevi and around

The tight web of narrow, apparently aimless streets of this part of town opens out just beyond the Accademia on one of Rome's more surprising sights, easy to stumble upon by accident – the **Fontana di Trevi**, a huge, very Baroque gush of water over statues and rocks built onto the backside of a Renaissance palace; it's fed by the same source that surfaces at the Barcaccia fountain in Piazza di Spagna. There was a Trevi fountain, designed by Alberti, around the corner in Via dei Crociferi, a smaller, more modest affair by all accounts, but Urban VIII decided to upgrade it in line with his other grandiose schemes of the time and employed Bernini, among others, to design an alternative. Work didn't begin, however, until 1732, when Niccolò Salvi won a competition held by Clement XII to design the fountain, and even then it took thirty years to finish the project. Salvi died in the process, his lungs shot by the time spent in the dank waterworks of the fountain. The Trevi fountain is now, of course, the place you come to chuck in a coin if you want to guarantee your return to Rome, though you might remember Anita Ekberg throwing herself into it in *La Dolce Vita* (there are police here to discourage you from doing the same thing). Newly restored, it's one of the city's most vigorous outdoor spots to hang out.

Accademia di San Luca

A short walk from the fountain, towards Via del Tritone, the **Accademia di San Luca** (Mon–Sat 10am–12.30pm; free) is Rome's **school of art** first and foremost. But it has a small gallery of pictures that is open to the public. The building itself is worth visiting for its Borromini ramp, which spirals up from the main lobby instead of a staircase. The paintings include a fresco by Raphael, a *Venus* by Guercino and a couple of pictures by Titian and Rubens.

Santi Vincenzo ed Anastasio

Directly opposite the Trevi fountain, the grubby little church of **Santi Vincenzo ed Anastasio** is the parish church of the Quirinal Palace, and, bizarrely, holds in marble urns the hearts and viscera of the 22 popes who used the palace as a **papal residence**. Two tablets – one either side of the high altar – record each of the popes whose bits and pieces lie downstairs, from Sixtus V, who died in 1590, to Leo XIII, who passed away in 1903.

Museo Nazionale delle Paste Alimentari

Two minutes walk from the Trevi fountain at Piazza Scanderberg 114–120, the **Museo Nazionale delle Paste Alimentari** (daily 9.30am–5.40pm; €9; Ⓦwww.pastainmuseum.com) is not nearly as grand as it sounds, a small, homely exhibition that follows the history of **pasta** from its earliest mentions in twelfth-century Palermo to the present day, with displays of both artisanal and industrial kneaders, presses and suchlike, adverts, and lots of cartoons and photos of famous people eating pasta. It covers the various regional traditions of Italy, and gives us the lowdown on how pasta is the superfood to beat them all – high in carbohydrates, cheap and easy to cook, and easy to digest. But to be honest it's all a bit of a yawn, and at €9 can presumably be here only to cash in on the Trevi tourist trade.

Galleria Colonna

A short stroll south brings you to the **Galleria Colonna**, Via della Pilotta 17 (Sat 9am–1pm, closed August; €7), part of the Palazzo Colonna complex and, although outranked by many of the other Roman palatial collections, worth forty minutes or so if you happen by when it's open, if only for the chandelier-decked **Great Hall** where most of the paintings are displayed. Best on the whole is the gallery's collection of landscapes by Dughet (Poussin's brother-in-law), but other works that stand out are Carracci's early – and unusually spontaneous – *Bean Eater* (though this attribution has since been questioned), a *Narcissus* by Tintoretto and a *Portrait of a Venetian Gentleman* caught in supremely confident pose by Veronese.

Santi Apostoli

The back of the Palazzo Colonna is in fact taken up by the large church of **Santi Apostoli** (daily 7am–noon & 4–7pm), an originally sixth century basilica whose ancient origins are hard to detect now, encased as it is in an eighteenth-century shell and Napoleonic facade, and completely done up in Baroque finery inside, Still, it's a wide, airy church, looked after by the **Franciscan friars** who pad soundlessly around while you take in its clash of Byzantine, Renaissance and Baroque architectural styles. Its statue-encrusted portico is perhaps its most impressive feature, looking over to the equally grandiose Palazzo Odelscalchi opposite, renovated by none other than Bernini in the 1660s.

Ancient Rome

T here are remnants of the era of ancient Rome all over the city, and some key ones that lie just outside this area*, but the most concentrated and central grouping, which for simplicity's sake we've called **Ancient Rome**, is the area that stretches southeast from the Capitoline Hill. It's a reasonably traffic-free, and self-contained, part of the city. But it wasn't always like this: Mussolini ploughed **Via dei Fori Imperiali** through here in the 1930s with the idea of turning it into one massive archeological park – which, to some extent, it is – and you can spend a good half-day, perhaps longer, lazily picking your way through the rubble of what was once the heart of the ancient world. The most obvious place to start is with the original, republican-period **Forum**, immediately below the Capitoline Hill, taking in the various, later **Imperial Forums** that lie nearby before heading up to the greener heights of the **Palatine Hill** or continuing straight on for the **Colosseum**, which lies just beyond the Forum, and the **Celian Hill**, which sits next door.

The Roman Forums

Immediately beyond the Vittoriano, and just off Via dei Fori Imperiali to the right, the original **Roman Forum** was basically the centre of the Rome of the republican era. Even in ancient times Rome was a very large city, stretching out as far as the Aurelian Wall in many places in a sprawl of apartment blocks or *insulae*. But the Forum was its centre, home to its political and religious institutions, its shops and market stalls, and a meeting-place for all and sundry – which it remained until the imperial era, when Rome's increased importance as a world power led to the building of the **Imperial Forums** nearby. Julius Caesar began the expansion in around 50 BC, building a new Senate building, and, beyond it to the northeast, a series of basilicas and temples – work that was continued after his assassination by his nephew and successor Augustus, and later by the Flavian emperors – Vespasian, Nerva and finally Trajan. The Forum never really recovered from its downgrading, and it's odd to think that during the time when the empire was at its height, neglect had already set in. A fire in the third century AD destroyed many of the buildings, and although the damage was repaired, Rome was by this time in a general state of decay, the coming of Christianity only serving to accelerate the process, particularly

---

* The most obvious ones are the Circus Maximus, Baths of Caracalla and the Domus Aurea.

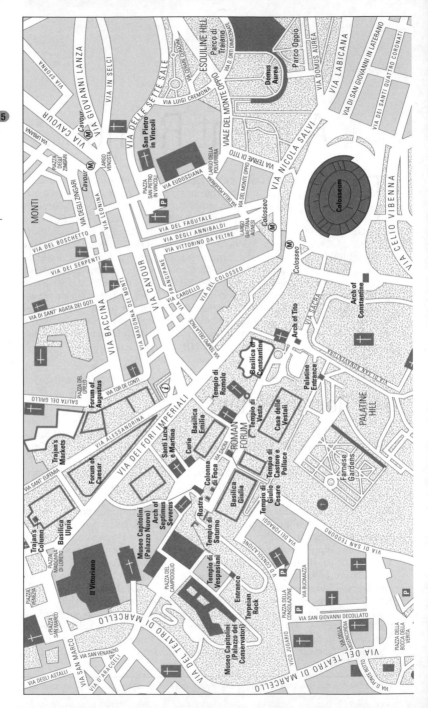

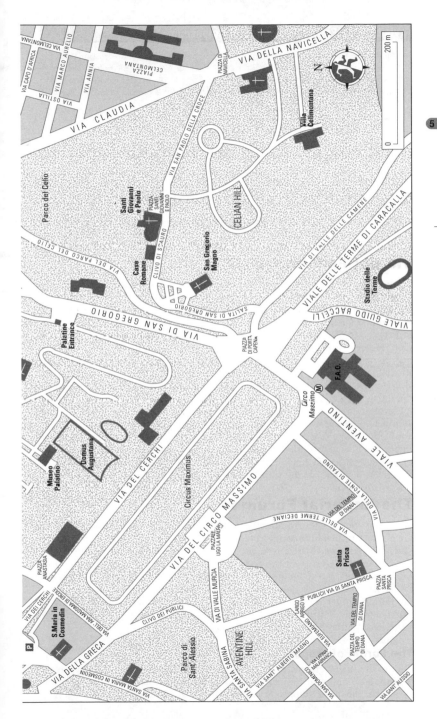

The **Forum**, **Palatine** and **Colosseum** are open daily: summer 9am–6.15pm; winter 9am–4.30pm; last entries one hour before closing. Entry to the Forum is free; however, entry to the Palatine and Colosseum costs €8, or €20 for a ticket that includes both, plus the Baths of Caracalla, Crypta Balbi and most of the Via Appia Antica sights.

with regard to its pagan temples and institutions. After the later fall of the city to various barbarian invaders, the whole area was left in ruin, its relics quarried for the construction of other parts of Rome during medieval and Renaissance times and for the odd church or tower built *in situ* out of the more viable piles. Excavation of the site didn't start until the beginning of the nineteenth century, since when it has continued pretty much without stopping: you'll notice a fair part of the site, especially up on the Palatine Hill, closed off for further digs.

Via dei Fori Imperiali

From Piazza Venezia **Via dei Fori Imperiali** cuts south through the heart of Rome's ancient sites, a soulless boulevard imposed on the area by Mussolini in 1932. Before then this was a warren of medieval streets that wound around the ruins of the ancient city centre, but, as with the Via della Conciliazione up to St Peter's (see Chapter 11), the Duce preferred to build something to his own glory rather than preserve that of another era. There has been a long-standing plan to make the entire ancient part of the city into a huge archeological park stretching right down to the catacombs on the Via Appia Antica. However, although excavations have been undertaken in recent years, they are continuing slowly. It's a dilemma for the city planners: Via dei Fori Imperiali is a major traffic artery, a function which must be preserved; one way around this is to dig a tunnel under the road – an expensive option but one that is apparently being considered. For the moment, if you want a tranquil stroll between the major sights, you'll have to settle for coming on a Sunday, when a long stretch from Piazza Venezia to Via Appia Antica is closed to traffic and pedestrians take to the streets to stroll past the ruins of the ancient city.

The Imperial Forums

Nowadays there's a lot of interest along Via dei Fori Imperiali itself, where a lot of the **Imperial Forums** have been excavated since work started in the mid-1990s and much is now open to the public. The Forum of Trajan and the Forum of Augustus on the north side have most of interest, and are most easily accessible, but there are forums, to Vespasian and Nerva, next door, and to Caesar on the south side, that might also detain you before moving on to the Forum proper. A **Visitor Centre**, opposite the church of Santi Cosma e Damiano (daily 9.30am–6.30pm; guided tours Sat at 11am & 3pm; €6), has more information if you need it, and a café to rescue your aching feet.

The Forum of Trajan

One of the major victims of Mussolini's plan for the area was the **Forum of Trajan**, a complex of basilicas, monuments, apartments and shops that was in its day the most sumptuous of the Imperial Forums, built at what was probably the very pinnacle of Roman power and prestige, after Trajan returned from conquering Dacia (modern Romania) in 112 AD. It's currently fairly unreco-gnizable, the main section no more than a sunken area of scattered columns to the left of the road, fronting the semicircle of the **Markets of Trajan** (Tues–Sun 9am–6pm; €8), a tiered ancient Roman shopping centre that's also accessible from Via IV Novembre. Down below the markets, the Basilica Ulpia was a central part of the Forum of Trajan, an immense structure, with five aisles and a huge apse at either end, that measured 176m long by 59m wide; the central nave is discernible from the large paved area in the centre, and the column stumps give an idea of its former dimensions.

At the head of the basilica, the enormous **Column of Trajan** was erected to celebrate the emperor's victories in Dacia, and is covered top to bottom with reliefs commemorating the highlights of the campaign. The carving on the base shows the trophies brought back and there's an inscription saying that the column was dedicated by the Senate and People of Rome in 113 AD in honour of Trajan. The statue on the top is St Peter, placed here by Pope Sixtus V in the late sixteenth century, and made from the bronze doors of Sant' Agnese fuori le Mura on Via Nomentana (see p.111).

Behind the Forum of Trajan, the **Torre delle Milizie** (summer Sat & Sun 9am–7pm; €4) is fondly imagined to be the tower from which Nero watched Rome burning, although it's actually a twelfth-century fortification left over from days when Rome was divided into warring factions within the city walls. The top was destroyed by a blast of lightning in the fifteenth century.

The Forum of Augustus

Back on Via dei Fori Imperiali, to the left, across the field of ruins, the round brick facade you can see now houses the Order of Malta but was once part of the **Forum of Augustus**. Just beyond, the monumental staircase and platform was Augustus's Temple of Mars the Avenger, put up by Augustus in memory of his uncle and adoptive father, Julius Caesar, after the last of his assassins had been killed. The temple is backed by a large wall in grey stone that was erected to prevent fire from spreading into the forums from the densely inhabited adjacent neighbourhood of Subura.

The Roman Forum

The **Roman Forum** is very near the top of most visitors' things to see in Rome. However, for many it's also one of the city's most disappointing sights, and you need an imagination and some small grasp of history really to

---

The decline and fall of the Forum

In 667 AD, Costans II, ruler of the Eastern empire, paid a state visit to Rome. He came to the Forum, and, seeing all the temples and basilicas held together with bronze and iron cramps, decided that the metal would serve better in his war against encroaching Islam, and ordered all the metal to be transported back home and forged into spearpoints, arrowheads and armour for his forces. It took just twelve days to dismantle the metal props, and, although everything was captured en route to Constantinople by Saracen raiders, the columns and arches supporting all the buildings in the Forum fell down with the next earth tremor. By the early ninth century hardly anything remained standing – ripe for the looters of later years, and one reason why so little is left today.

appreciate the place at all. Certainly it holds some of the most ruined Roman ruins you'll see: the area was abandoned (and looted) for so long that very little is anything like intact. But these five or so acres were once the heart of the Mediterranean world, and are a very real and potent testament to a power that held a large chunk of the earth in its thrall for close on five centuries, and whose influence reverberates right up to the present day – in language, in architecture, in political terms and systems, even in the romance that the last couple of hundred years have lent to its ruins.

The Via Sacra

Immediately inside the main entrance, take some time to get orientated. Sit down on the three long steps that flank the other side of the **Via Sacra**, which runs directly through the core of the Forum, from below the Capitoline Hill in the west to the far eastern extent of the site and the Arch of Titus (where there's a handy exit for the Colosseum). It was the best-known street of ancient Rome, along which victorious emperors and generals would ride in procession to give thanks at the Capitoline's Temple of Jupiter. It's possible, however, that this wasn't the original Via Sacra at all, and in fact was renamed in the 1550s, when the Holy Roman Emperor, Charles V, visited Pope Paul III and the only triumphal arch they could find to march under was the Arch of Septimius Severus, a couple hundred metres to your left.

The Regia and around

The steps you're sitting on are part of the **Regia**, or house of the kings, an extremely ancient – and ruined – group of foundations that date probably from the reign of the second king of Rome, Numa, who ruled from 715 to 673 BC. There was a shrine of Mars here, housing the shields and spears of the god of war, which generals embarking on a campaign rattled before setting off. If the shields and spears rattled of their own accord it was a bad omen, requiring purification and repentance rites. The Regia later became the residence of

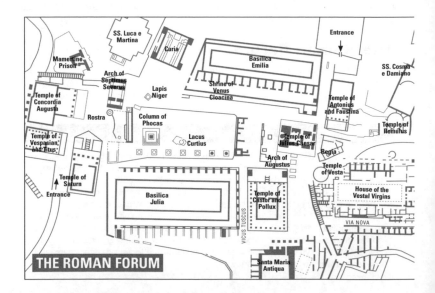

Julius Caesar, who moved in here in 45 BC – an imperious act which at least in part led to his downfall. On the other side of the road from the Regia, the Temple of Antoninus and Faustina is the best-preserved temple in the Forum, mainly because of its preservation since the seventh century as the church of **San Lorenzo in Miranda**. The six huge Corinthian columns across its front are still connected by an inscribed lintel, dedicating the temple, by order of the Senate, to the god Antonino and the goddess Faustina – the parents of Marcus Aurelius (Roman emperors were always considered to be deities). Above the inscription was the roof architrave, along the sides of which can be seen the original frieze of griffins, candelabra and acanthus scrolls. Otherwise, the brick stairs leading up to the floor of the temple are a modern reconstruction, while the facade of the church dates from 1602.

Next to the Regia, the pile of rubble immersed in cement with the little green roof is all that remains of the grandeur and magnificence that comprised the **temple to Julius Caesar** – the round brick stump under the roof marks the spot where Caesar was cremated, and around which the temple was built. You may hear tour guides declaiming Mark Antony's "Friends, Romans, countrymen" speech from here; if you do, bear in mind that not only was the speech made up by Shakespeare, but also that apparently Mark Antony only read Caesar's will, and that he would have done it from the Rostra (see below).

The football pitch of broken columns to the right of the Via Sacra marks the site of the **Basilica Emilia**, built in the second century BC to house law courts, and, in the little booths and boutiques flanking it on the Via Sacra side, moneychangers. Close by, a little marble plaque dedicated to **Venus Cloacina** marks the site of a small shrine dedicated to Venus where the Cloaca Maxima canal drained the Forum, which was originally marshland. The Cloaca Maxima reaches all the way to the Tiber from here, and still keeps the area drained.

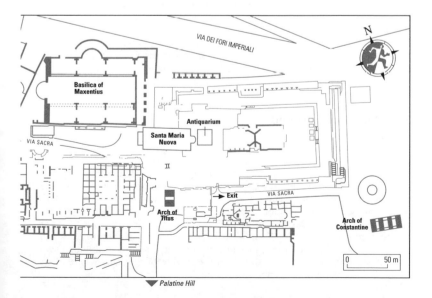

The Curia and around

A little way beyond, the large cube-shaped building is the **Curia**, built on the orders of Julius Caesar as part of his programme for expanding the Forum – it connects up with the Forum of Caesar outside – although what you see now is a 3rd-century AD reconstruction built during the era of the emperor Diocletian. The Senate met here during the republican period, and augurs would come to announce the wishes of the gods. For centuries the Curia served as a church, reverting to its original form only earlier this century, when it was restored, and its bronze doors – which had been removed in the seventeenth century to San Giovanni in Laterno, where they remain – were replaced with reproductions.

Inside, three wide stairs rise left and right, on which about three hundred senators could be accommodated with their folding chairs. In the centre is the speaker's platform, with a porphyry statue of a togaed figure. Otherwise, apart from the floor, elegantly patterned in red, yellow, green and white marble, there's not much left of its ancient decor, only the grey and white marble facing each side of the speaker's platform, which would once have covered the entire hall. The ceiling is a modern replacement, and in Roman times would have been gilded. The large marble reliefs here, the so-called **Plutei of Trajan** – found outside and brought here for safekeeping – show Trajan in the midst of public-spirited acts, forgiving the public debt owed by citizens to the state (porters carry large register books and place them before the seated emperor, where they will be burnt) and, on the right giving a woman a sack of money, a representation of Trajan's welfare plan for widows and orphans. Look closely at the reliefs and you can see how parts of the Forum would have looked at the time: in one, a fig tree, the columns and arches of the Basilica Julia, the facade of the Temple of Saturn, a triumphal arch and the Temple of Vespasian and Titus; in the other, the columns and eaves of the Temple of Castor and Pollux, and the Arch of Augustus.

Nearby, the black, fenced-off paving of the **Lapis Niger** marks the traditional site of the tomb of Romulus, the steps beneath (usually closed) leading down to a monument that was considered sacred ground during classical times. Across the travertine pavement from the Curia, the **Column of Phocas** is one of a few commemorative columns here that retains its dedicatory inscription. To the right, the **Arch of Septimius Severus** was constructed in the early third century AD by his sons Caracalla and Galba to mark their father's victories in what is now Iran. The friezes on it recall Severus and in particular Caracalla, who ruled Rome with undisciplined terror for seven years. There's a space where Galba was commemorated – Caracalla had him executed in 213 AD, and his name expediently removed from the arch altogether.

The Rostra and around

To the left of the arch, the low brown wall is the **Rostra**, facing the wide-open scatter of paving, dumped stones and beached columns that makes up the central portion of the Forum, the place where most of the life of the city was carried on, and which, in ancient times, was usually crowded with politicians, tribunes and traders. Facing the central part of the Forum, the Rostra was the place where important speeches were made, and it was from here that Mark Antony most likely spoke about Caesar after his death. Left of the Rostra are the long stairs of the **Basilica Julia**, built by Julius Caesar in the 50s BC after he returned from the Gallic Wars. All that remains are a few column bases and one nearly complete column, and you can't mount the stairs – although you can still see the gameboards scratched in the marble of the stairs where idlers in the Forum played their pebble-toss games.

△ Temple of Castor and Pollux

A bit further along, on the right, the guard rails lead into a kind of alcove in the pavement, which marks the site of the **Lacus Curtius** – the spot where, according to legend, a chasm opened during the earliest days and the sooth-sayers determined that it would be closed only when Rome had sacrificed its most valuable possession into it. Marcus Curtius, a Roman soldier who declared that Rome's most valuable possession was a loyal citizen, hurled himself and his horse into the void and it duly closed. Further on, you reach the **Temple of Saturn** – the oldest temple in the Forum, dating originally from 497 BC, although the base and eight columns you see today are the result of a series of restorations carried out between 42 BC and as late as 380 AD. The temple was also the Roman treasury and mint. To the right of the temple, three columns still stand from the **Temple of Vespasian and Titus** of the 80s AD. Still further to the right, behind the Arch of Septimius Severus, the large pile of brick and cement rubble is all that remains of the **Temple of Concordia Augusta**, dedicated by Tiberius in 10 AD.

Santa Maria Antiqua and the Temple of Castor and Pollux

Retracing your steps past the Forum proper takes you to **Vicus Tuscus**, "Etruscan Street", at the end of which are public toilets and a water fountain, and the church of **Santa Maria Antiqua**, which formed the vestibule to the emperor Domitian's palace on the Palatine Hill, and was the first ancient building to be converted for Christian worship – recently open again after many years. Back around the corner to the right, the enormous pile of rubble topped by three graceful Corinthinan columns is the **Temple of Castor and Pollux**, dedicated in 484 BC to the divine twins or Dioscuri, the offspring of Jupiter by Leda, who appeared miraculously to ensure victory for the Romans in a key battle. The story goes that a group of Roman citizens were gathered around a water fountain on this spot fretting about the war, when Castor and Pollux appeared and reassured them that the battle was won – hence the temple, and their adoption as the special protectors of Rome.

House of the Vestal Virgins

Beyond here, the **House of the Vestal Virgins** is a second-century AD recon-struction of a building originally by Nero. Vesta was the Roman goddess of the hearth and home, and her cult was an important one in ancient Rome. Her temple was in the charge of the so-called **Vestal Virgins**, who had the responsibility of keeping the sacred flame of Vesta alight, and were obliged to remain chaste for the thirty years that they served (they usually started at around age 10). If the flame should go out, the woman responsible was scourged; if she should lose her chastity, she was buried alive (her male partner-in-crime was flogged to death in front of the Curia). Because of the importance of their office, they were accorded special privileges; a choice section in the Colosseum was reserved for them; only they and the empress could ride in a wheeled vehicle within the confines of the city; and they had the right to pardon any criminal who managed to get close enough to one of them to beseech their mercy. A vestal virgin could resign her post if she wished, and she had the benefit of residing in a very comfortable palace: four floors of rooms around a central courtyard, with the round **Temple of Vesta** at the near end. The rooms are mainly ruins now, though they're fairly recognizable on the Palatine side, and you can get a good sense of the shape of the place from the remains of the courtyard, still with its pool in the centre and fringed by the statues or inscribed pedestals of the women themselves.

The Basilica of Maxentius

Opposite the vestals' house, the curved facade of the **Temple of Romulus** (the son of the emperor Maxentius), dating from 309 AD, has been sanctified and serves as vestibule for the church of **Santi Cosma e Damiano** behind, which sports a wide and majestic sixth-century apse mosaic showing Christ and the Apostles (entrance on Via dei Fori Imperiali). Just past the temple, a shady walkway to the left leads up to the **Basilica of Maxentius**, sometimes called the Basilica of Constantine, which rises up towards the main road – in terms of size and ingenuity probably the Forum's most impressive remains. By the early fourth century, when this structure was built, Roman architects and engineers were expert at building with poured cement. Begun by Maxentius, it was continued by his co-emperor and rival, Constantine, after he had defeated him at the Battle of the Milvian Bridge in 312 AD. It's said that Michelangelo studied the hexagonal coffered arches here when grappling with the dome of St Peter's, and apparently Renaissance architects frequently used its apse and arches as a model.

The Antiquarium and Arch of Titus

Back on the Via Sacra, past the church of Santa Maria Nova, the **Antiquarium of the Forum** (daily except Mon 9am–5pm; free) houses a collection of statue fragments, capitals, tiles, mosaics and other bits and pieces found around the Forum – none of it very interesting, apart from a number of skeletons and wooden coffins exhumed from an Iron Age necropolis found to the right of the Temple of Antoninus and Faustina.

From the basilica the Via Sacra climbs more steeply, past a grassy series of ruins that no one has been able to positively identify, to the **Arch of Titus**, which stands commandingly on a low arm of the Palatine Hill, looking one way down the remainder of the Via Sacra to the Colosseum, and back over the Forum proper. The arch was built by Titus's brother, Domitian, after the emperor's death in 81 AD, to commemorate his victories in Judaea in 70 AD, and his triumphal return from that campaign. It's a much restored structure, and you can see, in reliefs on the inside, scenes of Titus riding in a chariot with Nike, goddess of Victory, being escorted by representatives of the Senate and Plebs, and, on the opposite side, spoils being removed from the Temple in Jerusalem. It's a long-standing tradition that Jews don't pass under this arch.

The Colosseum and the Palatine and Celian hills

Beyond the Forum, a lake lay where the **Colosseum** stands now, drained by a small stream that wove between the **Palatine** and **Celian hills**, curving to empty into the Tiber close by. The slopes of the Palatine and Celian hills were inhabited by people living in shanties and huts until the great fire of 64 AD, when Nero incorporated the area into his grand design for the city, building a gigantic nymphaeum or courtyard to support his planned gardens on the Celian Hill, part of his Domus Aurea (see p.113), and cleaning up the slopes of the two hills. Eventually a temple to the deified Claudius was built on the

Celian Hill, and the Palatine became the residence of the emperors, fed by water brought by the arched span of the Aqua Claudia.

The Palatine Hill

Turning right at the Arch of Titus takes you up to the ticket booth and main entrance to the **Palatine Hill** – there's another entrance on Via San Gregorio. The Palatine is supposedly where the city of Rome was founded, by Romulus and Remus, and holds some of its most ancient remnants. In a way it's a more pleasant site to tour than the Forum, larger, greener and more of a park – a good place to have a picnic and relax after the rigours of the ruins below. In the days of the Republic, the Palatine was the most desirable address in Rome (the word "palace" is derived from Palatine), and the big names continued to colonize it during the imperial era, trying to outdo each other with ever larger and more magnificent dwellings.

Along the main path up from the Forum, the **Domus Flavia** was once one of the most splendid residences, and, although it's now almost completely ruined, the peristyle is easy enough to identify, with its fountain and hexagonal brick arrangement in the centre. To the left, the top level of the gargantuan **Domus Augustana** spreads to the far brink of the hill – not the home of Augustus as its name suggests, but the private house of any emperor

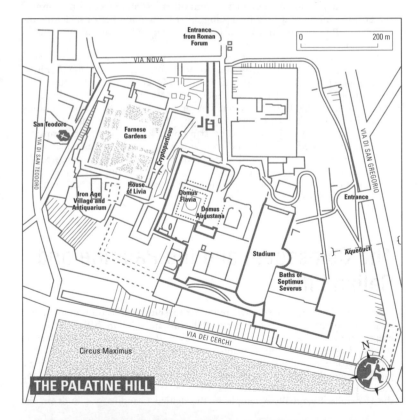

ANCIENT ROME | The Colosseum and the Palatine and Celian hills

(or "Augustus"). You can look down from here on its vast central courtyard with maze-like fountain and wander to the brink of the deep trench of the **Stadium**. On the far side of the stadium, the ruins of the **Baths of Septimius Severus** cling to the side of the hill, the terrace giving good views over the Colosseum and the churches of the Celian Hill opposite.

In the opposite direction from the Domus Flavia, steps lead down to the **Cryptoporticus**, a long passage built by Nero to link the vestibule of his Domus Aurea (see p.112) with the Domus Augustana and other Palatine palaces, and decorated along part of its length with well-preserved Roman stucco-work. You can go either way along the passage: a left turn leads to the **House of Livia**, originally believed to have been the residence of Livia, the wife of Augustus, though now identified as simply part of Augustus's house (the set of ruins beyond). Its courtyard and some of the inner rooms are decorated with scanty frescoes.

Turn right down the passage and up some steps on the left and you're in the **Farnese Gardens**, among the first botanical gardens in Europe, laid out by Cardinal Alessandro Farnese in the mid-sixteenth century and now a tidily planted, shady retreat from the exposed heat of the ruins. The terrace here looks back over the Forum, while the terrace at the opposite end looks down on the church of San Teodoro, across to St Peter's, and down on the new excavations immediately below – the traces of an **Iron Age village** that perhaps marks the real centre of Rome's ancient beginnings. The large grey building here houses the Palatine **Antiquarium**, which contains a vast assortment of statuary, pottery, terracotta antefixes and architectural fragments that have been excavated on the Palatine during the last 150 years. As in the Forum Antiquarium, its most interesting exhibits are the very oldest, including models of how the Palatine looked in the Iron Age.

The Arch of Constantine

Leaving the Forum by way of the Via Sacra, under the Arch of Titus (see p.79), you see the huge **Arch of Constantine** to your right, placed here in the early decades of the fourth century AD after Constantine had consolidated his power as sole emperor. The arch demonstrates the deterioration of the arts during the late stages of the Roman Empire, in that there were hardly any sculptors around who could produce original work and most of the sculptural decoration here had to be removed from other monuments. The builders were probably quite ignorant of the significance of the pieces they borrowed: the round medallions are taken from a temple dedicated to the emperor Hadrian's lover, Antinous, and show Antinous and Hadrian engaged in the hunt. The other pieces, removed from the Forum of Trajan, show Dacian prisoners captured in Trajan's war there. The large inscription in the centre was made for the arch, and dedicates the arch to Constantine for his wisdom – presumably in making Christianity the official religion of the Empire, although no one really knows what this refers to.

Between the Arch of Constantine and the Colosseum, at a pivotal point in the Via Sacra, stood a monumental fountain or **Meta Sudans**, the outline of which can still be seen today in the form of a series of recently excavated low brick walls. A "Meta" was the marker in the centre of a racecourse, and was usually an obelisk or some other large, easily visible object. In this case it was a conical fountain that was probably dedicated to Apollo, and produced a slow supply of water that resembled sweat – hence its name the "Sweating Meta".

The Colosseum

Across the way from here, the **Colosseum** is perhaps Rome's most awe-inspiring ancient monument, and one which – unlike the Forum – needs little historical knowledge or imagination to deduce its function. This enormous structure was so solidly built that despite the depredations of nearly two thousand years of earthquakes, fires, riots, wars, and, not least, its plundering for its seemingly inexhaustible supply of ready-cut travertine blocks (the Barberini and Cancelleria palaces, even St Peter's, all used stone from here), it still stands relatively intact – a readily recognizable symbol not just of the city of Rome, but of the entire ancient world. It's not much more than a shell now, eaten away by pollution and cracked by the vibrations of cars and metro; around the outside, the arches would originally have held statues, and there are gaping holes where metal brackets linked the great blocks together. The basic structure of the place is easy to see, however, and has served as a model for stadiums around the world ever since. You'll not be alone in appreciating it, and during summer the combination of people and scaffolding can make a visit more like touring a modern building-site than an ancient monument. But visit late in the evening or early morning before the tour buses have arrived, go up a level to get a real sense of the size of the building, and the arena can seem more like the marvel it really is.

The Colosseum: past and present

Originally known as the Flavian Amphitheatre (the name Colosseum is a much later invention), it was begun around 72 AD by the emperor **Vespasian**, who was anxious to extinguish the memory of Nero, and so chose the site of Nero's outrageous Domus Aurea (see p.112) for the stadium; the Colosseum is sited on a lake that lay in front of the vestibule of the palace, where Nero had erected a huge statue of himself as sun god. The lake was drained, and the Colosseum was – incredibly, given the size of the project – inaugurated by Vespasian's son Titus about eight years later, an event celebrated by a hundred days of continuous games; it was finally completed by Domitian, Titus's brother, the third of the Flavian emperors.

Up until this time gladiatorial and other bloody games had been conducted in a makeshift stadium in the Roman Forum, near the Curia. The stands were temporary and constructed of wood, and had to be erected and taken down every time there were games. It is said that seventy thousand Hebrew slaves did the heavy work at the Colosseum. Fifty thousand cartloads of pre-cut travertine stone was hauled from the quarries at Tivoli, a distance of 27km. In the depths of what must have been the muddy bottom of the lake, a labyrinth was laid out, walling in passages for the contestants and creating areas for assembling and storing sets, scenery and other requirements for gladiatorial contests.

The overall structure was tastefully designed, with close attention paid to decoration. On the outside, the arena's three arcades rose in strict classical fashion – with Ionic, topped by Doric, topped by Corinthian, columns – to a flat surface at the top punctuated only by windows, where there was a series of supports for masts that protruded at the upper limit. These masts, 240 in total, were used to array a canvas awning over the spectators inside the arena. Inside, beyond the corridors that led up to the seats, lavishly decorated with painted stuccoes, there was room for a total of around 60,000 people seated and 10,000 or so standing; and the design is such that all 70,000 could enter and be seated in a matter of minutes – surely a lesson for designers of modern stadiums.

The seating was allocated on a strict basis, with the emperor and his attendants naturally occupying the best seats in the house, and the social class of

Beastly happenings at the Colosseum

The Romans flocked to the Colosseum for many things, but **gladiatorial contests** were the big attraction. Gladiatorial combat as a Roman tradition was a direct import from the Etruscans, who thought it seemly to sacrifice a few prisoners of war or slaves at the funeral games of an important person. By the second century BC gladiatorial games had become so institutionalized in Rome that a gladiatorial school, or Ludus, was installed in the city – a rather grim affair, consisting of a barracks for gladiators and a ring in which they could practise with blunt weapons under supervision.

Gladiatorial combat was probably the greatest and cruellest of all bloodsports. At the start of the games the gladiators would enter through the monumental door at the eastern end of the arena. They would make a procession around the ring and halt in front of the emperor's box, where they would make their famous greeting, "Hail Caesar, we who are about to die salute you." Gladiators were divided into several classes, to perform different types of combat. There was the heavily armed "Samnite", named after the types of arms that the Romans had captured on the defeat of that tribe in 310 BC, equipped with heavy armour, an oblong bronze shield, a visored helmet with crest and plumes, and a sword (gladius). Usually a Samnite would be pitted against a combatant without armour, who was equipped only with a cast net and a trident, whose main protection was that he was unencumbered and thereby could be fleet of foot. He had, however, only one cast of his net in which to entangle the Samnite and kill him with his trident. He was not allowed to flee from the arena, and, once captured, the roaring mob would be asked whether he should be killed or be allowed to live. If he had put up a good fight he would usually be spared; if he had not fought as valiantly as he should, however, he would be slaughtered on the spot. The advent of Christianity brought a gradual end to the gladiatorial games (contrary to popular opinion, Christians were never fed to the lions here), and in 404 AD the emperor Honorius abolished them altogether.

The other activities conducted in the Colosseum involved **animals**. In the hundred-day games that inaugurated the Colosseum, something like 9000 beasts were massacred – roughly twelve killings a minute – and during the 450 years of activity here several breeds of African elephant and lion were rendered extinct. There were also gladiatorial games which involved "hunting" wild animals, and sometimes animals would be pitted against each other – bears would be tied to bulls and have to fight to the finish, lions would take on tigers, dogs would be set against wolves, and so on. The last games involving animals were conducted in the year 523 AD, after which the Colosseum gradually fell into disuse and disrepair.

the spectators diminishing as you got nearer the top. There were no ticket sales as we conceive of them; rather, tickets were distributed through – and according to the social status of – Roman heads of households. These "tickets" were in fact wooden tags, with the entrance, row, aisle and seat number carved on them.

Inside the amphitheatre, the labyrinth below was covered over with a wooden floor, punctuated at various places for trap doors which could be opened as required and lifts to raise and lower the animals that were to take part in the games. The floor was covered with canvas to make it waterproof and the canvas was covered with several centimetres of sand to absorb blood; in fact, our word "arena" is derived from the Latin word for sand.

The Celian Hill

Some of the animals that were to die in the Colosseum were kept in a zoo up on the **Celian Hill**, just behind the arena, the furthest south of Rome's seven hills and probably its most peaceful, still clothed almost entirely in woodland

and with the park of Villa Celimontana at its heart; the entrance is on **Piazza della Navicella**, a little way down Via Claudia, and you could do worse than take a stroll through, before moving on to a couple of worthwhile churches, and the remains of a Roman dwelling nearby.

Santi Giovanni e Paolo

Continuing up to the summit of the hill, you'll come to the church of **Santi Giovanni e Paolo** (daily 8.30am–11.30am & 3.30–6pm), marked by its colourful campanile and set in a once-peaceful square that's been invaded by adolescent autograph hunters since Silvio Berlusconi's TV studios moved in opposite. Originally founded by a Roman senator called Pammachius, the church is in a way a memorial to conscientious objection, dedicated to two dignitaries in the court of Constantine who were beheaded here in 361 AD after refusing military service. The relics of what is believed to be their house are now open to the public (see below). Inside the church's dark interior, thronged with chandeliers, a railed-off square in mid-nave marks the shrine where the saints were martyred and buried.

The Case Romane

Another Roman attraction that has just opened after a long period of restoration, the so-called **Case Romane**, around the corner from the church on Clivio di Scauro (daily except Tues & Wed 10am–1pm & 3–6pm; €6), was believed to be the relatively lavish residence of Giovanni and Paolo – the two prominent citizens who were martyred during the third century AD and commemorated in the church (see above). It's made up of around twenty rooms in all, and in fact is more likely to be a series of dwellings, separated by a narrow lane, rather than a single residence. Patchily frescoed with pagan and Christian subjects, most of the chambers are relatively dark, poky affairs which need some imagination to see as the no doubt palatially appointed living quarters they were. However, there are standouts, including the Casa dei Genii, frescoed with winged youths and cupids, and the courtyard or nymphaeum, which has a marvellous fresco of a goddess being attended on and poured a drink, sandwiched between cupids in boats, fishing and loading supplies. The antiquarium, too, beautifully pulls together finds from the site, among them a *Christ with Saints* fresco, and ceramics, amphorae and some fascinating small domestic artefacts – an intact imperial age spoon, a bronze reel, bone sewing needles and almost perfect oil lamps.

San Gregorio Magno

The road descends from the church and Roman house under a succession of brick arches to the church of **San Gregorio Magno** on the left (daily 9am–noon & 3–6.30pm), in a commanding position above the traffic drone of the road below, and looking over to the lollipop pines of the Palatine Hill opposite. Again, it's the story behind the church that's most interesting. It was from here that St Gregory dispatched St Augustine in the early seventh century to convert England to Christianity, and although the rather ordinary Baroque interior shows little evidence of it, the chapel of the saint does have a beautifully carved altar showing scenes from his life, and there's a room containing his marble throne.

More impressive is the structure to the left of the church, made up of three chapels and surrounded by cypress trees. **Santa Silvia** and **Sant'Andrea** contain **frescoes** by Guido Reni, Domenichino and Pomarancio, while **Santa Barbara** treasures the table at which St Gregory fed twelve paupers daily with his own hands for years.

The Aventine and south central Rome

T he area south of the Forum and Palatine has some of the city's most atmospheric and compelling Christian and ancient sights, from the relatively central **Circus Maximus** and **Baths of Caracalla** – one of the city's grandest ruins, and the venue of occasional but usually inspirational performances of opera – to the **catacombs** on the ancient Via Appia on the city's outskirts, with quite a lot that's worth seeing in between. It also has some of its most pleasant corners, in particular up on the still green and peaceful **Aventine Hill**, while just below the Aventine **Via Ostiense** linked Rome to its port of Ostia. It's home to a more recent, nineteenth-century attraction in the **Protestant Cemetery**, where the poets Keats and Shelley are buried. Around here are Rome's trendiest neighbourhoods, **Testaccio** – a working-class enclave that has become increasingly hip and gentrified over the past decade or so, and **Ostiense** itself, whose regeneration is more recent, spurred on by the conversion of the **Centrale Montemartini** electricity generating plant to an amazing new gallery. Beyond lies the magnificent rebuilt basilica of **Sant Paolo fuori le Mura** and Rome's futuristic 1930s experiment in extra-urban town planning, **EUR**.

The Circus Maximus

At the end of Via San Gregorio, the southern side of the Palatine Hill drops down to the **Circus Maximus**, a long, thin, green expanse bordered by heavily trafficked roads that was the ancient city's main venue for chariot races. At one time this arena had a capacity of up to 400,000 spectators, and if it were still intact it would no doubt match the Colosseum for grandeur. As it is, a litter of stones at the Viale Aventino end is all that remains, together with – at the southern end – a little medieval tower built by the Frangipani family, and, behind a chain-link fence traced out in marble blocks, the outline of the **Septizodium**, an imperial structure designed to show off the glories of the city and its empire to those arriving on the Via Appia. The huge obelisk that now stands in front of the church of San Giovanni in Laterno – at 385 tonnes and over 30m high the largest in the world – was once the central marker of the arena, and it's known that the obelisk now in Piazza del Popolo stood here too.

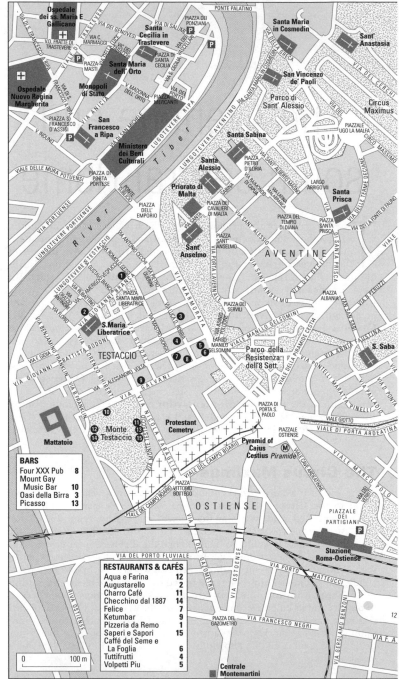

PONTE PALATINO

Ospedale dei ss. Maria E Gallicano

VIA DEI GENOVESI

VIA DI SALUMI

PIAZZA DEI PONZIANI

Santa Cecilia in Trastevere

VIA DI S. FRANCESCO A RIPA

V.D. FRATTE DI TRASTEVERE

VIA C. MARMAGGI

Santa Maria in Cosmedin

Sant' Anastasia

VIA DELLA GRECA

VIA DEI CERCHI

PIAZZA MASTAI

Santa Maria dell'Orto

PIAZZA DI SANTA CECILIA

VIA S. GIOIA

San Vincenzo de' Paoli

Ospedale Nuovo Regina Margherita

Monopoli di Stato

VIA MADONNA DELL'ORTO

PIAZZA PORTO MERCANTI

Parco di Sant' Alessio

Circus Maximus

PIAZZA S. FRANCESCO D'ASSISI

San Francesco a Ripa

V INDUNO

VIA ANICIA

San Michele

Ministero dei Beni Culturali

Tiber

LUNGOTEVERE RIPA

Santa Sabina

PIAZZA UGO LA MALFA

CIRCO MASSIMO

VIALE DELLE MURA POTUENSI

PIAZZA DI PORTA PORTESE

PONTE SUBLICIO

River

Santa Alessio

Priorato di Malta

PIAZZA DEI CAVALIERI DI MALTA

PIAZZA PIETRO D'ILLIRIA

VIA S. ALBERTO MAGNO

VIA RAIMONDO DI CAPUA

LARGO ARRIGO VII

Santa Prisca

VIA DELLE TERME DECIANE

LUNGOTEVERE PORTUENSE

PIAZZA DELL'EMPORIO

VIA SANTA

Sant' Anselmo

PIAZZA SANT'ANSELMO

PIAZZA DEL TEMPIO DI DIANA

PIAZZA SANTA PRISCA

VIA DI SANTA PRISCA

VIA ANTONIO CECCHI

VIA MARMORATA

AVENTINE

VIALE

LUNGOTEVERE TESTACCIO

S.Maria Liberatrice

PIAZZA SANTA MARIA LIBERATRICE

PIAZZA DEI SERVILI

PIAZZA ALBANIA

S. Saba

TESTACCIO

LARGO MANLIO GELSOMINI

Parco della Resistenza dell'8 Sett.

VIA ANNIA FAUSTINA

VIA GALVANI

PIAZZA DI PORTA S. PAOLO

Mattatoio

Monte Testaccio

Protestant Cemetery

Pyramid of Caius Cestius Piramide

PIAZZALE OSTIENSE

VIALE GIOTTO

VIALE DI PORTA ARDEATINA

VIALE MARCO POLO

OSTIENSE

PIAZZA VITTORIO BOTTEGO

PIAZZALE DEI PARTIGIANI

Stazione Roma-Ostiense

VIA DEL PORTO FLUVIALE

VIA FRANCESCO NEGRI

RIVA OSTIENSE

PIAZZA DEL GAZOMETRO

BARS	
Four XXX Pub	8
Mount Gay Music Bar	10
Oasi della Birra	3
Picasso	13

RESTAURANTS & CAFÉS	
Aqua e Farina	12
Augustarello	2
Charro Café	11
Checchino dal 1887	14
Felice	7
Ketumbar	9
Pizzeria da Remo	1
Saperi e Sapori	15
Caffé del Seme e La Foglia	6
Tuttifrutti	4
Volpetti Piu	5

0   100 m

Centrale Montemartini

San Paolo fuori le Mura (1 km) ▼

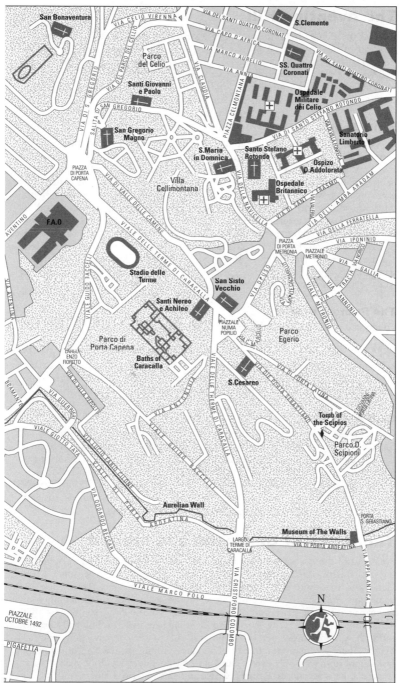

Domine Quovadis (300 m) & Catacombs of San Callisto (1 km) ▼

The Aventine Hill

Beyond the Circus Maximus you can scale the **Aventine Hill** – the south-ernmost of the city's seven hills and the heart of plebeian Rome in ancient times. These days the working-class quarters of the city are further south, and the Aventine is in fact one of the city's more upscale residential areas, covered with villas with large gardens that lend a leafy, suburban feel, and make it one of the few places in the city centre where you can escape the traffic.

Santa Sabina

A short way up Via Santa Sabina, the church of **Santa Sabina** (daily 7am–12.45pm & 3.30–6pm) is a strong contender for Rome's most beautiful basilica: high and wide, its nave and portico restored back to their fifth-century appearance in the 1930s. Look especially at the main doors, which are contemporary with the church and boast eighteen panels carved with Christian scenes, forming a complete illustrated Bible, which includes one of the oldest representations of the Crucifixion in existence. Santa Sabina is also the principal church of the Dominicans, and it's claimed that the orange trees in the garden outside which you can glimpse on your way to the restrained cloister are descendants of those planted by St Dominic himself. Whatever the truth of this, the views from the gardens are splendid – right across the Tiber to the centre of Rome and St Peter's.

The Priorato di Malta

Follow the road south past the **Priorato di Malta**, one of several buildings in the city belonging to the Knights of Malta – now known simply as the "Order of Malta", which has a celebrated view of the dome of St Peter's through the keyhole of its main gate. The little piazza in front of the main gate has marble triumphal insignia designed and placed here by Piranesi (who also designed the the church of Santa Maria inside) to celebrate the knights' dramatic history.

Sant'Anselmo

Opposite the Priorato di Malta, spare five minutes or so for the church of **Sant'Anselmo**, a Benedictine complex of church and college with nice gardens and a shop selling all manner of produce, Benedictine and otherwise – *limoncello*, *grappa*, *amaro*, as well as chocolate, beer, books, CDs and toiletries. The church itself is a plain basilica built in the last decade of the nineteenth century – not of much interest really, but known for its Gregorian chorus and reasonably regular concerts, usually held on Sunday evenings.

The Baths of Caracalla and around

Southeast of the Aventine, beyond the large UN Food and Agriculture build-ing, the **Baths of Caracalla** at Viale Terme di Caracalla 52 (summer Mon 9am–1pm, Tues–Sun 9am–6.30pm; winter Mon & Sun 9am–1pm, Tues–Sat 9am–3pm; €5) give a far better sense of the scale and monumentality of Roman architecture than most of the extant ruins in the city – so much so that Shelley was moved to write *Prometheus Unbound* here in 1819. The baths are no more than a shell now, but the walls still rise to very nearly their original height. There are many fragments of mosaics – none spectacular, but quite a few bright and well preserved – and it's easy to discern a floor plan. As for Caracalla, he was one of Rome's worst and shortest-lived rulers, and it's no

△ Baths of Caracalla

wonder there's nothing else in the city built by him. The baths were for many years used for occasional opera performances during the summer (one of Mussolini's better ideas), but these were stopped a few years ago due to damage to the site. Watch out for their re-emergence, though – it's a thrilling and inexpensive way to see the baths at their most atmospheric.

San Saba

A few minutes' walk from the Caracalla baths, **San Saba** (daily 9am–noon & 4–7pm) is an ancient church, originally built in the tenth century over a seventh-century structure built by monks who had fled here from the Middle East to escape the Arab invaders. Topped with an old, fifteenth-century loggia and fronted by a pleasant if scruffy walled garden, it's worth visiting for its wonderful cosmati-work door and floor and a beautifully proportioned apse.

Testaccio

On the far side of Via Marmorata, below, the solid working-class neighbourhood of **Testaccio** groups around a couple of main squares, a tight-knit community with a market and a number of bars and small trattorias that was for many years synonymous with the slaughterhouse that sprawls down to the Tiber just beyond. In the last couple of decades the area has become a trendy place to live, property prices have soared, and some uneasy contradictions have emerged, with vegetarian restaurants opening their doors in an area still known for the offal dishes served in its traditional trattorias, and gay and alternative clubs standing cheek-by-jowl with the car-repair shops gouged into Monte Testaccio.

The slaughterhouse, or **Mattatoio**, once the area's main employer, is now home to the Centro Sociale and "Villaggio Globale", a space used for concerts, raves and the like, along with stabling for the city's horse-and-carriage drivers, a gymnasium and a small Gypsy camp. For years there has been talk of sprucing it up into a chichi affair of shops and restaurants, but so far nothing has happened, and it's likely to remain as it is for some time to come. Meanwhile, it also houses something called the **Museum of Contemporary Art of Rome** (MACRO; Tues–Sun 9am–6.30pm; €5), just inside the main gate, which stages temporary exhibitions of a radical and adventurous nature.

Opposite the slaughterhouse, **Monte Testaccio**, which gives the area its name, is a 35-metre-high mound created out of the shards of Roman amphorae that were dumped here over several centuries. The ancients were not aware of the fact that the terracotta amphorae could be recycled, and consequently broke them up into small shards and lay them down in an orderly manner, sprinkling quicklime on them to dissolve the residual wine or oil and so creating the mountain you see today. It's an odd sight, the ceramic curls clearly visible through the tufts of grass that crown its higher reaches, the bottom layers hollowed out by the workshops of car and bike mechanics – and, now, clubs and bars.

The Protestant Cemetery

On the far side of Monte Testaccio, off Via Marmorata, on Via Caio Cestio X, the **Protestant Cemetery** (Tues–Sat 9am–5pm, Sun 9am–4pm; donation expected) isn't in fact a Protestant cemetery at all, but is reserved for non-Roman Catholics of all nationalities, so you'll also find famous Italian atheists, Christians of the Orthodox persuasion, and the odd Jew or Muslim, buried here. It is nonetheless one of the shrines to the English in Rome, and a fitting conclusion to a visit to the Keats-Shelley Memorial House on Piazza di Spagna (see Chapter 4), since it is here that both poets are buried, along with a handful of other well-known names. Most visitors come to see the grave of Keats, who lies next to his friend, the painter Joseph Severn, in a corner of the old part of the cemetery near the pyramid, his stone inscribed as he wished with the words "here lies one whose name was writ in water". Severn died much later than Keats but asked to be laid here nonetheless, together with his brushes and palette.

Shelley's ashes were brought here at Mary Shelley's request and interred, after much obstruction by the papal authorities, in the newer part of the cemetery, at the opposite end – the Shelleys had visited several years earlier, the poet praising it as "the most beautiful and solemn cemetery I ever beheld". It had been intended that Shelley should rest with his young son, William, who died while they were in Rome and was also buried here, but his remains couldn't be found (although his small grave remains nearby). It's worth knowing that Mary Shelley was so broken-hearted by the deaths of both her son and husband, that it was twenty years before she could bring herself to visit this place.

Among other famous internees, Shelley's great friend, the writer and adventurer Edward Trelawny, lies next door, the political writer and activist, Antonio Gramsci, on the far right-hand side in the middle, to name just two – though if you're at all interested in star-spotting you should either borrow or buy the booklet from the entrance.

The Piramide Cestia

Overlooking the cemetery, the most distinctive landmark in this part of town is the **Piramide Cestia**, the mossy pyramidal tomb of one Caius Cestius, who died in 12 BC. Cestius had spent some time in Egypt, and part of his will decreed that all his slaves should be freed, and the white pyramid you see today was thrown up by them in only 330 days of what must have been joyful building. It's open to the public on the second and fourth Saturday of each month, though you can visit the cats who live here, and the volunteers who care for them, any afternoon between 2.30pm and 4.30pm.

Ostiense

Immediately south of Testaccio, the industrial neighbourhood of **Ostiense** is perhaps the city's most up-and-coming area, home to those who can no longer afford to live in already gentrified Testaccio. There was until a few years ago no real reason to come here at all, unless you were on your way down the basilica of San Paolo (see below), but nowadays the Capitoline collections at **Centrale Montemartini** alone make it worth the trip, as well as the clubs, bars and restaurants that are beginning to spring up to serve the media types and companies that are moving in. This will be even more true if the **Mercati Generale**, Rome's vast former wholesale food market on Via Ostiense, currently derelict, are developed into a brand-new retail and shopping district as planned.

Centrale Montemartini

For the moment it's the **Centrale Montemartini**, Via Ostiense 106 (Tues–Sun 9.30am–7pm; €4.20, €9 for Capitoline Museums as well) that has done the most to put Ostiense on the map, a former electricity generating station that was requisitioned to display the cream of the Capitoline Museums' sculpture while the main buildings were being renovated, and that was so popular that it has become a permanent outpost of the venerable institution. Ten minutes' walk from Piramide metro station, the huge rooms of the power station are ideally suited to showing off ancient sculpture, although checking out the massive turbines and furnaces has a fascination of its own, and more than competes for your attention.

The size of the building is the thing, most obviously in the **Machine Hall**, where there's the head, feet and an arm from a colossal statue, once 8m high, found in Largo Argentina. Elsewhere in the chamber are various heads, some of emperors – Claudius, Tiberius, Domitian – a large Roman copy of *Athena*, and fine statue of a Roman soldier from the Esquiline Hill tucked away in a corner. In the next room, the **Furnace Hall**, the most obvious features are the furnace itself at the far end and a fragmented mosaic of hunting scenes that occupies half the floor; a walkway gives a good view of the latter's deer and boar, and figures both on horseback and crouching to trap their prey in nets. Among the sculptures on display is the milk-white *Esquiline Venus* and an amazing statue of a girl seated on a stool with legs crossed, from the third century BC. There's also a figure of Hercules and next to it the soft *Muse Polymnia*, the former braced for activity, the latter leaning on a rock and staring thoughtfully into the distance. Look out, too, for a wonderful pair of statues of magistrates, one old, one young, but both holding the handkerchief they would use to herald the start of competitions and circuses.

San Paolo fuori le Mura

Two kilometres or so south of the Porta San Paolo, the basilica of **San Paolo fuori le Mura** or "St Paul's Outside-the-Walls" (daily 7.30am–6.30pm) is one of the five patriarchal basilicas of Rome, occupying the supposed site of St Paul's tomb, where he was laid to rest after being beheaded at Tre Fontane (see below). Of the five, this basilica has probably fared the least well over the years. It was apparently once the grandest, connected to the Aurelian Wall by a colonnade, over a kilometre in length, made up of eight hundred marble columns, but a ninth-century sacking by the Saracens and a devastating fire in 1823 (a couple of cack-handed roofers spilt burning tar, almost entirely destroying the church) means that the building you see now is largely a nineteenth-century reconstruction, sited in what is these days a rather unenticing neighbourhood.

For all that, it's a very successful if somewhat clinical rehash of the former church, succeeding where St Peter's tries (but ultimately fails) by impressing with sheer size and grandeur: whether you enter by way of the cloisters or the west door, it's impossible not to be awed by the space of the building inside, its crowds of columns topped by round-arched arcading. Also, of all the basilicas of Rome, this one gives you the feel of what an ancient Roman basilica must have been like: the huge, barn-like structure, with its clerestory windows and roof beams supported by enormous columns, has a powerful and authentic sense of occasion.

Some parts of the building did survive the fire. In the south transept, the **paschal candlestick** is a remarkable piece of Romanesque carving, supported by half-human beasts and rising through entwined tendrils and strangely human limbs and bodies to scenes from Christ's life, the figures crowding in together as if for a photocall; it's inscribed by its makers, Nicolo di Angelo and Pietro Bassalletto. The bronze aisle doors were also rescued from the old basilica and date from 1070, as was the thirteenth-century tabernacle by Arnolfo di Cambio, under which a slab from the time of Constantine, inscribed "Paolo Apostolo Mort", is supposed to lie – although it's hard to get a look at this. The arch across the apse is original, too, embellished with

mosaics (donated by the Byzantine queen Galla Placidia in the sixth century) that show Christ giving a blessing, angels, the symbols of the Gospels, and saints Peter and Paul. There's also the cloister, just behind here – probably Rome's finest piece of Cosmatesque work, its spiralling, mosaic-encrusted columns enclosing a peaceful rose garden. Just off here, the **Relics Chapel** houses a dustily kept set of relics, and the **Pinacoteca** shows engravings depicting San Paolo before and after the fire.

The Aurelian Wall

Rather than heading south from Piazza di Porta San Paolo, you can make a long detour back into the city centre following the **Aurelian Wall**, built by the emperor Aurelian (and his successor Probus) in 275 AD to enclose Rome's seven hills and protect the city from invasion. The Aurelian Wall surrounds the city with a circumference of about 17km, and, if you really are an enthusiast, the entire distance can be walked in an eight-hour day with a pause for lunch. However, for a taster, one of the best-preserved stretches runs between Porta San Paolo and Porta San Sebastiano, following Via Porta Ardeatina: cross the road from Piramide station and turn right and follow the walls, keeping them always on your left.

It is around two kilometres from Porta San Paolo to **Porta San Sebastiano**, built in the fifth century, where the **Museo delle Mura** (Tues–Sat 9am–5pm; €2.60), occupying a couple of floors of the gate, has displays of Aurelian's original plans and lots of photos of the walls past and present that are helpful in showing what is original and what medieval additions, and how different structures have been incorporated into the walls over the years. The museum tells you more about the walls and the various gates than you ever thought you might need to know, but you can climb up to the top of the gate for great views over the Roman *campagna* beyond, and walk a few hundred metres along the walls themselves – towards the east – before having to return to the museum.

From Porta San Sebastiano you are a short walk from the Baths of Caracalla, back up Via di Porta San Sebastiano, on the way to which, if you're in no hurry, you could stop off at the **Tomb of the Scipios** (though this was closed at the time of writing). The tomb was discovered in 1780 and the Etruscan-style sarcophagus found here transported to the Vatican, where it is on display (see Chapter 11). For the moment, though, you have to make do with peeking into the small entrance or looking down from the scruffy park just above.

Failing that, continue following the walls by walking along Via delle Mura Latine to Piazzale Metronio, from where you're just a short walk from San Giovanni in Laterano (see Chapter 8).

Via Appia Antica and the catacombs

Starting at the Porta San Sebastiano, the **Via Appia Antica** is the most famous of Rome's consular roads that used to strike out in each direction from the ancient city, basically leading from here straight as an arrow to the port of Brindisi 590km south. The road was built by the censor Appio Claudio in 312 BC, and is the only Roman landmark mentioned in the Bible. During classical times it was the most important of all the Roman trade routes, the so-called "Queen of Roads", carrying supplies right down through Campania to the port of Brindisi. It's no longer the main route south out of the city – that's Via Appia Nuova from nearby Porta San Giovanni – but it remains an important part of early Christian Rome, its verges lined with numerous pagan and Christian sites, including most famously the underground burial cemeteries or **catacombs** of the first Christians. Laws in ancient Rome forbade burial within the city walls – most Romans were cremated – and there are catacombs in other parts of the city (those attached to the church of Sant'Agnese on Via Nomentana are some of the best). But this is by far the largest concentration – five complexes in all, dating from the first century to the fourth century, almost entirely emptied of bodies now but still decorated with the primitive signs and frescoes that were the hallmark of the then-burgeoning Christian movement. Despite much speculation, no one really knows why the Christians decided to bury their dead in these tunnels: the rock here, tufa, is soft and easy to hollow out, but the digging involved must still have been phenomenal, and there is no real reason to suppose that the burial places had to be secret – they continued to bury their dead like this long after Christianity became the established religion. Whatever the reasons, they make intriguing viewing now. The three principal complexes are within walking distance of each other, though it's not really worth trying to see them all – the layers of shelves and drawers aren't particularly gripping after a while. If you only go for one, you'd do best to focus on San Sebastiano (and maybe San Callisto) and explore the other attractions nearby.

Domine Quo Vadis

About 500m from Porta San Sebastiano, where the road forks, the church of **Domine Quo Vadis** is the first most obvious sight, and signals the start of the catacomb stretch of road. Legend has this as the place where St Peter saw Christ while fleeing from certain death in Rome and asked, "Where goest thou, Lord ?", to which Christ replied that he was going to be crucified once more, leading Peter to turn around and accept his fate. The small church is ordinary enough inside, except for its replica of a piece of marble that is said to be marked with the footprints of Christ (the original is in the church of San Sebastiano).

Catacombs of San Callisto

A kilometre or so further on, down a walled and often traffic–choked stretch of road, you reach the **Catacombs of San Callisto** (daily except Wed 8.30am–noon & 2.30–5pm; €5). The largest of Rome's catacombs, they were founded in the second century AD, and many of the early popes (of whom

St Callisto was one) are buried here in the papal crypt. St Callisto was in fact the guardian of the cemetery before he became pope; he was later killed in a riot and buried here in 222 AD. The site also features some well-preserved seventh- and eighth-century frescoes, and the crypt of Santa Cecilia, who was buried here after her martyrdom, before being shifted to the church dedicated to her in Trastevere (see Chapter 10).

Catacombs of San Domitilla

A little way west of here, down Via Ardeatina at Via delle Sette Chiese 282 (bus #218), the **Catacombs of San Domitilla** (daily except Tues 8.30am–noon & 2.30–5.30pm; €5) are quieter than those of San Callisto and adjoin the remains of a fourth-century basilica erected here to the martyrs Achilleus and Nereus. They were the servants of Domitilla, niece of Domitian, and with her fled south of Rome to escape the persecutions of Hadrian, but were killed and eventually buried here. The network itself is huge, stretching for around 17km in all, and contains more frescoes and early wall etchings, as well as the tombs of Nereus and Achilleus and a relief showing their martyrdom.

Catacombs of San Sebastiano

The **Catacombs of San Sebastiano** (daily except Sun 9am–noon & 2.30–5pm; €5), 500m further on from San Callisto, are situated under a much renovated basilica that was originally built by Constantine on the spot where the bodies of the Apostles Peter and Paul are said to have been laid for a time. In the church, the first chapel on the left holds a statue of the saint as he lay dying, built above his original tomb, while opposite is the original slab of marble imprinted with the feet of Christ that you may have seen in the church of Domine Quo Vadis. Downstairs, half-hour tours wind around the catacombs, dark corridors showing signs of early Christian worship – paintings of doves and fish, a contemporary carved oil lamp and inscriptions dating the tombs themselves. The most striking features, however, are not Christian at all, but three pagan tombs (one painted, two stuccoed) discovered when archeologists were burrowing beneath the floor of the basilica upstairs. Just above here, Constantine is said to have raised his chapel to Peter and Paul, and although St Peter was later removed to the Vatican, and St Paul to San Paolo fuori le Mura, the graffiti above records the fact that this was indeed, albeit temporarily, where the two Apostles rested.

The Circus of Maxentius and Tomb of Romulus

A couple of hundred metres further on from the San Sebastiano catacombs, the group of brick ruins trailing off into the fields to the left are the remains of the **Villa and Circus of Maxentius** (April–Sept daily 9am–7pm, Oct–March Mon–Sat 9am–4.30pm, Sun 9am–3.30pm; €2.60), a large complex built by the emperor in the early fourth century AD before his defeat by Constantine. It's a clear, long oval of grass, similar to the Circus of Maximus (see above) back in town, but slightly better preserved and in a more bucolic location – making it a fantastic place to eat a picnic, lolling around in the grass or perching on the ruins. Clambering about in the ruins, you can make out the twelve starting gates to the circus, or racetrack, and the enormous towers that contained the mechanism for lifting the gates at the beginning of the races, and the remains of a basilica. Other structures surround it, including, closer to the road, the ruins of what was once a magnificent mausoleum of an unknown person or persons, the so-called **Tomb of Romulus**, in the middle of a huge quadrangle of walls.

The Tomb of Cecilia Metella and beyond

Further along the Via Appia is the circular **Tomb of Cecilia Metella** (Tues–Sun 9am–6.3pm; €2) from the Augustan period, converted into a castle in the fourteenth century. Known as "Capo di Bove" for the bulls on the frieze around it, the tomb itself, a huge brick-built drum, is little more than a large pigeon coop these days; various fragments and finds are littered around the adjacent, later courtyards, and down below you can see what's left of an ancient lava flow from thousands of years earlier.

Between here and the eleventh milestone is the best-preserved section of the ancient Via Appia, littered with remains and reconstructions of Roman tombs and fragments of the original paving. This, combined with impressive countryside to either side of the narrow road, makes it worth persevering, even though there's no bus service out here and the traffic can be heavy at times.

EUR

From San Paolo, Via Ostiense leads south to join up with Via Cristoforo Colombo which in turn runs down to **EUR** (pronounced "eh-oor") – the acronym for the district built for the "Esposizione Universale Roma".

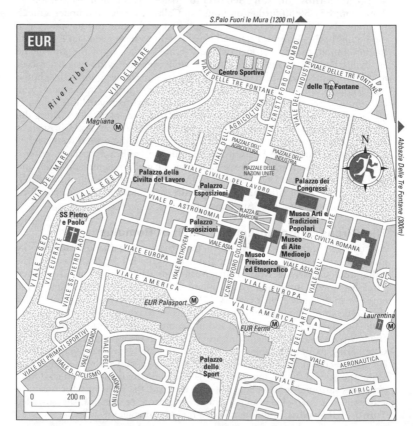

△ Palazzo della Civiltà del Lavoro

Reachable by bus #714 from Termini or taking metro line B, this is not so much a neighbourhood as a statement in stone: planned by Mussolini for the aborted 1942 World's Fair and not finished until well after the war, it's a cold, soulless grid of square buildings, long vistas and wide processional boulevards linked tenuously to the rest of Rome by metro but light years away from the city in feel. Come here for its numerous museums, some of which *are* worth the trip, or if you have a yen for modern city architecture and planning; otherwise, stay well clear.

Exploring EUR

The great flaw in EUR is that it's not built for people: the streets are wide thoroughfares designed for easy traffic flow and fast driving; shops and cafés are easily outnumbered by offices. Of the buildings, the postwar development of the area threw up bland office blocks for the most part, and it's the prewar, Fascist-style constructions that are of most interest. The **Palazzo della Civiltà del Lavoro** in the northwest corner stands out, Mussolini-inspired architecture at its most assured – the "square Colosseum" some have called it, which sums up its mixing of modern and classical styles perfectly. To the south, **Piazza Marconi** is the nominal centre of EUR, where the wide, classically inspired boulevards intersect to swerve around an obelisk in the centre.

All of EUR's museums are within easy reach of here. On the square itself, the **Museo Nazionale delle Arti e delle Tradizioni Popolari** (Tues–Sat 9am–8pm; €4) is a run-through of applied arts, costumes and religious artefacts from the Italian regions – though everything is labelled in Italian; bring a dictionary. The **Museo Nazionale Preistorico ed Etnografico Luigi Pigorini**, Viale Lincoln 1 (daily 9am–8pm; €4), is arranged in manageable and easily comprehensible order, but its prehistoric section is mind-numbingly exhaustive; the ethnographic collection does something to relieve things, however, with artefacts from South America, the Pacific and Africa. In the same building, further down the colonnade, at Viale Lincoln 3, is the **Museo dell'Alto Medioevo** (Tues–Sat 9am–2pm; €2), which concentrates on artefacts from the fifth century to the tenth century – local finds mainly, including some beautiful jewellery from the seventh century and a delicate fifth-century gold *fibula* found on the Palatine Hill. But of all the museums, the most interesting is the **Museo della Civiltà Romana**, Piazza Agnelli 10 (Tues–Sat 9am–6.45pm, Sun 9am–1.30pm; €6.20), which has, among numerous ancient Roman finds, a large-scale model of the fourth-century city – perfect for setting the rest of the city in context.

The Abbazia delle Tre Fontane

The perfect antidote to EUR is just a short, ten-minute walk away – follow Via Cristoforo Colombo north and take a right on Via delle Tre Fontane. The **Abbazia delle Tre Fontane** is a complex of churches founded on the spot where St Paul was martyred; it's said that when the saint was beheaded his head bounced and three springs erupted where his head touched the ground. In those days this was a malarial area, and it was all but abandoned during the Middle Ages, but in the second half of the nineteenth century Trappist monks drained the swamp and planted eucalyptus trees in the vicinity; they still distil a eucalyptus-based chest remedy here, as well as an exquisite liqueur and wonderful chocolate bars – all sold at the small shop by the entrance.

The abbey churches

As for the churches, they were rebuilt in the sixteenth century and restored by the Trappists. They're not particularly outstanding buildings, appealing more for their peaceful location, which is relatively undisturbed by visitors, than any architectural distinction.

The first church, originally built in 625 and rebuilt and finally restored by the Trappists, is the church of **Santi Vincenzo e Anastasio**; this has a gloomy atmosphere made gloomier by the fact that most of the windows are of a thick marble that admits little light – although the stained-glass ones, dating from the Renaissance with papal heraldry from that period, are beautiful. The three fountains in the floor are supposedly the ones of the bouncing head of the saint but they have long since run dry.

Further on, to the right, the church of **Santa Maria Scala Coeli** owes its name to a vision St Bernard had here: he saw the soul he was praying for ascend to heaven; the Cosmatesque altar where this is supposed to have happened is down the cramped stairs, in the crypt, where St Paul was allegedly kept prior to his beheading. Beyond, the largest of the churches, **San Paolo alle Tre Fontane**, holds the pillar to which St Paul was tied and a couple of mosaic pavements from Ostia Antica. Try to be here, if you can, in the early morning or evening, when the monks come in to sing Mass in Gregorian chant – a moving experience.

On the way out, the **gatehouse** near the chocolate and liqueur shop contains ceiling frescoes from the thirteenth century that show the possessions of the abbey at the time. They're in a pretty bad state, but the ones that remain have been restored and are still very interesting, showing as they do a kind of picture map of Italy in the thirteenth century.

The Quirinale and east central Rome

O f the hills that rise up on the eastern side of the centre of Rome, the **Quirinale** is perhaps the most appealing. It was the first to be properly developed, when, in the seventeenth century, those who could afford it moved up to the higher ground from the city centre, and the popes made their home here in the **Palazzo del Quirinale**. Nowadays this is the residence of the president of the Italian Republic, and not accessible most of the time (see below). But, that aside, the district holds some of the city's most compelling sights, such as the enormous **Palazzo Barberini**, home of some of the best of Rome's art, and, just beyond, the **Palazzo Massimo**, where a good deal of the city's ancient Roman treasure is on display. This district, around **Stazione Termini**, is also where you might end up staying, home as it is to a good portion of the city's hotels. Beyond here, just outside the city centre, **Via Nomentana** also hosts a couple of churches – Sant'Agnese fuori le Mura and Santa Costanza – that are well worth making the trip out to; and the district of **San Lorenzo** forms a hub for the city's students and a handful of clubs and restaurants.

Piazza Barberini

Piazza Barberini is a traffic junction at the top end of the busy shopping street of Via del Tritone, named after Bernini's **Fontana del Tritone**, whose god of the sea gushes a high jet of water from a conch shell in the centre of the square. The recently restored fountain lends a unity to the square in more ways than one: traditionally, this was the Barberini quarter of the city, a family who were the greatest patrons of Bernini, and the sculptor's works in their honour are thick on the ground around here. He finished the Tritone fountain in 1644, going on shortly after to design the **Fontana delle Api** ("Fountain of the Bees") which you can see at the bottom end of Via Veneto. Unlike the Tritone fountain you could walk right past this, a smaller, quirkier work, its broad scallop shell studded with the bees that were the symbol of the Barberinis.

Santa Maria della Concezione

A little way up Via Veneto, on the right, the Capuchin church of **Santa Maria della Concezione** was another sponsored creation of the Barberini (founded in 1626), though it's not a particularly significant building in itself, numbering only Guido Reni's androgynous *St Michael Trampling on the Devil* among its treasures. The devil in the picture is said to be a portrait of Innocent X, whom the artist despised and who was apparently a sworn enemy of the Barberini family. Take a look at the tomb of the founder of the church, Antonio Barberini, which has an inscription – "Here lies dust, ashes, nothing" – that is quite at odds with the worldly, wealthy impression you get of the Barberinis elsewhere in the city. The **Capuchin cemetery**, attached to the right of the church, continues the deathly theme, home as it is to the bones of 4000 monks set into the walls of a series of chapels, a monument to "Our Sister of Bodily Death", in the words of St Francis, that was erected in 1793. The bones appear in abstract or Christian patterns or as fully clothed skeletons, their faces peering out of their cowls in various twisted expressions of agony – somewhere between the chilling and the ludicrous, and one of the more macabre and bizarre sights of Rome.

Via Veneto

Via Veneto, which bends north from Piazza Barberini up to the southern edge of the Villa Borghese, is a cool, materialistic antidote to the murky atmosphere of the Capuchin grotto. The pricey bars and restaurants lining the street were once the haunt of Rome's Beautiful People, made famous by Fellini's *La Dolce Vita*, but they left a long time ago, and Via Veneto, despite being home to some of the city's fanciest hotels, has never quite recovered the cachet it had in the Sixties and Seventies. Nonetheless, its pretty tree-lined aspect, its pavement cafés, swanky stores and uniformed hotel bellmen, lend it an upscale European air that is quite unlike anywhere else in the city.

Palazzo Barberini

On the other side of Piazza Barberini, the **Palazzo Barberini**, Via Barberini 18, is home to (among other things) a series of apartments that were once occupied by the Barberinis and, most importantly, the **Galleria di Arte Antica** (Tues–Sun 8.30am–7.30pm; €6; apartment tours leave every 45min), consisting of a rich patchwork of mainly Italian art from the early Renaissance to late Baroque period in the palace's converted rooms. The gallery has been undergoing a massive restoration for as long as most people can remember, and consequently some things may have moved, or be back on display by the time you read this. But broadly the collection proceeds chronologically across three floors of the building, starting with the first floor and ending on the third.

It's an impressive collection, and highlights include works by Titian, El Greco and Caravaggio. But perhaps the most impressive feature of the gallery is the building itself, worked on at different times by the most favoured architects of the day – Bernini, Borromini, Maderno – and the epitome of Baroque grandeur. The **first floor** Gran Salone, certainly, is guaranteed to impress, its ceiling frescoed by Pietro da Cortona in one of the best examples of exuberant Baroque trompe l'oeil work there is, a manic rendering of *The Triumph of Divine Providence* that almost crawls down the walls to meet you. Note the bees flying towards the figure of Providence – the Barberini family symbol again. The displays here are mainly seventeenth-century works for the moment – paintings by the Dutch Mannerists, Terbrugghen and Van Bronckhorst, Caravaggio's *Judith and Holofernes*, as well as a number of striking portraits of various saints: Spada's *St Jerome*, and another, more anguished depiction of the same saint by Guercino, Ribera's intense, staring *St James* and Saraceni's depictions of *St Gregory* and *St Francis*.

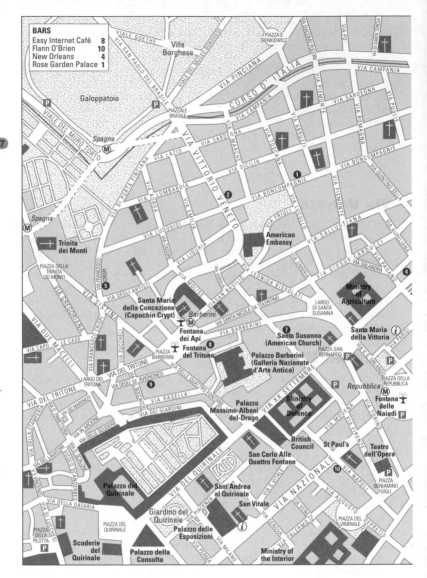

BARS
Easy Internet Café	8
Flann O'Brien	10
New Orleans	4
Rose Garden Palace	1

Next door there are later, frothier works by Boucher and Canaletto, among others, while across the hall a series of rooms display early Renaissance works, notably Fra' Filippo Lippi's warmly maternal *Madonna and Child*, painted in 1437 and introducing background details, notably architecture, into Italian religious painting for the first time. Next to it is a richly coloured and beautifully composed *Annunciation* by the same artist. In a further room on this floor, Raphael's beguiling *Fornarina* sits centre stage, a painting of the daughter of a Trasteveran baker thought to have been Raphael's mistress (Raphael's name

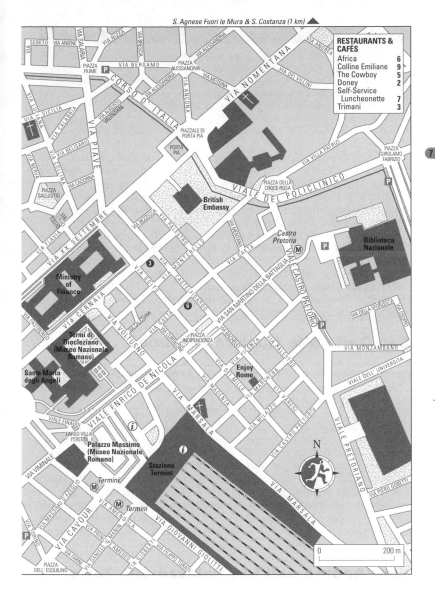

RESTAURANTS & CAFÉS

Africa	6
Colline Emiliane	9
The Cowboy	5
Doney	2
Self-Service Luncheonette	7
Trimani	3

appears clearly on the woman's bracelet), although some experts claim the painting to be the work of a pupil. Next to it is Sodoma's dark *Mystical Marriage of St Catherine* and also in the same room a beautifully composed *Pietà* by Giacomo Francia – one of the most overlooked works in the collection. Subsequent rooms hold a number of portraits, notably Bronzino's rendering of the marvellously erect *Stefano Colonna*, and a portrait of *Henry VIII* by Hans Holbein which feels almost as well known – probably because the painter produced so many of the monarch. Painted on the day of his marriage to his

More or less opposite Palazzo Barberini, **Via Rasella** was the scene of an ambush of a Nazi military patrol in 1944 that led to one of the worst Italian wartime atrocities – the reprisal massacre of 35 innocent Romans at the Ardeatine Caves outside the city walls. A memorial now stands on the sight of the executions, and the event is commemorated every March 24. Oddly enough, Mussolini had a flat on Via Rasella in which he would entertain his mistresses.

fourth wife, Anne of Cleves, he's depicted as a rather irritable but beautifully dressed middle-aged man – a stark contrast to the rather ascetic figure of *Erasmus of Rotterdam* by Quentin Matsys, which sometimes hangs nearby. Look out also, in the end room, for Tintoretto's *Christ taken in Adultery*, and two unusually small paintings by El Greco, *The Baptism of Christ* and *Adoration of the Shepherds*, as well as Titian's lively *Venus and Adonis*.

If you've still got the energy, you can take a tour of the Barberini apartments on the **second floor** – worth doing not so much for the dusty, painted Rococo rooms themselves (though the so-called Room of the Battles, showing various members of the Barberini and Colonna families engaged in glorious strife, is impressive) as for the circular staircase you cilmb to get there: the work of Borromini, and in sharp contrast to the huge and stately Bernini staircase you take to reach the paintings on the other side.

San Carlo alle Quattro Fontane

Continue on down Via delle Quattro Fontane and you're at a seventeenth-century landmark, the church of **San Carlo alle Quattro Fontane** (Mon–Sat 10am–1pm & 3–6pm, Sat noon–1pm & 3–6pm). This was Borromini's first real design commission, and in it he displays all the ingenuity he later became known for, cramming the church elegantly into a tiny and awkwardly shaped site that apparently covers roughly the same surface area as one of the main columns inside St Peter's. Tucked in beside the church, the cloister is also squeezed into a tight but elegant oblong, topped with a charming balustrade.

Outside the church are the **four fountains** that give the street and church their name, each cut into a niche in a corner of the crossroads that marks this, the highest point on the Quirinal Hill. They were put here in 1593, and represent the Tiber and Aniene rivers, and *Strength* and *Fidelity* and they make a fine if busy spot to look back down towards the Trinità dei Monti obelisk in one direction and the Santa Maria Maggiore obelisk in the other – all part of Sixtus V's grand city plan.

Sant'Andrea and the Palazzo del Qurinale

There's another piece of design ingenuity a few steps southwest of here, on Via del Quirinale, which is flanked on the left by public gardens and the domed church of **Sant'Andrea al Quirinale** (daily except Tues 8am–noon & 4–7pm), a flamboyant building that Bernini planned as a kind of flat oval shape to fit into its wide but shallow site.

Opposite is the featureless wall – the so-called "manica lunga" or "long sleeve" – of the **Palazzo del Quirinale** (open the 2nd & 4th Sun morning each month 8am–1pm; €5; @www.quirinale.it), a sixteenth-century structure that was the official summer residence of the popes until Unification, when it became the royal palace. It's now the home of Italy's president (a largely ceremonial role), but you can appreciate its exceptional siting from the **Piazza del Quirinale** at the far end on the right, from which views stretch right across the centre of Rome. The main feature of the piazza is the huge statue of the **Dioscuri**, or Castor and Pollux – massive five-metre-high Roman copies of classical Greek statues, showing the two godlike twins, the sons of Jupiter, who according to legend won victory for the Romans in an important battle (see also p.78). The statues originally stood at the entrance of the Baths of Constantine, the ruins of which lay nearby, and were brought here by Pope Sixtus V in the early sixteenth century to embellish the square – part of the pope's attempts to dignify and beautify the city with many large, vista-laden squares and long straight avenues. Nowadays it forms an odd concoction with the obelisk, which tops the arrangement, originally from the Mausoleum of Augustus, and the vast shallow bowl in front, which was apparently once resident at the Roman Forum – all in all a classic example of how Renaissance Rome and later periods made the most out of the classical debris that littered the city.

The Scuderie del Quirinale

The eighteenth-century **Scuderie del Quirinale** faces the palace from across the square, completing the triangle of buildings that make up the piazza. Originally the papal stables, it has been imaginatively restored as display space for some of the major travelling exhibitions that come to the city (opening times and prices vary). You'll probably want to visit only if there's something on that you specifically wish to see, but it costs nothing to call into the excellent art bookshop on the ground floor and to glimpse the equestrian spiral staircase that winds up from here to the main exhibition rooms. Plus, the modern glass staircase added to the side of the building gives the Quirinale's best view over Rome by far.

Via XX Settembre

Via XX Settembre spears out towards the Aurelian Wall from Via del Quirinale – not Rome's most appealing thoroughfare by any means, flanked by the deliberately faceless bureaucracies of the national government, erected after Unification in anticipation of Rome's ascension as a new world capital. It was, however, the route by which Italian troops entered the city on September 20, 1870, and the place where they breached the wall is marked with a column. Halfway up, just north of Piazza della Repubblica, the church of **Santa Susanna** (daily 9am–noon & 4–7pm) is one of an elegant cluster of facades, although behind its well-proportioned Carlo Maderno frontage it isn't an especially auspicious building, except for some bright and soothing frescoes. The headquarters of American Catholics in Rome, it looks across the busy junction to the **Fontana dell' Acqua Felice**, playfully fronted by four basking lions, and focusing on a massive, bearded figure of Moses, in the central one of three arches. Marking the end of the Acqua Felice aqueduct, the fountain forms part of Pope Sixtus V's late-sixteenth-century attempts to spruce up the city centre with large-scale public works (see p.120).

Santa Maria della Vittoria

Immediately opposite the fountain, the church of **Santa Maria della Vittoria** (daily 7am–noon & 3.30–7pm) was also built by Carlo Maderno and it has an interior that is one of the most elaborate examples of Baroque decoration in Rome: almost shockingly excessive to modern eyes, its ceiling and walls are pitted with carving, and statues are crammed into remote corners as in an over-stuffed attic. The church's best-known feature, Bernini's carving of the *Ecstasy of St Teresa*, the centrepiece of the sepulchral chapel of Cardinal Cornaro, continues the histrionics – a deliberately melodramatic work featuring a theatrically posed St Teresa of Avila against a backdrop of theatre-boxes on each side of the chapel, from which the Cornaro cardinals murmur and nudge each other as they watch the spectacle. St Teresa is one of the Catholic Church's most enduring mystics, and Bernini is basically recording an occasion, indeed the very moment, when in 1537 she had a vision of an angel piercing her heart with a dart. It is a very Baroque piece of work in the most populist sense – not only is the event quite literally staged, but St Teresa's ecstasy verges on the worldly as she lays back in groaning submission beneath a mass of dishevelled garments and drapery.

Via Nazionale

A couple of minutes' walk downhill from the Quirinale Palace, **Via Nazionale** connects Piazza Venezia and the centre of town with the area around Stazione Termini and the eastern districts beyond. A focus for much development after Unification, its heavy, overbearing buildings were constructed to give Rome some semblance of modern sophistication when it became capital of the new country, but most are now occupied by hotels and bland shops and boutiques.

At the corner of Via Nazionale and Via Napoli is the American Episcopal church of **St Paul's-within-the-Walls** (daily 9am–1pm & 4–7pm), the first Protestant church to be built within the walls of the city after the Unification of Italy in 1870. Dating from 1879, it was built in a neo-Gothic style by the British architect, G.E. Street, and is worth a quick peek inside for its apse mosaics by Burne-Jones, which depict one of the church's founders, the American financier J.P. Morgan, as St Paul, alongside his family, Garibaldi, General Ulysses Grant, and Abraham Lincoln.

Piazza della Repubblica and around

At the top of Via Nazionale, **Piazza della Repubblica** (formerly Piazza Esedra) is typical of Rome's nineteenth-century regeneration, a stern and dignified semicircle of buildings that was until recently rather dilapidated but is now – with the help of the new and very stylish *Hotel Exedra* – once again resurgent. The arcades make a fine place to stroll, despite the hum of traffic, which roars ceaselessly around the centrepiece Fontana delle Naiadi of languishing nymphs and sea monsters.

Santa Maria degli Angeli

The piazza actually follows the semicircular outline of the exedra of the Baths of Diocletian, the remains of which lie across the piazza and are partially contained in the church of **Santa Maria degli Angeli** (daily 7.30am–12.30pm & 4–7pm) – not Rome's most welcoming church by any means but giving the best impression of the size and grandeur of Diocletian's bath complex. It's a huge, open building, with an interior standardized by Vanvitelli into a rich eighteenth-century confection after a couple of centuries of piecemeal adaptation (started by an aged Michelangelo). The pink

△ Bernini staircase, Palazzo Barberini

granite pillars, at 3m in diameter the largest in Rome, are original, and the main transept formed the main hall of the baths; only the crescent shape of the facade remains from the original caldarium (it had previously been hidden by a newer facing), the vestibule (the tepidarium) and main transept. The meridian that strikes diagonally across the floor here was, until 1846, the regulator of time for Romans (now a cannon shot fired daily at noon from the Janiculum Hill).

Around Piazza della Repubblica

The buildings that surround Santa Maria degli Angeli are also recycled parts of Diocletian's baths, including the round church of **San Bernardo alle Terme**, off via XX Settembre, and the round building, now an *albergo diurnale*, at the corner of Via Viminale and Via di Terme di Diocleziano. Immediately to the left of Santa Maria degli Angeli, another caldarium was formerly used as a planetarium and is now the **Aula Ottagona** (Octagonal Hall), part of the Museo Nazionale Romano (Mon–Sat 9am–2pm, Sun 9am–1pm; same ticket) – a large domed room which contains marble statues taken from the Baths of Caracalla and Diocletian, and two remarkable statues of a boxer and athlete from the Quirinal Hill. Excavations underground – accessible by stairs – show the furnaces for heating water for the baths and the foundations of another building from the time of Diocletian.

Museo delle Terme di Diocleziano

The rest of the baths – the huge halls and courtyards on the side towards Termini – have been renovated and it and the Carthusian monastery attached to the church now hold what is probably the least interesting part of the Museo Nazionale Romano, the **Museo delle Terme di Diocleziano** (Tues–Sun 9am–7pm; €5). (The best are across the street in Palazzo Massimo – see below – and in Palazzo Altemps – see Chapter 2.) Fronted by a fragrant garden, open to all, which centres on a large *krater* fountain with little cupids holding up its rim, the museum's most evocative part is the large cloister of the church whose sides are crammed with statuary, funerary monuments and sarcophagi and fragments from all over Rome. There's a lot to pick through, around three hundred bits and pieces in all, but standouts include the animal heads, found in the Forum of Trajan, a fine headless seated statue of Hercules from the second century AD, and a nice, if again damaged, statue of a husband and wife. Meanwhile there's an upstairs gallery that wraps around the cloister and includes finds to the seventh century BC, and a downstairs section with more Roman finds: busts, terracotta statues, armour and weapons found in Roman tombs – all nicely, if rather academically, presented, but hardly compulsory viewing.

Palazzo Massimo

Across from Santa Maria degli Angeli, the snazzily restored **Palazzo Massimo**, Largo di Villa Perretti 1, is home to one of the two principal parts of the Museo Nazionale Romano (the other is in the Palazzo Altemps) – a superb collection of Greek and Roman antiquities, second only to the Vatican's, which has been entirely reorganized and features many pieces that have remained undisplayed for decades (Tues–Sun 9am–7pm; €6; timed tours for the second floor – you may have to wait for the next one in English).

Basement

This has displays of exquisite gold jewellery from the second century AD – necklaces, rings, brooches, all in immaculate condition – and some fine gold imperial hairnets. There's also – startlingly – the mummified remains of an 8-year-old girl, along with a fantastic **coin collection**, from the first bronze coinage of the fourth century BC to the surprisingly sophisticated coins of the Republic and imperial times, right up to the lira and concluding with a display devoted to the Euro. It's all shown in glass cases equipped with magnifying glasses on runners, controlled by the buttons mounted on the front of each case.

The ground floor

The ground floor of the museum is devoted to statuary of the **early Empire**, including a gallery with an unparalleled selection of unidentified busts found all over Rome; their lack of clear identity is no barrier to appreciating them – they're amazing pieces of portraiture, and as vivid a representation of patrician Roman life as you'll find. At the far end of the gallery there are more busts, this time identifiable: a bronze of Germanicus, a marvellous small bust of Caligula, several representations of Livia and a hooded statue of Augustus. Look out also for the so-called *Statue of the Tivoli General*, the face of an old man mounted on the body of a youthful athlete – sometimes believed to be a portrait of L. Munatius Plancus, the military officer who named Octavian "Augustus" (literally "Reverend") and so officially started the cult of the emperor. Further on, there's a painted frieze discovered on the Esquiline Hill that dates from the first century BC and shows scenes from the Trojan War and the later legendary story of the founding of Rome. There are also some superb examples of Roman copies of Greek statuary – an altar found on Via Nomentana stands out, decorated with figures relating to the cult of Bacchus, as well as statues of Aphrodite and Melpomene.

The first floor

The museum really gets going on the first-floor gallery, with groupings of the various **imperial dynasties** in roughly chronological order, and starting with the Flavian emperors – the craggy determination of Vespasian, the pinched nobility of Nerva, leading on to Trajan in the next room, who appears with his wife Plotina as Hercules, next to a bust of his cousin Hadrian. The most successful years of the empire were around this time, continuing with the Antonine emperors – Antonius Pius in a heroic nude pose and in several busts, flanked by likenesses of his daughter Faustina Minor. Faustina was the wife of Antonius's successor, Marcus Aurelius, who appears in the next room. Also here is Commodus, the last of the Antonine emperors. Further on are the Severans, with the fierce-looking Caracalla looking across past his father Septimius Severus to his brother Geta, whom he later murdered.

Just beyond the Severan emperors a hyper-realistic sarcophagus from 190 AD shows Roman victories over barbarians, while other rooms hold any number of astonishing pieces, many of them copies of Greek originals – figures of Apollo and Dionysus, a sleeping hermaphrodite, an amazon and barbarian, full of movement and vigour, as well as more dynastic busts discovered at Hadrian's villa in Tivoli, not least youthful likenesses of Marcus Aurelius and Antonius Pius and a beautiful statue of a young girl holding a tray.

The second floor

You can visit the second floor only by way of an organised tour. These last 45 minutes take in some of the finest **Roman frescoes and mosaics** ever found. There is a stunning set of frescoes from the Villa di Livia, specifically depicting an orchard dense with fruit and flowers and patrolled by partridges, doves and other feathered friends, and wall paintings rescued from what was perhaps the riverside villa of Julia and Agrippa, including an entire room painted with garlands and an Egyptian-style frieze. Further on there are floor mosaics showing naturalistic scenes – sea creatures, people boating – and some from the so-called Villa di Baccano on Via Cassia, a sumptuous mansion probably owned by the imperial Severi family, and including four mosaic panels taken from a bedroom, featuring four chariot drivers and their horses, so finely crafted that from a distance they look as if they've been painted. Others come from Anzio; notable is one showing a reclining Hercules holding a cup and club while a wild boar emerges from a nearby cave, while in the adjoining room is a very rare example of *opus sectile*, a mosaic technique imported from the Eastern provinces in the first century AD. Inlaid pieces of marble, mother-of-pearl, glass and hard stone are used instead of tesserae, the parts cut so as to enhance detail and give perspective depth.

Stazione Termini

Across the street from the museum is the low white facade of **Stazione Termini** (so named for its proximity to the Baths of Diocletian, nothing to do with being the terminus of Rome's rail lines) and the vast, bus-crammed hubbub that is Piazza dei Cinquecento in front. The station is great, an ambitious piece of modern architectural design that was completed in 1950 and still entirely dominates the streets around with its low-slung, self-consciously futuristic lines – it's nicknamed "the dinosaur" for its low, curved front canopy. It has recently received a huge and sleek renovation that has converted part of its cavernous ticket hall to retail and restaurant space and upgraded the building in general – making it a nice spot for a browse and a wander, and a marvellous place to catch a train. It's got a great bookstore, a branch of the UPIM department store, even an exhibition space. As for **Piazza dei Cinquecento**, it's a good place to find buses and taxis, but otherwise it and the areas around are pretty much low-life territory, and although not especially dangerous, not particularly a place to hang around for long either.

Via Nomentana

At the north end of Via XX Settembre, the **Porta Pia** was one of the last works of Michelangelo, erected under Pope Pius IV in 1561. To the left of the gate is the busy Corso d'Italia (in effect forming part of the central ring road that girdles the city centre), while to the right is the low-slung modern home of the British Embassy; straight on is the wide boulevard of **Via Nomentana**, lined with luxury villas that have long been home to some of the city's more illustrious names.

A kilometre down Via Nomentana on the right is the nineteenth-century **Villa Torlonia**, which the banker Prince Giovanni Torlonia turned over to Mussolini to use as long as he needed it. You can't visit the house – which has seen better days – but the grounds are open to the public (daily 7am–1hr before sunset). If you do venture out this way, stop by at the **Casina delle Civette**, Via Nomentana 70 (April–Sept Tues–Sun 9am–6.30pm; Oct–March

9am–4.30pm; €2.60) – the "small house of the owls" – a lovely building designed by Valadier at the beginning of the eighteenth century. It was carefully restored and opened to the public in 1997 and houses an unusual museum of notable stained-glass windows.

Sant'Agnese fuori le Mura

Further up Via Nomentana is the church of **Sant'Agnese fuori le Mura** (Mon 9am–noon, Tues–Sat 9am–noon & 4–6pm, Sun 4–6pm) dedicated to the 13-year-old saint who was martyred in Domitian's Stadium in 303 AD (see Chapter 2). It's part of a small complex of early Christian monuments that includes the church, the catacombs underneath and the neighbouring church of Santa Costanza. To get into the church, walk down the hill and through the courtyard to the narthex of the building, which apart from some very out-of-place later fixtures is much as it was built by Pope Honorius I in the seventh century, when he reworked Constantine's original structure that had been built over St Agnes's grave. Inside, the church proper has been updated in Baroque style, but the apse mosaic is contemporary with Honorius's building, showing Agnes next to the pope, who holds a model of his church, in typical Byzantine fashion.

Out of the narthex the custodian will lead you down into the **catacombs** (same hours as church; €5) that sprawl below the church, which are among the best-preserved and most crowd-free of all the city's catacombs. Indeed, if you have time for only one set of catacombs during your stay in Rome (and they really are all very much alike), these are among the best. The custodian also sells little terracotta lamps in the shape of fish, or conventional Roman-style lamps with the "Chi-Rho" sign on – probably the most ancient symbol of Christianity. They are very reasonably priced and make a nice souvenir of the place.

Santa Costanza

After the catacombs the guide will show you the church of **Santa Costanza** (usually open the same hours as Sant'Agnese; free), which more than any other building in Rome, perhaps, illustrates the transition from the pagan to Christian city in its decorative and architectural features. Built in 350 AD as a mausoleum for Constantia and Helena, the daughters of the emperor Constantine, it's a round structure which follows the traditional shape of the great pagan tombs (consider those of Hadrian and Augustus elsewhere in the city), and the mosaics on the vaulting of its circular ambulatory – fourth-century depictions of vines, leaves and birds – would have been as at home on the floor of a Roman *domus* as they were in a Christian church. Unfortunately, the porphyry sarcophagus of Santa Costanza herself has been moved to the Vatican, and what you see in the church is a plaster copy.

San Lorenzo

South and east of Via Nomentana, a short walk from Termini, the neighbourhood of **SAN LORENZO** spreads from the main campus of Rome's university, on the far side of Via Tiburtina, to the railway tracks – a solidly working-class district that retains something of the air of a local neighbourhood, quite different from the rest of the city centre. It's home to some good and often inexpensive local restaurants, and is also the location of the enormous **Campo Verano** cemetery – since 1830 the largest Catholic burial-place in Rome, and in itself worth a visit for the grandiose tombs in which many have been laid to rest.

San Lorenzo fuori le Mura

The area takes its name from the church of **San Lorenzo fuori le Mura** on Via Tiburtina right by the cemetery (daily: summer 7am–noon & 4–7.30pm; winter closes 5.30pm) – one of the seven great pilgrimage churches of Rome, and a typical Roman basilica, fronted by a columned portico and with a lovely twelfth-century cloister to its side. The original church here was built by Constantine over the site of St Lawrence's martyrdom – the saint was reputedly burned to death on a gridiron, halfway through his ordeal apparently uttering the immortal words, "Turn me, I am done on this side." Where the church of San Lorenzo differs is that it's actually a combination of three churches built at different periods – one a sixth-century reconstruction of Constantine's church by Pelagius II, which now forms the chancel, another a fifth-century church from the time of Sixtus III, both joined by a basilica from the thirteenth century by Honorius II.

Because of its proximity to Rome's railyards, the church was bombed heavily during World War II, but it has been rebuilt with sensitivity, and remains much as it was originally. Inside there are features from all periods: a Cosmati floor, thirteenth-century pulpits and a paschal candlestick. The mosaic on the inside of the triumphal arch is a sixth-century depiction of Pelagius offering his church to Christ; while below stairs, catacombs (closed at present for restoration) – where St Lawrence was apparently buried – lead a dank path from the pillars of Constantine's original structure. There's also a Romanesque cloister with well-tended garden that you can get into through the sacristy.

Monti and San Giovanni

Immediately north of the Colosseum, and east of Via Cavour, the **Esquiline Hill** is the highest and largest of the city's seven hills. Formerly a sparsely populated area, with vineyards, orchards and olive groves stretching out to the Aurelian Wall, it was one of the most fashionable residential quarters of ancient Rome. In fact it consists of four separate summits: the *Oppian* (the part nearest the Colosseum, now a small park); the *Subura*, which was ancient Rome's most notorious inner-city suburb; the *Fagutalis* and – the highest (65m) and largest – the *Cispius*, which is the site of the basilica of Santa Maria Maggiore. Immediately to the west, stretching over as far as the shopping street of Via Nazionale, the **Viminale Hill** is less rich in interest, the smallest of Rome's hills and known as the home of Italy's interior ministry and not much else. Together, the central parts of the two hills form a district known as "**Monti**", an appealing quarter of cobbled streets and neighbourhood bars and restaurants, mixed in with the busy streets and ponderous nineteenth-century buildings around **Via Nazionale** (see Chapter 7) and **Via Cavour** – the latter the main spine of the area, a busy artery that ferries traffic from Termini down to the area around the Colosseum and Roman Forums.

Overall this is a part of town that most travellers to Rome encounter at some point – not just because of key sights such as Nero's **Domus Aurea** and the basilica of **Santa Maria Maggiore**, but also because it's close to the lion's share of Rome's budget hotels around Termini. Also, not far away to the east, are other ancient churches: triple-layered **San Clemente**, a short walk from the Colosseum, the complex of **San Giovanni in Laterano**, which gives its name to the district – **San Giovanni** – and nearby **Santa Croce in Gerusalemme**.

The Domus Aurea and around

The Esquiline's most visited sight by far, the **Domus Aurea**, is also the most accessible, situated as it is just across the road from the Colosseum. Some people stop at that, but even if you're not going to explore the area in any depth at all, it's worth at least walking a few minutes beyond to the church of **San Pietro in Vincoli**, for one of the city's greatest Renaissance treasures. And

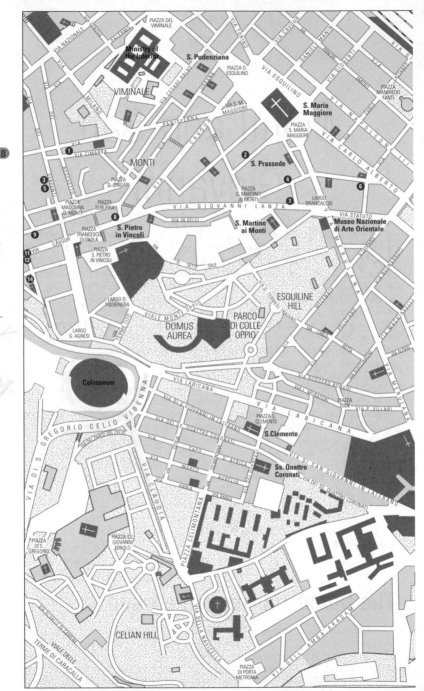

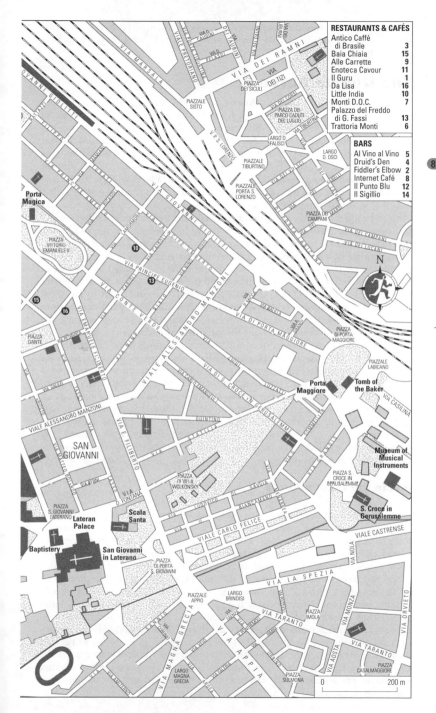

RESTAURANTS & CAFÉS

Antico Caffé di Brasile	3
Baia Chiaia	15
Alle Carrette	9
Enoteca Cavour	11
Il Guru	1
Da Lisa	16
Little India	10
Monti D.O.C.	7
Palazzo del Freddo di G. Fassi	13
Trattoria Monti	6

BARS

Al Vino al Vino	5
Druid's Den	4
Fiddler's Elbow	2
Internet Café	8
Il Punto Blu	12
Il Sigillio	14

8

MONTI AND SAN GIOVANNI

once there you're poised to explore the more picturesque corners of **Monti**, across the busy thoroughfare of **Via Cavour**, around Via dei Serpenti and Via del Boschetto, in more detail.

The Domus Aurea

The entrance to Nero's **Domus Aurea** or "Golden House" (daily except Tues 9am–6.45pm, guided tours in English or Italian obligatory; €5, plus €1.50 booking fee; ☎06.3996.7700, ⓦwww.romeguide.it/domus_aurea) is off Via Labacana, in the Parco di Colle Oppio, almost opposite the Colosseum. (If you find yourself in the main part of the park, you've gone too far.) One of the city's most intriguing sights, the "house" was a vast undertaking built on the summit of the Oppian and into its sides after a fire of 64 AD (allegedly started by Nero) devastated this part of Rome. It was not intended to be a residence at all; rather it was a series of banqueting rooms, nymphaeums, small baths, terraces and gardens, facing what at the time was a small lake fed by the underground springs and streams that drained from the surrounding hills. Rome was used to Nero's excesses, but it had never seen anything like the Golden House before. The facade was supposed to have been coated in solid gold, there was hot and cold running water in the baths, one of the dining rooms was rigged up to shower flower petals and natural scent on guests, and the grounds – which covered over two square kilometres – held vineyards and game. Nero didn't get to enjoy his palace for long – he died a couple of years after it was finished, and Vespasian tore a lot of the exposed facade down in disgust, draining its lake and building the Colosseum on top. Later Trajan built his baths on top of the rest of the complex, and it was pretty much forgotten until its wall paintings were discovered by Renaissance artists, including Raphael. When these artists first visited these rooms, they had to descend ladders into what they believed at first was some kind of mystical cave, or **grotto** – giving us the word *grotesque*, which they used to describe their attempts to imitate this style of painting in their own work.

Today it is possible to visit parts of the Golden House. Tours start by taking you down a long corridor into the excavated rooms of the palace. The temperature always hovers at around 10°C and this, and the almost 100 percent humidity, makes it necessary to wear a sweater or jacket even in the middle of the Roman summer.

Inside the Domus Aurea

Tours can at first be confusing, as you become aware of just how much Trajan set out to obliterate the palace with his baths complex – the baths' foundations merge into parts of the palace, and vice versa – but a free plan, not to mention the guide, helps you sort it out. There are various covered fountains, service corridors, terraces and, most spectacularly, the **Octagonal Room**, domed, with a hole in the middle, which is supposed to have rotated as the day progressed to emulate the passage of the sun. Most of the rooms are decorated in the so-called Third Pompeiian style, with fanciful depictions of people looking back through windows at the viewer, garlands of flowers, fruit, vines and foliage, interspersed with mythical animals. Perhaps the best preserved frescoes are in the **Room of Achilles at Skyros**, and illustrate Homer's story of Achilles being sent to the island of Skyros disguised as a woman to prevent him being drawn into the Trojan Wars. In one fresco, Achilles is in drag at the Skyros court; another shows him putting his female clothes aside and picking up a shield, brought to him by Ulysses (in the crested helmet) to catch him out and betray his disguise.

Parco di Colle Oppio

Outside the entrance to the Golden House, the **Parco di Colle Oppio** is dotted with remnants of the various Roman structures that once stood here: various piles of rubble, the remains of **Trajan's Baths**, and a number of round brick stumps – well-heads that led down into the Golden House. These apart, the park is a pretty unsavoury spot, a gathering place for street people and fascist youths, and as such not particularly safe after dark.

San Pietro in Vincoli

Steps lead up from Colosseum metro station to Via Terme di Tito and left into Via Eudossia, which leads past Rome university's faculty of engineering to the tranquil piazza in front of the recently restored church of **San Pietro in Vincoli** (daily 7am–12.30pm & 3.30–6pm) – one of Rome's most delightfully plain churches, built to house an important relic, the chains ("vincoli") that held St Peter when he was in Jerusalem and those that held him in Rome, which miraculously joined together. During the papacy of Sixtus IV, it was the cardinal seat of the pope's nephew, Giuliano della Rovere, who became Pope Julius II, of Sistine Chapel ceiling fame.

The chains of St Peter can still be seen in the confessio beneath the high altar, in a beautiful gold and rock crystal reliquary, but most people come for the **tomb** of Pope Julius II at the far end of the southern aisle, which occupied Michelangelo on and off for much of his career and was the cause of many a dispute with Julius and his successors. Michelangelo reluctantly gave it up to paint the Sistine Chapel, and never again found the time to return to it for very long, being always at the beck and call of successive popes – who understandably had little interest in promoting the glory of one of their predecessors.

No one knows how the tomb would have looked had it been finished – it's generally assumed that Moses would have been on one end and the risen Christ on the other, with a statue of Julius himself surmounting the whole thing – and the only statues that Michelangelo completed are the *Moses*, *Leah* and *Rachel*, which remain here in the church, and two *Dying Slaves* which are now in the Louvre. The figure of Moses, however, pictured as descended from Sinai to find the Israelites worshipping the golden calf, and flanked by the gentle figures of Leah and Rachel, is one of the artist's most captivating works, the rest of the composition – completed by later artists – seeming dull and static by comparison. Because of a medieval mistranslation of scripture, Moses is depicted with satyr's horns instead of the "radiance of the Lord" that Exodus tells us shone around his head. Nonetheless, this powerful statue is so lifelike that Michelangelo is alleged to have struck its knee with his hammer and shouted, "Speak, damn you!". The rest of the group was finished by Michelangelo's pupils, while the statue of Julius II at the top, by Maso del Bosco, modelled on an Etruscan coffin lid, sadly fails to evoke the character of this apparently active, courageous and violent man.

San Martino ai Monti

Turn right outside the church and follow Via delle Sette Sale – named after the seven water cisterns of the nearby Baths of Trajan – to the church of **San Martino ai Monti**, another place of worship that dates back to the earliest days of Christianity. It was dedicated to the saints Sylvester and Martin in the sixth century, and incorporates an ancient Roman structure, but it was almost entirely rebuilt in the 1650s, and sports a ceiling from that time that is strangely modern in appearance, parts of it reminiscent of 1920s brushed stainless steel. The ceiling also shows the arms of the Medicis, specifically the family's last pope, Leo XI, who ruled briefly in 1605, and has a series of frescoes depicting scenes of the Roman Campagna and the interiors of the old Roman basilicas of St Peter and San Giovanni before they were gussied up in their present Baroque splendour – St Peter's is at the far end of the north aisle, San Giovanni near the door.

Museo Nazionale di Arte Orientale

It's a short walk from San Martino to the busy Largo Brancaccio, and the nineteenth-century thoroughfare of Via Merulana, where the imposing Palazzo Brancaccio houses the **Museo Nazionale di Arte Orientale**, Via Merulana 248 (Mon, Wed & Sat 8.30am–1.30pm, Tues & Thurs 8.30am–7pm, closed 1st & 3rd Mon of every month; €4) – a first-rate collection of oriental art (Italy's best) that has recently been restored. Beginning with Marco Polo in the thirteenth century, the Italians have always had connections with the Far East, and the quality of this collection of Islamic, Chinese, Indian and Southeast Asian art reflects this fact – not to mention making a refreshing break from the multiple ages of Western art you are exposed to in Rome. There are finds dating to 1500–500 BC from a necropolis in Pakistan; architectural fragments in painted wood, and art works and jewellery, from Tibet, Nepal and Pakistan; and a solid collection from China, with predictable Buddhas and vases, but also curiosities such as imperial warming plates. Take a look, too, at the Luristan bronzes from eighth-century BC Iran, and marvel at the similarities between these and some of the Etruscan bronzes of the same age you may well have seen elsewhere in the city.

Piazza Vittorio Emanuele II

Cross Largo Leopardi outside the museum, and walk a few metres up Via Leopardi to **Piazza Vittorio Emanuele II**, the centre of a district which became known as the "quartiere piemontese" when the government located many of its major ministries here after Unification. The arcades of the square, certainly, recall central Turin, as do the solid palatial buildings that surround it. It's more recently become the immigrant quarter of Rome, with a heavy concentration of African, Asian and Middle Eastern shops and restaurants. You'll easily hear a dozen different languages spoken as you pass through, although sadly the open-air **market** that used to surround the piazza is no more.

Close to the northern end of the piazza, an eighteen-metre-high pile of Roman bricks is what is left of a monumental public fountain known as the **Nymphaeum of Alexander Severus** (emperor 222–235 AD) – a distribution point for water arriving in the city by a branch of the Aqua Claudia aqueduct.

Santa Maria Maggiore and around

A short walk northwest from Piazza Vittorio Emanuele II, following Via Carlo Alberto, the basilica of **Santa Maria Maggiore** is one of the city's five great basilicas, and has one of Rome's best-preserved Byzantine interiors – a fact belied by its dull eighteenth-century exterior. Nearby, too, are some of Rome's most beautiful and precious Byzantine mosaics in the churches of **Santa Prassede** and **Santa Pudenziana**.

Santa Maria Maggiore

Unlike the other great places of pilgrimage in Rome, **Santa Maria Maggiore** (daily 7am–7pm) was not built on any special Constantinian site, but instead went up during the fifth century after the Council of Ephesus recognized the **cult of the Virgin** and churches venerating Our Lady began to spring up all over the Christian world. According to legend, the Virgin Mary appeared to Pope Liberius in a dream on the night of August 4, 352 AD, telling him to build a church on the Esquiline Hill, on a spot where he would find a patch of newly fallen **snow** the next morning. The snow would outline exactly the plan of the church that should be built there in her honour – which of course is exactly what happened, and the first church here was called Santa Maria della Neve ("of the snow"). The present structure dates from about 420 AD, and was completed under the reign of St Sixtus III, who was pope between 432 AD and 440 AD.

Santa Maria Maggorie is noted for two special ceremonies. One, on August 5, celebrates the miraculous snowfall: at midday Mass white rose petals are showered on the congregation from the ceiling, and at night the fire department operates an artificial snow machine in the piazza in front and showers the area in snow that, naturally, melts immediately. The other takes place on Christmas morning, when the reliquary containing the crib is processed around the church and then displayed on the high altar.

The Basilica

The **basilica** was encased in its eighteenth-century shell during the papacy of Benedict XIV, although the campanile, the highest in Rome, is older than this – built in 1377 under Pope Gregory XI. Inside, however, the original building survives intact, its broad nave fringed on both sides with strikingly well-kept mosaics (binoculars help), most of which date from the time of Pope Sixtus III and recount, in comic-strip form, incidents from the Old Testament. The ceiling, which shows the arms of the Spanish Borgia Popes, Calixtus III and Alexander VI, was gilded in 1493 with gold sent by Queen Isabella as part payment of a loan from Innocent VIII to finance the voyage of Columbus to the New World.

The chapel in the right transept holds the elaborate tomb of Sixtus V – another, less famous, **Sistine Chapel**, decorated with marble taken from the Roman Septizodium, and with frescoes and stucco reliefs portraying events from his reign. The chapel also contains the tomb of another zealous and reforming pope, Pius V, whose statue faces that of Sixtus; he's probably best known as the pope who excommunicated Queen Elizabeth I of England, in 1570.

Outside the Sistine Chapel is the tomb slab of the Bernini family, including Gian Lorenzo himself, while opposite, the **Pauline Chapel** is even more sumptuous than the Sistine Chapel, home to the tombs of the Borghese pope, Paul V, and his immediate predecessor Clement VIII. The floor, in *opus sectile*, contains the Borghese arms, an eagle and dragon, and the magnificently gilded ceiling shows glimpses of heaven. The altar, of lapis lazuli and agate, contains a *Madonna and Child* dating from the twelfth or thirteenth century.

Sixtus V

Although he reigned only five years, from 1585 to 1590, **Sixtus V**'s papacy was one of Rome's most memorable. He laid out several new streets – the long, straight thoroughfare that runs from the top of Trinità dei Monti to Santa Maria Maggiore (at various points Via Sistina, Via delle Quattro Fontane and Via de Pretis) is one example; he erected many of the present obelisks that dot the city, notably those in Piazza San Pietro and Piazza San Giovanni; and he launched an attack on bandits in the surrounding countryside and criminal gangs in the city. As a priest at the time remarked: "I am in Rome after an absence of ten years, and do not recognize it, so new does all appear to me to be: monuments, streets, piazzas, fountains, aqueducts, obelisks and other wonders, all the works of Sixtus V." Sixtus was, like Julius II, a man of action and a Franciscan friar. He was perhaps most famously responsible for the execution of Beatrice Cenci (see p.56). But his reign was also notorious for his stripping the Roman Forum of its marbles and the Colosseum of its stone for St Peter's. He also demolished the so-called *Septizodium,* at the southeast end of the Palatine, marble from which decorated his tomb.

Between the two chapels, the **confessio** contains a kneeling statue of Pope Pius IX, and, beneath it, a reliquary that is said to contain fragments of the crib of Christ, in rock crystal and silver. The high altar, above it, contains the relics of St Matthew, among other Christian martyrs, but it's the **mosaics** of the arche that really dazzle, a vivid representation of scenes from the life of Christ – *The Annunciation, The Adoration of the Magi* (in which Christ is depicted not as a child, unusually, but as a king himself) and *The Massacre of the Innocents* on the left, and *The Presentation in the Temple* and *Herod receiving the Magi* on the right. The central apse mosaics are later, but are no less impressive, commissioned by the late-thirteenth-century pope, Nicholas IV, and showing *The Coronation of the Virgin*, with angels, saints and the pope himself.

The Museum and Loggia

There's a **museum** underneath the basilica (daily 9.30am–6.30pm; €2), which sports what even by Roman standards is a wide variety of relics – a hair of the Virgin and the arms of saints Luke and Matthew – as well as the usual liturgical garments and so on, but it's not really worth the money. Better to save it for the **Loggia** above the main entrance, with its thirteenth-century mosaics of *Pantocrator and the Legend of the Snow,* and for the nativity scene or *Presepio* which is the work of Arnolfo di Cambio, (€2.70). These tend to be erratically open and you'll have to wait for someone to take you, but the crib scene especially, originally created to decorate a chapel to hold the basilica's holy crib relics, is well worth catching.

Santa Prassede

Behind Santa Maria Maggiore, off Via Merulana, the ninth-century church of **Santa Prassede** (daily 7am–12.30pm & 4–6.30pm) occupies an ancient site, where it's claimed St Prassede harboured Christians on the run from the Roman persecutions. She apparently collected the blood and remains of the martyrs and placed them in a well where she herself was later buried; a red marble disc in the floor of the nave marks the spot. In the southern aisle, the chapel of Saint Zeno was built by Pope Paschal I as a mausoleum for his mother, Theodora, and is decorated with marvellous ninth-century mosaics that make it glitter like a jewel-encrusted box. You'll need €0.50 to light them; Theodora is depicted on the left-hand arch. The chapel also contains a fragment of a column supposed to be the one to which Christ was tied when he was scourged. In the apse are more ninth-century mosaics, showing Christ between, on the right, saints Peter, Pudenziana and Zeno and on the left saints Paul, Praxedes and Paschal I. Note that Paschal's halo (like Theodora's) is in a rectangular form, indicating that he was alive when the mosaics were placed here.

Santa Pudenziana

On the other side of Via Cavour, the church of **Santa Pudenziana**, down below street level on Via Urbana (daily 8am–noon & 4–6pm), has equally ancient origins, dedicated to St Prassede's supposed sister and for many years believed to have been built on the site where St Peter lived and worshipped – though this has since been entirely discredited, snd it's now thought to have simply been the site of a Roman bathhouse. There were for years two relics in the church, the chair that St Peter used as his throne and the table at which he said Mass, though both have long gone – to the Vatican and the Lateran, respectively. But the church still has one feature of ancient origin, the superb fifth-century apse mosaics – some of the oldest Christian figurative mosaics in Rome, though they've been tampered with and restored over the years. They're still fluid and beautiful works centring on a golden enthroned Christ surrounded by the Apostles – not quite all of them, you'll notice, due to the fact that the mosaic was reduced in size when the church was restored in the sixteenth century and they cut off one from either side. Nonetheless the mosaic is marvellous, not least the graphic arrangement of the Apostles that remain, and the expressiveness of their faces, each one of which is purposefully different from the next.

San Giovanni in Laterano and around

The area immediately south and east of the Esquiline and the Colosseum is known as **San Giovanni**, after the basilica that lies at the end of Via Merulana. This is offically the city's cathedral, and was, before the creation of the separate Vatican city state, the headquarters of the Catholic Church. It's a mixed area, mainly residential, but it has some compelling sights in the basilica of San Giovanni itself, the church of Santa Croce in Gerusalemme just beyond; and, back towards the Colosseum, the amazing church of San Clemente.

San Giovanni in Laterano

The basilica of **San Giovanni in Laterano** (daily 7am–6.45pm) is officially Rome's cathedral and the seat of the pope as bishop of Rome, and was for centuries the main papal residence. However, when the papacy returned from Avignon at the end of the fourteenth century, the Lateran palaces were in ruin and uninhabitable, and the pope moved across town to the Vatican, where he has remained ever since. The Lateran Treaty of 1929 accorded this and the other patriarchal basilicas extraterritorial status.

△ San Giovanni in Laterano

There has been a church on this site since the fourth century, the first established by Constantine, and the present building, reworked by Borromini in the mid-seventeenth century, evokes – like San Clemente or San Stefano – Rome's staggering wealth of history, with a host of features from different periods. The doors to the church, oddly enough, were taken from the Curia or Senate House of the Roman Forum, while the obelisk that stands on the north side of the church is the oldest in Rome, dating from the fifteenth century BC and brought here from Thebes by Constantine, originally for the Circus Maximus, but raised here by Sixtus V.

The Basilica

The **interior** of San Giovanni has been extensively reworked over the centuries. Much of what you see today dates from 1600, when the Aldobrandini family pope, Clement VIII, had the church remodelled for that Holy Year. The gilded ceiling of the nave has as its centrepiece the papal arms of Pope Pius VI, from the late 1700s; the ceiling in the crossing bears, on the left, the Aldobrandini insignia, and on the right the remembrances of Pope Innocent III, who died in 1216 and was buried here in the late 1800s at the behest of Pope Leo XIII, when he had this wing of the crossing remodelled. Leo XIII himself, who died in 1903, is buried opposite. The first pillar on the left of the right-hand aisle shows a fragment of Giotto's fresco of Boniface VIII, proclaiming the first Holy Year in 1300, a gentle work with gorgeous colours that's oddly overshadowed by the immensity and grandeur of the rest of the building. On the next pillar along, a more recent monument commemorates Sylvester I – "the magician pope", bishop of Rome during much of Constantine's reign – and incorporates part of his original tomb, said to sweat and rattle its bones when a pope is about to die. Kept secure behind the papal altar are the heads of St Peter and St Paul, the church's prize relics.

The Cloisters

Outside the church, the **cloisters** (daily 9am–6pm; €2) are one of the most pleasing parts of the complex, decorated with early thirteenth-century Cosmati work and with fragments of the original basilica arranged around. Rooms off to the side form a small museum, with, in no particular order, a remarkable papal throne assembly and various papal artefacts (not least the vestments of Boniface VIII).

The Lateran Palace and Baptistry

Adjoining the basilica is the **Lateran Palace**, home of the popes in the Middle Ages and also formally part of Vatican territory. Next door, the **Baptistry** (daily 7am–12.30pm & 3.30–7.30pm; free) has been carefully restored, along with the side of the church itself, after a car bombing in 1993. It is the oldest surviving baptistry in the Christian world, an octagonal structure built during the fifth century that has been the model for many such buildings since. Oddly, it doesn't really feel its age, although the mosaics in the side chapels and the bronze doors to the chapel on the right, brought here from the Baths of Caracalla, quickly remind you where you are.

The Scala Santa and Sancta Sanctorum

There are more ancient remains on the other side of the church, on Piazza di Porta San Giovanni, foremost of which is the **Scala Santa** (April–Sept daily

6.15am–noon & 3.30–6.45pm; Oct–March daily 3–6.15pm), claimed to be the staircase from Pontius Pilate's house down which Christ walked after his trial. It was said to have been brought to Rome by St Helena and was placed here by Pope Sixtus V, who also moved the chapel here – it was formerly the pope's private place of worship. The 28 steps are protected by boards, and the only way you're allowed to climb them is on your knees, which pilgrims do regularly – although there are staircases either side for the less penitent. At the top, **Sancta Sanctorum**, or chapel of San Lorenzo, holds an ancient (sixth- or seventh-century) painting of Christ said to be the work of an angel, hence its name – *acheiropoeton*, or "not done by human hands". You can't enter the chapel, and, fittingly perhaps, you can only really get a view of it by kneeling and peering through the grilles.

Santi Quattro Coronati

Not far from San Giovanni in Laterano, back towards the Colosseum, the church of **Santi Quattro Coronati** (daily 9am–noon & 4–6pm) is dedicated to four soldier martyrs who died because they refused to worship a statue of Aesculapius during the persecutions of Diocletian. Originally built in 1110 by Pope Paschal II, the church is a prime example of a medieval Christian building, though with an extra-wide apse and a sanctuary that contains a *matroneum* or women's gallery – something rarely seen nowadays. A cloistered convent of Augustinian nuns lives here now, and it's them you have to ask for the key to get into the chapel of St Sylvester, which contains the oldest extant frescoes in Rome – painted in 1248 and relating the story of how the fourth-century pope cured the emperor Constantine of leprosy and then baptized him.

San Stefano Rotondo

Not far from Quattro Coronati, over towards the Celian Hill on Via della Navicella, the round church of **San Stefano Rotondo** (daily 9am–1pm & 3.30–6pm) is another truly ancient structure, built in the 460s AD and consecrated by Pope Simplicius to commemorate Christianity's first martyr. Recently open again after a lengthy restoration, its four chapels form the shape of a cross in a circle, moodily lit by the 22 windows of the clerestory. The interior has a labyrinthine feel, but the feature that will really stick in your mind is the series of stomach-turning frescoes on the walls of the outer ring: various saints being martyred in different ways: impalings, pinchings, drawings and quarterings, disembowelments, boilings in oil, hangings, beheadings – you name it.

San Clemente

Back on Via San Giovanni in Laterano, the church of **San Clemente** (Mon–Sat 9am–12.30pm & 3–6pm, Sun opens 10am; €3 for the earlier church and temple), a cream-coloured twelfth-century basilica that perhaps encapsulates better than any other the continuity of history in the city – being in fact a conglomeration of three places of worship from three very different eras in the history of Rome. Pope St Clement I, to whom the church is dedicated, was the third pope after St Peter (and in fact is said to have been ordained by him), and he reigned from 90 AD until 99 AD, when he was exiled and martyred in the Crimea. His relics are kept in this church, and have been venerated here from the very earliest times.

The Basilica

The **ground-floor church** is a superb example of a medieval basilica: its facade and courtyard face east in the archaic fashion, and there are some fine, warm mosaics in the apse and a chapel with frescoes by Masolino. The choir is partitioned off with beautiful white marble slabs bearing the earliest papal insignia in the city, the monogram of Pope John II, who reigned from 533 to 535. The gilded ceiling bears the arms of Pope Clement XI, from the early years of the eighteenth century, during whose papacy the church was remodelled.

The early church and Mithraic temple

Downstairs there's the nave of an **earlier church**, dating back to 392 AD, with a frescoed narthex depicting, among other things, the *Miracle of San Clemente*. And at the eastern end of this church, steps lead down to a third level, the remains of a Roman house – a labyrinthine set of rooms including a dank **Mithraic temple** of the late second century, set among several rooms of a Roman house built after the fire of 64 AD. In the temple is a statue of Mithras slaying the bull and the seats upon which the worshippers sat during their ceremonies. The underground river that formerly fed the lake in front of the Domus Aurea can be heard rushing to its destination in the Tiber, behind the Circo Massimo, a reminder that Rome is built on very shaky foundations indeed.

Next door to the Roman house, across a narrow alleyway, are the ground-floor **rooms** of a first-century imperial building, all of which can be explored by the spooky light of fluorescent tubes set in the ceiling and along the mossy brick walls.

Porta Asinaria and the Aurelian Wall

In the opposite direction from San Giovanni in Laterano, across the far side of the square in front of the church, the **Porta Asinaria**, one of the city's grander gateways, marks the Aurelian Wall. If you're here in the morning, you could visit the new and second-hand clothing market on **Via Sannio** (Mon–Sat until about 1.30pm). Once you've seen the market, you could continue on for five minutes to **Piazzale Metronio**, from where you have the best oppor-tunity to follow the line of the **Aurelian Wall** as far as **Porta San Sebastiano** and the Aurelian Wall museum (see p.93) – a twenty-minute walk.

Santa Croce in Gerusalemme

Otherwise follow the wall on the city side by way of Viale Carlo Felice for five minutes to another key Roman church, **Santa Croce in Gerusalemme** (daily 6.45am–7.30pm), one of the seven pilgrimage churches of Rome. Santa Croce, despite its later Renaissaance and Baroque adornments, feels a very ancient church – and it is, for it is supposed to stand on the site of the palace of Constantine's mother St Helena. It houses the relics of the true cross she had brought back from Jerusalem, stored in a surreal Mussolini-era chapel up some steps at the end of the left aisle. The Renaissance apse frescoes show the discovery of the fragments, under a seated Christ, and are very fine indeed – a beautiful, technicolour, naturalistic scene showing trees and mountains and the saint at the centre, with the true cross and a kneeling cardinal. Steps behind lead down to the original level of Helena's house – now a chapel dedicated to the saint and decorated with Renaissance mosaics; the tiles on the stairs down are an inscription relating to the true cross discovery and were done at the same time as the apse frescoes.

National Museum of Musical Instruments

The first floor of the palace next door to Santa Croce is the home of the **National Museum of Musical Instruments** (Tues–Sat 8.30am–7.30pm; €2), a good display of Italian and other European instruments with good information, much of it in English. There are early Roman and Etruscan pieces, lots of stringed instruments, and others divided into mechanical instruments, instruments used by travelling musicans, church instruments and early pianofortes. Not what you came to Rome for, perhaps, but worth a look if you're in this part of town.

Porta Maggiore

North of here towards the rail tracks, the **Porta Maggiore** is probably the most impressive of all the city gates, built in the first century AD to carry water into Rome from the aqueducts outside, and incorporated into the Aurelian walls. The **aqueducts** that converge here are the **Aqua Claudia**, which dates from 45 AD, and the **Aqua Marcia** from 200 BC. The Roman engineers built them one on top of the other at this point to channel the water of the Aqua Claudia into the city in a manner not to interfere with the pre-existing Aqua Marcia – a feat recounted in the monumental tablet over the central arches.

The famous **Tomb of the Baker**, in white travertine, just outside the gate, is a monument from about 30 AD. The baker in question was a public contractor who made a fortune selling bread to the imperial government. The round holes in the tomb represent the openings of the baker's ovens – a style that strangely enough was picked up in the Mussolini era and can be seen time and again in Fascist architecture.

The Villa Borghese and north central Rome

The area outside the Aurelian walls, to the north and northeast of the city, was once a district of market gardens, olive groves and patrician villas abutting the Via Salaria and Via Nomentana before trailing off into open country. During the Renaissance, these vast tracts of land were appropriated as summer estates for the city's wealthy, particularly those affiliated in some way to the papal court. One of the most notable of these estates, the **Villa Borghese**, was the summer playground of the Borghese family and is now a public park, and home to the city's most significant concentration of museums. Foremost among these are the **Galleria Borghese**, housing the resplendent art collection of the aristocratic family – a Roman must-see in anyone's book – and the **Villa Giulia**, built by Pope Julius III for his summer repose and now the National Etruscan Museum. North of Villa Borghese stretch Rome's post-Unification residential districts – not of much interest in themselves, except perhaps for **Foro Italico**, which is worth visiting either to see Roma or Lazio play at its Olympic Stadium, or simply to admire Mussolini's stylish, of-its-time sports complex.

Villa Borghese

Immediately above Piazza del Popolo, the hill known as the Pincio (see p.64) marks the edge of the city's core and the beginning of a collection of parks and gardens that forms Rome's largest central open space – the **Villa Borghese**, made up of the grounds of the seventeenth-century palace of Scipione Borghese, which were bought by the city at the turn of the twentieth century; it celebrated its centenary in 2003 with lots of events and renovation work, and has an informative website worth checking at Ⓦwww.villaborghese.it. It's a huge area, and its woods, lake and grass, criss-crossed by roads, are about as near as you can get to peace in the city centre without making too much effort. There are any number of attractions for those who want to do more than just stroll or sunbathe:

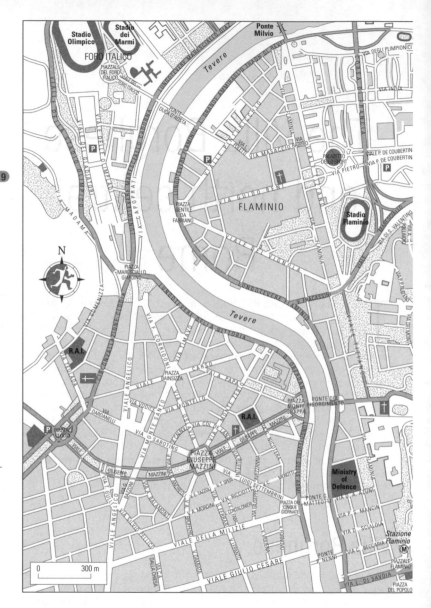

a tiny boating lake, a zoo – renamed the "Bioparco" in an attempt to re-brand a previously poor image (see Chapter 21, "Kids' Rome") – and some of the city's finest museums. Stop also at the equestrian ring of the Galoppatoio, just beyond the Pincio Gardens, which is home to a large hot-air balloon that gives twenty-minutes-worth of one of the best views of the city centre you'll find (daily 9.30am–dusk).

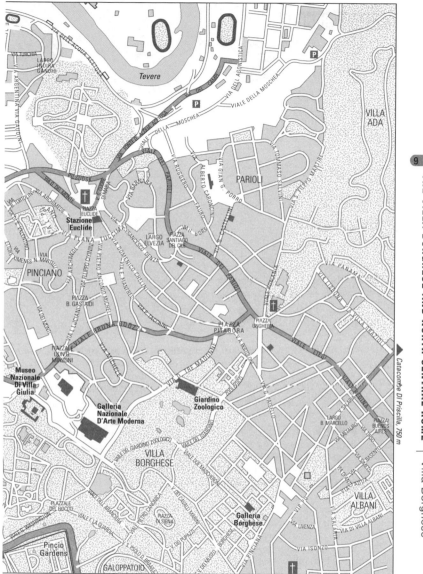

Catacombe Di Priscilla, 750 m

The Museo e Galleria Borghese

The best place to make for first, if you want some focus to your wanderings, is the Casino Borghese itself, on the far eastern side, which was built in the early seventeenth century and turned over to the state when the gardens became city property in 1902 as the **Museo e Galleria Borghese**, Piazza le

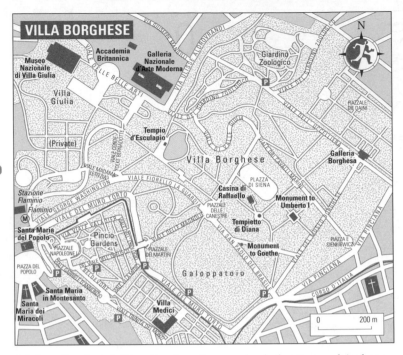

Scipione Borghese 5 (Tues–Sun 9am–7pm; pre-booked visits are advised, as a limited number of people are allowed in every 2hr; ☎06.32.810, Mon–Fri 9am–7pm, Sat 9am–1pm; €8.50; Ⓦwww.galleriaborghese.it). Reopened several years ago after a lengthy restoration, the Borghese has taken its place as one of Rome's great treasure houses and should not be missed.

Some history

When Camillo Borghese was elected pope and took the papal name Paul V in 1605, he elevated his favourite nephew, Scipione Caffarelli Borghese, to the cardinalate and put him in charge of diplomatic, ceremonial and cultural matters at the papal court. Scipione possessed an infallible instinct for recognizing artistic quality, and, driven by ruthless passion, he used fair means or foul to acquire the most prized works of art. He was also shrewd enough to patronize outstanding talents such as Gian Lorenzo Bernini, Caravaggio, Domenichino, Guido Reni and Peter Paul Rubens. To house the works of these artists, as well as his collection of antique sculpture and other pieces, he built the Casino, or summer house, and predictably he spared no expense. The palace, which was built in the early 1600s, is a celebration of the ancient splendour of the Roman Empire: over the years its art collection has been added to, and its rooms redecorated – most notably during the last quarter of the eighteenth century, when the ceilings were re-done to match thematically the artworks of each room. The recent restoration of the sumptuous interior seemed to go on forever, but now the gallery's Roman-era mosaics, rich stucco decorations and trompe l'oeil ceilings provide the perfect surroundings in which to enjoy the artworks which Cardinal Scipione Borghese collected so voraciously.

The porch and entrance hall

Entrance is through a **porch**, which displays classical sculpture, notably several large statues of Dacian prisoners from the time of the emperor Trajan. Inside, the **entrance hall** has a splendid ceiling by Marino Rossi, painted in 1775–78, depicting the foundations and early history of Rome – Jupiter in the centre surrounded by various moral and spiritual attributes, and historical and mythological characters such as Romulus, Remus and the she-wolf. On the floor, a series of Roman mosaics from about 320 AD depict gladiators fighting and killing various animals and each other – a circle with a line drawn through it next to the name indicates the deceased, and blood gushes gruesomely from the pierced throats and hearts of the animals. Among a number of notable statues, there's a *Bacchus* from the second century AD, a *Fighting Satyr*, and, on the wall facing the entrance door, a melodramatic piece in marble of Marcus Curtius flinging himself into the chasm (see p.78) – his horse is a Roman sculpture and the figure is by Bernini's father. Bernini himself also makes an appearance with a late, in fact unfinished work, *Truth Revealed in Time*, done late in his career when he had been accused of faulty architectural work in part of St Peter's. Truth, with a sappy look on her face, clutches the sun, representing time, to her breast. There are also colossal heads of the emperors Hadrian and Antoninus Pius, and a female head of the Antonine period, with a lotus flower to represent Isis.

The ground floor

The **ground floor** beyond the entrance hall contains sculpture, a mixture of ancient Roman items and seventeenth-century works, roughly linked together with late-eighteenth-century ceiling paintings showing scenes from the Trojan War. The first room off the entrance hall, whose paintings depict the *Judgement of Paris*, has as its centrepiece Canova's famous statue of *Pauline Borghese* posed as Venus, with flimsy drapery that leaves little to the imagination.

The second ground-floor room, the **Room of the Sun**, has a marvellous statue of *David* by Bernini, finished in 1624, when the sculptor was just 25. The face is a self-portrait of the sculptor, said to have been carved with the help of a mirror held for him by Scipione Borghese himself. There's more work by Bernini in the next room, where his statue of *Apollo and Daphne* is a dramatic, poised work that captures the split second when Daphne is transformed into a laurel tree, with her fingers becoming leaves and her legs tree trunks. Briefly, Apollo had made fun of Cupid, who had taken revenge by firing a golden arrow which infused immediate and desperate love into the breast of Apollo, and by shooting Daphne with a leaden one designed to hasten the rejection of

Pauline Borghese

Pauline Borghese, the sister of Napoleon and married (reluctantly) to the reigning Prince Borghese, was a shocking woman in her day, with grand habits. There are tales of her jewels and clothes, of the Negro who used to carry her from her bath, of the servants she used as footstools, and, of course, her long line of lovers. The statue of her in the Villa Borghese was considered outrageous by everyone but herself: when asked how she could have posed almost naked, she simply replied, "Oh, there was a stove in the studio." Interestingly, the couch on which she reposes originally had a kind of clockwork mechanism inside, which allowed the statue to rotate while the viewer remained stationary.

amorous advances. Daphne, the daughter of a river god, called on her father to help her avoid being trapped by Apollo, who was in hot pursuit; her father changed her into a laurel tree just as Apollo took her into his arms – a desperately sad piece of drama to which Bernini's statue does full justice. This statue also caused a great scandal when it was unveiled. The poet and playwright, Maffeo Barberini, who later became Pope Urban VIII, wrote a couplet in Latin, which is inscribed on the base, claiming that all who pursue fleshly lusts are doomed to end up holding only ashes and dust.

Next door, the walls of the **Room of the Emperors** are flanked by seventeenth- and eighteenth-century busts of Roman emperors, facing another Bernini sculpture, *The Rape of Proserpine* dating from 1622, a coolly virtuosic work that shows in melodramatic form the story of the carrying off to the underworld of the beautiful nymph Proserpine, daughter of Gaia, goddess of the earth. The brutal Pluto grasps the girl in his arms, his fingers digging into the flesh of her thigh as she fights off his advances, while the three-headed form of Cerberus snaps at their feet.

In the small room next door, there's a marvellous statue of a sleeping hermaphrodite, from the first century AD, and a large porphyry Roman bathtub whose feline feet are almost modern in style. But it's back to the Berninis in the following room, where a larger-than-life statue of Aeneas, carrying his father, Anchises, out of the burning city of Troy, was sculpted by both father and his then 15-year-old son in 1613. The statue portrays a crucial event in Roman history, when after the defeat of the Trojans, Aeneas escaped with his family and went on a long voyage that ended up on the shores of what became Latium – his descendants eventually founding the city of Rome. The old man carries the statues representing their family household gods; the small boy carrying a flaming pot with what became the Vestal Fire is Aeneas's son Ascanius.

The **Egyptian Room**, beyond, contains artefacts, paintings and mosaics with an Egyptian theme and a statue of a satyr on a dolphin dating from the first century AD, while further on, the **Room of Silenus** contains a variety of paintings by Cardinal Scipione's faithful servant Caravaggio – notably the *Madonna of the Grooms* from 1605, a painting that at the time was considered to have depicted Christ far too realistically to hang in a central Rome church, so Cardinal Scipione happily bought it for his collection. Look also at *St Jerome*, captured writing at a table lit only by a source of light that streams in from the upper left of the picture, and his *David holding the Head of Goliath*, sent by Caravaggio to Cardinal Scipione from exile in Malta, where he had fled to escape capital punishment for various crimes. The cardinal managed to get the artist off, but Caravaggio died of malaria after landing in Italy at Porto Ercole, north of Rome, in 1610; the head of Goliath is believed to be a self-portrait.

The first floor

Upstairs houses the Galeria Borghese's **Pinacoteca**, literally one of the richest collections of paintings in the world, although unfortunately you're only allowed half an hour up here before having to leave. Given this, you'd do well to make a second trip if possible.

First off are several important paintings by **Raphael**, his teacher Perugino and other masters of the Umbrian School from the late fifteenth and early sixteenth centuries, not least Raphael's *Deposition*, done in 1507 for a noble of Perugia in memory of her son, and pillaged from Perugia cathedral by associates of Cardinal Scipione. Look also for the *Lady With a Unicorn*, and

Portrait of a Man, both also by Raphael but misattributed earlier this century, and, over the door, a copy of the artist's portrait of a tired-out Julius II, painted in the last year of the pope's life, 1513.

The next room contains more early-sixteenth-century paintings, prominent among which is Cranach's *Venus and Cupid with a Honeycomb*, of 1531, and Brescianino's *Venus and Two Cupids*, from about 1520 – both remarkable at the time for their departure from classical models for their subjects. The Cranach *Venus*, dressed in a diaphanous robe, shows Cupid carrying a honeycomb, demonstrating the dangers of carnal love. Further into the gallery, look out for two early-sixteenth-century copies of Leonardo's *Leda and the Swan* (the original has been lost), Lorenzo Lotto's touching *Portrait of a Man*, a soulful study that hints at grief over a wife lost in childbirth symbolized by the tiny skull and rose petals under his right hand, and, in the **Gallery of Lanfranco**, at the back of the building, a series of self-portraits done by Bernini at various stages of his long life. Next to these are a lifelike bust of Cardinal Scipione executed by Bernini in 1632, portraying him as the worldly connoisseur of fine art and fine living that he was, and a smaller bust of Pope Paul V, also by Bernini.

Further on there is a painting of *Diana* by Domenichino showing the goddess and her attendants celebrating and doing a bit of target practice – one of them has just shot a pheasant through the head and everybody else is jumping with enthusiasm; in the foreground a young nymph, lasciviously bathing, looks out with a lustful expression. From here, if you can get to the **Room of Psyche** before the guards start herding you out, you will be able to see, along with works by Bellini and the other Venetians of the early 1500s, Titian's *Sacred and Profane Love*, painted in 1514 when he was about 25 years old, to celebrate the marriage of the Venetian noble Nicolo Aurelio (whose coat of arms is on the sarcophagus). It shows his bride, Laura Bagarotto, dressed in white representing Sacred Love, and Venus, representing Profane Love, carrying a lamp symbolizing the eternal Love of God. The bride cradles a bowl of jewels that refer to the fleeting happiness of life on earth.

The Galleria Nazionale d'Arte Moderna

The Villa Borghese's two other major museums are situated on the other side of the park, along the Viale delle Belle Arti, in the so-called "Academy Ghetto" – the Romanian, British, Dutch, Danish, Egyptian and other cultural academies are all situated here. Of these, the **Galleria Nazionale d'Arte Moderna**, Via delle Belle Arti 131 (Tues–Sun 9am–7.30pm; €6.50; ⓦwww.gnam.arti .beniculturali.it) is probably the least enticing, a huge, lumbering, Neoclassical building housing a collection that isn't really as grand as you might expect, made up of a wide selection of nineteenth- and twentieth-century Italian (and a few foreign) names. However, it can make a refreshing change after several days of having the senses bombarded with Etruscan, Roman and Renaissance art. The nineteenth-century collection contains a splendid group of paintings by the Tuscan Impressionists (the Macchiaioli School including Fattori, Lega, Segantini), as well as paintings by Courbet, Van Gogh and Cézanne, but really isn't that compelling unless this is one of your areas of interest. The twentieth-century collection on the upper level is more appealing, and includes work by Modigliani, De Chirico, Giacomo Balla, Boccioni and other Futurists, along with the odd Mondrian and Klimt, and some postwar canvases by the likes of Mark Rothko and Jackson Pollock and Cy Twombly, Rome's own American artist, who lived in the city most of his life. There is also a reasonably priced

△ Galleria Borghese

café, the *Caffè delle Arti*, out the back door at Via Gramsci 73, which is part of the gallery complex and is much the best place to grab something to eat and drink if you're wilting from a tour of Villa Borghese.

Museo Nazionale Etrusco di Villa Giulia

The **Villa Giulia**, five minutes' walk away in the direction of Via Flaminia, a harmonious collection of courtyards, loggias, gardens and temples put together in a playful Mannerist style for Pope Julius III in the mid-sixteenth century, is perhaps more of an essential stop than the Modern Art Museum. It's home to the **Museo Nazionale Etrusco di Villa Giulia**, Piazzale Villa Giulia 9 (Tues–Sun 8.30am–7.30pm; €4), the world's primary collection of Etruscan treasures (along with the Etruscan collection in the Vatican), and a good introduction – or conclusion – to the Etruscan sites in Lazio, which between them contributed most of the artefacts on display here. It's not an especially large collection, but it's worth taking the trouble to see the whole.

The east wing

The entrance room of the **east wing** houses two pieces of Etruscan sculpture, one showing a man astride a seahorse, a recurring theme in ancient Mediterranean art, and an oddly amateurish centaur – basically a man pasted to the hindquarters of a horse – both from Vulci and dating from the sixth century BC. The next rooms contain bronze objects dating from the seventh and sixth centuries BC – urns used to contain the ashes of cremated persons, among which a beautiful bronze example, in the shape of a finely detailed dwelling hut, stands out – and a number of terracotta votive offerings of anatomical parts of the human body, their detail alluding to the Etruscans' accomplishments in medicine. A gold dental bridge shows their skill at dentistry too.

The next room displays items found in Veio – among them Apollo and Hercules disputing over the sacred hind which Apollo had shot and Hercules claimed. Next door, in the octagonal room, the remarkable *Sarcophagus of the Married Couple* (dating from the sixth century BC, and actually containing the ashes of the deceased rather than the bodies), is from Cerveteri, and is one of the most famous pieces in the museum – a touchingly lifelike portrayal of a husband and wife lying on a couch. He has his right arm around her; she is offering him something from her right

The Etruscans

The **Etruscans** remain something of a historical mystery. We know that they lived in central Italy – in Etruria – from around 900 BC until their incorporation into the Roman world in 88 BC. However, whether they were native to the region, or whether they had originally migrated here from overseas, specifically from Asia Minor, remains a matter of debate even now. And very little is known about them overall. The Romans borrowed heavily from their civilization, and thus in many ways the influence of the Etruscans is still felt today: our alphabet, for example, is based on the Etruscan system; and bishops' crooks and the "fasces" symbol, of a bundle of rods with an axe – found, among other places, behind the speaker's rostrum in the US House of Representatives – are just two other Etruscan symbols that endure. The Etruscans were also masters of working in terracotta, gold and bronze, and accomplished carvers in stone, and it is these skills – together with their obvious sensuality and the ease with which they enjoyed life – that make a visit to the Villa Giulia so beguiling.

hand, probably an egg – a recurring theme in Etruscan art. Their clothes are modelled down to the finest detail, including the laces and soles of their shoes, and the pleats of the linen and lacy pillowcases. In case you're wondering, the holes in the backs of their heads, and at other spots, are ventilation holes to prevent the terracotta from exploding when the hollow piece was fired. Beyond are more finds from Cerveteri: hundreds of vases, pots, drinking vessels and other items. Most interesting is a portrait of a man, complete with cauliflower right ear, and a finely stitched cut to the right of his mouth – clearly a tough customer.

Upstairs, in the balcony over the married couple sarcophagus, there are displays on the Etruscan language, and the *cistae* recovered from tombs around Praeneste – drum-like objects, engraved and adorned with figures, that were supposed to hold all the things needed for the care of the body after death – including a special area devoted to the famous *Ficorini Cista*, made by an Etruscan craftsman named Novios Plautios for a lady named Dindia Malconia and probably a wedding present. In the same room, look too at the marvellously intricate pieces of gold jewellery, delicately worked into tiny horses, birds, camels and other animals. Further on you'll find mostly bronzes, mirrors, candelabra, religious statues and tools used in everyday life. Notice, particularly, the elongated statues of priests and priestesses, some of whom hold eels in their hands engaged in some kind of rite. There is also a realistic bronze statuette of a ploughman at work plodding along behind his oxen.

After this hall you are at the bottom of the "U" curve that forms the building's outline, and a an enormous collection of jewellery – all of it fascinating. Branching off are items and reconstructions from the enormous temple excavated at Pyrgi, Cerveteri's seaport, in the 1960s, including replicas of gold foil plates thought at one time to be the Rosetta Stone for the Etruscan language – the plates are in three different languages, Etruscan, Punic and Greek, and represent the oldest pre-Roman inscriptions ever found. In the rooms to the west of here are items from the very earliest Etruscan collections, together with the story of how everything was brought together in the Villa Giulia, a model of the villa, and original architectural drawings by, among others, Michelangelo.

The atrium and beyond

Exiting the U-shaped room you will find several hundred examples of Etruscan pottery, terracottas and bronze items, including charcoal braziers and pieces of armour, and, remarkably, a trumpet that has not sounded for two thousand years. This gallery will lead you to the steps down to the upper floor of the west wing, which is devoted to the **Faliscians**, a people from northeast Lazio who spoke a dialect of Latin but were culturally Etruscans. This part of the museum was reorganized in 1998 and is clearly labelled in English, with good information in each room from the excavations at Narce, Falerii Nuovi, Civita Castellana and other sites in the Faliscian area. The displays include a drinking horn in the shape of a dog's head that is so lifelike you almost expect it to bark; a *holmos*, or small table, to which the maker attached 24 little pendants around the edge; and a bronze disc breastplate from the seventh century BC decorated with a weird, almost modern abstract pattern of galloping creatures.

In the atrium, two storeys high, are finds from the temples at Sassi Caduti and the Sanctuary of Apollo in Civita Castellana – Etruscan artistry at its best, with gaudily coloured terracotta figures that leer, run, jump and climb; a beautiful, lifelike torso of Apollo, dating from around the turn of the fourth century BC;

and a bust of Juno which has the air of a dignified matron, the flower pattern on her dress still visible, as are her earrings, her necklace and her crown. Further on you will see further display cases containing articles found outside Etruria but obviously of Etruscan origin or Etruscan influence.

The west wing ground floor

The ground floor of the **west wing** of the museum displays artefacts found outside Etruria proper but of obvious Etruscan provenance or heavily influenced by the Etruscans. The Etruscans had close relations with North Africa, and there are ostrich eggs, an Etruscan symbol of resurrection and rebirth, and mirrors, some of which have mythological events etched on their backs, from there. The next series of galleries has items from southern Lazio – Lake Nemi and the Alban Hills: an oak log that was used as a coffin, and cases of terracotta votive offerings – anatomical parts, babies in swaddling clothes, models of temples and houses. And there are more *cistae*, gold breastplates and belt buckles, bronze pots with griffins' heads looking in to see what's cooking, and a wonderful bronze throne with elaborately worked scenes of hunting, military parades and horse racing.

Parioli and north

The area north of Villa Borghese is the posh **PARIOLI** district, whose quiet, winding streets populated by large villas and their lush, leafy gardens make up one of Rome's wealthier neighbourhoods. However, it's of little interest to anyone who doesn't live there, or who isn't dining at one of its top restaurants. Immediately east stretches the enormous public park of the **Villa Ada**, connected with Villa Borghese by Via Salaria – the old trading route between the Romans and Sabines, so called because the main product transported along here was salt. The Villa Ada was once the estate of King Vittorio Emanuele III and is a nice enough place in which to while away an afternoon, with a bucolic atmosphere that is a world away from the busy streets of the city centre. But otherwise it's not really worth the special journey from the centre of town, unless you want to visit the Egyptian embassy, or Rome's only mosque, housed in its grounds.

The Catacombe di Priscilla

The **Catacombe di Priscilla** (Tues–Sun 8.30am–noon & 2.30–5pm; €4), which you can reach from Via Salaria, are the only real thing to see in the Villa Ada – a frescoed labyrinth of tunnels that is visitable on regular (obligatory) guided tours. No one quite knows why these catacombs are here, and whether they are Christian or pagan in origin. The so-called Greek Chapel has a number of obviously Christian frescoes – Daniel in the lions' den, the resurrection of Lazarus, Noah, the sacrifice of Isaac – painted between the second and fourth centuries AD. However, other paintings, including something that is claimed as the earliest known depiction of the *Virgin and Child*, could in fact simply be a picture of a mother and child, both of whom were probably buried here.

Ponte Milvio

On the far side of the Parioli district the Tiber sweeps around in a wide hook-shaped bend. These northern outskirts of Rome aren't particularly enticing, though the **Ponte Milvio**, the old, originally Roman, footbridge where the emperor Constantine defeated Maxentius in 312 AD, still stands and provides wonderful views of the meandering Tiber, with the city springing up green on the hills to both sides and the river running fast and silty below. Inside a **guardhouse** on the right (northern) bank of the Tiber a marble plaque bears the arms of the Borgia family – including, in the centre, the papal badge and shield of Callisto III, on the right – featuring a bull – and on the left the arms of Rodrigio Borgia, who later became Pope Alexander VI but was at the time his father's secretary of state. On the northern side of the river, **Piazzale di Ponte Milvio** sports a cheap and cheerful market (Mon–Sat 8am–1.30pm) and a handful of bars and restaurants.

Foro Italico

It's just ten minutes' walk from the Ponte Milvio – past the huge Italian Foreign Ministry building – to the **Foro Italico** sports centre, one of the few parts of Rome to survive intact pretty much the way Mussolini planned it. This is still used as a sports centre, but it's worth visiting as much for its period feel and architecture as anything else. Its centrepiece is perhaps the **Ponte Duca di' Aosta**, which connects Foro Italico to the town side of the river, and is headed by a white marble obelisk capped with a gold pyramid that is engraved MUSSOLINI DUX in beautiful 1930s calligraphy. The marble finials at the side of each end of the bridge show soldiers in various heroic acts, loading machine guns and cannons, charging into the face of enemy fire, carrying the wounded and so forth, each bearing the face of Mussolini himself – a very eerie sight indeed.

Beyond the bridge, an avenue patched with more mosaics revering the *Duce* leads up to a fountain surrounded by mosaics of muscle-bound figures revelling in healthful sporting activities. Either side of the fountain are the two main stadiums: the larger of the two, the **Stadio Olimpico** on the left, was used for the Olympic Games in 1960 and is still the venue for Rome's two soccer teams on alternate Sundays (see Chapter 20, "Sports and Outdoor Activities"). The smaller, the **Stadio dei Marmi** ("stadium of marbles"), is ringed by sixty great male statues, groins modestly hidden by fig leaves, in a variety of elegantly macho poses – each representing both a sport and a province of Italy. It's a typically Fascist monument in many ways, but in the end a rather ironic choice for what was a notoriously homophobic government.

Trastevere and the Janiculum Hill

A cross the river from the centre of town, on the right bank of the Tiber, is the district of **TRASTEVERE**. A smallish district sheltered under the heights of the Janiculum Hill, it was the artisan area of the city in classical times, neatly placed for the trade that came upriver from Ostia and was unloaded nearby. Outside the city walls, Trastevere (the name means literally "across the Tiber") was for centuries heavily populated by immigrants, and this uniqueness and separation lent the neighbourhood a strong identity that lasted well into this century. Nowadays the area is a long way from the working-class quarter it used to be, and although you're still likely to hear Trastevere's strong Roman dialect here, you'll probably also bump into some of its many foreign residents, lured by the charm of its narrow streets and closeted squares. However, even if the local *Festa de' Noantri* ("celebration of we others"), held every July, seems to symbolize the slow decline of local spirit rather than celebrate its existence, there is good reason to come to Trastevere. It is among the more pleasant places to stroll in Rome, particularly peaceful in the morning, and lively come the evening, as dozens of trattorias set tables out along the cobblestone streets (Trastevere has long been known for its restaurants). The neighbourhood has also become the focus of the city's alternative scene and is home to much of its most vibrant and youthful nightlife. See Chapters 14–16 for details.

East of Viale di Trastevere

The quietest part of Trastevere lies on the southeastern side of **Viale di Trastevere**, the wide boulevard that cuts through the centre of the district. Just the other side of the Tiber from the Aventine Hill, and Testaccio, it feels oddly cut off from the city centre, a small knot of peeling streets and echoing squares that are a peaceful contrast to the relatively spruced-up nature of Trastevere proper, across the other side of the main spine.

Porta Portese

On a Sunday it's worth apporaching Trastevere by walking over the Ponte Sublicio to Porta Portese, from which the **Porta Portese** flea market

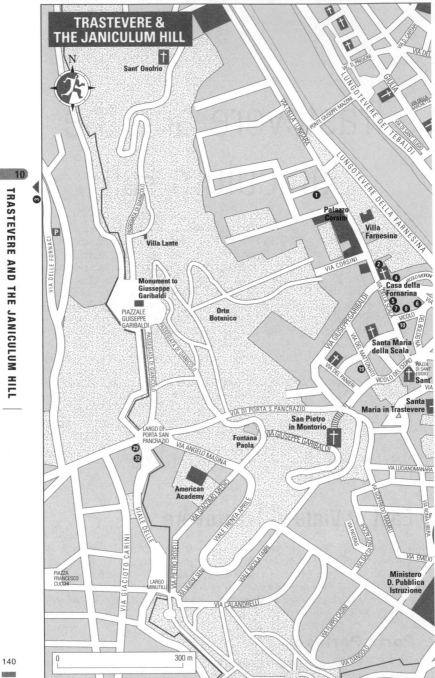

TRASTEVERE &
THE JANICULUM HILL

N

Sant' Onofrio

Villa Lante

Monument to
Giuseppe
Garibaldi

PIAZZALE
GUISEPPE
GARIBALDI

Orte
Botanico

Palazzo
Corsini

Villa Farnesina

Casa della
Fornarina

Santa Maria
della Scala

Santa
Maria in Trastevere

San Pietro
in Montorio

Fontana
Paola

LARGO DI
PORTA SAN
PANCRAZIO

American
Academy

PIAZZA
FRANCESCO
CUCCHI

LARGO
MINUTILLI

Ministero
D. Pubblica
Istruzione

VIA DELLE FORNACI

PASSEGIATA DI GIANICOLO

VIA DELLA LUNGARA

PONTE GIUSEPPE MAZZINI

LUNGOTEVERE DEI TEBALDI

LUNGOTEVERE DELLA FARNESINA

GIULIA

VIA CORSINI

VIA GIUSEPPE GARIBALDI

VIA DELLA SCALA

VIA DEL MATTONATO

VIA DEL PANIERI

VICOLO DEL CEDRO

PIAZZA
DI SANT'
EGIDIO

VIA DI PORTA S. PANCRAZIO

VIA GIUSEPPE GARIBALDI

VIA ANGELO MASINA

VIA GIACOMO MEDICI

VIA PIETRO ROSELLI

VIALE GLAUCO CARINI

VIALE DELLE

VIALE TRENTA APRILE

VIALE NICOLA FABRI

VIA ULISSE SENI

VIA CALANDRELLI

VIA LUCIANO MANARA

VIA GOFFREDO MAMELI

VIA ROMA LIBERA

VIA EMILIO

0   300 m

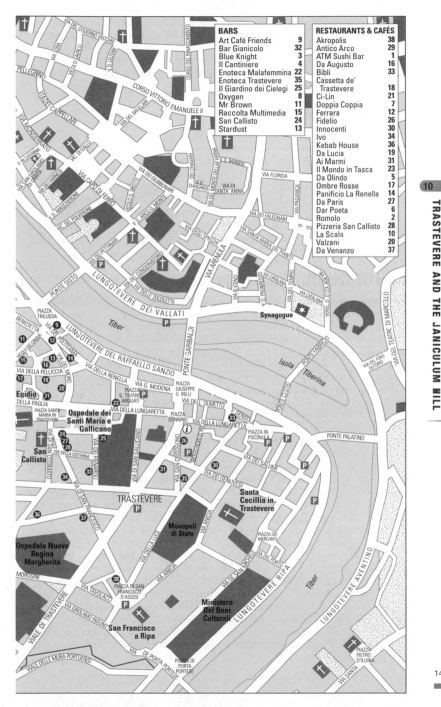

BARS

Art Café Friends	9
Bar Gianicolo	32
Blue Knight	3
Il Cantiniere	4
Enoteca Malafemmina	22
Enoteca Trastevere	35
Il Giardino dei Cielegi	25
Oxygen	8
Mr Brown	11
Raccolta Multimedia	15
San Callisto	24
Stardust	13

RESTAURANTS & CAFÉS

Akropolis	38
Antico Arco	29
ATM Sushi Bar	1
Da Augusto	16
Bibli	33
Cassetta de' Trastevere	18
Ci-Lin	21
Doppia Coppia	7
Ferrara	12
Fidelio	26
Innocenti	30
Ivo	34
Kebab House	36
Da Lucia	19
Ai Marmi	31
Il Mondo in Tasca	23
Da Olindo	5
Ombre Rosse	17
Panificio La Renella	14
Da Paris	27
Dar Poeta	6
Romolo	2
Pizzeria San Callisto	28
La Scala	10
Valzani	20
Da Venanzo	37

stretches down Via Portuense to Trastevere train station in a congested medley of antiques, old motor spares, cheap clothing, trendy clothing, cheap *and* trendy clothing, and assorted junk. Haggling is the rule, and keep a good hold of your wallet or purse. Come early if you want to buy, or even move – most of the bargains have gone by 10am, by which time the crush of people can be intense.

San Francesco a Ripa

Not far from Piazza di Porta Portese, the fairly ordinary church of **San Francesco a Ripa** (daily 7am–noon & 4–7.30pm) is best known for two things: the fact that St Francis himself once stayed here – if it's open, which it often isn't, you can see the actual room he stayed in – and the writhing, orgasmic statue of a minor saint, the Blessed Ludovica Albertoni, that Bernini sculpted towards the end of his career. As a work of Baroque sauciness, it bears comparison with his more famous *Ecstasy of St Teresa* in the church of Santa Maria in Vittoria; indeed it's perhaps even more shameless in its depiction of an earthily realised divine ecstasy – the woman is actually kneading her breasts.

Santa Cecilia in Trastevere

Further north, on its own quiet piazza off Via Anicia, is the church of **Santa Cecilia in Trastevere** (daily 9.30am–1pm & 4–7.15pm), a cream, rather sterile church – apart from a pretty front courtyard – whose antiseptic eighteenth-century appearance belies its historical associations. A church was originally built here over the site of the second-century home of St Cecilia, whose husband Valerian was executed for refusing to worship Roman gods and who herself was subsequently persecuted for her Christian beliefs. The story has it that Cecilia was locked in the caldarium of her own baths for several days but refused to die, singing her way through the ordeal (Cecilia is the patron saint of music). Her head was finally half hacked off with an axe, though it took several blows before she finally succumbed. Below the high altar, under a Gothic baldachino, Stefano Maderno's limp, almost modern statue of the saint shows her incorruptible body as it was found when exhumed in 1599, with three deep cuts in her neck – a fragile, intensely human piece of work that has helped make Cecilia one of the most revered Roman saints. Behind all this presides an apse mosaic from the ninth century showing Paschal I, who founded the current church, being presented to Christ by St Cecilia flanked by various saints.

The excavations of the baths and the rest of the Roman house are on view in the crypt below (€2.50) – a series of dank rooms with some fragments of mosaic and a gaudily decorated chapel at the far end. More alluring by far is the singing gallery above the nave of the church (Mon–Sat 10.15am–12.15pm, Sun 11.15am–12.15pm; €2.50, ring the bell to the left of the church door to get in), where Pietro Cavallini's late-thirteenth-century fresco of the Last Judgement is all that remains of the decoration that once covered the entire church. It's a powerful painting, an amazingly fluid, naturalistic piece of work for the time, with each of the Apostles, ranked six each side of Christ, captured as an individual portrait, while Christ sits in quiet, meditative majesty in the centre, flanked by angels.

West of Viale Trastevere

The most obvious way to approach Trastevere is to cross over from Isola Tiberina or from the pedestrian Ponte Sisto at the end of Via Giulia, both of which leave you five minutes from the heart of the neighbourhood.

There's a bit more life on this west side of **Viale Trastevere**, centred – during the day at least – around two main squares. The first of these, **Piazza di San Cosimato**, holds a medium-sized produce market (Mon–Sat 8am–1pm), while the other, **Piazza Santa Maria in Trastevere**, a short walk north, is the heart of old Trastevere, named after the church in its northwest corner.

Santa Maria in Trastevere

The church of **Santa Maria in Trastevere** (daily 7am–9pm) is held to be the first Christian place of worship in Rome, built on a site where a fountain of oil is said to have sprung on the day of Christ's birth. The greater part of the structure now dates from 1140, after a rebuilding by Innocent II, a pope from Trastevere. These days many people come here for the church's mosaics, which are among the city's most impressive: those on the cornice by Cavallini were completed a century or so after the rebuilding and show the Madonna surrounded by ten female figures with lamps – once thought to represent *The Wise and Foolish Virgins*. Inside, there's a nineteenth-century copy of a Cosmatesque pavement of spirals and circles, and apse mosaics contemporary with the building of the church – Byzantine-inspired works depicting a solemn yet sensitive parade of saints thronged around Christ and Mary. Beneath the high altar on the right, an inscription – "FONS OLIO" – marks the spot where the oil is supposed to have sprung up, close by which there is a chapel that is crowned with the crest of the British monarchy – placed here by Henry, cardinal of York, when he and his family, the Stuarts, lived in exile in Rome.

Piazza Sant'Egidio and Santa Maria della Scala

A short walk from Santa Maria in Trastevere, the long triangle of **Piazza Sant' Egidio** is home to the small **Museo di Roma in Trastevere** (Tues–Sun 10am–7pm; €2.60), a recently refurbished collection of artefacts illustrating Roman folklore – paintings of eighteenth-century life, models of popular Roman sights, and, best of all, life-sized tableaux showing scenes of Roman life. All in all it's much more accessible and engaging than the displays of its counterpart in the city centre. Beyond the square, the church of **Santa Maria della Scala** is often closed, but is worth a look, if open, for its eighteenth-century pharmacy, with its beautiful wooden cabinets and ceramic jars, which can be seen on request.

Palazzo Corsini

Cutting north through the backstreets towards the Tiber, the **Galleria Nazionale d'Arte di Palazzo Corsini**, Via della Lungara 10 (Tues–Sun 8.30am–7.30pm; €4), is an unexpected cultural attraction on this side of the river. Built originally for Cardinal Riario in the fifteenth century, the palace was totally renovated in 1732–36 by Ferdinando Fuga for the cardinal and art

△ Garibaldi Monument, Janiculum Hill

collector Neri Maria Corsini, who gathered most of the paintings on display. It's rather a highbrow collection, perhaps of more interest to the art historian than the layperson, but among its highlights are works by Rubens, Van Dyck, Guido Reni and Caravaggio.

Among a host of paintings from the late 1400s and early 1500s, there is a particularly gruesome *St George and the Dragon* by Francesco Raibolini, and, in the next room, a *St John the Baptist* by Caravaggio and *Madonna and Child* by Gentileschi, along with a charming double portrait of Clement XII with his nephew, the gallery's founder Neri Corsini. Beyond here, look out for a depiction of the Pantheon by Charles Clérisseau, when there was a market held in the piazza outside – though it's a rather fanciful interpretation, squeezing the Pyramid of Cestius and Arch of Janus into the background. You can also visit the **chambers of Queen Christina**, who renounced Protestantism, and, with it, the Swedish throne in 1655, and brought her library and fortune to Rome, to the delight of the Chigi pope, Alexander VII. She died here, in the palace, in 1689, and she is one of only three women to be buried in St Peter's. Her bedroom is decorated with frescoes by an unknown artist – grotesques with scenes of the miracles of Moses as well as the Riario coat of arms.

Later rooms are chock-full of paintings from the seventeeth and eighteenth centuries, but apart from a famous portrayal of *Salome With the Head of St John the Baptist* by Guido Reni, and *Prometheus Chained* by Salvatore Rosa – the latter one of the most vivid and detailed expositions of human internal anatomy you'll see – the main thing to look for is the curious **Corsini Throne**, thought to be a Roman copy of an Etruscan throne of the second or first century. Cut out of marble, its back is carved with warriors in armour and helmets, below which is a boar hunt, with wild boars the size of horses pursued by hunters. The base is decorated with scenes of a sacrifice, notably the minotaur devouring a human being – only discernible by the kicking legs that protrude from the feasting beast.

The Orto Botanico

The park of the Palazzo Corsini is now the site of the **Orto Botanico** (Tues–Sat 9.30am–6.30pm; €2), which, after Padua's botanical gardens, is the most important in Italy – and a good example of eighteenth-century garden design. It's a pleasantly neglected expanse these days, a low-key bucolic treat in the heart of Rome, clasping the side of the Janiculum Hill. You can clamber up to high stands of bamboo and ferns cut by rivulets of water, stroll through a wood of century-old oaks, cedars and conifers, and a grove of acclimatized palm trees in front of the so-called Fountain of the Tritons, a rather grand name for the relatively small-scale fountain that forms the centrepiece of the lower part of the gardens. There's a herbal garden with medicinal plants, a collection of orchids that bloom in springtime and early summer – and, a nice touch, a garden of aromatic herbs put together for the blind people; the plants can be identified by their smell or touch, and are accompanied by signs in Braille. The garden also has the distinction of being home to one of the oldest plane trees in Rome, between 350 and 400 years old, situated by the slightly decrepit monumental staircase.

Villa Farnesina

More interesting is the **Villa Farnesina** (Mon–Sat 9am–1pm; €4.50), across the road from the Palazzo Corsini, built during the early sixteenth century by

Baldassare Peruzzi for the Renaissance banker Agostino Chigi – a unique building known for its Renaissance frescoes, and contributed to by some of the masters of the Renaissance. Chigi situated his villa here so as to be close to the papal court and away from his business cronies. Most people come here to view the Raphael-designed painting of *Cupid and Psyche* in the now glassed-in loggia (in fact at the original front of the building, though now at the back), completed in 1517 by the artist's assistants, Giulio Romano, Francesco Penni and Giovanni da Udine. The painter and art historian Vasari claims Raphael didn't complete the work because his infatuation with his mistress – "La Fornarina", whose father's bakery was situated nearby – was making it difficult to concentrate, and says that Chigi arranged for her to live with the painter in the palace while he worked on the loggia. More likely he was simply so overloaded with commissions that he couldn't possibly finish them all.

Whoever was responsible, it's mightily impressive, a flowing, animated work bursting with muscular men and bare-bosomed women. Actually it would have made even more of an impact originally because the blue would have been much brighter – this is just the preparatory colour. The only part Raphael is said to have completed is the female figure with her back turned on the lunette to the right of the door leading out to the east. He did, however, apparently manage to finish the *Galatea* in the room next door, which he fitted in between his Vatican commissions for Julius II: "the greatest evocation of paganism of the Renaissance," Kenneth Clark called it, although Vasari claims that Michelangelo, passing by one day while Raphael was canoodling with La Fornarina, finished the painting for him. It's more of a mixed bag thematically, with bucolic country scenes interspersed with Galatea on her scallop-shell chariot and a giant head once said to have been painted by Michelangelo in one of the lunettes – which otherwise feature scenes from Ovid's *Metamorphoses* by Sebastiano del Piombo; the ceiling illustrates Chigi's horoscope constellations, frescoed by the architect of the building, Peruzzi, who also decorated the upstairs Salone delle Prospettive, where trompe l'oeil balconies give views onto contemporary Rome – one of the earliest examples of the technique. This room leads through to Chigi's bedroom, decorated with Sodoma's bold and colourful scenes from the life of Alexander the Great.

The Janiculum Hill

It's about a fifteen-minute walk up Via Garibaldi (bus #870 goes up from Piazza della Rovere) to the summit of the **Janiculum Hill** – not one of the original seven hills of Rome, but the one with the best and most accessible views of the centre. If you don't want to take the main road, follow Vicolo del Cedro from Via della Scala and take the steps up from the end, cross the main road, and continue on the steps that lead up to San Pietro in Montorio.

San Pietro in Montorio

Now part of a complex that includes the Spanish Academy and Spanish ambassador's residence, the church of **San Pietro in Montorio** (daily 7.30am–noon & 4–6pm) was built on a site once – now, it's thought, wrongly – believed to have been the place of the saint's crucifixion. The compact interior is particularly intimate – it's a favourite for weddings – and features some first-rate paintings, among them Sebastiano del Piombo's graceful *Flagellation*. Don't miss Bramante's little **Tempietto** (daily 9am–noon & 4–6pm) in the courtyard on the right, one of the seminal works of the Renaissance, built on what was supposed to have been the precise spot of St Peter's martyrdom. The small circular building is like a classical temple in miniature, perfectly proportioned and neatly executed.

Up to Porta San Pancrazio

The Janiculum was the scene of a fierce 1849 set-to between Garibaldi's troops and the French, and the white marble **memorial** around the corner from the church is dedicated to all those who died in the battle. A little further on, the **Fontana di Acqua Paola** – constructed for Paul V with marble from the Roman Forum and currently under reconstruction – gushes water at a bend in the road.

At the top of the hill, the city gate of **Porta San Pancrazio** was built during the reign of Urban VIII, destroyed by the French in 1849, and rebuilt by Pope Pius IX five years later. It has recently been restored to house the new Museum of the Roman Republic 1848–49 – yet to open at the time of writing. On the far side is **Piazzale Aurelio**, start of the old Roman Via Aurelia, and close by the numerous buildings of the **American Academy in Rome**. Beyond is the entrance to the grounds of the **Villa Doria Pamphilj**, which stretch down the hill, the largest and most recent of Rome's parks, laid out in 1650 and acquired for the city in the Seventies. It's a good place for a picnic.

The Passeggiata del Gianicolo

However, most people turn right before they reach the crest of the hill, following the **Passeggiata del Gianicolo** along the ridge to **Piazzale Garibaldi**, where there's an equestrian monument to Garibaldi – an ostentatious work from 1895. Just below is the spot from which a cannon is fired at noon each day for Romans to check their watches. Further on, the statue of **Anita Garibaldi** recalls the important part she played in the 1849 battle – a fiery, melodramatic work (she cradles a baby in one arm, brandishes a pistol with the other, and is galloping full speed on a horse) which also marks her grave. Spread out before her are some of the best views over the city.

Close by, the Renaissance **Villa Lante** is a jewel of a place that is now the home of the Finnish Academy in Rome and gives a panoramic view of the city. Descending from here towards the Vatican and St Peter's, follow some steps off to the right and, next to a small amphitheatre, you'll find the gnarled old oak tree where the sixteenth-century Italian poet **Tasso**, friend of Cellini and author of *Orlando Furioso*, is said to have whiled away his last days. Further down the hill, past the Jesuit children's hospital, the church of **Sant'Onofrio** (Sun 9am–1pm) sits on the road's hairpin, its L-shaped portico fronting the church where Tasso is buried. To the right of the church is one of the city's most delightful small cloisters; you can visit the poet's cell, which holds some manuscripts, his chair, his death mask and personal effects.

The Vatican and around

O n the west bank of the Tiber, directly across from Rome's historic centre, the **VATICAN CITY** was established as an independent sovereign state in 1929, a tiny territory with a population of around a thousand, surrounded by high walls on its far, western side and on the near side opening its doors to the rest of the city and its pilgrims in the form of St Peter's and its colonnaded piazza.

The Latin name *Mons Vaticanus* (Vatican Hill) is a corruption of an Etruscan term, indicating a good place for observing the flights of birds and lightning on the horizon that was believed to prophesy the future. It's believed that later St Peter himself was buried in a pagan cemetery here, giving rise to the building of a basilica to venerate his name and the siting of the headquarters of the Roman Catholic Church here. After reaching an uneasy agreement with Mussolini, the Vatican became a sovereign state in 1929, and nowadays has its own radio station, daily newspaper (*L'Osservatore Romano*), its own version of the euro complete with the pope's head (collector's items, incidentally, should you be given one), postal service, and indeed security service in the colourfully dressed Swiss Guards. However, its relationship with the Italian state is not surprisingly anything but straightforward.

Vatican practicalities

The **Vatican Museums** and the **Basilica of San Pietro (St Peter's)** are open to visitors (no shorts or bare shoulders for St Peter's), and it's also possible to visit the **Vatican Gardens,** though only on one guided tour a day (Mon–Tues & Thurs–Sat except religious holidays 10am; €12); visits last about two hours and tickets must be bought a few days ahead from the **Vatican Information Office** in Piazza San Pietro (Mon–Sat 8.30am–6pm; ☏06.6988.4466; ⊛www.vatican.va); you pay when you pick your tickets up on the day. The gardens are lovely and the views of St Peter's are great. You can also, if you wish, attend a **papal audience**: these happen once a week, usually on Wednesdays at 11am in the Audiences Room, and are by no means one-to-one affairs – you'll be with dozens of others. It's often possible to get a place on one if you apply not more than a month and not less than two days in advance, by sending a fax with your name, your home address, your Rome address, and your preferred date of audience, to the Prefettura della Casa Pontificia (☏06.6988.3273, 🖷06.6988.5863). Finally, if you want to send a postcard with a Vatican postmark, there are Vatican **post offices** on the north side of Piazza San Pietro and inside the Vatican Museums.

Apart from entering St Peter's or the museums, you wouldn't know at any point that you had left Rome and entered the Vatican; indeed the area around it, known as the **Borgo**, holds one or two sights that are technically part of the Vatican (like Castel Sant'Angelo) but is one of the most cosmopolitan districts of Rome, full of hotels and restaurants, and scurrying tourists and pilgrims – as indeed it always has been since the king of Wessex founded the first hotel for pilgrims here in the eighth century. You may find yourself staying in one of many mid-range hotels located here, or in the neighbouring nineteenth-century district of **Prati** just to the north, although unless you're a pilgrim it's a better idea to base yourself in the more atmospheric city centre and travel back and forth on the useful bus #64. However much you try, one visit is never anywhere near enough.

Castel Sant'Angelo and around

The best route to the Vatican and St Peter's is across **Ponte Sant'Angelo**, flanked by angels carved to designs by Bernini (his so-called "breezy maniacs"). On the far side is the great circular hulk of the **Castel Sant'Angelo** (Tues–Sun 9am–8pm; €6.50 free guided tours in English Sat & Sun 4:30pm), designed and built by the emperor Hadrian as his own mausoleum (his ashes were interred here until a twelfth-century pope appropriated the sarcophagus, which was later destroyed in a fire). It was a grand monument, faced with white marble and surrounded with statues and topped with cypresses, similar in style to Augustus's mausoleum across the river. It was renamed in the sixth century, when Pope Gregory the Great witnessed a vision of St Michael here that ended a terrible plague. The mausoleum's position near the Vatican was not lost on the papal authorities, who converted the building for use as a fortress and built a passageway to link it with the Vatican as a refuge in times of siege or invasion – a route utilized on a number of occasions, most notably when the Medici pope, Clement VII, sheltered here for several months during the Sack of Rome in 1527.

Inside, from the monumental entrance hall, a spiral ramp leads up into the centre of the mausoleum itself, passing through the chamber where the emperor was entombed, over a drawbridge, one of the defensive modifications made by the Borgia pope, Alexander VI, in the late fifteenth century, to the main level at the top, where a small palace was built to house the papal residents in appropriate splendour. After the Sack of Rome, Pope Paul III had some especially fine renovations made, including the beautiful *Sala Paolina*, which features frescoes by Pierno del Vaga, among others. The gilded ceiling here displays the Farnese family arms, and on the wall is a trompe-l'oeil fresco of one of the family's old retainers, whose name is unknown, coming through a door from a darkened room. You'll also notice Paul III's personal motto, *Festina Lente* ("make haste slowly"), scattered throughout the ceilings and in various corners of all his rooms. Elsewhere, rooms hold swords, armour, guns and the like; others are lavishly decorated with grotesques and paintings (don't miss the bathroom of Clement VII on the second floor, with its prototype hot and cold water taps and mildly erotic frescoes). Below are dungeons and storerooms (not visitable), which can be glimpsed from the spiralling ramp, testament to the castle's grisly past as the city's most notorious Renaissance prison – Benvenuto Cellini and Cesare Borgia are just two of its more famous

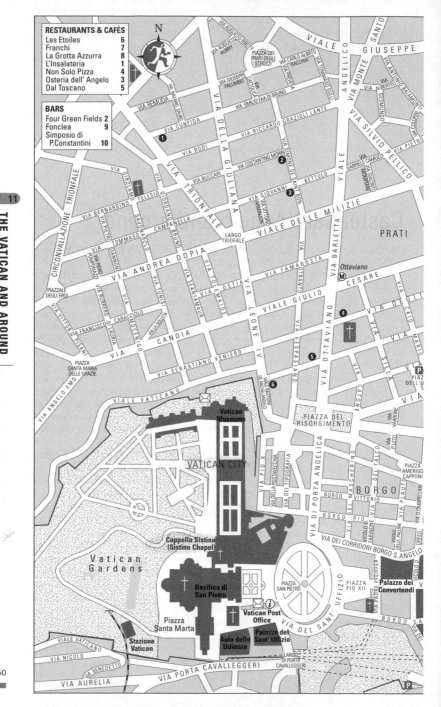

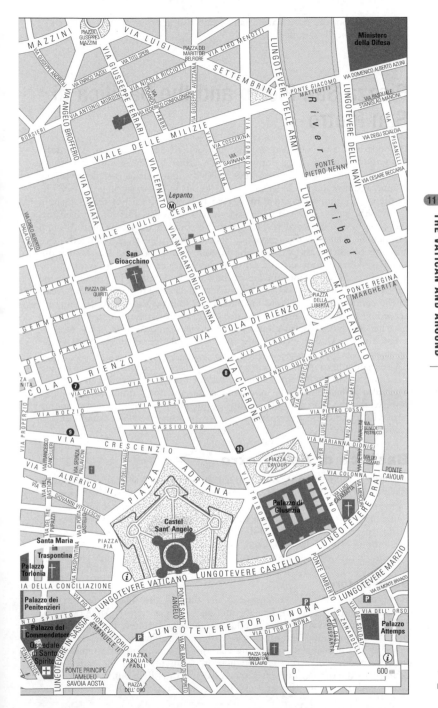

detainees. From the quiet bar upstairs you'll also get one of the best views of Rome and excellent coffee.

Piazza San Pietro and the Basilica di San Pietro

Beyond the Castel Sant'Angelo, the approach to St Peter's – on **Via della Conciliazione** – is disappointing: typically, Mussolini swept away the houses of the previously narrow street and replaced them with this wide, sweeping avenue, and nowadays St Peter's somehow looms too near as you get closer. The vastness of Bernini's **Piazza San Pietro** is, however, still not really apparent until you're right on top of it. In fact, in tune with the spirit of the Baroque, the church was supposed to be even better hidden than it is now: Bernini planned to complete the colonnade with a triumphal arch linking the two arms, so obscuring the view until you were well inside the square, but this was never carried out and the arms of the piazza remain open, symbolically welcoming the world into the lap of the Catholic Church. The obelisk in the centre was brought to Rome by Caligula in 36 AD, and it stood for many years in the centre of Nero's Circus on the Vatican Hill (to the left of the church); according to legend, it marked the site of St Peter's martyrdom. It was moved here in 1586, when Sixtus V ordered that it be erected in front of the basilica, a task that took four months and was apparently done in silence, on pain of death.

The matching fountains on either side are the work of Carlo Maderno (on the right) and Bernini (on the left). In between the obelisk and each fountain, a circular stone set into the pavement marks the focal points of an ellipse, from which the four rows of columns on the perimeter of the piazza line up perfectly, making the colonnade appear to be supported by a single line of columns.

Basilica di San Pietro

The piazza is so grand that you can't help but feel a little let down by the **Basilica di San Pietro**, better known to many as St Peter's (daily: summer 7am–7pm; winter 7am–6pm), its facade – by no means the church's best feature – obscuring the dome that signals the building from just about everywhere else in the city. Amid a controversy similar to that surrounding the restoration of the Sistine Chapel a few years ago, the facade has also recently been restored, leaving the previously sober travertine facade a decidedly yellowish grey.

Some history

Built to a plan initially conceived at the turn of the fifteenth century by Bramante and finished off, heavily modified, over a century later by Carlo Maderno, St Peter's is a strange hotchpotch of styles, bridging the gap between the Renaissance and Baroque eras with varying levels of success. It is, however, the principal shrine of the Catholic Church, built as a replacement for the rundown structure erected here by Constantine in the early fourth century on the site of St Peter's tomb. As such it can't help but impress, having been worked on by the greatest Italian architects of the sixteenth and seventeenth centuries, and occupying a site rich with historical significance. In size, certainly, St Peter's beats most other churches hands down (although it's not officially the largest in terms of area – that honour belongs to the Basilica of Our Lady of Peace, Côte d'Ivoire). Bramante had originally conceived a Greek cross plan rising to a high central dome, but this plan was altered after his death and revived only with the (by then) very elderly Michelangelo's accession as chief architect. Michelangelo was largely responsible for the dome, but he too died shortly afterwards, in 1564, before it was completed. He was succeeded by Vignola, and the dome was completed in 1590 by Giacomo della Porta. Carlo Maderno, under orders from Pope Paul V, took over in 1605, and stretched the church into a Latin cross plan, which had the practical advantage of accommodating more people and followed more directly the plan of Constantine's original basilica. But in so doing he completely unbalanced all the previous designs, not least by obscuring the dome (which he also modified) from view in the piazza. The inside, too, is very much of the Baroque era, largely the work of Bernini, who created many of the most important fixtures. The church was finally completed and reconsecrated on November 18, 1626, exactly 1300 years to the day after the original basilica was first consecrated.

Inside St Peter's

You need to be properly dressed to enter St Peter's, which means no bare knees or shoulders – a rule that is very strictly enforced. Inside on the right is Michelangelo's other legacy to the church, his **Pietà**, completed at the opposite end of his career when he was just 24. Following an attack by a vandal a few years back, it sits behind glass, strangely remote from the life of the rest of the building. When you look at the piece, its fame comes as no surprise: it's a sensitive and individual work, and an adept one too, draping the limp body of a grown man across the legs of a woman with grace and ease. Though you're much too far away to read it, etched into the strap across Mary's chest are words proclaiming the work as Michelangelo's – the only piece ever signed by the sculptor and apparently done after he heard his work, which had been placed in Constantine's basilica, had been misattributed by onlookers. You can see it properly on the plaster cast of the statue in the Pinacoteca of the Vatican Museums.

As you walk down the **nave**, the size of the building becomes more apparent – and not just because of the bronze plaques set in the floor that make comparisons with the sizes of other churches. For the record, the length of the nave is 186m from the door sill to the back of the apse; the width at the crossing is 137m, and of the nave at its narrowest part 60m. In the north transept is the wonderful gilded Baroque **Chapel of the Blessed Sacrament**, designed by Borromini with work by Pietro da Cortona, Domenichino and Bernini. This chapel is not open to the casual sightseer but it is worthy of a visit, which can be managed if you go there to pray along with the clergy, who maintain a vigil there during the time the basilica is open.

The **dome** is breathtakingly imposing, rising high above the supposed site of St Peter's tomb. With a diameter of 44m it is only 1.5m smaller than the Pantheon (the letters of the inscription inside its lower level are nearly 2m high); it is supported by four enormous piers, decorated with reliefs depicting the basilica's so-called "**major relics**": St Veronica's handkerchief, which was used to wipe the face of Christ, and is adorned with his miraculous image; the lance of St Longinus, which pierced Christ's side; and a piece of the True Cross, in the pier of St Helen (the head of St Andrew, which was returned to the

Eastern Church by Pope Paul VI in 1966, was also formerly kept here). On the right side of the nave, near the pier of St Longinus, the bronze statue of **St Peter** is another of the most venerated monuments in the basilica, carved in the thirteenth century by Arnolfo di Cambio and with its right foot polished smooth by the attentions of pilgrims. On holy days this statue is dressed in papal tiara and vestments.

Bronze was also the material used in Bernini's **baldacchino**, the centrepiece of the sculptor's Baroque embellishment of the interior, a massive 26m high (the height, apparently, of Palazzo Farnese), cast out of 927 tonnes of metal removed from the Pantheon roof in 1633. To modern eyes, it's an almost grotesque piece of work, with its wild spiralling columns copied from columns in the Constantine basilica. But it has the odd personal touch, not least in the female faces expressing the agony of childbirth and a beaming baby carved on the plinths – said to be done for a niece of Bernini's patron (Urban VIII), who gave birth at the same time as the sculptor was finishing the piece.

Bernini's feverish sculpting decorates the apse, too, his bronze **Cattedra** enclosing the supposed (though doubtful) chair of St Peter in a curvy marble and stucco throne, surrounded by the doctors of the Church (the two with bishops' mitres are St Augustine of Hippo and St Ambrose, representing the Western Church; the two to the rear are portraits of St John Chrysostom and St Athanasius of the Eastern Church). Puffs of cloud surrounding the alabaster window displaying the dove of the Holy Spirit (whose wingspan, incidentally, is 2m) burst through brilliant gilded sunbeams. On the right, the **tomb of Urban VIII**, also by Bernini, is less grand but more dignified. On the left, the **tomb of Paul III**, by Giacomo della Porta, was moved up and down the nave of the church before it was finally placed here as a counter to that of Urban VIII. More interesting is Bernini's **monument to Alexander VII** in the south transept, with its winged skeleton struggling underneath the heavy marble drapes, upon which the Chigi pope is kneeling in prayer. The grim reaper significantly clutches an hourglass – the Baroque at its most melodramatic, and symbolic. On the left sits *Charity*, on the right, *Truth Revealed in Time*; to the rear are *Hope* and *Faith*.

There are innumerable other tombs and works of art in the basilica, and you could spend days here if you tried to inspect each one. Further down the south transept, on the east side of the crossing is an enormous **mosaic** of Raphael's *Transfiguration*, significantly larger than the original painting – which is in the Vatican Pinacoteca (oil paintings would be ruined by the dampness caused by the high water table under St Peter's). Under the next to last arch in the south transept is Antonio Pollaiuolo's tomb of the

---

St Peter's tomb

The baldacchino and confessio just in front are supposed to mark the exact spot of the **tomb of St Peter**, and excavations earlier this century did indeed turn up – directly beneath the baldacchino and the remains of Constantine's basilica – a row of Roman tombs with inscriptions confirming that the Vatican Hill was a well-known burial ground in classical times. Whether the tomb of St Peter was found is less clear: a shrine was discovered, badly damaged, that agrees with some historical descriptions of the saint's marker, with a space in it through which ancient pilgrims placed their heads in prayer. Close by, the bones of an elderly but physically fit man were discovered and later claimed as the relics of the Apostle, although speculation ever since has been rife. It is possible to take an English-language tour of the Vatican necropolis; contact the Vatican Information Office (see p.148) for details.

late-fifteenth-century pope, **Innocent VIII** – banker to Queen Isabella of Spain and financier of Columbus's voyage to the New World – which is the only tomb to survive from the Constantinian basilica. In the upper statue of the monument the pope holds what looks like a mason's trowel but is in fact the spearpoint of Longinus, given to him by the Ottoman sultan Bajazet II to persuade him to keep the sultan's brother and rival in exile in Rome. In the last arch of the south transept is an austere monument by Canova depicting the last of the **Stuart pretenders** to the English throne. Over the door to the lift is the monument to **Clementina Sobieska**, the wife of James III (Stuart pretender to the English throne) – one of only three women buried in St Peter's.

The Treasury

An entrance off the aisle leads to the steeply priced **Treasury** (daily: summer 9am–6pm; winter 9am–5pm; €4). Along with more recent additions, this holds artefacts from the earlier church: a spiral column (the other survivors form part of the colonnade around the interior of the dome); a wall-mounted tabernacle by Donatello; a rich blue-and-gold dalmatic that is said once to have belonged to Charlemagne (though this has since been called into question); the vestments and tiara for the bronze statue of St Peter in the nave of the basilica; and the massive, though fairly ghastly, late-fifteenth-century bronze tomb of Sixtus IV by Pollaiuolo – said to be a very accurate portrait.

The Grottoes

Back at the central crossing, steps lead down under Bernini's statue of St Longinus to the **Grottoes** (daily: summer 8am–6pm; winter 7am–5pm), where a good number of popes are buried, though to be honest none is particularly interesting.

Ascending to the roof and dome

Far better is the **ascent to the roof and dome** (daily: May–Sept 8am–6pm; Oct–April 8am–5pm; €5 with lift, €4 using the stairs); the entrance is in the northern courtyard between the church and the Vatican Palace, on your way out as you exit through the crypt. You'll probably need to queue and, even with the lift, it's a long climb up a narrow stairway that spirals up the dome. The views from the gallery around the interior of the dome give you a sense of the enormity of the church. From there, the roof grants views from behind the huge statues onto the piazza below, before the ascent to the lantern at the top of the dome, from which the views over the city are as glorious as you'd expect. Remember that it is over three hundred fairly claustrophobic steps through the double shell of the dome to reach the lantern; indeed you should probably give it a miss if you're either in ill health or uneasy with heights or confined spaces.

The Vatican Museums

A fifteen-minute walk out of the northern side of the piazza takes you up to the only part of the Vatican Palace you can visit independently, the **Vatican Museums**, at Viale Vaticano 13 – quite simply, the largest, richest, most compelling and perhaps most exhausting museum complex in the world (Dec–March Mon–Sat 8.45am–12.45pm, last exit 1.45pm; rest of year Mon–Sat 8.45am–3.45pm, last exit 4.45pm; €12, reduced rate €8. Closed Sun, hols and religious holidays, except the last Sunday of each month when admission is free; Ⓦwww.vatican.va provides up-to-date info on what's open, what's closed, etc). If you have found any of Rome's other museums

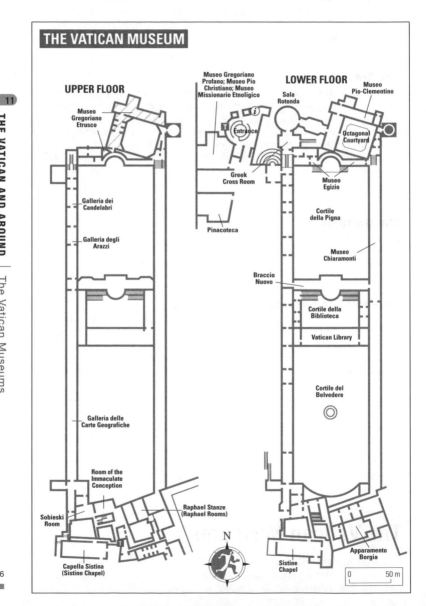

The museums' layout

The Vatican Museums are composed of four principal structures: the **Vatican Palace** itself, at the end nearest St Peter's, the oldest part of the complex; the **Belvedere Palace** to the north, constructed in the late 1400s by Pope Innocent VIII, as a summer casino amidst the meadows that in those days surrounded this part of the city (and from which the modern neighbourhood, Prati, – "pastures" – gets its name); and the two long **galleries** built in the 1500s to make passage between the two palaces easier.

In the middle of all this are three **courtyards**: the **Cortile del Belvedere** at the southern end, the small **Cortile della Biblioteca** in the middle, created by the construction of the Vatican Library and Braccio Nuovo and, the northernmost of the three, the **Cortile della Pigna** – named after the huge bronze pine cone ("pigna" in Italian) mounted in the niche at the end, an ancient Roman artefact that was found close to the Pantheon. In classical times this was a fountain with water pouring out of each of its points. Also in this courtyard is a large modern bronze sculpture of a sphere within a sphere, which occasionally rotates – though to an erratic schedule. If you're on a guided tour, you'll stop here to be talked through the Sistine Chapel paintings before going in, as it's forbidden to speak inside. Even if you're not, it can be worth listening in, if there's one being given in English, but be discreet.

The old **main entrance** to the museums was created by Pope Pius XI, in 1932, and its huge bronze spiral staircase, the work of one Giuseppe Momo, made a fittingly monumental prelude to the ticket offices above. On it are displayed the heraldic arms of all the popes from 1447 (Nicholas II) to Pius XI's predecessor (Benedict XV), while the staircase is in the form of a double helix, one half ascending, the other descending – an idea that Frank Lloyd Wright copied when designing the Guggenheim in New York. Sadly, perhaps, the museum entrance has recently been updated and restructured, and you now enter through a door in the bastion wall to the left of Pius XI's monumental entrance – through a large hall and a new monumental marble staircase. An escalator carries you up to the actual museum.

One final thing: bear in mind that the collections of the Vatican Museums are in a constant state of restoration, and are often closed and shifted around with little or no notice. The most important departments are usually open but don't be surprised if some things are off limits or in a different position to the one given in our account; again the website can help with this.

disappointing, the Vatican is probably the reason why: so much booty from the city's history has ended up here, from both classical and later times, and so many of the Renaissance's finest artists were in the employ of the pope, that not surprisingly the result is a set of museums so stuffed with antiquities as to put most other European collections to shame.

As its name suggests, the complex actually holds a collection of museums on very diverse subjects – displays of classical statuary, Renaissance painting, Etruscan relics, Egyptian artefacts, not to mention the furnishings and decoration of the palace itself. There's no point in trying to see everything, at least not on one visit. Once inside, you have a choice of official **routes**, but the only features you really shouldn't miss are the Raphael Stanze and the Sistine Chapel. Above all, decide how long you want to spend here, and what you want to see, before you start; you could spend anything from 45 minutes to the better part of a day here, and it's easy to collapse from museum fatigue before you've even got to your most important target of interest. Be conservative – the distances between different sections alone can be vast and very tiring.

Museo Pio-Clementino

To the left of the entrance, the small **Museo Pio-Clementino** and its octagonal courtyard is home to some of the best of the Vatican's **classical statuary**, including two statues that influenced Renaissance artists more than any others – the serene *Apollo Belvedere*, a Roman copy of a fourth-century BC original, and the first-century BC *Laocoön*. The latter was discovered near Nero's Golden House in 1506 by a ploughman who had inadvertently dug through the roof of a buried part of Trajan's Baths. It depicts the prophetic Trojan priest being crushed with his sons by serpents sent to punish him for warning his fellow citizens of the danger of the Trojan horse. It is perhaps the most famous classical statue ever, referred to by Pliny who thought it carved from a single piece of marble, and written about by Byron – who described its contorted realism as "dignifying pain". It was restored by Michelangelo, who replaced the missing right arm – since in turn replaced by the original, which was found in the 1950s.

Also in the museum, the frescoed Hall of the Muses has as its centrepiece the so-called *Belvedere Torso*, which was found in the Campo de' Fiori during the reign of Julius II. It's signed by one Apollonius the son of Nestor, a Greek sculptor of the first century BC, and is generally thought to be a near-perfect example of male anatomy. Its portrayal, either of Hercules sitting on his lion skin or Ajax resting, was studied by most key Renaissance artists, including Michelangelo, who incorporated its turning pose as Christ's in the *Last Judgement* in the Sistine Chapel.

The Sala Rotonda

A brief corridor leads next to the **Sala Rotonda**, whose floor is paved with a second-century AD Roman mosaic from the town of Otricoli, north of Rome, depicting battles between men and sea monsters. There is more classical statuary around the room, notably a huge gilded bronze statue of a rather dim-witted looking Hercules also from the second century AD, the only surviving gilded bronze statue on display in the Vatican Museums. Each side of the statue are busts of the emperor Hadrian and his lover, Antinous – who is also depicted in the same room as a huge statue dressed as Bacchus. There is also a beautiful white marble statue of Claudius, in the guise of Jupiter, with his oak leaf crown and an eagle.

The Greek Cross Room

Beyond here, the **Greek Cross Room** is decorated in Egyptian style, although the pharaonic statues flanking the entry door are nineteenth-century imitations. There's another Roman mosaic, showing the phases of the moon, from the second century AD, and two huge porphyry boxes – the sarcophagi of queens Helen and Costanza. On Helen's, soldiers vanquish their enemies, a reference to the fact that she was the mother of Constantine, while that of Costanza, the daughter of the emperor, shows putti carrying grapes, loaves of bread and lambs – a reference to the eucharist, as she was a devout Christian. Look behind the sarcophagus, on the left, at the lifesize statue of a striding woman – believed to be the only surviving likeness of Cleopatra.

Museo Gregoriano Egizio

The **Museo Gregoriano Egizio**, founded in the nineteenth century by Gregory XVI, isn't one of the Vatican's main highlights. But this says more

△ Piazza San Pietro

about the rest of the Vatican than the museum, which has a distinguished collection of ancient Egyptian artefacts. It holds some vividly painted mummy cases (and two mummies), along with *canopi*, the alabaster vessels into which the entrails of the deceased were placed. There is also a partial reconstruction of the Temple of Serapis from Hadrian's Villa near Tivoli, along with another statue of his lover, Antinous, who drowned close to the original temple in Egypt and so inspired Hadrian to build his replica. The Egyptian-style statues in shiny black basalt next door to the mummies were also found in Tivoli, and are also Roman imitations, although Hadrian collected some original Egyptian bits and pieces, too, some of which are housed in the room which curves around the niche containing the pine cone – various Egyptian deities including the laughing fat ogre, Bes. The next rooms contain Egyptian bronzes from the late pharaonic period and early days of the Roman Empire, including a group of items from the cult of Isis which became popular in Rome itself. There is also, beyond here, a series of rooms with clay tablets inscribed in cuneiform writing from Mesopotamia, and Assyrian, Sumerian and Persian bas-reliefs on stone tablets.

Museo Gregoriano Etrusco

Past the entrance to the Egyptian Museum a grand staircase, the Simonetti Stairs, leads up to the **Museo Gregoriano Etrusco**, which holds sculpture, funerary art and applied art from the sites of southern Etruria – a good complement to Rome's specialist Etruscan collection in the Villa Giulia, although you have to be keen on the Etruscans to visit both. Especially worth seeing are the finds from the Regolini-Galassi tomb, from the seventh century BC, discovered near Cerveteri, which contained the remains of three Etruscan nobles, two men and a woman; the breastplate of the woman and her huge *fibula* (clasp) are of gold. Take a look at the small ducks and lions with which they are decorated, fashioned in the almost microscopic beadwork for which Etruscan goldsmiths were famous. There's also armour, a bronze bedstead, a funeral chariot and a wagon, as well as a great number of enormous storage jars, in which food, oil and wine were contained for use in the afterlife.

Beyond here are Etruscan bronzes, including weapons, candelabra, barbecue sets (skewers and braziers); beautiful women's makeup cases known as *cistae*, and, most notably, the so-called *Mars of Todi*, a three-quarters lifesize votive statue found in the Umbrian town of Todi. On a flap of the figure's armour an inscription gives the name of the donor. Further on, there is a large collection of Etruscan sarcophagi and stone statuary from Vulci, Tarquinia and Tuscania in northern Lazio. Particularly interesting here are the finely carved horses' heads from Vulci and the sarcophagus of a magistrate from Tarquinia which still bears traces of the paint its reliefs were coloured with. There are also two rooms of Etruscan jewellery, with exquisite goldsmith work, crowns of golden oak and laurel leaves, necklaces, earrings and rings set with semiprecious stones and a *fibula* complete with the owner's name etched on it in such small writing that a magnifying glass is provided for you to read it.

If you haven't had your fill of the Etruscans by now, go back downstairs to see another huge collection, housed in a series of large rooms on the north side of the Belvedere Palace which offer stunning views of Monte Mario, and comprising lots of vases, assorted weapons and items of everyday household use, and a magnificent terracotta statue of Adonis melodramatically lying on a lacy couch, found near the town of Tuscania in the 1950s. Finally, don't miss the Greek *krater*, among a lot of Greek pottery found in Etruscan tombs, which shows Menelaus and Ulysses asking the Trojans for the return of Helen. It's housed in a special display case and can be rotated by pressing the electrical switch on the bottom of the case.

The Galleria dei Candelabri and Galleria degli Arazzi

Outside the Etruscan Museum, a large monumental staircase leads back down to the main route, taking you first through the **Galleria dei Candelabri**, the niches of which are adorned with huge candelabra taken from imperial Roman villas. This gallery is also stuffed with ancient sculpture, its most memorable piece being a copy of the famous statue of *Diana of Ephesus*, whose multiple breasts are, according to the Vatican official line, in fact bees' eggs. Beyond here the **Galleria degli Arazzi** (Tapestries) has on the left Belgian tapestries to designs by the school of Raphael which show scenes from the life of Christ, and on the right tapestries made in Rome at the Barberini workshops during the 1600s, showing scenes from the life of Maffeo Barberini, who became Pope Urban VIII.

The Galleria delle Carte Geografiche and Hall of the Immaculate Conception

Next, the **Galleria delle Carte Geografiche** (Maps), which is as long (175m) as the previous two galleries put together, was decorated in the late sixteenth century at the behest of Pope Gregory XIII, the reformer of the calendar, to show all of Italy, the major islands in the Mediterranean, the papal possessions in France, as well as the Siege of Malta, the Battle of Lepanto and large-scale maps of the maritime republics of Venice and Genoa. This gallery is considered by many to be the most beautiful in the entire Vatican Museums, and its ceiling frescoes, illustrating scenes that took place in the area depicted in each adjacent map, are perhaps one reason why.

After the Gallery of the Maps, there is a hall with more tapestries, and, to the left, the **Hall of the Immaculate Conception**, which sports nineteenth-century frescoes of Pope Pius IX declaring the Doctrine of the Immaculate Conception of the Blessed Virgin Mary on December 8, 1854. From here all visitors are directed to a covered walkway suspended over the palace courtyard of the Belvedere which leads through to the Raphael Rooms.

The Raphael Stanze (Raphael Rooms)

The **Raphael Stanze** (Raphael Rooms) are, apart from the Sistine Chapel perhaps, the Vatican's greatest work of art. This set of rooms formed the private apartments of Pope Julius II, and when he moved in here he commissioned Raphael to redecorate them in a style more in tune with the times. Raphael died before the scheme was complete, but the two rooms that were completed by him, as well as others completed by pupils, stand as one of the highlights – perhaps *the* highlight – of the Renaissance.

The Stanza di Constantino

The first of the Raphael Stanze that you come to, the **Stanza di Constantino**, was not in fact done by Raphael at all, but painted in part to his designs about five years after he died, by his pupils, Giulio Romano, Francesco

Penni and Raffello del Colle, between 1525 and 1531. It shows scenes from the life of the emperor Constantine, who made Christianity the official religion of the Roman Empire. The enormous painting on the wall opposite the entrance is the *Battle of the Milvian Bridge* by Giulio Romano and Francesco Penni – a depiction of a decisive battle in 312 AD between the warring co-emperors of the West, Constantine and Maxentius. With due regard to the laws of propaganda, the victorious emperor is in the centre of the painting mounted on his white horse while the vanquished Maxentius drowns in the river to the right, clinging to his black horse. The painting to your left as you enter, the *Vision of Constantine* by Giulio Romano, shows Constantine telling his troops of his dream-vision of the Holy Cross inscribed with the legend "In this sign you will conquer". Opposite, the *Baptism of Constantine*, by Francesco Penni, is a flight of fancy – Constantine was baptized on his deathbed about thirty years after the battle of the Milvian Bridge.

The Sala dei Chiaroscuri

Beyond the Stanza di Constantine, the **Sala dei Chiaroscuri** was originally painted by Raphael, but curiously Pope Gregory XIII had those paintings removed and the room repainted in the rather gloomy style you see today – although there is a magnificent gilded and painted ceiling which bears the arms of the Medici.

The Capella di Niccolo V and Stanza di Eliodoro

A small door from here leads into the little **Capella di Niccolo V**, with wonderful frescoes by Beato Angelico painted between 1448 and 1450, showing scenes in the lives of saints Stephen and Lawrence. But the real attraction is to head straight through the souvenir shop to the **Stanza di Eliodoro**, the first of the Raphael rooms proper, in which the fresco on the right of the entrance, *The Expulsion of Heliodorus from the Temple*, tells the story of Heliodorus, the agent of the eastern king, Seleucus, who was slain by a mysterious rider on a white horse while trying to steal the treasure of Jerusalem's Temple. It's an exciting piece of work, painted in the years 1512–14 for Pope Julius II, and the figures of Heliodorus, the horseman and the flying men are adeptly done, the figures almost jumping out of the painting into the room. The group of figures on the left, however, is more interesting – Pope Julius II, in his papal robes, Giulio Romano, the pupil of Raphael, and, to his left, Raphael himself in a self-portrait

On the left wall as you enter, the *Mass of Bolsena* is a bit of anti-Lutheran propaganda, and relates a miracle that occurred in the town in northern Lazio in the 1260s, when a German priest who doubted the transubstantiation of Christ found the wafer bleeding when he broke it during a service. (The napkin onto which it bled is preserved in Orvieto's cathedral.) The pope facing the priest is another portrait of Julius II. The composition is a neat affair, the colouring rich, the onlookers kneeling, turning, gasping, as the miracle is realized. On the window wall opposite is the *Deliverance of St Peter*, showing the saint being assisted in a jail-break by the Angel of the Lord – a night scene, whose clever chiaroscuro predates Caravaggio by nearly one hundred years. It was painted by order of Pope Leo X, as an allegory of his imprisonment after a battle that took place in Ravenna a few years earlier. Finally, on the large wall opposite *The Expulsion of Heliodorus from the Temple*, there is *Leo I Repulsing Attila the Hun*, an allegory of the difficulties that the papacy was going through in the early 1500s, showing the chubby cardinal, Giovanni de' Medici, who succeeded Julius II as Leo X in 1513. Leo later had Raphael's pupils paint a portrait of himself as Leo I, so, confusingly, he appears twice in this fresco, as pope and as the equally portly Medici cardinal just behind.

The Stanza della Segnatura

The next room, the **Stanza della Segnatura** or Pope's study, is probably the best known – and with good reason. Painted in the years 1508–11, when Raphael first came to Rome, the subjects were again the choice of Julius II, and, composed with careful balance and harmony, it comes close to the peak of the painter's art. *The School of Athens*, on the near wall as you come in, steals the show, a representation of the triumph of scientific truth (to pair with the *Disputation over the Sacrament* opposite, which is a reassertion of religious dogma), in which all the great minds from antiquity are represented. Plato and Aristotle discuss philosophy at the centre of the painting: Aristotle, the father of scientific method, motions downwards; Plato, pointing upward, indicating his philosophy of otherworldly spirituality, is believed to be a portrait of Leonardo da Vinci. On the far right, the crowned figure holding a globe was meant to represent the Egyptian geographer, Ptolemy; to his right is Raphael, the young man in the black beret, while in front, demonstrating a theorem to his pupils on a slate, the figure of Euclid is a portrait of Bramante. Spread across the steps is Diogenes, lazily ignorant of all that is happening around him, while to the left Raphael added a solitary, sullen portrait of Michelangelo – a homage to the artist, apparently painted after Raphael saw the first stage of the Sistine Chapel almost next door. Other identifiable figures include the beautiful youth with blonde hair looking out of the painting, Francesco Maria della Rovere, placed here by order of Julius II. Della Rovere also appears as the good-looking young man to the left of the seated dignitaries, in the painting opposite, the *Disputation over the Sacrament*, an allegory of the Christian religion and the main element of the Mass, the Blessed Sacrament – which stands at the centre of the painting being discussed by all manner of popes, cardinals, bishops, doctors, even the poet Dante.

The Stanza Incendio

The last room, the **Stanza Incendio**, was the last to be decorated, to the orders and general glorification of Pope Leo X, and in a sense it brings together three generations of work. The ceiling was painted by Perugino, Raphael's teacher, and the frescoes were completed to Raphael's designs by his pupils (notably Giulio Romano). The most striking of them is the *Fire in the Borgo*, facing the main window – an oblique reference to Leo X restoring peace to Italy after Julius II's reign but in fact describing an event that took place during the reign of Leo IV, when the pope stood in the loggia of the old St Peter's and made the sign of the cross to extinguish a fire. As with so many of these paintings, the chronology is deliberately crazy: Leo IV is in fact a portrait of Leo X, while on the left, Aeneas carries his aged father Anchises out of the burning city of Troy, two thousand years earlier. This last Raphael Room is connected to the **Sala Sobieski**, with its nineteenth-century painting of the Polish king driving Turks out of Europe, by the small **Chapel of Urban VI**, with frescoes and stuccoes by Pietro da Cortona.

The Appartamento Borgia

Outside the Raphael Stanze, on the other side of the Sistine Chapel steps, the **Appartamento Borgia** was inhabited by Julius II's hated predecessor, Alexander VI – a fact which persuaded Julius to move into the new set of rooms he called upon Raphael to decorate. Nowadays host to a large collection of modern religious art (see below), the Borgia rooms were almost exclusively decorated by Pinturicchio in the years 1492–95, on the orders of Alexander VI. The ceiling frescoes in the Sala dei Santi are especially worth seeing, typically rich in colour and detail and depicting the legend of Osiris and the Apis bull – a reference to the Borgia family symbol. Among other images is a scene showing St Catherine of Alexandria disputing with the emperor Maximilian, in which Pinturicchio has placed his self-portrait behind the emperor – and also, clearly visible in the background, the Arch of Constantine. The figure of St Catherine is said to be a portrait of Lucrezia Borgia, and the room was reputedly the scene of a decidedly un-papal party to celebrate the first of Lucrezia's three marriages, which ended up with men tossing sweets down the fronts of the women's dresses.

The religious collection in the next forty or so rooms includes a variety of works by some of the most famous names in the **modern art** world – liturgical vestments designed by Matisse; a fascinating *Landscape with Angels* by Salvador Dalí, donated by King Juan Carlos of Spain; one of Francis Bacon's studies of Innocent X after Velázquez (a list is available at the door) – but really isn't that interesting by comparison.

The Capella Sistina (Sistine Chapel)

Steps lead up from here to the **Capella Sistina (Sistine Chapel)**, a huge barn-like structure built for Pope Sixtus IV between 1473 and 1481. It serves as the pope's official private chapel and the scene of the conclaves of cardinals for the election of each new pontiff. The ceiling paintings here, and the *Last Judgement* on the wall behind the altar, together make up arguably the greatest masterpiece in Western art, and the largest body of painting ever planned and executed by one man – Michelangelo. They are also probably the most viewed paintings in the world: it's estimated that on an average day about 15,000 people trudge through here to take a look; and during the summer and on special occasions the number of visitors can exceed 20,000. It's useful to carry a pair of binoculars with you in order to see the paintings better, but bear in mind that it is strictly forbidden to take pictures of any kind in the chapel, including video, and it is also officially forbidden to speak – although this is something that is rampantly ignored.

The wall paintings

Upon completion of the structure, Sixtus brought in several prominent painters of the Renaissance to decorate the **walls**. The overall project was under the management of Pinturicchio and comprised a series of paintings showing (on the left as you face the altar) scenes from the life of Moses and, on the right, scenes from the life of Christ. There are paintings by, among others, Perugino, who painted the marvellously composed cityscape of *Jesus giving St Peter the Keys to Heaven*, Botticelli – *The Trials of Moses* and *Cleansing of the Leper* – and Ghirlandaio, whose *Calling of St Peter and St Andrew* shows Christ calling the two fishermen to be disciples, surrounded by onlookers, against a fictitious medieval landscape of boats, birds, turrets and mountains. Some of the paintings were in fact collaborative efforts, and it's known that Ghirlandaio and Botticelli in particular contributed to each other's work. Anywhere else they would be pored over very closely indeed. As it is, they are entirely overshadowed by Michelangelo's more famous work.

When construction was completed in 1483 during the reign of Pope Sixtus IV, the Sistine Chapel ceiling was painted as a blue background with gold stars to resemble the night sky. Over the altar there were two additional paintings by Perugino and a large picture of the Virgin Mary. Sixtus IV was succeeded by Innocent VIII, who was followed by Alexander VI, the Borgia pope, who was later, in 1503, after the brief reign of Pius III, succeeded by Giuliano della Rovere, who took the name **Julius II**. Though a Franciscan friar, he was a violent man with a short temper, and his immediate objective as pope was to try to regain the lands that had been taken away from the papacy during the reigns of Innocent VIII and Alexander VI by the French, Germans and Spanish. For this purpose he started a series of wars and secret alliances.

Julius II was also an avid collector and patron of the arts, and he summoned to Rome the best artists and architects of the day. Among these artists was **Michelangelo**, who, through a series of political intrigues orchestrated by Bramante and Raphael, was assigned the task of decorating the Sistine Chapel. Work commenced in 1508. Oddly enough, Michelangelo hadn't wanted to do the work at all: he considered himself a sculptor, not a painter, and was more eager to get on with carving Julius II's tomb (now in San Pietro in Vincoli, see p.117) than the ceiling, which he regarded as a chore. Pope Julius II, however, had other plans, drawing up a design of the twelve Apostles for the vault and hiring Bramante to design a scaffold for the artist from which to work. Michelangelo was apparently an awkward, solitary character: he had barely begun painting when he rejected Bramante's scaffold as unusable, fired all his staff, and dumped the pope's scheme for the ceiling in favour of his own. But the pope was easily his match, and there are tales of the two men clashing while the work was going on Michelangelo would lock the doors at crucial points, ignoring the pope's demands to see how it was progressing; and legend has the two men at loggerheads at the top of the scaffold one day, resulting in the pope striking the artist in frustration.

The ceiling paintings

Michelangelo's **frescoes** depict scenes from the Old Testament, from the *Creation of Light* at the altar end to the *Drunkenness of Noah* over the door. The sides are decorated with prophets and sibyls and the ancestors of Jesus. Julius II lived only a few months after the Sistine Chapel ceiling was finished, but the fame of the work he had commissioned soon spread far and wide. Certainly, it's staggeringly impressive, all the more so for its recent restoration (financed by a Japanese TV company to the tune of $3 million in return for three years' world TV rights), which has lifted centuries of accumulated soot and candle grime off the ceilings to reveal a much brighter, more vivid painting than anyone thought existed. The restorers have also been able to chart the progress of Michelangelo as he moved across the vault. Images on fresco must be completed before the plaster dries, and each day a fresh layer of plaster would have been laid, on which Michelangelo would have had around eight hours or so before having to finish for the day. Comparing the different areas of plaster, it seems the figure of Adam, in the key *Creation of Adam* scene, took just four days; God, in the same fresco, took three days. You can also see the development of Michelangelo as a painter when you look at the paintings in reverse order. The first painting, over the door, the *Drunkenness of Noah*, is done in a stiff and formal style, and is vastly different from the last painting he did, over the altar, the *Creation of Light*, which shows the artist at his best, the perfect master of the technique of fresco painting.

Entering from behind the altar, you are supposed, as you look up, to imagine that you are peering into heaven through the arches of the fictive architecture

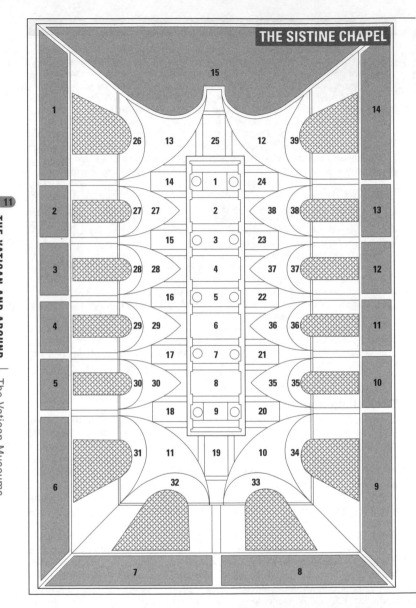

that springs from the sides of the chapel, supported by little putti caryatids and *ignudi* or nudes, bearing shields and Della Rovere oakleaf garlands. Look at the pagan sibyls and biblical prophets which Michelangelo also incorporated in his scheme – some of the most dramatic figures in the entire work, and all clearly labelled by the painter, from the sensitive figure of the Delphic Sibyl, to the hag-like Cumaean Sibyl, whose biceps would put a Bulgarian shotputter to

WALL PAINTINGS

1 Perugino
Moses' Journey into Egypt

2 Botticelli
The Trials of Moses

3 Rosselli
Crossing of the Red Sea

4 Rosselli
Moses and the Law

5 Botticelli
Punishment of the Rebels

6 Signorelli
Testament and Death of Moses

7 Matteo da Lecce
Fight over the Body of Moses

8 Arrigo Palludano
Resurrection of Christ

9 Rosselli
Last Supper

10 Perugino
*Jesus giving St Peter
the Keys of Heaven*

11 Roselli
Sermon on the Mount

12 Ghirlandaio
*Calling of St Peter
and St Andrew*

13 Botticelli
Cleansing of the Leper

14 Perugino
Baptism of Christ

15 Michelangelo
The Last Judgement

CEILING PAINTINGS

1 The Creation of Light
2 The Creation of the Sun and the Moon
3 The Separation of Land and Water
4 The Creation of Adam
5 The Creation of Eve
6 The Temptation and Expulsion from the Garden of Eden
7 The Sacrifice of Noah
8 The Story of the Flood
9 The Drunkenness of Noah

10 David and Goliath
11 Judith and Holofernes
12 The Punishment of Haman
13 The Brazen Serpent

14 The Libyan Sibyl
15 Daniel
16 The Cumaean Sibyl
17 Isaiah
18 The Delphic Sibyl
19 Zachariah

20 Joel
21 The Erythraean Sibyl
22 Ezekiel
23 The Persian Sibyl
24 Jeremiah
25 Jonah

26 Aminadab
27 Salmon, Booz, Obed
28 Rohoam, Abia
29 Ozias, Joatham, Achaz
30 Zorobabel, Abiud, Elichiam
31 Achim, Eliud
32 Jacob, Joseph
33 Eleazar, Matthan
34 Azor, Sadoch
35 Josias, Jechonias, Salathiel
36 Ezekias, Manasses, Amon
37 Asa, Josophat, Joram
38 Jesse, David, Solomon
39 Naasson

shame. Look out, too, for the figure of the prophet Jeremiah – a brooding self-portrait of an exhausted-looking Michelangelo.

We've detailed the paintings of the central panels in the chart (see above), but, specifically, they start with a large portrait of *Jonah and the Whale*, and move on, consecutively, to *God Separating Light from Darkness* – his arms bowed, beard flowing, as he pushes the two qualities apart; *God Creating the Sun, the Moon and the Planets* – in which Michelangelo has painted God twice, once with his back to us hurling the moon into existence and simultaneously displaying another moon to the audience; *God Separating Land from Water*; and, in the fourth panel, probably most famous of all these paintings, the *Creation of Adam*, in which God sparks Adam into life with the touch of his finger. God's cape billows behind him, where a number of figures stand – representatives of all the unborn generations to come after Adam. The startled young woman looking at Adam is either Eve or the Virgin Mary, here as a witness to the first events in human history.

The fifth panel from the altar shows the *Creation of Eve*, in which Adam is knocked out under the stump of a Della Rovere oak tree and God summons Eve from his side as he sleeps. She comes out in a half-crouch position with her hands clasped in a prayer of thanksgiving and awe. The sixth panel is the powerful *Temptation and Expulsion from the Garden of Eden*, with an evil spirit, depicted as a serpent, leaning out from the tree of knowledge and handing the fruit to Adam. On the right of this painting the angel of the Lord, in swirling red robes, is brandishing his sword of original sin at the nape of Adam's neck as he tries to fend the angel off, motioning with both hands. The eighth panel continues the story, with the *Story of the Flood*, and the unrighteous bulk of mankind taking shelter under tents from the rain while Noah and his kin make off for the Ark in the distance. Panel seven shows Noah and his family making a *Sacrifice of Thanksgiving* to the Lord for their safe arrival after the flood; one of the sons of Noah kneels to blow on the fire to make it hotter, while his wife brings armloads of wood. Lastly, there's the *Drunkenness of Noah* in which Noah is shown getting drunk after harvesting the vines and exposing his genitals to his sons (it is strictly prohibited in the Hebrew canon that a father should show his organs of reproduction to his children) – although oddly enough Noah's sons are naked too.

The Last Judgement

The **Last Judgement**, on the altar wall of the chapel, was painted by Michelangelo more than twenty years later, between 1535 and 1541. Michelangelo wasn't especially keen to work on this either – he was still engaged on Julius II's tomb, under threat of legal action from the late pope's family – but Pope Paul III, an old acquaintance of the artist, was keen to complete the decoration of the chapel. Michelangelo tried to delay by making demands that were likely to cause the pope to give up entirely, insisting on the removal of two paintings by Perugino and the closing of a window that pierced the end of the chapel. Furthermore, he insisted that the wall be replastered, with the top 15cm out of the perpendicular to prevent the accumulation of soot and dust.

The painting took five years, again single-handed, but it is probably the most inspired and most homogeneous large-scale painting you're ever likely to see, the technical virtuosity of Michelangelo taking a back seat to the sheer exuberance of the work. The human body is fashioned into a finely captured set of exquisite poses: even the damned can be seen as a celebration of the human form. Perhaps unsurprisingly, the painting offended some, and even before it was complete Rome was divided as to its merits, especially regarding the etiquette of introducing such a display of nudity into the pope's private chapel. But Michelangelo's response to this was unequivocal, lampooning one of his fiercer critics, the pope's master of ceremonies at the time, Biago di Cesena, as Minos, the doorkeeper of hell, with ass's ears and an entwined serpent in the bottom right-hand corner of the picture. Later the pope's zealous successor, Pius IV, objected to the painting and would have had it removed entirely had not Michelangelo's pupil, Daniele da Volterra, appeased him by carefully – and selectively – adding coverings to some of the more obviously naked figures, earning himself forever the nickname of the "breeches-maker". During the recent work, most of the remaining breeches have been discreetly removed, restoring the painting to its former glory.

Briefly, the painting shows the last day of existence, when the bodily resurrection of the dead takes place and the human race is brought before Christ to be either sent to eternity in Paradise or condemned to suffer in Hell. The centre is occupied by Christ, turning angrily as he gestures the condemned to the underworld. St Peter, carrying his gold and silver keys, looks on in astonishment at his Lord filled with rage, while Mary averts her eyes from the scene. Below Christ a group of angels blasts their trumpets to summon the dead from their sleep. Somewhat amusingly, one angel holds a large book, the book of the damned, while another carries a much smaller one, the book of the saved. On the left, the dead awaken from their graves, tombs and sarcophagi (one apparently has the likeness of Martin Luther) and are levitating into the heavens or being pulled by ropes and the napes of their necks by angels who take them before Christ. At the bottom right, Charon, keeper of the underworld, swings his oar at the damned souls as they fall off the boat into the waiting gates of hell. Among other characters portrayed are many martyred saints, the Apostles, Adam, and, peeking out between the legs of the saint on the left of Christ, Julius II, with a look of fear and astonishment.

The Library of Sixtus V

Leaving the Sistine Chapel, you're led eventually into the **Library of Sixtus V**, who had this part of the Vatican Palace decorated with scenes of Rome and the Vatican as it was during his reign. Over the doors of the corridor you can see the facade of St Peter's as it was in the late 1500s, before Maderno's extension of the nave. Over the next door you can see the erection of the obelisk outside in the Piazza San Pietro, showing the men, ropes, animals and a primitive derrick, with the obelisk being drawn forward on a sled. Otherwise, there are sometimes exhibits of books from the main Vatican Library here.

Braccio Nuovo and Museo Chiaramonti

The **Braccio Nuovo** and **Museo Chiaramonti** both hold classical sculpture, although be warned that they are the Vatican at its most overwhelming – close on a thousand statues crammed into two long galleries – and you need a keen eye and much perseverance to make any sense of it all. The **Braccio Nuovo** was built in the early 1800s to display classical statuary that was particularly prized, and it contains, among other things, probably the most famous extant image of Augustus, and a bizarre-looking statue depicting the Nile, whose yearly flooding was essential to the fertility of the Egyptian soil. It is this aspect of the river that is represented here: crawling over the hefty river god are sixteen babies, thought to allude to the number of cubits the river needed to rise to fertilize the land.

The 300-metre-long **Chiaramonti gallery** is especially unnerving, lined as it is with the chill marble busts of hundreds of nameless, blank-eyed ancient Romans, along with the odd deity. It pays to have a leisurely wander, for there are some real characters here: sour, thin-lipped matrons with their hair tortured into pleats, curls and spirals; kids, caught in a sulk or mid-chortle; and ancient old men with flesh sagging and wrinkling to reveal the skull beneath. Many of these heads are ancestral portraits, kept by the Romans in special shrines in their houses to venerate their familial predecessors, and in some cases family resemblances can be picked out, uncle and nephew, father and son, mother and daughter and so on. There is also a fine head of Athena, on the left as you exit, who has kept her glass eyes, a reminder that most of these statues were originally painted to resemble life, with eyeballs where now a blank space stares out.

The Pinacoteca

The **Pinacoteca** is housed in a separate building on the far side of the Vatican's main spine and ranks possibly as Rome's best picture gallery, with works from the early to High Renaissance right up to the nineteenth century.

Among early works, there are pieces by Crivelli, Lippi and the stunning Simoneschi triptych by Giotto of the *Martyrdom of SS Peter and Paul*, painted in the early 1300s for the old St Peter's, where it remained until 1506 when it was removed for the rebuilding of the new church. Beyond the rich backdrops and elegantly clad figures of the Umbrian School painters, Perugino and Pinturicchio, Raphael has a room to himself, including three very important oil paintings, and, in climate-controlled glass cases, the tapestries that were made to his designs to be hung in the Sistine Chapel during conclave. (The cartoons from which these tapestries were made are now in the Victoria and Albert Museum in London.) Of the three paintings, there is the *Transfiguration*, which he had nearly completed when he died in 1520, and which was finished by his pupils; the *Coronation of the Virgin*, done when he was only 19 years old; and, on the left, the *Madonna of Foglino*, showing saints John the Baptist, Francis of Assisi, and Jerome – painted as an offering from the donor for his life being spared after his house was struck by a cannonball (seen flying into the house in the centre of the painting).

Leonardo's *St Jerome*, in the next room, is unfinished, too, but it's a remarkable piece of work, with Jerome a rake-like ascetic torn between suffering and a good meal. Look closely at this painting and you can see that a 25cm square, the saint's head, has been reglued to the canvas after the painting was used as upholstery for a stool in a cobbler's shop in Rome for a number of years. Caravaggio's *Descent from the Cross* in the next room but one, however, gets more attention, a warts 'n' all canvas that unusually shows the Virgin Mary as a middle-aged mother grieving over her dead son, while the men placing Christ's body on the bier are obviously models that the artist recruited from the city streets – a realism that is imitated successfully by Reni's *Crucifixion of St Peter* in the same room. Take a look also at the most gruesome painting in the collection, Poussin's *Martyrdom of St Erasmus*, which shows the saint stretched out on a table with his hands bound above his head in the process of having his small intestine wound onto a drum – basically being "drawn" prior to "quartering".

The Musei Gregoriano Profano, Pio Cristiano and Missionario Etnologico

Leaving the Pinacoteca, you're well placed for the further grouping of museums in the modern building next door. The **Museo Gregoriano Profano** holds more classical sculpture, mounted on scaffolds for all-round viewing, including mosaics of athletes from the Baths of Caracalla and Roman funerary work, notably the Haterii tomb friezes, which show backdrops of ancient Rome and realistic portrayals of contemporary life. It's thought the Haterii were a family of construction workers and that they grabbed the opportunity to advertise their services by incorporating reliefs of the buildings they had worked on (including the Colosseum), along with a natty little crane, on the funeral monument of one of their female members.

The adjacent **Museo Pio Cristiano** has intricate early Christian sarcophagi and, most famously, an expressive third-century AD statue of the *Good Shepherd*. And the **Museo Missionario Etnologico** displays art and artefacts from all over the world, collected by Catholic missionaries, and seems to be inspired by the Vatican's desire to poke fun at non-Christian cults as well as pat itself on the back for its own evangelical successes.

Out from the city

You may find there's quite enough of interest in Rome to keep you occupied during your stay. But it can be a hot, oppressive city, its surfeit of churches and museums sometimes intensely wearying, and if you're around long enough you really shouldn't feel any guilt about freeing yourself from its weighty history to see something of the countryside around. Two of the main attractions visitable on a day-trip are, admittedly, ancient Roman sites, but just the process of getting to them can be energizing. And there are other attractions further afield that may even tempt you to stay overnight – though to visit the places we've included here this isn't necessary. **Tivoli**, about an hour by bus east of Rome, is a small provincial town famous for the travertine quarries nearby and also for two villas – one Renaissance, one Roman, both of them complete with landscaped gardens and parks. **Ostia**, in the opposite direction from the city near the sea, and similarly easy to reach on public transport, is the city's main seaside resort (though one worth avoiding), but was also the site of the port of Rome in classical times, the ruins of which – **Ostia Antica** – are well preserved and worth seeing. North of Rome, the Etruscan site of **Cerveteri** is an atmospheric alternative to the archeology of the city itself, while **Bracciano** has the airy location on its lake and the appeal of an Italian provincial town to lure you. South of Rome, the **Castelli Romani** provide the closest and most appealing stretch of countryside close to Rome; and the coastal towns of **Anzio and Nettuno** its most accessible seaside resorts.

Tivoli

Just 40km from Rome, perched high on a hill and looking back over the plain, **TIVOLI** has always been something of a retreat from the city, due to its fresh mountain air and pleasant position on the Aniene River. In classical days it was a retirement town for wealthy Romans; later, during Renaissance times, it again became the playground of the moneyed classes, attracting some of the city's most well-to-do families out here to build villas. Nowadays the leisured classes have mostly gone, but Tivoli does very nicely on the fruits of its still-thriving travertine business, exporting the precious stone worldwide (the quarries line the main road into town from Rome), and supports a small airy centre that preserves a number of relics from its ritzier days. To do justice to the gardens and villas – especially if Villa Adriana is on your list – you'll need time; set out *early*.

Rome's nearest **beach** is at **Lido di Ostia**, half an hour away by train, and this is where the tourist board will try to point you. However, as you'll see from the account on p.177, it's not the best place to head for. The beaches on the road **south from Ostia** towards Torvaianica and Capocotta have recently been cleaned up and can be a bit quieter; to get there, take the Ostia train to the Cristoforo Colombo stop, then take bus #071 or #061. Also, if you're making a day of it, it's worth travelling south to **Anzio** or **Nettuno** – an hour away by frequent train from Termini (every hour), where you'll find clean, if fairly crowded, beaches – and, in Anzio, a nice selection of seafood restaurants.

Villa d'Este

Most people head first for **Villa d'Este** (summer daily 9am–1hr before sunset; winter Tues–Sun 9am–1hr before sunset; €9), across the main square of Largo Garibaldi – the country villa of Cardinal Ippolito d'Este that was transformed from a convent by Pirro Ligorio in 1550 and is now often thronged with visitors even outside peak season. The villa itself is worth a visit. It has been recently restored to its original state with beautiful Mannerist frescoes in its seven rooms showing scenes from the history of the d'Este family in Tivoli. But it's the garden that most people come to see, peeling away down the hill in a succession of terraces: probably the most contrived garden in Italy, but also the most ingenious, almost completely symmetrical, its carefully tended lawns, shrubs and hedges interrupted at decent intervals by one playful fountain after another. In their day some of these were quite amazing – one was a water organ, the air for the pipes being forced by water valves, another imitated the call of birds – though nowadays the emphasis is on the quieter creations. Newly restored and once again fully open to the public, they're collectively unique and a must-see if you're in Tivoli; just make sure that you don't *touch or drink* the water in the fountains – it comes directly from the operating sewers of Tivoli.

Among the fountains, the central, almost Gaudí-like Fontana del Bicchierone, by Bernini, is one of the simplest and most elegant; on the far left, the Rometta or "Little Rome" has reproductions of the city's major buildings and a boat holding an obelisk; while perhaps the best is the Fontana dell'Ovato on the opposite side of the garden, fringed with statues, behind which is a rather dank arcade, in which you can walk.

Villa Gregoriana

The downside of Villa d'Este being open again is that it's the turn of Tivoli's other main attraction, the **Villa Gregoriana**, to be closed for restoration. However, this park with waterfalls – created when Pope Gregory XVI diverted the flow of the river here to ease the periodic flooding of the town in 1831 – is at least as interesting and beautiful, but in a very different way. Less well known and less visited than the d'Este estate, it has none of the latter's conceits – its vegetation is lush and overgrown, descending into a gashed-out gorge over 60m deep.

There are two main waterfalls – the larger Grande Cascata on the far side, and a small Bernini-designed one at the neck of the gorge. The path winds down to the bottom of the canyon, passing ruined Roman resting pavilions and scales the drop on the other side past two grottoes, where you can get right up close to the

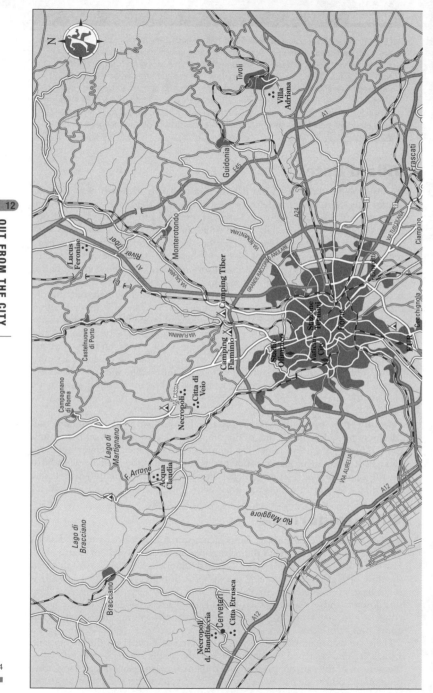

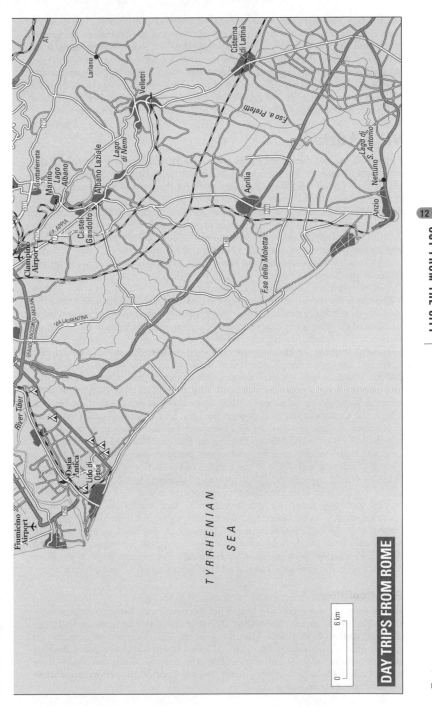

TYRRHENIAN SEA

DAY TRIPS FROM ROME

0 _____ 6 km

roaring falls. The dark, torn shapes of the rock glower overhead. It's harder work than the Villa d'Este – if you blithely saunter down to the bottom of the gorge, you'll find that it's a long way back up the other side – but it is in many ways more rewarding; the path leads up on the far side to an exit and the substantial remains of a **Temple of Vesta**, which you'll have seen clinging to the side of the hill. This is now incorporated into the gardens of a restaurant, but it's all right to walk through and take a look, and the view is probably Tivoli's best – down into the chasm and across to the high green hills that ring the town.

Villa Adriana

Once you've seen these two sights you've really seen Tivoli – the rest of the town is nice enough but there's not that much to it. But just outside town, at the bottom of the hill, fifteen minutes' walk off the main Rome road (ask the Rome–Tivoli bus to drop you or take the local CAT #4 from Largo Garibaldi), **Villa Adriana** (daily 9am–1hr before sunset; €6.50) casts the invention of the Tivoli popes and cardinals very much into the shade. This was probably the largest and most sumptuous villa in the Roman Empire, the retirement home of the emperor Hadrian for a short while between 135 AD and his death three years later, and it occupies an enormous site. You need time to see it all; there's no point in doing it at a gallop and, taken with the rest of Tivoli, it makes for a long day's sightseeing.

The site is one of the most soothing spots around Rome, its stones almost the epitome of romantic, civilized ruins. The imperial palace buildings proper are in fact one of the least well preserved parts of the complex, but much else is clearly recognizable. Hadrian was a great traveller and a keen architect, and parts of the villa were inspired by buildings he had seen around the world. The massive Pecile, for instance, through which you enter, is a reproduction of a building in Athens. The Canopus, on the opposite side of the site, is a liberal copy of the sanctuary of Serapis near Alexandria, its long, elegant channel of water fringed by sporadic columns and statues leading up to a temple of Serapis at the far end.

Near the Canopus a museum displays the latest finds from the usually on-going excavations, though most of the extensive original discoveries have found their way back to Rome and many museums in Europe. Walking back towards the entrance, make your way across the upper storey of the so-called Pretorio, a former warehouse, and down to the remains of two bath complexes. Beyond is a fishpond with a *cryptoporticus* (underground passageway) winding around underneath. It is great to walk through the cryptoporticus and look up at its ceiling, picking out the names of the seventeenth- and eighteenth-century artists (Bernini, for one) who visited and wrote their signatures here using a smoking candle when before excavation the cryptoporticus was filled in to the surface level. Behind this are the relics of the emperor's imperial apartments. The Teatro Maríttimo, adjacent, with its island in the middle of a circular pond, is the place to which it's believed Hadrian would retire at siesta time to be sure of being alone.

Practicalities

Buses leave Rome for Tivoli and Villa Adriana every twenty minutes from Ponte Mammolo metro station (line B) – journey time fifty minutes. In Tivoli, the **bus station** is in Piazza Massimo near the Villa Gregoriana, though you can get off earlier, on the main square of Largo Garibaldi, where you'll find the **tourist office** (Mon 9am–3pm, Tues–Fri 9am–6.30pm, Sat 9am–3pm; ☎0774.334.522), which has free maps and information on **accommodation** if you're planning to stay over.

Ostia

There are two Ostias: one an overvisited seaside resort, the so-called **Lido di Ostia**, which is well worth avoiding; the other, one of the finest ancient Roman sites – the excavations of the port of **Ostia Antica** – which are on a par with anything you'll see in Rome itself and easily merit a half-day journey out.

Lido di Ostia

The **LIDO DI OSTIA**, reachable by overground train from Magliana metro station on line B, has for many years been the number-one seaside resort for Romans. The beaches are OK, and have recently been cleaned up, but the town is on the whole a poor outpost of the city, with little, if anything, to recommend it – you're probably better off making the slightly longer journey to Anzio or Nettuno if you want to swim (see p.184). If you do come here, the water is most inviting along the coastal road between Ostia and Torvaianica, and there are nudist areas around the 8 or 9km marker.

Ostia Antica

The stop before Lido di Ostia on the train from Rome, the site of **OSTIA ANTICA** marked the coastline in classical times, and the town which grew up here was the port of ancient Rome, a thriving place whose commercial activities were vital to the city further upstream – until they were curtailed by the silting up of the harbour. The **excavations** (Tues–Sun 9am–1hr before sunset; €4) remain relatively unvisited; indeed until the 1970s the site was only open one day a week and few people realized how well the port had been preserved by the Tiber's mud. Still relatively free of the bustle of tourists, it's an evocative site, and it's much easier to reconstruct a Roman town from this than from any amount of pottering around the Forum – or even Pompeii. It's also very spread out, so be prepared for a fair amount of walking; and carry some water, so as to avoid the rather pricey snack bar in the back of the museum.

From the entrance, the **Decumanus Maximus**, the main street of Ostia, leads west, past the **Baths of Neptune** on the right (where there's an interesting mosaic) to the town's commercial centre, otherwise known as the **Piazzale delle Corporazioni** for the remains of shops and trading offices that still fringe the central square. These represented commercial enterprises from all over the ancient world, and the mosaics just in front denote their trade – grain merchants, ship-fitters, ropemakers and the like.

Flanking one side of the square, the **theatre** has been much restored but is nonetheless impressive, enlarged by Septimius Severus in the second century AD to hold up to four thousand people; it sometimes hosts performances of classical drama during summer. On the left of the square, the **House of Apulius** preserves mosaic floors and, beyond, a dark-aisled *mithraeum* with more mosaics illustrating the cult's practices. Behind here – past the substantial remains of the *horrea* or warehouses that once stood all over the city – the **House of Diana** is probably the best-preserved private house in Ostia, with a dark, mysterious set of rooms around a central courtyard, and again with a *mithraeum* at the back. You can climb up to its roof for a fine view of the rest of the site, afterwards crossing the road to the **Thermopolium** – an ancient Roman café, complete with seats outside, a high counter, display shelves and even wall paintings of parts of the menu.

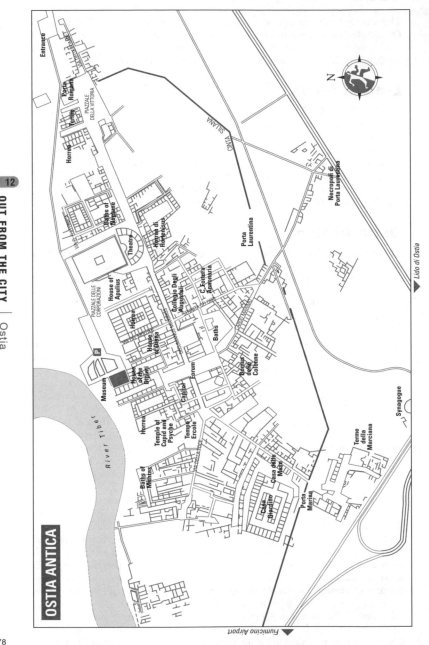

OSTIA ANTICA

River Tibet

Entrance

Porta Romana

Horrea

PIAZZALE DELLA VITTORIA

Baths of Neptune

Theatre

Horrea di Hortensius

Museum

House of the Dioseuri

Horrea

House of Apulius

House of Diana

PIAZZALE DELLE CORPORAZIONI

Collegio Dagli Alundual

C. Fontana Annonaria

Baths

Porta Laurentina

Horrea

Temple of Cupid and Psyche

Tempe Ercole

Capitol

Forum

Domus delle Colonne

Baths of Mithras

Casa Giardino

Casa della Muse

Porta Marina

Terme della Marciana

Synagogue

Necropoli di Porta Laurentina

CINTA SILLANA

N

Lido di Ostia

Fiumicino Airport

North of the Casa di Diana, the **museum** holds a variety of articles from the site, including wall paintings depicting domestic life in Ostia and some fine sarcophagi and statuary, notably one of *Mithras Slaying the Bull* from one of Ostia's mithraeums. Left from here, the **Forum** centres on the **Capitol** building, reached by a wide flight of steps, and is fringed by the remains of baths and a basilica. Continuing on down the main street, more **horrea**, superbly preserved and complete with pediment and names inscribed on the marble, merit a detour off to the right; although you can't enter, you can peer into the courtyard. Beyond, the **House of Cupid and Psyche** has a courtyard you can walk into, its rooms clearly discernible on one side, a colourful marbled floor on the other.

Cerveteri

The town of **CERVETERI**, around 30km northwest of Rome, isn't much in itself. But the necropolis just outside provides the most accessible Etruscan taster if you're commuting from Rome – though be warned that the railway station (at Ladispoli) is 7km away from the centre. Buses are more convenient, leaving from the Lepanto metro station (line A) in Rome every thirty minutes and dropping you at Piazza Aldo Moro in Cerveteri (a 1hr 20min journey). There's been a settlement here since the tenth century BC, when it was already known to the Greeks as an important trading centre. Cerveteri, the Roman Caere, was among the top three cities in the twelve-strong Etruscan federation, its wealth derived largely from the mineral riches of the Tolfa hills to the northeast – a gentle range which give the plain a much-needed touch of scenic colour. In its heyday the town spread over 8km (something like thirty times its present size), controlling territory that stretched for 50km up the coast. The rot set in from 351 BC, when it became a dependency of Rome, having failed, like most of Etruria, to maintain a neutrality with the new power.

The Necropolis and Museum

The present town is a thirteenth-century creation, dismissed by D.H. Lawrence – and you really can't blame him – as "forlorn beyond words". On arrival, make straight for the Etruscan **necropolis** (Tues–Sun: May–Sept 9am–7pm; Oct–April 9am–4pm; €4.15), just a kilometre away and signposted from the central piazza. The Etruscans constructed a literal city of the dead here, weird and fantastically well preserved, with complete streets and houses, some formed as strange round pillboxes carved from the living rock, others still covered in earth to create the tumuli effect that ripples over the surrounding plateau. The general span of the graves is seventh to first century BC: as far as anyone can make out, women were buried in separate small chambers within the "house" – easy to distinguish – while the men were laid on death beds (occasionally in sarcophagi) hewn directly from the stone. Slaves were cremated and their ashes placed in urns alongside their masters – civilized by comparison with the Romans, who simply threw their slaves into mass burial pits. The twelve or so show-tombs, lying between the two roads that bisect the city, are grouped together beyond the entrance; they close in random rotation, so it's difficult to know in advance which ones are going to be open. If possible don't miss the **Tomba Bella** (Tomb of the Bas-Reliefs), **Tomba dei Letti Funebri** (Tomb of the Funeral Beds) and the **Tomba dei Capitelli**.

If the tombs whet your appetite (and you could spend several hours wandering about), you might head back to town and stop at the little **trattoria** *Tulchulcha* on the road to the necropolis, where they serve a hearty meal of country-style cooking backed up by crisp Cerveteri white wines and, in summer, outside seating on a terrace overlooking the town.

The **Museo Nazionale di Cerveteri** is at the top of the old quarter in the sixteenth-century Castello Ruspoli (Tues–Sun 9am–7pm; free). It has four large rooms containing a fraction of the huge wealth that was buried with the Etruscan dead – vases, sarcophagi, terracottas and a run of miscellaneous day-to-day objects; most of the best stuff has been whisked away to Villa Giulia in Rome.

Bracciano

The closest of northern Lazio's lakes to Rome, **Lago di Bracciano** fills an enormous volcanic crater, a smooth, roughly circular expanse of water that's popular – but not too popular – with Romans keen to escape the summer heat of the city. It's nothing spectacular, with few real sights and a landscape of rather plain, rolling countryside, but its shores are fairly peaceful even on summer Sundays, and you can eat excellent lake fish in its restaurants.

The lake's main settlement is the town of **BRACCIANO** on the western shore, about half an hour by train from Rome San Pietro (direction Viterbo). It's a small town, dominated by the imposing **Castello Orsini–Odelscalchi** (April–Sept Tues–Fri 10am–7pm, Sat & Sun 9am–12.30pm & 3–7.30pm; Oct–March Tues–Fri 10am–5pm, Sat & Sun 10am–noon & 3–5pm; €6), a late-fifteenth-century structure now privately owned by the Odelscalchi family. The outer walls, now mostly disappeared, contained the rectangular piazza of the medieval town; nowadays it's rather run-down, its interior home to rusting suits of armour and faded frescoes, but the view from the ramparts is worth the admission price alone.

The best place to **swim** in the lake is from the beach at Via Argenti, below Bracciano town. You can rent a boat and picnic offshore; and the nearby trattorias are good and inexpensive. The shore between Trevignano and Anguillara also boasts fine swimming spots, as well as good **restaurants** in both of the towns. One of the best is the *Casina Bianca*, Via della Rena 100 (closed Mon), Trevignano, which is inexpensive and serves fresh fish on a terrace overlooking the lake.

The Castelli Romani

Just free of the sprawling southern suburbs of Rome, the thirteen towns that make up the **Castelli Romani** date back to medieval times, since when these hills – the Colli Albani – have served as an escape for the rich and powerful from the summer heat of the city. It's a wine-growing area (the vines grow easily on the volcanic soil) and is now pretty heavily built-up, with most of the historic centres ringed by unprepossessing suburbs; and summer weekends can see Romans trooping out in huge numbers for lunch at local trattorias. But if you avoid the rush-hour times and peak-season holidays, the region is still visitable as a day-trip from Rome or on the way south through Lazio. On public transport, COTRAL buses for the area (every 30min; a 35min journey) leave Rome from the terminus upstairs from the metro station Anagnina (line A).

Frascati and around

At just 20km from Rome, **FRASCATI** is the nearest of the Castelli towns and also the most striking, dominated by the majestic **Villa Aldobrandini**, built by Giacomo della Porta in 1598 for one Cardinal Aldobrandi. Since it still belongs to the family you can't actually get inside, but the **gardens** are open to the public (Mon–Fri: summer 9am–1pm & 3–6pm; winter 9am–1pm & 3–5pm; free). These are somewhat neglected these days, and sadly the potentially spectacular water garden at the rear of the villa is often switched off. But the view from the terrace in front of the house is superb, with Rome visible on a clear day. Frascati is also about the most famous of the Colli Albani wine towns: ask at the **tourist office** on Piazza Marconi 1 (Tue–Fri 8am–2pm & 4–7pm, Sat 8am–2pm; ☎06.942.0331) for details of local wine producers that run tours and tastings, or simply indulge in lunch at one of the many trattorias in town. Better yet, pick up a *porchetta* (whole roasted pork) sandwich from one of the stands on Piazza del Mercato and head for one of the town's many *cantine* – you can take food in with you – where wine is sold by the litre from giant wooden barrels.

Three kilometres or so down the road, **GROTTAFERRATA** is also known for its wine and its eleventh-century **Abbey** – a fortified Basilian (Greek Orthodox) monastery surrounded by high defensive walls and a now empty moat (daily: summer 6am–12.30pm & 3.30–7pm: winter 6am–12.30pm & 3.30pm–sunset; free). It's a timeless spot, the little church of Santa Maria inside with a Byzantine style interior decorated with thirteenth century mosaics and, in the chapel of St Nilo off the right aisle, frescoes by Domenichino. Through the inner courtyard there's a small museum (closed for restoration) displaying classical and medieval sculptures.

East of Lago Albano

The scenic Via dei Laghi skirts the eastern rim of **Lago Albano** until a winding road leads up to **Monte Cavo** (949m), the second highest of the Colli Albani and topped with the masts and satellite dishes of the Italian military – who operate from nearby Ciampino airport. There used to be a hotel here, a former Passionist convent, but the building is now derelict, and the summit is much less of a tourist attraction than it used to be. A temple to Jupiter once stood here, but now the only extant antiquity is the Via Sacra, which, about 1000m from the top, emerges from dense undergrowth, snaking down through the woods for a kilometre or so before disappearing again into thick bush.

On the far side of Monte Cavo, the road bears right for **ROCCA DI PAPA**, at 680m the highest of the Castelli Romani towns and one of its most picturesque, with a medieval quarter tumbling down the hill in haphazard terraces, and motor traffic kept to a strictly enforced minimum. The large main square, Piazza Repubblica, is modern and dull; instead, make for the small Piazza Garibaldi, a lively place in summer with a bar and restaurant, and soak up the views.

△ Lago Albano

Castel Gandolfo and west of Lago Albano

The old Roman Via Appia travels straight as an arrow down the west side of Lago Albano to **CASTEL GANDOLFO**, named after the castle owned by the powerful twelfth-century Genoese Gandolfi family and now best known as the summer retreat of the pope – though John Paul II is said to prefer visiting the mountains further north during the heat of the summer, much to the disgruntlement of the town. At over 400m above the rim of Lago Albano, it's a pleasantly airy place, but inevitably papal business predominates, especially on those Sundays between July and September when the pope traditionally gives a midday address from the courtyard of the Papal Palace. Unless you actually want to see the pope, it's best to avoid this. Better, if it's hot, to take advantage of the lake: there's a pleasant **Lido** just below the town, from where, if you've the energy, you can walk right around the lake in about two hours.

From Castel Gandolfo a panoramic road leads to **ALBANO LAZIALE**, probably the most appealing of the towns along the Via Appia, its large Piazza Mazzini looking south to the lovely Villa Comunale park, with sketchy remains of a villa that once belonged to Pompey. The town also has other Roman remains. Along the high street, Corso Matteotti, the church of **San Pietro** was built over the foundations of the baths of a Roman garrison, which you can see built into the walls. Near the church of Santa Maria della Stella is the **museo civico** (Mon–Sat 9am–12.30pm, Sun 9am–noon, plus Wed & Thurs 4–7pm; €2), with a small but high-quality archeological collection, including Etruscan and Roman artefacts found locally. Walk along Via della Stella to the **Tomb of Horatii and the Curiatii**, just outside town on the Ariccia road, whose strange "chimneys" date from the republican era. There's an **amphitheatre**, too, on the hill above – in heavy ruin now, and currently closed, but once with room for 15,000 spectators.

South of Lago Albano

GENZANO, 2km further on, also has a pleasant medieval centre, built around Piazza Frasconi, from where a road leads to the edge of Lago Albano's crater and sweeps down to the shore through dense woods. The town is the scene of the yearly *Infiorata on Corpus Domini*, usually in June, when Via Italo Belardi, which scales the hill from the piazza, is carpeted with flowers. A detour east will take you to **NEMI**, built high above the tiny crater **lake** of the same name. The village itself isn't much to write home about, but a cobbled road leads down to fields of strawberries that lie between the steep walls of the crater and the shores of the lake and make a good place to picnic. The town is known for its year-round strawberry harvest, in fact, and celebrates this on the first Sunday in June in the *Sagra delle Fragole*. On the northern shore of the lake you'll notice a large hangar-like building, the local **museum** (daily 9am–6pm; €2), which contains the scanty remains of two Roman pleasure boats said to have been built by Caligula. In ancient times they caught fire and sank. They were raised in the 1930s by the Mussolini government and placed in the specially constructed hangars, prime examples of reinforced concrete engineering and fascist architecture. In the last days of the German occupation in 1944 they were set on fire again so what you see is the ruins of a ruin. Much of the bronze fittings of these boats have been transferred to Palazzo Massimo in Rome but there are always interesting exhibitions of recent local archeological finds on display.

Further southeast, **VELLETRI**, though larger, is scarcely more interesting, its largely modern centre rebuilt after extensive war damage and with a Baroque cathedral, the fourteenth-century Torre del Trivio and a small archeological museum among its scant sights.

Anzio and Nettuno

About 40km south of Rome, and easily seen on a day-trip, **ANZIO** is the centre of a lengthy spread of settlement that focuses on a lively central square and a busy fishing industry. Much of the town was damaged during a difficult Allied landing here on January 22, 1944, to which two military cemeteries (one British, another, at nearby Nettuno, American) bear testimony. But despite a pretty thorough rebuilding it's a likeable resort, still depending as much on fish as tourists for its livelihood. The town's seafood **restaurants**, crowding together along the harbour and not unreasonably priced, are reason enough to come – try *Pierino* at Piazza C. Battisti 3 (closed Mon) – while the **beaches**, which edge the coast on either side, don't get unbearably thronged outside August. Anzio is also a possible route on to the lovely small island of Ponza, for which **hydrofoils** leave daily in summer – ask for timings at the **tourist office** on Piazza Pia 19 (daily 9am–1pm & 3.30–6pm; ☎06.984.5147).

NETTUNO, a couple of kilometres down the coast (and walkable by the coast road), is more of the same, but with slightly less beach space and water that's not quite so clear and calm. Again, it's a mostly modern town, but there's a well-preserved old quarter, still walled, with a couple of **trattorias** on the main square – information from the **tourist office** at the port (summer daily 9.30am–12.30pm & 5–7.30pm; winter closed Sun afternoon; ☎06.980.3335).

Listings

Listings

Accommodation

A s you might expect, there is plenty of **accommodation** in Rome, and for much of the year you can usually find something without too much trouble. However, it's always worth booking in advance if you want to snag a bargain, especially when the city is at its busiest – from Easter to the end of October, and during the Christmas and New Year period. Since the Jubilee Year 2000, the makeover that Rome underwent seems to have dramatically enhanced the city's allure for all sorts of visitors, not just pilgrims, and the amount of accommodation at all levels has increased significantly. You're sure to find something to suit within your budget, but don't leave it too late.

If for some reason you haven't booked, the **Enjoy Rome** office is your best bet (see p.17); or try the **Free Hotel Reservation Service** (daily 8am–10pm; ☎06.699.1000), where multilingual staff will check out vacancies for you. The rooms offered by the **touts** at Termini are rarely a good deal, and can often be rather dodgy; if you do take the bait, be sure to establish the (full) price beforehand, in writing if necessary, and use them only as a last resort.

Hotels and pensions

Many of the city's cheaper **hotels** are located conveniently close to **Termini**, and you could do worse than hole up in one of these, so long as you can tolerate the relative seediness of this district. The streets both sides of the station – Via Amendola, Via Principe Amedeo, Via Marghera, Via Magenta, Via Palestro – are stacked full of bargain hotels, and some buildings have several pensions to choose from. It's far from Rome's most attractive quarter, but the area has improved dramatically since Termini itself and nearby Piazza Vittorio have been spruced up – a phenomenon most obviously manifest in the appearance on the scene of Rome's trendiest new designer hotel, the *Es* (see p.192). However, especially if you're a woman travelling alone, use your common sense in avoiding the more obvious dives. If you want to stay somewhere more central and picturesque, there are many hotels in the **centro storico** and around **Campo de' Fiori**; some of them are not that expensive, but they fill quickly – best phone in advance before heading down there. For more luxury surroundings, **Tridente** and the area east of Via del Corso, towards **Via Veneto** and around the **Spanish Steps**, is the city's prime hunting-ground for beautiful, upscale accommodation, although there are still a few affordable options close by Piazza di Spagna. Consider also staying across the river in **Prati**, a pleasant neighbourhood, nicely distanced from the hubbub of the city centre proper and handy for the Vatican and St Peter's. Also on the west bank of the river, **Trastevere** boasts many new lodging options, all located within easy walking distance of the centre of town and all the sights.

Accommodation price codes

Hotel accommodation is listed by area and graded on a scale from 1 to 9 (see below); all are high-season rates and indicate the cost of the cheapest double room with en-suite private bath. Exact prices are given for youth hostels and are per person and assume Hostelling International (HI) membership.

❶ Up to €80
❷ €90–120
❸ €120–140
❹ €140–180
❺ €180–200

❻ €200–300
❼ €300–400
❽ €400–600
❾ €600 and above

Centro Storico, Campo de' Fiori and the Ghetto

Arenula Via S. Maria de' Calderari 47 ☎06.687.9454, ⊛www.hotclarcnula.com. Bus #63, 630, 780, H or Tram #8. Simple, clean rooms, each with its own bath, television and telephone. No lift, and the top-floor rooms are quite a climb. But a great, convenient location, just a few minutes' walk from Trastevere, the Jewish Ghetto, and Campo de' Fiori. ❷

Abruzzi Piazza della Rotonda 69 ☎06.679.2021, ⊛www.hotelabruzzi.it. Bus #30, 40, 46, 62, 63, 64, 70, 81, 87, 492, 628, 630, 780, 916 or Tram #8. This hotel used to be a very old-fashioned *pensione* right in the heart of the centro storico, but now it too has been refashioned into something that more closely resembles modern comfort and style. The knockout views of the Pantheon are still the main reason to stay here – unbeatable at any price. ❷

Campo de' Fiori Via del Biscione 6 ☎06.6880.6865, ⊛www.hotelcampodefiori.com. Bus #30, 40, 46, 62, 64, 70, 81, 87, 116, 186, 204, 492, 628, 916. A friendly place in a nice location close to Campo de' Fiori. Rooms come in all shapes and colours but are all clean and pleasant. Climb the six floors of stairs and catch your breath – and some great views – on their large roof terrace. ❹

Cesàri Via di Pietra 89a ☎06.679.9701, ☎06.6749.7030, ⊛www.venere.it/roma/cesari. Bus #62, 63, 81, 85, 95, 117, 119, 160, 175, 492, 628, 630, 850. In a perfect position close to the Pantheon, the *Cesàri* has been a hotel since 1787; as they will be sure to tell you, Stendhal stayed here once. Totally renovated in 1999, the rooms are quiet and comfortable, and have all the modern touches. ❹

Della Lunetta Piazza del Paradiso 68 ☎06.686.1080, ☎06.689.2028. Bus #30, 40, 46, 62, 64, 70, 81, 87, 116, 186, 204, 492, 628, 916. An unspectacular hotel, but in a nice location close to Campo de' Fiori. Simple, smallish rooms surround a green courtyard, and if you look up you will see the dome of San Andrea della Valle looming above. No breakfast. ❷

Due Torri Vicolo del Leoneto 23 ☎06.6880.6956 or 06.687.6983, ⊛www.hotelduetorriroma.com. Bus #30, 70, 81, 87, 116, 492, 628. Quietly elegant these days, this fine little hotel was once a residence for cardinals, following which it served as a brothel. Completely remodelled very recently, it retains a homely feel and is very near Piazza Navona and many of the city's greatest sights. Some rooms have private terraces with rooftop views. ❺

Genio Via G. Zanardelli 28 ☎06.683.219 or 06.683.3781, ☎06.6830.7246. Bus #30, 70, 81, 87, 116, 492, 628. Perfectly located for Piazza Navona and the rest of the centro storico, as well as for the Vatican sights, this comfortable, recently redone hotel draws tourist groups as well as individual travellers. The view from the rooftop terrace is superb, and there are also a few rooms available with the same view. ❺

In Parione Via dei Chiavari 32 ☎06.6880.2560, ☎06.683.4094, ⊛www.inparione.com. Bus #30, 40, 46, 62, 64, 70, 81, 87, 116, 186, 204, 492, 628, 916. In a nice part of town, central but very quiet, quite close to Campo de' Fiori, this place has recently been refurbished and all rooms have private bath and satellite TV. Many rooms look down to a bakery below and enjoy the smell of freshly baked bread. Run by a sweet, efficient Italian couple, who keep their pleasant, clean rooms to a high standard. ❸

Mimosa Via Santa Chiara 61 ☎06.6880.1753, ⓦwww.hotelmimosa.net. Bus #30, 40, 46, 62, 63, 64, 70, 81, 87, 492, 628, 630, 780, 916 or Tram #8. Clean, if slightly scruffy rooms, most without bathrooms. In a good position, on a quiet street, close to Santa Maria sopra Minerva and the Pantheon, and popular with groups of visiting students. Rooms are charged per person, not per room. No credit cards. ❷ with bath – cheaper without.

Navona Via dei Sediari 8 ☎06.686.4203, ⓦwww.hotelnavona.com. Bus #30, 70, 81, 87, 116, 492, 628. Completely renovated *pensione*-turned-hotel housed in a building that dates back to the first century AD, built on the ancient Roman baths of Agrippa. Very close to Piazza Navona and run by a friendly Italian-Australian couple. ❸

Nazionale a Montecitorio Piazza Montecitorio 131 ☎06.695.001, ⓦwww .nazionaleamontecitorio.it. Bus #62, 63, 81, 85, 95, 116, 117, 119, 160, 170, 204, 492, 628, 630, 850. Luxury hotel housed in a sixteenth-century *palazzo*, perfectly located between the Piazza Navona and Piazza di Spagna, in peaceful Piazza Montecitorio. Inevitably, given its position next door to the Italian parliament, it's popular with visiting politicians and dignitaries, and the rooms are accordingly luxurious, with every modern convenience. ❼

Pantheon Via Pastini 131 ☎06.678.7746, ⓦwww.venere.lt/roma/pantheon. Bus #62, 63, 81, 85, 95, 117, 119, 160, 175, 492, 628, 630, 850. This comfortable four-star is, as you might expect from the name, a stone's throw from the Pantheon. The well-equipped rooms range from the pleasant, with beamed wooden ceilings, to the exquisite – some on two levels, with an upstairs portion given over to a skylighted sitting room. ❼

Pomezia Via dei Chiavari 13 ☎06.686.1371, ⓦwww.hotelpomezia.it. Bus #30, 40, 46, 62, 64, 70, 81, 87, 116, 186, 204, 492, 628, 916. Down the street from the *In Parione*, slightly more expensive, and also recently refurbished. A small bar occupies half of the reception area, and Maurizio, the owner, keeps it open all night for those who want it. ❸

Portoghesi Via dei Portoghesi 1 ☎06.686.4231, ⓦwww.hotelportoghesiroma.com. Bus #30, 70, 81, 87, 116, 492, 628. Decent, well-equipped modern rooms in a great central location, five minutes from most places in the centro storico you might want to go. Breakfast is included and is served on the roof terrace upstairs. ❹

Residenza Farnese Via del Mascherone 59 ☎06.6889.1388, ⓕ06.6821.0980. Bus #30, 40, 46, 62, 64, 70, 81, 87, 116, 186, 204, 492, 628, 916. Situated on a quiet side street right by the massive Palazzo Farnese (French Embassy); rooms here are tastefully appointed and the staff very helpful. And the location is great for both the centro storico and lively Trastevere, just across the water by way of the Ponte Sisto footbridge. ❹

Santa Chiara Via Santa Chiara 21 ☎06.687.2979, ⓦwww.albergosantachiara.com. Bus #30, 40, 46, 62, 63, 64, 70, 81, 87, 492, 628, 630, 780, 916 or Tram #8. A friendly, stylish, family-run hotel in a great location, on a quiet piazza behind the Pantheon. Nice rooms, too, some of which overlook the church of Santa Maria sopra Minerva. It's hard to do better for the price, which includes breakfast. ❻

Smeraldo Via dei Chiodaroli 9–11 ☎06.687.5929 or 06.689.2121, ⓕ06.6880.5495. Bus #30, 40, 46, 62, 64, 70, 81, 87, 116, 186, 204, 492, 628, 916. Clean and comfortable hotel with a modern interior. All rooms have been fairly recently renovated, with shiny new baths, televisions and a/c. The terrace and some rooms have lovely views over Rome's rooftops. Breakfast is not included in the price but is available for €7. ❷

Sole Via del Biscione 76 ☎06.687.9446, ⓦwww.solealbiscione.it. Bus #30, 40, 46, 62, 64, 70, 81, 87, 116, 186, 204, 492, 620, 916. Almost overlooking Piazza del Campo de' Fiori, this place enjoys one of the best locations in the centre, and has pleasant rooms with televisions and phones. The real treat here, though, is the small roof terrace with a spectacular view of the domed churches of San Andrea delle Valle and San Carlo ai Catinari. No breakfast, no credit cards. ❸

Teatro di Pompeo Largo del Pallaro 8 ☎06.687.2812 or 06.6830.0170, ⓕ06.688.05531. Bus #30, 40, 46, 62, 64, 70, 81, 87, 116, 186, 204, 492, 628, 916. Built above the remains of Pompey's ancient Roman theatre, in a quiet piazza close to Campo de' Fiori, the rooms here are classy and comfortable, with high beamed wooden ceilings, marble-topped furniture and some with great views. ❺

Zanardelli Via G. Zanardelli 7 ☎06.6821.1392, ⓦwww.hotelnavona.com. Bus #70, 87, 116, 204, 280. A brand-new hotel run by the same family as the *Navona* – to which it is the more lavish alternative. Located just north of Piazza Navona, the building used to be

ACCOMMODATION | Hotels and pensions

a papal residence and has many original fixtures and furnishings. The rooms are elegant, with antique iron beds, silk-lined walls, and modern amenities, but still decently priced. ❸

Tridente, Quirinale, Via Veneto

Albergo Internazionale Via Sistina 79 ☎06.6994.1823 or 06.678.4686, ⓦwww .hotelinternazionale.com. Metro A Barberini or Bus #52, 53, 61, 62, 63, 80, 95, 116, 119, 175, 492, 630. In the first century AD this site was part of Lucullus' villa, and original elements can still be seen in the present hotel. Since Lucullus' day it has been home to nuns, an abbot, artists and musicians – and most recently has been thoroughly updated while retaining its ancient grace and atmosphere. Very good value for this level of style and comfort. Don't overlook the fourth-floor terrace views. ❻

Aleph Via San Basilio 15 ☎06.422.901, ⓦwww.boscolohotels.com. Metro A Barberini or Bus #52, 53, 61, 62, 63, 80, 95, 116, 119, 175, 492, 630. One of the newest of the city's luxury options, done up royally in the most opulent Roman tradition. The work of an American architect, the decor was loosely inspired by Dante's *Divine Comedy* – with evocations of Heaven, Purgatory and Hell, the latter most particularly by the hotel's restaurant, called simply *Sin*. ❼

Ambasciatori Palace Via Vittorio Veneto 62 ☎06.47.493, ⓦwww.ambasciatoripalace.com, Metro A Barberini or Bus #52, 53, 61, 62, 63, 80, 95, 116, 119, 175, 492, 630. Built in the 1920s, this has a more sophisticated atmosphere than its grand turn-of-the-century neighbours, with large rooms furnished in an Art Deco style without a lot of clutter; most overlook the lush green courtyard, while some have views of the centre of Rome. Don't miss the murals in the bar, some of which depict Mussolini's mistress Clara Petacci. ❾

Dei Borgognoni Via del Bufalo 126 ☎06.6994.1505, ⓦwww.hotelborgognoni.it. Bus #52, 53, 61, 62, 63, 80, 95, 116, 119, 175, 492, 630. Nicely situated four-star that has pleasant big rooms that have been well renovated. Surprisingly large, considering its location tucked down a side street not far from Piazza di Spagna. Handy for this part of town and for the centro storico. ❻

Carriage Via delle Carozze 36 ☎06.699.0124, ⓕ06.678.8279, ⓦwww.hotelcarriage.net. Good

location, friendly English-speaking staff make this Spanish steps area hotel one of the best choices for this part of town. Rooms are decent and have balconies – and breakfasts are excellent.

Condotti Via Mario de' Fiori 37 ☎06.679.4661, ⓕ06.679.0457. Metro A Spagna or Bus #52, 53, 61, 62, 63, 80, 95, 116, 119, 175, 492, 630. A cosy and inviting hotel with comfortable rooms, if a bit devoid of personality, although this is somewhat compensated for by the staff, who are cheery and welcoming. ❻

Eden Via Ludovisi 49 ☎06.478.121, ⓦwww .hotel-eden.it. Metro A Spagna or Bus #52, 53, 61, 62, 63, 80, 95, 116, 119, 175, 492, 630. Just off Via Veneto, this former private residence, on a quiet tree-lined street, is one of Rome's most enchanting hotels, with a lobby decorated with understated luxury – fresh flowers, marble floors, etc. All the rooms have everything you would expect from a luxury hotel, although those on the fifth floor are a bit more special – with private balconies offering spectacular views of the city. Even if you can't get one of these, the rooftop bar or restaurant is good compensation. ❾

Eliseo Via di Porta Pinciana 30 ☎06.487.0456 or 06.481.5474, ⓕ06.481.9629. Metro A Spagna or Bus #52, 53, 61, 62, 63, 80, 95, 116, 119, 175, 492, 630. This hotel's gracious facade looks out onto the ancient city walls and Villa Borghese, yet is only steps away from swanky Via Veneto. Inside, the decor is decidedly Rococo, with the emphasis on peaceful comfort. Great views of the city from the breakfast room. ❻

Eradelli Via due Macelli 28 ☎06.679.1265. Metro A Spagna or Bus #52, 53, 61, 62, 63, 80, 95, 116, 119, 175, 492, 630. A rather plain hotel with no-frills rooms, but well priced for its location just around the corner from the Spanish Steps. ❸

Firenze Via due Macelli 106 ☎06.679.4988, ⓕ06.678.5636. Metro A Spagna or Bus #52, 53, 61, 62, 63, 80, 95, 116, 119, 175, 492, 630. Just up the street from *Eradelli*, this recently renovated hotel is a bit more expensive but is worth it for its smart, large rooms. ❹

Grand Hotel Flora Via Vittorio Veneto 191 ☎06.489.929, ⓦwww.marriotthotels.com. Metro A Spagna or Bus #52, 53, 61, 62, 63, 80, 95, 116, 119, 175, 492, 630. This Marriott property combines traditional Roman grace and opulence with a squeaky-clean American feel that can make it a soothing haven for busy visitors. Fine antiques adorn the public and private spaces, and all rooms feature unique decor. ❼

Hassler Villa Medici Trinità dei Monti 6 ⓣ06.699.340, ⓦwww.hotelhasslerroma.com. Metro A Spagna or Bus #52, 53, 61, 63, 80, 95, 116, 119, 175, 492, 630. Location, location, location – at the top of the Spanish Steps, you can't get much closer to the heart of Rome than this. A luxury hotel, with simple, elegant rooms and every convenience a guest could possibly require, but what you are paying for above all is the location and its view. ❾

Homs Via della Vite 71–72 ⓣ06.679.2976, ⓦwww.hotelhoms.it. Metro A Spagna or Bus #52, 53, 61, 63, 80, 95, 116, 119, 175, 492, 630. Perfectly located for the Spanish Steps, Trevi Fountain, and all the elegant shops, this little boutique hotel boasts a roof terrace with marvellous views. The rooms have been recently refurbished, and there's a very friendly atmosphere – something that's not always guaranteed in the hotels of this ritzy neighbourhood. ❸

De Russie Via del Babuino 9 ⓣ06.328.881, ⓦwww.roccofortehotels.com. Metro A Flaminio or Bus #88, 95, 117, 119, 495, 628, 926 or Tram #2. Opened in the spring of 2000, the *Russie* quickly became the abode of choice for visiting movie stars in-the-know. Coolly elegant, gorgeously understated; its profound emphasis on comfort and quality, not to mention its stellar location just off Piazza del Popolo, make it first choice for the hip traveller spending someone's else's money. Don't miss the garden bar and the view from atop the Pincio. ❽

D'Inghilterra Via Bocca di Leone 14 ⓣ06.699.811, ⓦwww.hoteldinghilterraroma.it. Metro A Spagna or Bus #52, 53, 61, 63, 80, 95, 116, 119, 175, 492, 630. Billing itself as one of the world's finest 100 hotels, this old favourite, formerly the apartments of the princes of Torlonia, does not disappoint – and is surprisingly good value compared to similar pampering elsewhere in the city. Intimacy, opulence, exquisite antiques, frescoed rooms, and all the delights of the ancient city centre on your doorstep. ❼

Majestic Via Veneto 50 ⓣ06.421.441, ⓦwww.hotelmajestic.com. Metro A Barberini or Bus #52, 53, 61, 62, 63, 80, 95, 116, 119, 175, 492, 630. Opened in 1889, this is Via Veneto's oldest hotel, and, with its precious antiques and sumptuous furnishings, it set the standard for hotels that would follow on Rome's most fashionable street. The reception is as ostentatious as you would expect, with ceiling frescoes, silk hangings, and big, comfy couches. Each room is a bit different, but all are elegant and roomy, with huge marble baths. ❾

Manfredi Via Margutta 61 ⓣ06.320.7676, ⓦwww.hotelmanfredi.com. Metro A Spagna or Bus #52, 53, 61, 62, 63, 80, 95, 116, 119, 175, 492, 630. Occupying a sixteenth-century building, this is a first-class hotel with an ideal location on Via Margutta, moments from the Spanish Steps. ❻

Margutta Via Laurina 34 ⓣ06.322.3674, ⓕ06.320.0395. Metro A Flaminio or Bus #52, 53, 61, 62, 63, 80, 95, 116, 119, 175, 492, 630. Popular hotel handily located in the Corso/Piazza del Popolo shopping area. Three rooms have tiny private balconies. Reserve well ahead. ❸

Piazza di Spagna Via Mario de' Fiori 61 ⓣ06.679.3061, ⓦwww.hotelpiazzadispagna.it. Metro A Spagna or Bus #52, 53, 61, 62, 63, 80, 95, 116, 119, 175, 492, 630. A small hotel just a few minutes' walk from the Spanish Steps – a good alternative to the sumptuous palaces that characterize this area. Rooms are comfortable, all have a/c, minibar, phone, and some have Jacuzzis. Friendly staff, too. ❻

Plaza Via del Corso 126 ⓣ06.6992.1111, ⓦwww.grandhotelplaza.com. Metro A Spagna or Bus #52, 53, 61, 62, 63, 80, 95, 116, 119, 175, 492, 630. On the face of it one of the most sumptuous hotels in Rome, with huge rooms furnished with antiques and a fantastic lobby that's worth dropping into even if you're not staying here. But the rooms are very slightly on the worn side and that makes it a little cheaper than comparable options. Worth it for the atmosphere alone – and you couldn't be more central, bang on Via del Corso, and just around the corner from the shops and restaurants of the Spanish Steps district. ❼

La Residenza Via Emilia 22–24 ⓣ06.488.0789, ⓕ06.485.721. Metro A Spagna or Bus #52, 53, 61, 62, 63, 80, 95, 116, 119, 175, 492, 630. One of the great discoveries in the overpriced Via Veneto area, this place combines the luxuries and atmosphere of a grand hotel with the easygoing comforts and intimacy of a private home. It's also set off the busy main drag and is very tranquil. ❺

Scalinata di Spagna Piazza Trinità dei Monti 17 ⓣ06.679.3006, ⓦwww.hotelscalinata.com. Metro A Spagna or Bus #52, 53, 61, 63, 80, 95,

116, 119, 175, 492, 630. A wonderful location, just up from the Spanish Steps, and all the amenities you would expect at this price, plus a terrace for breakfast. Rooms have very plush decor, employing yards and yards of expensive fabric and antique accents – although the staff can be a little snooty. ❼

Victoria Via Campania 41 ☏06.473.931, ☏06.487.189. Metro A Spagna or Bus #52, 53, 61, 62, 63, 80, 95, 116, 119, 175, 492, 630. Newly remodelled in imperial Roman style, this Swiss-managed hotel is situated between the super-deluxe grandeur of Via Veneto and the verdant freedom of Villa Borghese. Many rooms enjoy views of the ancient walls and beyond. ❼

Westin Excelsior Via Veneto 125 ☏06.47.081, ☏06.482.6205. Metro A Spagna or Bus #52, 53, 61, 62, 63, 80, 95, 116, 119, 175, 492, 630. This grand white palace on Via Veneto was recently renovated to its original turn-of-the-century Empire style and is once again the choice of royalty when they visit Rome, who favour the antiques, crystal chandeliers, and tapestries that decorate each room – along with, of course, every modern-day convenience. ❾

Termini and around

Alpi Via Castelfidardo 84 ☏06.444.1235, ⓦ www.hotelalpi.com. Metro B Castro Pretorio or Bus #16, 38, 75, 86, 90, 92, 204, 217, 310, 360, 492, 649. One of the more peaceful yet convenient options close to Termini, recently renovated, and within easy walking distance of the easyJet bus stop. Pleasant if somewhat small rooms with bathrooms, and a great buffet breakfast – much better than you would normally expect in a hotel of this category. ❸

Apollo Via dei Serpenti 109 ☏06.488.5889, ☏06.488.1989. Metro B Cavour or Bus #40, 60, 64, 70, 75, 84, 85, 87, 117, 175, 186, 204, 810, 850, H or Tram #5, 14. The Monti area is getting more and more interesting of late, and this little hotel is one of its most attractive, located right in the heart of all the shops and restaurants that draw people here from all over Rome. It's also just a stone's throw away from such major sights as the Forum and the Colosseum. ❹

Astoria Garden Via Bachelet 8 ☏06.446.9908. ⓦ www.hotelastoriagarden.it. Metro Termini or Bus # 16, 36, 38, 40, 64, 75, 84, 86, 90, 92, 105,

170, 175, 217, 310, 360, 492, 649, 714, 910, H. In a peaceful area east of Termini, a recently renovated hotel that was once the home of an Italian count. Rooms are pleasant, quiet and some have balconies that look onto the large garden below. ❹

Britannia Via Napoli 64 ☏06.488.3153, ⓦ www.hotelbritannia.it. Metro A Repubblica or Bus # 40, 60, 61, 62, 64, 84, 90, 170, 175, 492, 910, H. A surprisingly peaceful hotel minutes from Termini and Piazza della Repubblica. The Neoclassical interior was renovated last year, and rooms have all modern amenities, lovely furnishings, and are decorated with pictures of ancient Rome. ❻

Cervia Via Palestro 55 ☏06.491.057, ⓦ www.hotelcerviaroma.com. Metro B Castro Pretorio or Bus #16, 38, 75, 86, 90, 92, 204, 217, 310, 360, 492, 649. Pleasant rooms in a lively *pensione* in the same building as the *Restivo* (see below). If you don't mind lugging your bags a few more steps, ask for the discounted rooms on the third floor. ❶

Des Artistes Via Villafranca 20 ☏06.445.4365, ⓦ www.hoteldesartistes.com. Metro B Castro Pretorio or Bus #16, 38, 75, 86, 90, 92, 204, 217, 310, 360, 492, 649. One of the better hotels in the Termini area. Exceptionally good value, spotlessly clean, and recently redecorated. Eat breakfast or recover from a long day of sightseeing on a breezy roof terrace; there's also email and free Internet services for guests' use. Also has dorm beds for €20. ❷

Elide Via Firenze 50 ☏06.474.1367, ☏06.4890.4318. Metro A Repubblica or Bus #40, 60, 61, 62, 64, 84, 90, 170, 175, 492, 910, H. A *pensione* for the last fifty years, with clean, simple rooms and a friendly staff, a few minutes' from Piazza della Repubblica. Several of the rooms are right on a busy street, though; if noise bothers you, ask for a room in the back. ❶

Es Hotel Via F. Turati 171 ☏06.444.841, ⓦ www.eshotel.it. Metro Termini or Bus #70, 71, 105 or Tram #5, 14. Rome's edgiest design hotel is also the flagship for the radical makeover that the area around Termini is undergoing; "Es" stands for Esquilino, the Roman hill on which it stands. Within walking distance of both Termini Station and the erstwhile down-at-the-heel market square Piazza Vittorio, this hotel makes a powerful fashion statement, with its stark aesthetic, multicoloured room lighting and state-of-the-art rooftop bar and spa. ❽

Fawlty Towers Via Magenta 39 ☎06.445.4802, ⦿www.fawltytowers.org. Metro Termini or Bus # 16, 36, 38, 40, 64, 75, 84, 86, 90, 92, 105, 170, 175, 217, 310, 360, 492, 649, 714, 910, H. Playfully named accommodation, owned by the people who run Enjoy Rome, this place has both dorm beds (€23) and clean and comfortable hotel rooms, some with private bath. There's a communal kitchen, Internet access, and a pleasant roof terrace. ❶

Grifo Via del Boschetto 144 ☎06.487.1395 or 06.482.7596, ℻06.474.2323. Metro B Cavour or Bus #40, 60, 64, 70, 75, 84, 85, 87, 117, 175, 186, 204, 810, 850, H or Tram #5, 14. This hotel is yet another new addition to the Monti district. The decor is crisply modern, but the terrace overlooks a timeless scene of medieval Rome at its most picturesque. ❹

Katty Via Palestro 35 ☎06.490.079, ℻06.444.1216. Metro B Castro Pretorio or Bus #16, 38, 75, 86, 90, 92, 204, 217, 310, 360, 492, 649. A good-value *pensione* located in one of the nicer buildings on the east side of Termini. Rooms are quite pleasant and some have shiny new bathrooms. If you want to spend a bit extra, go up a floor to *Katty 2*, where all rooms have private baths, minibar, TV, phone, and a/c. ❶

Magnifico Via Nazionale 243, scala B interno 6 ☎06.4782.5074, ⦿www.hotelmagnifico.com. Metro A Repubblica or Bus #40, 60, 61, 62, 64, 84, 90, 170, 175, 492, 910, H. With its Neoclassical entrance, the eighteenth-century building this small hotel occupies sets the tone. Inside, parquet floors, a gracious internal courtyard and warm wood furnishings continue the uniquely Roman feel. ❹

Marsala Via Marsala 36 ☎06.444.1262, ⦿www.hotelmarsala.it. Metro Termini or Bus #16, 36, 38, 40, 64, 75, 84, 86, 90, 92, 105, 170, 175, 217, 310, 360, 492, 649, 714, 910, H. Handily situated two-star hotel 50m east of the station. Very clean, good-value rooms, and a friendly English-speaking staff. ❷

Positano Via Palestro 49 ☎06.446.9101. ⦿www.hotelpositano.it. Metro Termini or Bus #16, 36, 38, 40, 64, 75, 84, 86, 90, 92, 105, 170, 175, 217, 310, 360, 492, 649, 714, 910, H. Not glamorous, but certainly reasonably priced, with comfortable rooms two minutes' walk from Termini. Helpful management, too. ❶

Restivo Via Palestro 55 ☎06.446.2172. Metro B Castro Pretorio or Bus #16, 38, 75, 86, 90, 92, 204, 217, 310, 360, 492, 649. Spotless rooms in a small *pensione* run by a sweet old lady.

She stays up until all guests are safely back home, so it's best avoided if you're planning to party into the small hours. No private bathrooms. ❶

Richmond Largo Corrado Ricci 36 ☎06.6994.1256, ⦿www.hotelrichmondroma.com. Metro B Colosseo or Bus #60, 75, 81, 85 87, 117, 175, 673, 810 or Tram #3. For devotees of Rome's most ancient splendours, this is the perfect choice; with its location right across the way from the Forums and the Colosseum, and a roof terrace for taking in the view, all of the ancient city is at your doorstep. Rooms are small, but well planned and newly freshened. ❺

Rosetta Via Cavour 295 ☎ & ℻06.4782.3069. Metro B Cavour or Colosseum or Bus #60, 75, 84, 85, 87, 117, 175, 186, 204, 810, 850. Family-run *pensione* in a nice location very close to the Colosseum. The small rooms are a bit shabby, but they're comfortable enough, and have private baths, TV, and telephone. No breakfast. ❶

St Regis Grand Via V.E. Orlando 3 ☎06.47.091 or 06.478.2740, ⦿www.stregis.com/grandrome. Metro A Repubblica or Bus #40, 60, 61, 62, 64, 84, 90, 170, 175, 492, 910, H. Originally the brainchild of legendary hotelier Caesar Ritz, a few years ago this truly grand property was fully restored to its glimmering gilded glory, all done up in Empire and Regency style with no luxury appointment omitted ❾

Salus Piazza Indipendenza 13 ☎06.444.0330, ⦿www.hotelsalus.crimar.it. Metro Termini or Bus #36, 38, 40, 60, 61, 62, 64, 75, 84, 90, 92, 105, 170, 175, 217, 310, 492, 714, 910, H. This modest establishment, just around the corner from Termini, has the virtues of being attractive, clean, efficiently run and friendly – things that can't always be said for the hotels in this neighbourhood – and it also has an internal garden for guests' use. ❶

Seiler Via Firenze 48 ☎06.485.550 or 06.488.0204, ℻06.488.0688. Metro A Repubblica or Bus #40, 60, 61, 62, 64, 84, 90, 170, 175, 492, 910, H. An elegant building just off one of Rome's main shopping streets houses this nicely decorated and friendly establishment. Characteristic touches include stone vaults and terracotta tile floors. ❸

Villa delle Rose Via Vicenza 5 ☎06.445.1788, ⦿www.villadellerose.it. Metro Termini or Bus #16, 36, 38, 40, 64, 75, 84, 86, 90, 92, 105, 170, 175, 217, 310, 360, 492, 649, 714, 910, H. This centuries-old aristocratic villa sits amidst its own tranquil rose gardens, belying the fact that it's only a block from Termini Station. Newly done up, it's quiet, pleasant and appealingly decorated, with a very friendly staff. ❹

Trastevere, Testaccio & the Aventine

Brunella Via Pacinotti 8 ☎06.557.7219, ℻06.557.1626. Bus #170, 780, H or Tram #3, 8. Good-value, comfortable small hotel situated at the end of Viale Trastevere, not far from the nightlife of the Testaccio area, but well connected to the historical centre by public transport. ❶

Carmel Via G. Mameli 11 ☎06.580.9921, ⓦwww.hotelcarmel.hotmail.com. Bus #23, 75, 280, 630, 780, H or Tram #8. Pleasant rooms, with private bathrooms and two with their own terrace, on the western side of Trastevere. There's also a leafy roof terrace for all guests. If you arrange it ahead of time they can provide a kosher kitchen for your personal use. Don't arrive on spec as the owner closes if she's not expecting anyone. ❶

Casa Kolbe Via di San Teodoro 44 ☎06.679.4974, ℻06.699.41550. Bus #44, 63, 81, 95, 170, 628, 715, 716, 781. In a quiet location not far from the Bocca della Verità, this is a favourite with students and tour groups, which means that the overworked staff can often be brusque. Its rooms are simple, clean, and good value for the location, while its best feature is the delightful cloister garden. Half- and full-board possible. ❶

Cisterna Via della Cisterna 7–9 ☎06.581.7212, ℻06.581.0091. Bus #23, 75, 280, 630, 780, H or Tram #8. Friendly hotel with a homely feel, bang in the middle of Trastevere. Twelve rooms, some with colourful tiled floors, wooden beamed ceilings, and all with private bathrooms. The peaceful terrace garden out the back is a treat when the weather is nice. ❷

Domus Tiberina Via in Piscinula 37 ☎06.580.3033, ⓦwww.domustiberina.com. Bus #23, 75, 280, 630, 780, H or Tram #8. Located on the quiet side of the popular Trastevere quarter, this boutique hotel nevertheless lies within a few minutes' walk of many of the area's best restaurants, as well as some of its most authentic sights. Rooms are small, but newly refurbished, as this is one of the several brand-new accommodation choices this side of the river. ❸

Grand Hotel del Gianicolo Viale delle Mura Gianicolensi 107 ☎06.5833.3405, ℻06.5817.9434. Bus #44, 75, 710, 870, 871. Commanding the heights above Trastevere and with views of the entire city, this former convent is just a few blocks away from the American Academy and the joys of Villa Pamphilj. In addition to the understated elegance of the hotel itself, the grounds sport a large swimming pool set amidst subtropical gardens. A wonderful choice if you want somewhere that feels far away from the hubbub of the city centre. ❺

San Francesco Via Jacopa de' Settesoli 7 ☎06.5830.0051, ⓦwww.hotelsanfrancesco.net. Bus #23, 44, 75, 280, 630, 780, H or Tram #3, 8. This new Trastevere option is well located – close enough to be everything but off on its own enough to be restful. It's located just across the river from Testaccio, too, making it an ideal base for Rome's major nightlife venues. Rooms are comfortable, if a little uninspired. ❺

Trastevere Via Luciano Manara 24a/25 ☎06.581.4713, ℻06.588.1016. Bus #23, 75, 280, 630, 780, H or Tram #8. The place to come if you want to be in the heart of Trastevere, this hotel was totally renovated in 1998, with all new furnishings, wood panelling, terracotta floors, and newly installed bathrooms in every room. Especially good value are their four apartments with kitchens and private entry. ❷

Trastevere House Vicolo del Buco 7, ☎ & ℻06.588.3774. Bus #23, 75, 280, 630, 780, H or Tram #8. This small seventeenth-century palace is home to one of Trastevere's newest lodging options, and it's been neatly done up, although many find the rooms a bit cramped. Located in a quiet corner of this bustling district, but just seconds away from all the nightlife and restaurants. ❸

Villa della Fonte Via della Fonte d'Olio 8, ☎06.580.3797, ⓦwww.villafonte.com. Bus #23, 75, 280, 630, 780, H or Tram #8. This attractive place has a hidden-away, almost secret feel to it, yet is just a few steps off the district's main square, Piazza Santa Maria in Trastevere, where every evening sees loads of action, from fire-eaters to musicians. Rooms are cosy and newly renovated, maintaining traditional medieval style. ❹

Villa San Pio Piazza Sant'Anselmo 2 ☎06.574.5231, ⓦwww.aventinohotels.com. Metro B Circo Massimo or Bus #60, 75, 81, 118, 160, 175, 628, 673, 715. Of the four hotels run by the Aventino S.Anselmo group, the *Villa San Pio* has been completely remodelled and is by far the most pleasant, but they are all quite bucolic and give you the feeling that the grit and cacophony of downtown Rome are nowhere near, even though major sights are only down the hill. ❻

Prati and the Vatican

Atlante Star Via Vitelleschi 34 ☎06.687.3233, ⓦwww.atlantehotels.com. Metro A Ottaviano or Bus #23, 32, 34, 40, 49, 62, 81, 280, 492, 590, 982 or Tram #19. Just steps away from the Vatican, this is a truly luxurious hotel. Rooms are decorated with rich wood panelling and antiques, and each marble bathroom has a Jacuzzi so you can completely unwind. Perhaps the most impressive feature of this hotel is the rooftop terrace, which offers a 360-degree view of Rome; it's also the home of the very popular *Les Etoiles* restaurant (see p.215). ❽ A nearby annexe, the *Atlante Garden*, Via Crescenzio 78 ☎06.687.2361, ⓕ06.687.2315, offers similar luxury at slightly lower rates – ❼.

Alimandi Via Tunisi 8 ☎06.3972.3948, ⓦwww.alimandi.org. Metro A Ottaviano or Bus #23, 32, 34, 40, 49, 62, 81, 280, 492, 590, 982 or Tram #19. Close to the Vatican, this place boasts a friendly staff, a rooftop garden, and nicely furnished, good-value doubles, all with telephone and TV. Airport pickup service available. ❹

Amalia Via Germanico 66 ☎06.3972.3356, ⓦwww.hotelamalia.com. Metro A Ottaviano or Bus #23, 32, 34, 40, 49, 62, 81, 280, 492, 590, 982 or Tram #19. Located on an attractive corner of this busy shopping zone near the Vatican Museums, this is an extremely good-value option, providing four-star amenities at three-star prices – including double glazing on all windows for maximum serenity. ❺

Arcangelo Via Boezio 15 ☎06.687.4143, ⓦwww.travel.it/roma/arcangelo. Metro A Ottaviano or Bus #23, 32, 34, 40, 49, 62, 81, 280, 492, 590, 982 or Tram #19. Clean, reliable hotel, with comfortable, elegant rooms in a quiet street not far from the Vatican. The lounges have a warm, clubby feel. ❹

Bramante Vicolo delle Palline 24 ☎06.6880.6426, ⓦwww.hotelbramante.com. Bus #23, 34, 40, 62, 280. This little hotel, located right next to the ancient wall running from the Vatican to Castel Sant'Angelo, was once home to the

sixteenth-century architect Domenico and later became an inn. Recently restored, its rooms are charmingly decorated with original wood-beam ceilings and antique appointments. ❺

Colors Via Boezio 31 ☎06.687.4030, ⓦwww.colorshotel.com. Metro A Ottaviano or Bus #23, 32, 34, 40, 49, 62, 81, 280, 492, 590, 982 or Tram #19. Run by the friendly people from Enjoy Rome, this is a smaller version of their popular *Fawlty Towers* (see p.193), a hostel/hotel in a quiet neighbourhood near the Vatican. Dorm beds (€20) and private rooms, are available. Everyone is very friendly, and there are kitchen facilities, a lounge with satellite TV, and a small terrace. ❶

Davos Via degli Scipioni 239 ☎06.321.7012, ⓕ06.323.0367. Metro A Lepanto or Bus #30, 70, 280, 913. Simple, affordable *pensione* on a quiet street not far from the Vatican. Rooms are clean and quite basic, but all except one have a private bath. No credit cards. ❶

Dei Consoli Via Varrone 2d ☎06.6889.2972, ⓦwww.hoteldeiconsoli.com. Metro A Ottaviano or Bus #23, 32, 34, 40, 49, 62, 81, 280, 492, 590, 982 or Tram #19. From the elegantly welcoming entrance, just around the corner from all the splendours of the Vatican, to the thoughtfully designed rooms, where every comfort is included, this is an excellent choice. The decor on each floor is thematically inspired by master oil paintings – the top floor, curiously adorned with battle scenes, is where honeymooners are usually lodged. ❻

Farnese Via Alessandro Farnese 30 ☎06.321.1953, ⓦwww.hotelfarnese.com. Metro A Lepanto or Bus #30, 70, 280, 913. Another grand aristocratic residence that has been turned into an upscale hotel. All the rooms have recently been renovated, adding touches such as soundproof windows and doors, handmade walnut furniture, and marble bathrooms. Some rooms have private balconies, and there is a rooftop terrace with a great view of the Vatican. ❺

Gerber Via degli Scipioni 241 ☎06.321.6485, ⓦwww.hotelgerber.it. Metro A Lepanto or Bus #30, 70, 280, 913. A friendly staff and elegant comfortable rooms make this hotel great value for its convenient location on a quiet street not far from the Vatican. Even better, they give a ten percent discount to *Rough Guide* readers. ❸

Giulio Cesare Via degli Scipioni 287 ☎06.321.0751, ⓦwww.hotelgiuliocesare.com. Metro A Lepanto or Bus #30, 70, 280, 913. This

Renting an apartment in Rome has many advantages; for families with children or small groups, it can be a cheaper option than a hotel. Short-term rentals are becoming very popular, however, so you must book well in advance. All the places listed below have helpful websites, with pictures of their accommodation in Rome, which ranges from small city-centre apartments to grand villas outside the city. You can also find a good array of options in the bi-weekly magazine, Wanted in Rome. If you really want to do things in style, you can rent the top-floor apartment of the Keats-Shelley House on Piazza di Spagna, which holds up to four people.

City Apartments Viale Opito Oppio 78 Rome 00174 ☏06.7698.3140, ⓦwww.roma.cityapartments.it.

Homes in Rome Via Valadier 36 Rome 00193 ☏06.323.0166, ⓦwww.homesinrome.com.

Landmark Trust Shittesbrooke, Maidenhead, Berks SL6 3LW ☏01628 825925, ⓦwww.landmarktrust.co.uk.

Rome Sweet Home Via delle Vite 32 Rome 00187 ☏06.6992.4833, ⓦwww.romesweethome.it.

The Tourist Friend ☏06.6821.0410, ⓦwww.bandbinrome.com.

charming hotel is no longer the *Villa Patricia,* home of an Italian countess, but you will feel like royalty once you step into the foyer, with its glistening golden ceiling. An attentive staff will lead you down mirror-lined hallways to elegantly decorated rooms with marble baths. ❻

Isa Via Cicerone 39 ☏06.321.2610, ⓦwww.hotelisa.com. Metro A Lepanto or Bus #30, 70, 280, 913. A fairly short walk from the Vatican; the grim exterior of this hotel is deceptive, hiding moderately large rooms

that have been nicely renovated with warm wooden panelling, brightly coloured beds and shiny marble basins. ❹

La Rovere Vicolo San Onofrio 4–5 ☏06.6880.6739, ⓦwww.hotellarovere.com. Bus #23, 34, 40, 62, 64, 81, 280. Just round the corner from St Peter's and across the bridge from Piazza Navona, this attractive, newly refurbished boutique hotel is itself tucked quietly away from all the bustle and offers a terrace garden and antique-filled settings for its guests to relax in. ❺

Hostels and convents

Alessandro Palace Hostel Via Vicenza 42 ☏06.446.1958, ⓦwww.hostelsalessandro.com. Metro Termini or Bus #36, 38, 40, 60, 61, 62, 64, 75, 84, 90, 92, 105, 170, 175, 217, 310, 492, 714, 910, H. This place has been voted one of the top hostels in Europe, and it sparkles with creative style. Pluses include no lock-out or curfew, free Internet access, free drinks all day, a free pizza party every Thurs and Sat, and a great free city map. Beds €22, doubles €80, w/bath. A few blocks away, you'll also find *Alessandro Indipendenza,* Via Curatone 12 (same numbers as above) and on the other side of Termini, *Alessandro Downtown,* Via C. Cattaneo

23 (☏06.4434.0147, same fax), both with dorm beds only, €20.

Casa di Santa Brigida Piazza Farnese 96 ☏06.6889.2596, ⓦwww.brigidine.org. Bus #30, 40, 46, 62, 64, 70, 81, 87, 116, 186, 204, 492, 628, 916. Located right on this sublime Renaissance square, this place is hard to beat – a bit staid perhaps, but clean and comfortable, and there's no curfew. Breakfast included. ❸

Casa di Santa Francesca Romana Via dei Vascellari 61 ☏06.581.2125, ℗06.588.2408. Bus #23, 75, 280, 630, 780, H or Tram #8. This former medieval palace and then convent has been newly restructured as a refined and cheerful accommodation option in the quieter half of Trastevere. Although the rooms are certainly spartan, the central courtyard is very inviting, and the curfew is not until 2am, with no lock-out during the day. Breakfast included. ❷

Ostello del Foro Italico Viale delle Olimpiadi 61 ☏ 06.323.6267, ⓦ www.ostellionline.org. Bus #32, 69, 224, 280 – ask the driver for the "ostello". Rome's official HI hostel, though not particularly central or easy to get to from Termini. You can call ahead to check out availability, but they won't take phone bookings. €16, including breakfast. You can join here if you're not a HI member already.

Ottaviano Via Ottaviano 6 ☏ 06.3973.7253, ⓦ www.pensioneottaviano.com. Metro A Ottaviano or Bus #23, 32, 34, 40, 49, 62, 81, 280, 492, 590, 982 or Tram #19. A simple *pensione*-cum-hostel near the Vatican that is very popular with the backpacking crowd; book well in advance, fluent English spoken. Dorm beds €18 w/shared bath, €20 w/pvt bath; double €70, w/shared bath.

Sandy Via Cavour 136 ☏ 06.488.4585, ⓦ www.sandyhostel.com. Metro B Cavour or Colosseum or Bus #60, 75, 84, 85, 87, 117, 175, 186, 204, 810, 850. Run by the same folk as the *Ottaviano*, but with dormitories only. No breakfast, but microwave and free Internet access; €18 per bed.

Suore Pallotini Viale della Mura Aurelle 7B ☏ 06.635.697, ⓕ 06.3936.6943. Bus #64. Simple, clean accommodation near the Vatican, run by nuns, but open to both

women and men. The first night you are there, there is a midnight curfew, 11pm in winter. €60 for a double without bath, €85 with bath, breakfast included.

Suore Pie Operaie Via di Torre Argentina 76 ☏ 06.686.1254. Bus #30, 40, 46, 62, 63, 64, 70, 81, 87, 186, 204, 492, 628, 630, 780, 810, 916 or Tram #8. For women only, this place offers the cheapest beds in the city centre, although you need to book well in advance and there's a 10.30pm curfew. Closed Aug. €18 per person in a double, €16 in a triple. No breakfast.

Villa Santa Cecilia Via Argeleto 54–58 ☏ 06.5237.1688, ⓕ 06.5237.0880. Metro B Magliana, where you change for Lido and the overground train to Vitinia. Thirty minutes by metro from Termini, a religious-run hostel/hotel (no curfew) with singles, doubles, triples and four-bedded rooms, all with private bathrooms. Singles €42; doubles €70; triples €90; quadruples €110. All include breakfast.

YWCA Via C. Balbo 4 ☏ 06.488.0460 or 06.488.3917, ⓕ 06.487.1028. Metro Cavour or Bus #16, 70, 71, 75, 84, 360, 649, 714. Though open only to women, this is more conveniently situated than the HI hostel, just ten minutes' walk from Termini. A range of singles to quadruples. Singles €47 with bath, €37 without; doubles €74 with bath, €62 without, triples and quads €26 per person, without bath; all rooms include breakfast except Sun mornings and August. Midnight curfew.

Camping

All Rome's **campsites** are some way out of the city, and, although easy enough to get to, are not especially cheap.

Camping Flaminio 8km north of the centre on Via Flaminia Nuova. ☏ 06.333.2604, ⓦ www .villageflaminio.com. Attractive site and the closest to the centre. From Piazzale Flaminio take Tram #2 to Piazza Mancini, then transfer to Bus #200 (ask the driver to drop you at the "*fermata più vicina al campeggio*") or, again from Piazzale Flaminio, take the Roma-Nord train to the Due Ponti stop. Year-round, €4.90 per tent plus €8.90 per person.

Camping Tiber on Via Tiberina at Km 1400 ☏ 06.3361.2314 or 06.3361.0733, ⓕ 06.3361.2314. Another good bet – spacious and friendly, with a bar/pizzeria, a swimming pool and really hot showers. It offers a free shuttle service (every 30min) to and from the nearby Prima Porta station, where you can catch the Roma-Nord service to Piazzale Flaminio (about 20min). March–Oct, €4.50 per tent plus €8.50 per person.

Eating

lthough Rome is undeniably a major-league cultural and historic city, it just doesn't compare to London or Paris for cutting-edge sophistication and trendiness. In many ways it's like an overgrown village. This can be bad news for nightlife, but it's great news for **food**. Romans, as a group, are still very much in touch with the land – many even have small farms of their own in the countryside nearby, or they return to their home villages regularly. So the city's denizens know a good deal about freshness and authenticity, and can be very demanding when it comes to the quality of the dishes they are served.

Consequently, eating out is a major, often hours-long, activity in Rome, and the meals you'll enjoy generally range from good to truly remarkable. You'll find that most city-centre **restaurants** offer standard Italian dishes, and some specialise purely in Roman fare, but there have been a few more adventurous places popping up of late. At the geographical centre of the country, the capital also has numerous establishments dedicated to a variety of **regional cuisines**, and a reasonable number of excellent **ethnic restaurants**, though many of these are in outlying areas. Rome is also blessed with an abundance of good, honest **pizzerias**, churning out thin, crispy-baked pizza from wood-fired ovens. House wine is usually drinkable, if rarely memorable, but there are also any number of *enoteche* – **wine bars** – who really know their business (we've listed some of the best of these in Chapter 15). We've also listed a range of places serving **snacks** and the best of the city's **gelaterie** and **pasticcerie**. **Vegetarians** will find plenty of options in virtually all Italian eateries. Many pasta dishes and pizzas, of course, are made entirely without meat; lentils and other beans and pulses are a part of traditional cookery; and wonderful fresh vegetables and cheeses are always available. Even so, there are a number of restaurants that specialize in vegetarian cuisine, and some of them are among the most appealing places in Rome.

One final caveat: generally speaking it's hard to find truly bad food and rip-off prices in Rome. However, it may be wise to avoid places that are adjacent to some major monuments, such as the Pantheon, Piazza Navona, or the Vatican. The food in these places can be poor, and the prices truly outlandish, sometimes as much as three times the going rate. Near major sights, use the guide!

Opening hours have been given for all restaurants and cafés; note, however, that many places are closed during August.

Lunch, snacks and sandwiches

Just about all **bars and cafés** in town sell snacks such as *tramezzini* and *pizza bianca*, with fillings such as mozzarella and prosciutto, mozzarella and

Eating Italian: the essentials

Most Italians start their day in a bar, their breakfast consisting of a coffee with hot milk (a cappuccino) and a *cornetto* – a jam-, custard- or chocolate-filled croissant. At other times of the day, **sandwiches** (panini) can be pretty substantial, and cost about €2–3; bars also offer *tramezzini*, ready-made sliced white bread with mixed fillings – less appetizing than the average panino but still tasty and slightly cheaper at around €2 a time. If you want hot takeaway food, it's possible to find slices of pizza (*pizza rustica* or *pizza al taglio*) pretty much everywhere, and you can get most things, plus spit-roast chicken, pasta, and hot meals, in a *rosticceria*. Italian **ice cream** (*gelato*) is justifiably famous; reckon on paying upwards of €2.50 for a cone (*un cono*) depending on how many scoops you want. Most bars have a fairly good selection, but for real choice go to a *gelateria*, where the range is a tribute to the Italian imagination and flair for display; we've listed our favourites at the end of this chapter.

An Italian meal traditionally starts with **antipasto** (literally "before the meal"), consisting of various cold cuts of meat, seafood and various vegetable dishes. A plateful of various antipasti from a self-service buffet will set you back €5–10 a head, an item chosen from the menu slightly less. Bear in mind that if you're moving onto pasta, let alone a main course, you may need quite an appetite to tackle this. The next course, **il primo**, consists of a soup or pasta dish, and it's fine to eat just this and nothing else; pasta dishes go for around €8–12. This is followed by **il secondo** – the meat or fish course, usually served alone, except for perhaps a wedge of lemon or tomato. Watch out when ordering fish, which will either be served whole or by weight: 250g is usually plenty for one person, or ask to have a look at the fish before it's cooked; main fish or meat courses will normally be anything between €10 and €20. Vegetables or salads – **contorni** – are ordered and served separately, and sometimes there won't be much choice: potatoes will usually come as chips (*patatine fritte*); salads are either green (*verde*) or mixed (*mista*). Afterwards you nearly always get a choice of fresh fruit (*frutta*) and a selection of desserts (*dolci*) – sometimes just ice cream, but often more elaborate items, such as *zuppa inglese* (spongecake or trifle).

Many Italians wouldn't dream of going out to eat and not ordering a full **five-course meal** — starter, first, second, vegetable, desert or fruit, plus wine, mineral water, coffee and a *digestivo*, such as an *amaro* (home-made herb liqueur) — but don't think you have to follow the pattern; you can order as little or as much as you want, and no one will raise an eyebrow. Roman restaurants keep pretty rigid **opening hours**, generally from noon to 3pm and from 7pm to midnight, although some stay open later, especially in summer. Early in the week tends to be quieter, and many places are closed in August. It's always a good idea to make a reservation, particularly towards the weekend. Getting the **bill** (*il conto*) can sometimes be a struggle – nothing moves fast in Rome when it comes to mealtimes – but, when you do, **service** of 10–15 percent will sometimes be included, and if so it will be clearly indicated. Otherwise a small tip is fine, rounding the bill up €2–3 or so, as waiters in Italy are paid well. Almost everywhere they add a **cover charge** of around €2 a head; on your bill it will normally be labelled as "pane", and is technically for the bread, which they bring automatically. So if you don't want it — and don't want to pay for what you don't eat — you can send it back.

spinach, and *bresaola e rughetta* (cured beef and wild arugula). **Rosticcerie** have a whole range of Roman specialities, including *supplì* (deep-fried rice balls), roast chicken and potatoes, and even green vegetables, and a complete meal for two can cost as little as €6. Expect to pay around €4 for a decent-sized pizza slice from one of the many **pizza al taglio** or **pizza rustica** outlets scattered throughout the city. If money is very tight you can picnic on bread, tomatoes, salad and ricotta cheese bought from street markets and bakeries. All **alimentari** will make up sandwiches for you, usually starting at about €3; for hot snacks, go to a **tavola calda** ("hot table") or **gastronomia**, but expect to pay quite a bit more.

Centro Storico, Campo de' Fiori and the Ghetto

See maps p.37 and pp.52–53

Brek Largo di Torre Argentina 1 ☎06.6821.0353. Bus #30, 40, 46, 62, 63, 64, 70, 81, 87, 492, 628, 630, 780, 916 or Tram #8. Daily 8am–midnight. Semi-fast-food joint with a colourful cinema-theme decor. Everything is actually prepared for you fresh, making it good for both a snack or a full meal, although it's not an environment that especially encourages you to linger.

Bruschetteria degli Angeli Piazza Benedetto Cairoli 2/a ☎06.6880.5789. Bus #23, 30, 40, 46, 62, 63, 64, 70, 81, 87, 492, 628, 630, 780, 916 or Tram #8. Lunch and dinner during the week, evenings only weekends. Lovely and large *birreria* that does a great line on large *bruschette* with all kinds of toppings to soak up the ale. Lots of other choices, too. Very good, very central – a good bet for lunch or even dinner. You'll pay €8 or so for a large *bruschetta*, which is enough for two as a snack.

Caffè Leonardo Piazza Mignanelli 21a ☎06.679.7310. Metro A Spagna or Bus #52, 53, 61, 71, 80, 85, 95, 116, 119, 160, 850. Daily 10.30am–8pm. In an ideal location just around from the Spanish Steps, this bistro offers sandwiches and dozens of big, satisfying salads at amazing prices for the chic area it's in. Beautifully decorated inside, with comfortable tables outside on one of Rome's finest piazzas.

Delfino Corso V. Emanuele 67 ☎06.686.4053. Bus #30, 40, 46, 62, 63, 64, 70, 81, 87, 492, 628, 630, 780, 916 or Tram #8. Daily 8am–9pm. A fairly ordinary but very central and busy cafeteria right on Largo Argentina, with huge choice of snacks and full meals. Good for a fast fill-up between sights.

Enoteca Corsi Via del Gesù 87–88 ☎06.679.0821. Bus #30, 40, 46, 62, 63, 64, 70, 81, 87, 492, 628, 630, 780, 916 or Tram #8. Lunch only, closed Sun. Tucked away between Piazza Venezia and the Pantheon, this is an old-fashioned Roman trattoria and wine shop where you eat what they happen to have cooked that morning.

They do a menu that changes each day, and it gets very busy at lunchtimes – so much so that you may have to wait for a table at the height of the midday rush. Very cheap – €7.50 for a main course, €4 for a *primo*.

Enoteca del Corso Corso Vittorio Emanuele 293 ☎06.6880.1594. Bus #30, 40, 46, 62, 64, 70, 81, 116, 492, 628. Closes at 9.30pm. Long-established wine shop that not only has a great selection of wines but also sells chocolate and does focaccia sandwiches and other snacks at lunchtime and early evening.

Il Forno di Campo de' Fiori Campo de' Fiori 22 ☎06.6880.6662. Bus #30, 40, 46, 62, 64, 70, 81, 87, 116, 186, 204, 492, 628, 916. Mon–Sat 7am–1.30pm & 5.30–8pm; closed Sat evening in summer, Thurs evening in winter. The *pizza bianca* here (just drizzled with olive oil on top) is a Roman legend and their *pizza rossa* (with a smear of tomato sauce) follows close behind. Get it hot from the oven. Always busy with devotees.

Le Pain Quotidien Via Tomacelli 24–25 (between Piazza di Spagna and the Tiber) ☎06.6880.7727. Bus #30, 70, 81, 87, 116, 117, 119, 492, 628, 913, 926. Tues–Sun 9am–midnight. Actually part of a Belgian chain, but its wonderful organic breads, French cheeses and hearty soups – along with communal-style dining *banquettes* – have quickly found their way into Roman hearts. Weekend brunches are ever-popular.

Rosa Rosae Via di Pietra 88 ☎06.678.6789. Bus #62, 63, 81, 85, 95, 117, 119, 160, 175, 492, 628, 630, 850. Daily 5am–3pm. Tucked just off overwhelming Via del Corso, this serves tea, snacks, and full lunches to both Romans and weary tourists.

La Scaletta Via della Maddalena 46–49 ☎06.679.2149. Bus #62, 63, 81, 85, 95, 116, 117, 119, 160, 170, 204, 492, 628, 630, 850. Daily noon–3.30pm & 6pm–12.30am. Very centrally placed *birreria* that's good for its great, reviving snacks, hot meals, or just a drink between sights.

Zi Fenizia Via Santa Maria del Pianto 64–65. No phone. Bus #23, 63, 280, 630, 780, H or Tram #8. Sun–Thurs 8am–8pm, Fri 8am–3pm. Classic snack joint in the heart of the

Jewish Ghetto that does kosher pizza to go, roasted chicken, *suppli*, burgers and *shawarma*. The speciality of the house is pizza filled with fresh anchovies and *indivia*, a kind of salad.

Tridente, Quirinale, Via Veneto

See maps p.61 and pp.102–103

Antico Forno Via delle Muratte 8 ☎06.679.2866. Metro A Barberini or Bus #52, 53, 61, 62, 63, 80, 95, 116, 119, 175, 492, 630. Daily 7am–9pm. The last thing you'd expect just by the Trevi Fountain: fresh pizza, a sandwich bar, fresh fruits and salads, a bakery and grocery store, all rolled into one – and open on Sundays!

Babington's Tea Rooms Piazza di Spagna 23 ☎06.678.6027. Metro A Spagna or Bus #52, 53, 61, 62, 63, 80, 95, 116, 119, 175, 492, 630. Daily 9am–8.30pm. Over one hundred years of tradition in the very heart of Rome. Light lunches, and scones and other English delicacies for tea. Rather expensive, but very handy. Does a great Sunday brunch too.

Ciampini al Café du Jardin Viale Trinità dei Monti (no street number) ☎06.678.5678. Metro A Spagna or Bus #52, 53, 61, 62, 63, 80, 95, 116, 119, 175, 492, 630. A secluded outdoor setting with a view, opposite Villa Medici, just up the Spanish Steps, a perfect place to relax if you're not too hungry. Salads, sandwiches, ice cream, and, of course, coffee, don't come cheap – resting your feet in Rome's most fashionable quarter has its price – but the location can't be beaten.

Defa Via del Corso 51 ☎06.679.3548. Metro A Flaminio or Bus #88, 95, 117, 119, 495, 628, 926 or Tram #2. Daily 8am–midnight. *Tavola calda* with *pizza al taglio*, to eat on the premises or take away.

Caffè Greco Via Condotti 86 ☎06.678.5474. Metro A Spagna or Bus #52, 53, 61, 71, 80, 85, 95, 116, 119, 160, 492, 630, 850. Mon–Sat 8am–9pm. Founded in 1742, and patronized by, among others, Casanova, Byron, Goethe and Stendhal. Now, however, it's a rather dubious tourist joint. Curiosity value only, although the *granita di caffè* (iced coffee) is a hit on a hot summer day.

Herbier Natura Via San Claudio 87 ☎06.678.5847. Metro A Spagna or Bus #52, 53, 61, 71, 80, 85, 95, 116, 119, 160, 492, 630, 850. Mon–Sat 8am–8pm. Just off Piazza San

Silvestro, inside a lovely inner courtyard, this is a real oasis of calm away from the hectic and fumy traffic. Offers snacks or even a full lunch.

Pizza House Via della Mercede 46 ☎06.679.7584. Metro A Spagna or Bus #52, 53, 61, 71, 80, 85, 95, 116, 119, 160, 492, 630, 850. Daily 11am–11pm. *Rosticceria* and *tavola calda* with seating inside. Good choices and prices, at least for this part of town.

Self-Service Luncheonette Salita di San Nicola da Tolentino 19/21 ☎06.474.0029. Metro A Barberini or Bus #52, 53, 61, 62, 63, 80, 95, 116, 119, 175, 492, 630. Mon–Sat 8am–3pm. Just up from Bernini's spouting Triton fountain at Piazza Barberini, this place has great food served cafeteria-style. It caters to the office workers in the area and so is delicious and cheap. It can be very crowded, so best get there early.

Termini and Around

See map pp.114–115

Caffè Fantini Via A. Depretis 77b ☎06.474.6866. Metro A Vittorio or B Cavour or Bus #16, 75, 84, 360, 649. Mon–Sat 6.30am–6pm. Cafeteria-style service, sandwiches, and a hot and cold buffet that's different every day. A convenient place to break after seeing Santa Maria Maggiore. Just go down the grand staircase at the back of the basilica, cross Via Cavour and continue straight on about a block. No-smoking policy during the lunch hour.

Enoteca Cavour 313 Via Cavour 313 ☎06.678.5496. Metro B Cavour or Bus #16, 75, 84, 360, 649. Mon–Sat 12.30–2.30pm & 7.30pm–12.30am. At the Forum end of Via Cavour, a lovely old wine bar that makes a handy retreat after seeing the ancient sites. Lots of wines and delicious (though not cheap) snacks and salads.

Trimani Via Cernaia 37b ☎06.446.9630. Metro Repubblica or Termini or Bus #36, 38, 40, 60, 61, 62, 64, 75, 84, 90, 92, 105, 170, 175, 217, 310, 492, 714, 910, H. Mon–Sat noon–midnight. Classy wine bar (Rome's biggest selection of Italian regional vintages) good for a lunchtime tipple and an indulgent snack. You'll spend around €15 to sample a range of good-quality cheeses and cured pork meat, or a soup and salad, including a glass of wine. Also has a wine shop outlet nearby – see p.246.

Trastevere and Testaccio

See maps pp.140–141 and pp.86–87

Akropolis Via S. Francesco a Ripa 103 ☎06.5833.2600. Bus #23, 63, 280, 630, 780, H or Tram #8. Tues–Sun noon–2.30pm & 7pm–midnight. Greek takeaway featuring *souvlaki* and all the usual snacks and honeyed sweets.

Fidelio Via degli Stefaneschi 3/7. No phone. Bus #23, 63, 280, 630, 780, H or Tram #8. Daily noon–2am. Tucked away just behind Piazza Sonnino in Trastevere, a *vineria* with lunch and dinner possibilities, too. Sandwiches go for €3, big salads for about €5. Offers a good selection of Italy's best wines. See also p.221.

Kebab House Via Natale del Grande 17 ☎06.581.9863. Bus #23, 44, 75, 280, 630, 780, H or Tram #3, 8. Daily noon–midnight. Mostly takeaway, but you can perch at the counters if you like. *Shawarma*, hummus, grilled chicken and veal, and all the traditional salads and sweets make this a delicious Trastevere way to eat and run.

Il Mondo in Tasca Via della Lungaretta 169 ☎06.588.6040. Bus #23, 63, 280, 630, 780, H or Tram #8. Tues–Sun 11am–3pm & 6pm–midnight. This great little place, whose name translates as "The World in Your Pocket", offers *shawarma*, felafel, hummus, curry, pizza, chili con carne, couscous, salads, tandoori, moussaka, goulash, and just about anything else you could think of. Plus you can check your email and get a tarot reading. Home-made pitta bread, too.

Ombre Rosse Piazza Sant'Egidio 12 ☎06.588.4155. Bus #23, 63, 280, 630, 780, H or Tram #8. Mon–Sat 7am–2.30am, Sun 5pm–2.30am. This has become something of a Trastevere institution, especially for a morning cappuccino, but also for interesting light meals. A great place to people-watch.

Panificio La Renella Via del Moro 15 ☎06.581.7265. Bus #23, 63, 280, 630, 780, H or Tram #8. Daily 8am–9pm. Arguably the best bakery in Rome, right in the heart of Trastevere. Superb *pizza al taglio*: ask for *pizza al tonno*, *pomodoro e rughetta* (tuna fish, tomatoes and wild arugula) or wait around to taste *pizza e patate* (with potatoes and rosemary) hot from the oven. Take a number and be prepared to wait at busy times.

Caffè del Seme e la Foglia Via Galvani 18 ☎06.574.3008. Bus #23, 30, 75, 95, 170, 280, 716, 781 or Tram #3. Mon–Sat 8am–1.30am, Sun 6pm–1.30am. Pleasantly low-key café popular with Testaccio trendies and students from the nearby music school. During the day it's good for sandwiches and big salad lunches – they do fairly exotic things such as avocados with shrimp or crab, and curried turkey sandwiches – and in the evenings a mellow place to relax before visiting the area's more energetic offerings.

Da Venanzo Via San Francesco a Ripa 137 ☎06.589.7110. Bus #23, 63, 280, 630, 780, H or Tram #8. Mon–Sat 11am–11pm, closed holidays. Located just half a block from Viale Trastevere, there's no sign outside this *pizza al taglio* hole-in-the-wall, which is ironic as it may very well have the best pizza by the slice in Rome. Also roast chickens and potatoes, *supplì* and all the usual *rosticceria* fare. Try their unique chopped spicy green olive pizza.

Volpetti Piu Via A. Volta 8. No phone. Bus #23, 30, 75, 95, 170, 280, 716, 781 or Tram #3. Mon–Sat 11am–9pm. *Tavola calda* that's attached to the famous deli a few doors down. Great pizza, *supplì*, chicken, deep-fried veg and much more.

Prati and the Vatican

See map pp.150–151

Franchi Via Cola di Rienzo 200 ☎06.686.4576. Metro A Lepanto or Ottaviano or Bus #23, 32, 34, 40, 49, 62, 81, 280, 492, 590, 982 or Tram #19. Mon–Sat 8am–9pm. One of the best delis in Rome — a triumph of cheeses, sausages and an ample choice of cold or hot food to go, including roast chicken. They'll make up customized lunches for you, and they also have the wines to go with it.

Non Solo Pizza Via degli Scipioni 95–97 ☎06.372.5820. Metro A Ottaviano or Bus #23, 32, 34, 40, 49, 62, 81, 280, 492, 590, 982 or Tram #19. Tues–Sun 8.30am–10pm. Try a slice of pizza with sausage and broccoli or with courgette flowers. There's also the whole range of Roman fritters — *supplì*, *olive ascolane*, *fiori di zucca*, *crocchette*, etc — and also a complete selection of hot dishes *tavola calda*-style. Starting at 7pm, they offer made-to-order round pizzas, too. No extra charge to sit, inside or out.

Coffee, cakes, ice cream

If you just want a **coffee** and a **pastry**, whether it's for breakfast or to keep you going between sights, Rome – like just about any other Italian city – has plenty of choices; it also has some excellent *gelaterie* in which to sample the delights of Italian **ice cream**. Below are some of our favourite venues for both activities. See relevant chapter maps for locations.

Antico Caffè di Brasile Via dei Serpenti 23 ℡06.488.2319. Mon–Sat 6am–8.30pm, Sun 7am–2pm. Reliable old Monti stand-by that has been selling great coffee, snacks and cakes for around a century. You'll know it by the old iron coffee roaster – no longer used – that stands towards the back, beyond which are a handful of seats and tables should you want to take the weight off.
Bernasconi Piazza Cairoli 16 ℡06.6880.6264. Bus #63, 630, 780, H or Tram #8. Tues–Sun 7am–8.30pm. Closed Aug. A great, family-run *pasticceria*, with *sfogliatelle* to die for and a host of other goodies. Good coffee, too.
Caffè Sant'Eustachio Piazza Sant' Eustachio 82. No phone. Tues–Sun 8.30am–1am. Just behind the Pantheon you'll find what many feel is absolutely Rome's best coffee, usually served Neapolitan-style – that is, very, very sweet. You can ask for it without sugar, but they'll think you're weird. They do a good line in coffee-based sweets and cakes.
Camilloni Piazza Sant'Eustachio 54 ℡06.686.4995. Bus #63 or #492. Tues–Sun 8.30am–midnight. The rival for Rome's best coffee, larger than the *Sant'Eustachio*, across the square, and with great cakes.
Cinque Lune Corso Rinascimento 89 ℡06.6880.1005. Bus #30, 70, 81, 87, 116, 492, 628. Tues–Sun 9am–1pm & 4–7pm. Traditional takeaway Roman pastries, including *baba* with whipped cream, and, at Christmas, perfect soft *torrone*. Just outside Piazza Navona.
La Dolceroma Via Portico d'Ottavia 20b ℡06.689.2196. Bus #23, 63, 280, 630, 780, H or Tram #8. Tues–Sun 9am–1pm & 4–7.30pm. First-class Austrian (Quark cake, plum crumble) and American classics – brownies, blueberry muffins and best of all, white chocolate chip cookies.
Dolci & Doni Via delle Carrozze 85 ℡06.678.2913. Metro A Spagna or Bus #52, 53, 61, 71, 80, 85, 95, 116, 119, 160, 850. Daily 8am–8pm. A truly sumptuous array of pastries right in the heart of the city, just a few steps away from Piazza di Spagna. Don't miss the lemon cheesecake. Tea and other snacks, too.

Doppia Coppia Via della Scala 51 ℡06.581.3174. Bus #23, 75, 280, 630, 780, H or Tram #8. Daily 1pm–midnight, later in summer. This Sicilian-owned Trastevere joint has some of the very best ice cream in town. Sublime consistency and unusual flavours such as cinnamon and cassata. The amarena and coconut are also great.
Il Forno del Ghetto Via del Portico d'Ottavia 1 ℡06.687.8637. Bus #23, 63, 280, 630, 780, H or Tram #8. Sun–Fri 8am–8pm. Marvellous kosher Jewish bakery whose unforgettable ricotta pies and *pizza giudia* (a hard cake, crammed with dried and candied fruit) draw quite a crowd.
Il Gelato di San Crispino Via della Panetteria 42 ℡06.7045.0412. Metro A Spagna or Barberini or Bus #52, 53, 61, 62, 63, 80, 95, 116, 119, 175, 492, 630. Wed–Mon noon–midnight. Considered by many to be the best ice cream in Rome, and certainly the most genuine. Wonderful flavours – all natural – will make the other *gelato* you've known pale by comparison. Worth paying a bit extra for. Not far from Trevi Fountain.
Giolitti Via Uffici del Vicario 40 ℡06.699.1243. Bus #30, 40, 46, 62, 63, 64, 70, 81, 116, 492, 628, 630. Tues–Sun 7am–2am. An Italian institution that once had a reputation — now lost — for the country's top ice cream. Still pretty good, however, with a choice of seventy flavours. And always very busy.
Innocenti Via della Luce 21 ℡06.580.3926. Bus #23, 75, 280, 630, 780, H or Tram #8. Mon–Sat 9am–1pm & 4–7.30pm, Sun 9am–1pm; closed Aug 15–Sept 15. Trastevere's – and maybe Rome's – best *biscottificio*, a family operation for 100 years. Wonderful, chewy *croccantini* — half chocolate, half vanilla. Plus *amarettii* (almond biscuits), *brutti ma buoni* (hazelnut biscuits), *straccetti* (almond and hazelnut biscuits) and dozens more varieties.
Palazzo del Freddo di Giovanni Fassi Via Principe Eugenio 65/7 ℡06.446.4740. Metro A Vittorio or Bus #16, 75, 84, 360, 649. Tues–Sun midday–midnight. A wonderful, airy 1920s ice-cream parlour (not far from Termini).

Brilliant fruit ice creams and good milk shakes.

Pascucci Via di Torre Argentina 20 ☎06.686.4816. Bus #30, 40, 46, 62, 63, 64, 70, 81, 87, 492, 628, 630, 780, 916 or Tram #8. **Daily 6.30am–midnight.** This tiny stand-up bar is *frullati* central for the centro storico. Your choice of fresh fruit whipped up with ice and milk — the ultimate Roman refreshment on a hot day.

La Tazza d'Oro Via degli Orfani 84/86 ☎06.679.2768. Bus #63, 492. **Mon–Sat 7am–8pm.** Straight off Piazza del Pantheon, this place is well named, since it is by common consent the home of one of Rome's best cups of coffee, plus decent iced coffee and sinfully rich *granita di caffè*, with double dollops of whipped cream.

Tre Scalini Piazza Navona 30 ☎06.6880.1996. Bus #30, 40, 46, 62, 64, 70, 81, 87, 116, 492, 628. **Thurs–Tues 8am–1.30am.** Piazza Navona institution that is renowned for its famous *tartufo* – death by dark chocolate.

Valzani Via del Moro 37 ☎06.580.3792. Bus #23, 75, 280, 630, 780, H or Tram #8. **Wed–Sun 10am–8.30pm; closed June–Sept 15; extended hours at Christmas and Easter.** One of the oldest of the city's pastry shops, still keeping up tradition with marvellous *mostaccioli* and *pangiallo* (both are traditional dried fruit and nut honey bars, the former chocolate covered), amazing *sachertorte* (classic Viennese double-chocolate cake with apricot filling), and, at Easter time, huge, gift-filled chocolate eggs which you can have your name etched on.

Da Vezio Via dei Delfini 23 ☎06.678.6036. Bus #23, 30, 44, 63, 81, 95, 160, 170, 280, 628, 630, 715, 716, 780, 781, 916, H or Tram #8. **Mon–Sat 7.30am–9pm.** Tiny bar tucked away across the street from the Capitoline Museums that is a shrine to the Italian Left, Castro and all aspects of the workers' struggle. Not the most welcoming bar in town, but it's worth lingering over a coffee to study the memorabilia that coats the walls.

Restaurants and pizzerias

There are lots of good places to eat in the **centro storico**, and it's still surprisingly easy to find places that are not tourist traps – **prices** in all but the really swanky places remain pretty uniform throughout the city. The area around Via Cavour and **Termini** is packed with cheap restaurants, although some of them are of dubious cleanliness; if you are not in a hurry, you might do better heading up to the nearby student area of **San Lorenzo**, where you can often eat far better for the same money. South of the centre, the **Testaccio** neighbourhood is also well endowed with good, inexpensive trattorias, and, across the river, **Trastevere** is Rome's traditional restaurant enclave. Even though the number of authentic "Trasté" trattorias has declined over recent years, you'll easily find good-to-great meals there, at all price levels.

Centro Storico, Campo de' Fiori and the Ghetto

See maps p.37 and pp.52–53

Acchiappafantasmi Via dei Cappellari 66 ☎06.687.3462. Bus #30, 40, 46, 62, 64, 70, 81, 87, 116, 186, 204, 492, 628, 916. **Daily 8pm–2am.** Fine "ghost-shaped" pizzas — the name of the place is Italian for "Ghostbusters" — appetizers, and a selection of Calabrian salamis. Always busy, with a very lively atmosphere, and service can suffer as a result.

Da Alfredo e Ada Via dei Banchi Nuovi 14 ☎06.687.8842. Bus #30, 40, 46, 62, 64, 70, 81,

116, 492 or 628. **Weekdays only, lunch and dinner.** There's no menu, and precious little choice, at this city-centre stalwart, at which Ada presides over an appreciative clientele of regulars, serving up pasta starters, followed by veal stew with peas, sausage and beans, or whatever they happen to have cooked that day. Dessert is biscuits from Ada's tin, dished out with grand-maternal generosity. €16 for three courses, including half a litre of wine.

Antica Birreria Peroni Via San Marcello 19 ☎06.679.5310. Bus #30, 40, 46, 62, 64, 70, 81, 116, 492, 628. **Mon–Sat noon–midnight.** Big bustling *birreria* with an excellent menu of simple food that's meant to soak up lots of

△ Antipasti at *La Carbonara*

Roman food and wine

Roman **cooking** is traditionally dominated by the offal-based, earthy cuisine of the working classes, with a little influence from the city's millennia-old Jewish population thrown in. Although you'll find all sorts of **pasta** served in Roman restaurants, spaghetti is probably the most popular, as it stands up well to the coarse, gutsy sauces the Romans prefer: *aglio e olio* (oil and garlic), *cacio e pepe* (pecorino and ground black pepper), *alla carbonara* (with beaten eggs, cubes of pan-fried *guanciale* — cured pork jowl — or bacon, and pecorino or parmesan), and *alle vongole* (best when a little peperoncino is added to give the clams an extra kick). There's also *maccheroni alla ciociara*, with *guanciale*, slices of sausage, prosciutto and tomato; *bucatini all'amatriciana* (thick spaghetti with tomato and *guanciale*); and *gnocchi*, usually with a meat sauce, which are traditionally eaten on Thursday.

Fish is an integral, though usually pricey, part of Roman cuisine, and is most frequently eaten in Rome as salt cod — *baccalà*; best eaten Jewish-style, deep-fried. **Offal** is also important and although it has been ousted from many of the more refined city-centre restaurants, you'll still find it on the menus of more traditional places, especially those in Testaccio. Most favoured is *pajata*, the intestines of an unweaned calf, but you'll also find *lingua* (tongue), *rognone* (kidney), *milza* (spleen — delicious as a pâté on toasted bread) and *trippa* (tripe). Look out, too, for *coda alla vaccinara*, oxtail stewed in a rich sauce of tomato and celery; *testerelle d'abbacchio*, lamb's head baked in the oven with herbs and oil; and *coratella*, lamb's heart, liver, lungs and spleen cooked in olive oil with lots of black pepper and onions. More conventional **meat dishes** include *abbacchio*, milk-fed lamb roasted to melting tenderness with rosemary, sage and garlic; *scottadito*, grilled lamb chops eaten with the fingers; and *saltimbocca alla romana*, thin slices of veal cooked with a slice of prosciutto and sage on top, served plain or with a Marsala sauce. Outside Rome there's quite a bit of game served — wild boar (*cinghiale*), hare (*lepre*), pigeon (*piccione*), rabbit (*coniglio*) and pheasant (*fagiano*).

Artichokes (*carciofi*) are the quintessential Roman **vegetable**, served "alla romana" (stuffed with garlic and roman mint and stewed) and in all their unadulterated glory as *alla giudea* — flattened and deep fried in olive oil. Another not-to-be-missed side dish is batter-fried squash or courgette blossom (*fiori di zucca*), stuffed with mozzarella and a sliver of marinated anchovy. Roman pizza has a thin crust and is best when baked in a wood-burning oven (*cotta a legna*), but you can also find pizza by the slice (*pizza al taglio*), always sold by weight.

Wine comes mainly from the Castelli Romani (most famously Frascati) to the south, and from around Montefiascone (Est! Est! Est!) in the north. Both are basic, straightforward whites, fine for sunny lunchtimes but otherwise not all that noteworthy. However, in most places you'll find a complete selection of Italy's best and most famous wines.

---

beer. There are the usual starters and pasta dishes, plus a good selection of meat dishes, *scamorza* and *wurstel* specialities. Its walls are decorated with a frieze full of slogans urging you to drink more beer – something that's very hard to resist in this lovely old wood-panelled turn-of-the-century restaurant full of photos of old Rome. Very fast service. **Armando al Pantheon** Salita de' Crescenzi 30 ☎06.6880.3034. Bus #30, 40, 46, 62, 63, 64, 70, 81, 87, 492, 628, 630, 780, 916 or Tram #8. **Mon–Fri 12.30–3pm & 7–11pm, Sat 12.30–3pm. Closed Sat pm and all day Sun.**

Surprisingly unpretentious surroundings and moderately priced hearty food in this long-standing staple close by the Pantheon (open since 1961).
Arnaldo ai Satiri Via di Grotta Pinta 8 ☎06.686.1915. Bus #30, 40, 46, 62, 63, 64, 70, 81, 87, 492, 628, 630, 780, 916 or Tram #8. **Wed–Mon 7.30pm–midnight.** One of Rome's cosiest hideaways, near Piazza Navona and the Pantheon. Couples can enjoy the cosy, candlelit setting with international ballet theme decor. Try the spaghetti sautéed with greens. No-smoking policy.

Il Bacaro Via degli Spagnoli 27 ☎06.686.4110. Bus #30, 40, 46, 62, 64, 70, 81, 116, 492, 628. Mon–Fri 12.30–2.30pm & 8–11.30pm, Sat 8–11.30pm. This tiny restaurant tucked away down a small side street off Via della Scrofa, has a small, focused menu featuring a delicious, interesting selection of antipasti and *primi*, and main courses focusing on meat dishes, particularly beef, in a variety of original sauces and servings. The feel of the place is rather romantic but it's really too cramped for a truly private liaison.

Da Baffetto Via del Governo Vecchio 114 ☎06.686.1617. Bus #30, 40, 46, 62, 64, 70, 81, 116, 492 or 628. Daily 7pm–midnight. A tiny, highly authentic pizzeria that has long been a Rome institution, though it now tends to be swamped by tourists. Amazingly it's still good value, and has tables outside in summer, though you will always have to queue. Especially good *bruschette* (toasted hunks of bread with savoury toppings).

Baronato Quattro Bellezze Via di Panico 23 ☎06.687.2865. Bus #30, 40, 46, 62, 64, 70, 81, 116, 492, 628. Daily 8pm–2am. A one-of-a-kind place, serving great home-cooked couscous in a wonderfully camp environment. Moderate prices. The owner-chef sings Piaf on Thursdays; see also p.238.

Dal Bolognese Piazza del Popolo 1 ☎06.361.1426. Metro A Flaminio or Bus #88, 95, 117, 119, 495, 628, 926 or Tram #2. Tues–Sun 12.45–3pm & 8.15–11pm. An elegant restaurant that is *the* place to go if you want to treat yourself to good Emilian cuisine; *tortellini in brodo* is a must if you like chicken soup. Reservations are recommended, especially if you'd rather eat outside and watch the passers-by in the piazza. Expensive.

Caffè Capranica Piazza Capranica 104 ☎06.679.0860. Bus #30, 40, 46, 62, 64, 70, 81, 116, 492, 628. Daily noon–midnight. This restaurant, *enoteca*, taverna and pizzeria all in one is admirably located on a fairly quiet piazza near the Pantheon. Standard fare, well prepared, and average prices, plus no serious limits on when you can eat.

La Campana Vicolo della Campana 18 ☎06.686. 7820. Bus #30, 70, 81, 87, 116, 492, 628. Tues–Sun 11.30am–3.30pm & 7.30pm–midnight. Packed with politicians and journalists, this is truly a trattoria of habitués. To newcomers, service can seem almost surly, but the Roman specialties – in what is said to be the oldest trattoria in the capital – are dependably good and hearty, featuring an abundance of fresh vegetables and fish and home-made desserts. The soups are all delicious, including the signature *pasta e fagioli*. There is also – unusually – a no-smoking room.

La Carbonara Campo de' Fiori 23 ☎06.686.4783. Bus #30, 40, 46, 62, 64, 70, 81, 87, 116, 186, 204, 492, 628, 916. Wed–Mon noon–3.30pm & 7pm–midnight. The most expensive of the square's restaurants, but still good value and always busy, with plenty of outdoor seating and an excellent selection of antipasti. Try their home-made ravioli, pappardelle in wild boar sauce, or their namesake *spaghetti alla carbonara*.

Ciccia Bomba Via del Governo Vecchio 76 ☎06.6880.2108. Bus #30, 40, 46, 62, 64, 70, 81, 116, 492, 628. Thurs–Tues noon–3pm & 7pm–1am. Mirrors and antique furniture make this versatile pizzeria/trattoria look pricey, but it isn't at all bad considering the quality. Rather in at the moment with the young chic set.

Il Convivio Vicolo dei Soldati 31 ☎06.686.9432. Bus #30, 40, 46, 62, 64, 70, 81, 116, 492, 628. Closed Monday at lunch, entirely Sun; otherwise open for lunch and dinner. Beautiful restaurant with tables set out in three vaulted rooms by the river near Piazza Navona. The food is

---

Italian regional cuisine

Not all Rome's restaurants just serve Roman specialities; in fact Rome offers a good sampling of the varied *cucina* of Italy's many distinct regions. See the listings for the full rundown on these places.

Acchiappafantasmi (Calabrian) (p.204)
Baia Chia (Sardinian) (p.212)
Dal Bolognese (Emilian) (see p.207)
Il Chianti (Tuscan) (p.211)
Colline Emiliane (Emilian) (p.211)

Il Dito e La Luna (Sicilian) (p.212)
Ferrara (Multiregional) (p.214)
Dal Toscano (Tuscan) (p.215)
El Toulà (Venetian) (p.210)
Tram Tram (Pugliese) (p.213)
Trattoria Monti (Le Marche) (p.213)

adventurous and exquisite with variations on in seasonal ingredients – the menu changes traditional Roman dishes such as *baccalà* and *fiori di zucca*, and a firm basis changes several times a year so it's hard to say what will be on offer. The prices make it one for a special night out, but you shouldn't be disappointed.

Filetti di Baccalà Largo dei Librari 88 ☎06.686.4018. Bus #30, 40, 46, 62, 64, 70, 81, 87, 116, 186, 204, 492, 628, 916. Mon–Sat 5.30–10.30pm; closed in August. A fish-and-chip shop without the chips. Paper-covered Formica tables (outdoors in summer), cheap wine, beer and fried cod, a timeless Roman speciality. Located a short walk from Campo de' Fiori, off busy Via Giubbonari. Service can be offhand, to say the least.

La Focaccia Via della Pace 11 ☎06.6880.3312. Bus #30, 40, 46, 62, 64, 70, 81, 116, 492, 628. Daily noon–3.30pm & 7.30pm–1am. A great location, just off Piazza Navona, and hearty, unusual dishes – and, of course, a dozen different kinds of focaccia. Try the one with sesame. Twenty-four different pizza offerings and big salads, plus original pastas. The *paccheri* on a bed of shredded smoked ricotta is especially delicious. For dessert, the pear tart smothered in amarena sauce is memorable. The red house wine is good, too. Tables outside in summer.

Da Francesco Piazza del Fico 29 ☎06.686.4009. Bus #30, 40, 46, 62, 64, 70, 81, 116, 492, 628. Mon & Wed–Sun 7pm–1am. Not just delectable pizzas in this full-on pizzeria in the heart of trendy Rome, but good antipasti, *primi* and *secondi* too. The service can be slapdash, but the food and atmosphere are second-to-none.

Osteria ar Galletto Piazza Farnese 102 ☎06.686.1714 Bus #30, 40, 46, 62, 64, 70, 81, 87, 116, 186, 204, 492, 628, 916. Mon–Sat 12.15–3pm & 7.30–11.15pm. This place is situated on one of Rome's stateliest piazzas, and just off one of its trendiest, too, and yet retains the feel of a provincial trattoria. It's been a local favourite for at least a quarter of a century and specializes in traditional Roman cookery with a homely touch. In winter, the atmospheric indoor setting is old Rome at its best; in warmer months, you can enjoy the magnificent Renaissance square from outside seating. Very good prices, too.

Da Giggetto Via del Portico d'Ottavia 21a–22 ☎06.686.1105. Bus #23, 63, 280, 630, 780, H or Tram #8. Tues–Sun noon–3.30pm & 7.30pm–midnight. Roman-Jewish fare in the Jewish Ghetto, featuring deep-fried artichokes, *baccalà*, and *rigatoni con pajata*, along with good non-offal pasta dishes, eaten outside in summer by the ruins of the Portico d'Ottavia. Not cheap, but worth the splurge. It's usually very crowded, but so huge you can almost always get a table.

Govinda Via Santa Maria del Pianto 15–16 ☎06.6889.1540. Bus #63, 630, 780, H or Tram #8. Sun–Fri 11.30am–3pm & 7.30–11pm; Sat evening only. This delightful, strictly Hindu vegetarian place is run by the Italian branch of the Hare Krishna movement. The atmosphere is light and refined, the food always delicious, and the service gracious. Between Largo Argentina and the Tiber.

Grappolo d'Oro Piazza della Cancelleria 80 ☎06.686.4118. Bus #30, 40, 46, 62, 64, 70, 81, 87, 116, 186, 204, 492, 628, 916. Mon–Sat noon–3pm & 8–11pm; closed August. Curiously untouched by the hordes in nearby Campo de' Fiori, this restaurant serves imaginative Roman cuisine in traditional trattoria atmosphere. Try the risotto with *tartufi* and *funghi*.

Alle Grotte Via delle Grotte 27 ☎06.686.4293. Bus #30, 40, 46, 62, 64, 70, 81, 87, 116, 186, 204, 492, 628, 916. Mon–Sat 11.30am–3.30pm & 7pm–midnight. An out-of-the-way, cosy trattoria with a traditional, limited menu and the deeply authentic feel of old Rome. Inexpensive, and with outdoor seating in summer, towards the river from Campo de' Fiori.

'Gusto Piazza Augusto Imperatore 9 ☎06.322.6273. Metro A Flaminio or Bus #88, 95, 117, 119, 495, 628, 926 or Tram #2. Daily 12.30–3pm & 7.30pm–2am. A slick establishment that's more like something you might find in San Francisco or Sydney. However, the food is unique and often wonderful, and the atmosphere very chic. There's a reasonably priced Mediterranean buffet lunch every day that is very popular. Otherwise, the restaurant upstairs offers true gourmet dishes: try the marinated chopped sea bass and tuna with ginger rice for starters. The tagliolini with *mazzan-colle* (a sort of Mediterranean crayfish), asparagus and star anise is sublime, as is the roasted breast of duck. Unusual, well-executed desserts, too, and a very complete wine list. See also Osteria della Frezza (below) and p.247 for the other options the 'Gusto empire offers.

L'Insalata Ricca Largo dei Chiavari 85/86
☎06.6880.3656. Bus #30, 40, 46, 62, 64, 70, 81, 87, 116, 186, 204, 492, 628, 916. Daily noon–3.30pm & 7pm–1am. An Anglo-American presence in a relaxed and slightly out-of-the-ordinary place, although it is just one of a Roman chain of six. Interesting, big salads, as the name suggests, whole-food options and reasonably priced Italian fare. A good choice for vegetarians. Nice setting, next to a church, between Piazza Navona and Campo de' Fiori. There's also another branch, very close by, on Piazza Pasquino, and one in Trastevere, too.

Il Leoncino Via del Leoncino 28
☎06.687.6306. Metro A Spagna or Bus #52, 53, 61, 62, 63, 80, 95, 116, 119, 175, 492, 630. Mon–Fri 1–2.30pm & 7pm–midnight, Sat & Sun 7pm–midnight. Cheap, hectic and genuine pizzeria, little known to out-of-towners. Really one of the very best for lovers of crispy Roman-style pizza, baked in wood ovens. Just off Via del Corso. No credit cards, and closed during August.

Maccheroni Piazza delle Coppelle 44
☎06.6830.7895. Bus #30, 40, 46, 62, 64, 70, 81, 116, 492, 628. Mon–Sat 12.30–3pm & 8pm–midnight. A friendly, relatively new restaurant that enjoys a wonderful location on this quiet piazza right in the heart of the centro storico. Inside is spartan yet comfy, with basic furniture and marble-topped counters, while the outside tables make the most of the pretty square-cum-intersection. The food is good, basic Italian fare, affordably priced and cheerfully served.

La Montecarlo Vicolo Savelli 12
☎06.686.1877. Bus #30, 40, 46, 62, 64, 70, 81, 116, 492, 628. Daily noon–3pm & 6.30pm–1am. Hectic pizzeria owned by the daughter of *Da Baffetto* (see p.207) and serving similar crisp, blistered pizza, along with good pasta dishes. Tables outside in summer, but be prepared to queue. Tucked off Corso Vittorio, not far from Piazza Navona.

Myosotis Via della Vaccarella 3–5
☎06.686.5554. Bus #62, 63, 81, 85, 95, 117, 119, 160, 175, 492, 628, 630, 850. Mon–Sat 12.30–2.45pm & 8–11pm. Excellent food, service and value at this upscale restaurant tucked away on a side street a short walk from the Pantheon, with excellent pasta, fish and roast meat dishes. Kind of snooty – the sort of place you choose for a posh night out.

Oliphant Vicolo delle Coppelle 31–32
☎06.686.1416. Bus #30, 40, 46, 62, 64, 70, 81, 87, 116, 492, 628. Daily noon–1am. American restaurant and bar, good for just a drink or a full meal if you're in the mood for their menu of steaks, burgers and Tex-Mex specials at €12 or so a time.

Osteria della Frezza Via della Frezza 1316
☎06.322.6273. Metro A Flaminio or Bus #88, 95, 117, 119, 495, 628, 926 or Tram #2. Part of the super-cool – and ultra-successful 'Gusto empire, this place is equally good for snacks such as cheese or salami plates or for full meals. There's a large wine list, and the whole thing is carried wit the usual 'Gusto panache – though the cool jazz sounds and gliding black-attired waiters tend to grate after a while. Not cheap, either.

Der Pallaro Largo del Pallaro 15
☎06.6880.1488. Bus #30, 40, 46, 62, 64, 70, 81, 87, 116, 186, 204, 492, 628, 916. Tues–Sun noon–3pm & 7pm–midnight. An old-fashioned trattoria serving a set daily menu for €20, including wine. A good option when you're starving. Located in a quiet piazza between Campo de' Fiori and Largo Argentina. No credit cards.

Roman Jewish Restaurants

Most, but not all, of the places specializing in traditional Roman Jewish cookery are in the Ghetto. Here are our favourites; full reviews can be found among the listings.

Il Forno del Ghetto (p.203)
Da Giggetto (p.208)
Da Lisa (p.212)
Da Paris (p.214)

Piperno (p.210)
Al Pompiere (p.210)
Sora Margherita (p.210)
Zi Fenizia (p.200)

Pizza Re Via di Ripetta 14 ☎06.321.1468. Metro A Flaminio or Bus #88, 95, 117, 119, 495, 628, 926 or Tram #2. Daily, except Sun lunch, noon–3pm & 7pm–midnight. Authentic Neapolitan pizzeria (thicker than Roman) made in a wood-stoked oven. Just up from Piazza del Popolo. Busy, so book.

Al Pompiere Via Santa Maria dei Calderari 38 ☎06.686.8377. Bus #23, 63, 280, 630, 780, H or Tram #8. Closed Sun, otherwise noon–3pm & 7pm–midnight. Housed in a frescoed old palace in the heart of the Ghetto, this fusty, old-fashioned restaurant exudes tradition and serves up some of the best Roman-Jewish food you'll find at decent prices. Its warren of high-ceilinged rooms is usually crowded, especially late on, and it's a good place to try *carciofi alla giudea* and *fiori fritti*.

Piperno Monte de Cenci 9 ☎06.6880.6629. Bus #23, 63, 280, 630, 780, H or Tram #8. Tues–Sat 12.30–2.15pm, Sun 12.30–2.15pm. A rather formal restaurant that makes one of the best opportunities to sample Jewish specialities. The cooking is exceptional, the prices moderate to high. An excellent choice for a big night out.

La Primavera Via del Sudario 37 ☎06.687.5417. Bus #30, 40, 46, 62, 63, 64, 70, 81, 87, 492, 628, 630, 780, 916 or Tram #8. Daily noon–3pm & 7pm–midnight. Chinese food isn't great in Italy, but this is a decent enough and rather elegant (by Roman standards) Chinese restaurant, just off Largo Argentina. Dinner is around €12, but you can buy food to take away. Reservations are recommended.

La Rosetta Via della Rosetta 9 ☎06.6830.8841. Bus #30, 40, 46, 62, 63, 64, 70, 81, 87, 492, 628, 630, 780, 916 or Tram #8. Mon–Fri noon–3pm & 8–11.30pm, Sat 8–11.30pm. Rome's premier fish restaurant, which all the others try to imitate. Set on a quiet side street a block from the Pantheon, it's an elegant dining experience, and well worth the – very expensive – prices.

Sora Margherita Piazza delle Cinque Scuole 30 ☎06.686.4002. Bus #23, 63, 280, 630, 780, H or Tram #8. Tues–Sun 12.30–3pm, Sat & Sun also 8.30–11pm. A tiny and famous trattoria in the heart of the Jewish quarter serving reasonably priced home-made pasta, gnocchi, and desserts. Great artichokes, Jewish-style, and stuffed squash blossoms. For something rare and delicious, try *ali-ciotti*, a casserole of fresh anchovies and curly endive. No sign outside — look for the doorway with red fuzzy plastic streamers.

Tapa Loca Via di Tor Millina, 4a–5 ☎06.683.2266. Bus #30, 40, 46, 62, 64, 70, 81, 116, 492, 628. Daily 8pm–2am (for meals). Moderately priced Spanish restaurant serving four different paellas (including vegetarian), tapas of all sorts, gazpacho, meat, fish and fish soup, and Spanish tortilla. Just off Piazza Navona in a very busy area, so reservations are a good idea. During the day, it's a bar with snacks.

Thien Kim Via Giulia 201 ☎06.6830.7832. Bus #23, 30, 40, 46, 62, 64, 70, 81, 87, 116, 186, 204, 280, 492, 628, 916. Mon–Sat 7.30–11pm. Perhaps Rome's only Vietnamese restaurant, but it's been here since the 1970s so it must be doing something right. Not expensive, and good if you want something different, but it's very small so you should probably book.

El Toulà Via della Lupa 29b ☎06.687.3498. Metro A Spagna or Bus #52, 53, 61, 62, 63, 80, 95, 116, 119, 175, 492, 630. Mon–Fri noon–3pm & 8–11.30pm, Sat 8–11.30pm. This is one of Rome's chicest and most beautiful

---

Ethnic restaurants

Chinese restaurants – most of them pretty average – abound. Otherwise there's a slowly growing list of international options in and around the centre. See our listings for full reviews.

Africa (Eritrean) (p.212)
Akropolis (Greek) (p.202)
ATM Sushi Bar (Japanese) (p.213)
Baronato Quattro Bellezze
  (Tunisian) (p.207)
Charro Café (Tex-Mex) (p.214)
Ci-Lin (Chinese) (p.214)
The Cowboy (Tex-Mex) (p.211)
Govinda (Indian) (p.208)

Il Guru (Indian) (p.212)
Hamasei (Japanese) (p.211)
Little India (Indian) (p.212)
Il Mondo in Tasca (Int'l-Snacks) (p.202)
Oliphant (Tex-Mex) (p.204)
La Primavera (Chinese) (210)
Tapa Loca (Spanish) (210)
Thien Kim (Vietnamese) (210)

restaurants, with a menu featuring some nostalgic Venetian recipes. Very expensive.

Tridente, Qurinale, Via Veneto

See maps p.61 and pp.102–103

Beltramme Via della Croce 39. No phone. Metro A Spagna or Bus #52, 53, 61, 62, 63, 80, 95, 116, 119, 175, 492, 630. Daily noon–3pm & 7–11pm. originally it sold only wine, by the *fiasco* or flask), two blocks from the Spanish Steps, is just about always packed and is fairly pricey, but if you want authentic Roman food, atmosphere and service the way it used to be, this is the place. Quite trendy. No credit cards.

Il Chianti Via del Lavatore 81–82a ☎06.678.7550. Metro A Spagna or Barberini or Bus #52, 53, 61, 62, 63, 80, 95, 116, 119, 175, 492, 630. Closed Sun. In the heart of tourist Rome, just metres from Trevi Fountain, this Tuscan specialist, both in wine and food, is a good find in a part of town not generally known for its good-value food and drink. It calls itself a *vineria* so you can just stop by for a drink or a full meal. There are good spreads of Tuscan cheese and cold meats, a good selection of beef and other meat dishes, the usual pasta dishes and decent pizzas. You can sit outside in summer if you can bear the travelling musicians who congregate to entertain the tourists.

Colline Emiliane Via degli Avignonesi 22 ☎06.481.7538. Metro A Barberini or Bus #52, 53, 61, 62, 63, 80, 95, 116, 119, 175, 492, 630. Sat–Thurs noon–3pm & 8–11.30pm. Many Italians consider the cuisine of the Emilia Romagna region to be the country's best. Try it for yourself, lovingly prepared by a family, oddly enough, from Le Marche. Located just down from Piazza Barberini, on a quiet backstreet parallel to Via del Tritone. Moderate prices.

The Cowboy Via Francesco Crispi 68 ☎06.488.3504. Metro A Spagna or Barberini or Bus #52, 53, 61, 62, 63, 80, 95, 116, 119, 175, 492, 630. Tues–Sun 11.30am–3pm & 6.30pm–1.30am. Inexpensive, old-guard Roman establishment, just above the Spanish Steps, offers Tex-Mex specialities, including various chilli dishes (including vegetarian), and hamburgers, and Mexican beer to go with it.

Doney Via Veneto 145 ☎06.4708.2805. Metro A Spagna or Barberini or Bus #52, 53, 61, 62, 63, 80, 95, 116, 119, 175, 492, 630. Mon–Sat noon–3.30pm & 7–11pm, Sun noon–3.30pm. An elegant *Dolce Vita*-era institution, serving buffet lunch and dinner and Sunday brunch, including salads, pasta dishes, meat and fish, and elaborate desserts. Eat inside or along the famous street, full of promenaders dressed to kill. Not as pricey as you might think.

Hamasei Via della Mercede 35/36 ☎06.679.2134. Metro A Spagna or Bus #52, 53, 61, 71, 80, 85, 95, 116, 119, 160, 850. Tues–Sun noon–2.30pm & 7pm–10.30pm. Medium-priced elegant Japanese restaurant right in the centre of town. Tranquil, refined atmosphere and a full range of Japanese dishes, including a sushi bar. A la carte prices are high, but there are economical luncheon specials.

Margutta Via Margutta 118 ☎06.3265.0577. Metro A Flaminia or Spagna or Bus #52, 53, 61, 62, 63, 80, 95, 116, 119, 175, 492, 630. Daily 12.30–3pm & 7.30–11.30pm. Good taste is not only about art and antiques on this famous street. There's also this upmarket, vegetarian restaurant that serves generous helpings – albeit at rather high prices. Try the Sunday brunch. They also have another branch near the Pantheon – *Margutta Vegetariano alle Cornacchie*, Piazza Rondanini 53 ☎06.6813.4544.

Naturist Club – L'Isola Via della Vite 14 (just off Via del Corso, a block away from Piazza San Silvestro, up on the fourth floor) ☎06.679.2509. Metro A Spagna or Bus #52, 53, 61, 71, 80, 85, 95, 116, 119, 160, 850. Mon–Sat 12.30–2.45pm & 7.30–10.30pm. A friendly, well-priced vegetarian, semi-self-service restaurant at lunchtime, *Naturist Club* features whole-grain risottos, vegetable pies and fresh juices. In the evenings it becomes L'Isola, a unique, but still affordable, restaurant, spe-cializing in fish dishes. Also offers wonderful organic wines, home-made ice creams and other delicious desserts.

Otello alla Concordia Via della Croce 81 ☎06.678.1454. Metro A Flaminia or Spagna or Bus #52, 53, 61, 62, 63, 80, 95, 116, 119, 175, 492, 630. Mon–Sat 11.30–3pm & 7.30–11pm. This place used to be one of Fellini's favourites – he lived just a few blocks away on Via Margutta – and remains an elegant yet affordable choice in the heart of Rome. A complete offering of Roman and Italian dishes, but ask for "spaghetti Otello" (never on the menu) for a taste of pure tradition – fresh tomatoes and basil with garlic.

Pizza Cir Via della Mercede 43/45 ☎06.678.6015. Metro A Spagna or Bus #52, 53, 61, 71, 80, 85, 95, 116, 119, 160, 850. Daily noon–3pm & 7pm–midnight. A big, friendly pizza place that also has first courses, main courses, and desserts. Try the *linguine al cir* which comes with seafood. Just up from Piazza San Silvestro.

Termini and around

See map pp.114–115

Africa Via Gaeta 26 ☎06.494.1077. Metro A Repubblica or Bus #40, 60, 61, 62, 64, 84, 90, 170, 175, 492, 910, H. Tues–Sun noon–3.30pm & 7.30–11pm. Arguably the city's most interesting ethnic food – Eritrean – and the first culinary sign of Rome's mostly recently arrived Ethiopian and Somalian population.

Arancia Blu Via dei Latini 57 ☎06.445.4105. Bus #71, 492 or Tram #3, 19. Daily 8.30pm–midnight. This ultra-trendy San Lorenzo vegetarian restaurant reckons itself a cut above. But in a city with very few vegetarians it doesn't have to try too hard. Good food using fresh ingredients in an imaginative fashion: specialities include various stuffed veggie pasta dishes – ravioli, cannelloni and the like – and decent salads.

Baia Chia Via Machiavelli 5 ☎06.7045.3452. Metro A Vittorio or Bus #16, 75, 84, 360, 649. Mon–Sat noon–3pm & 7.30pm–midnight. Closed Sun. Near Santa Maria Maggiore, this moderate Sardinian restaurant has lots of good fish starters and tasty first courses. The fish baked in salt is spectacular. For dessert don't fail to try the *sebadas*, hot pastries stuffed with cheese and topped with Sardinian honey.

Alle Carrette Via Madonna dei Monti 95 ☎06.679.2770. Metro B Cavour or Bus #40, 64, 70, 75, 117, 170, H. Daily 8pm–midnight. Inexpensive large pizzeria just up Via Cavour from the Imperial Forums. Expect to wait for the exceptional pizza here. Great home-made desserts.

Il Dito e La Luna Via dei Sabelli 49/51 ☎06.494.0726. Bus #71, 492 or Tram #3, 19. Mon–Sat 7.45–11pm. Creative Sicilian cuisine in a bistro-like San Lorenzo restaurant popular with thirty-something-ish Romans. Go early, as they tend to run out of dishes.

Formula 1 Via degli Equi 13 ☎06.445.3866. Bus #71, 492 or Tram #3, 19. Mon–Sat 7.30–midnight. Cheap and justifiably popular San Lorenzo pizzeria, with tables outside in summer. Delicious pizza all'Ortolana (with courgettes, aubergines and peppers) and good courgette flower fritters.

Il Guru Via Cimarra 4/6. ☎06.474.4110. Metro B Cavour or Bus #40, 64, 70, 75, 117, 170, H. Daily 7pm–1am. An elegant, inviting atmosphere and good northern Indian cuisine. Great location in an evocative, little-frequented neighbourhood, just above the Imperial Forums. Fixed menus vary from €16 to €20.

Da Lisa Via Foscolo 15 ☎06.7049.5456. Metro A Vittorio or Bus #16, 75, 84, 360, 649. Sun–Thurs noon–3pm & 7–11pm. Fri noon–3pm. Moderate kosher Israeli cuisine, including hummus, fish soup and kebabs, and also kosher home-made fettuccine prepared by Lisa herself. Reasonable prices, simple atmosphere. No credit cards.

Little India Via Principe Amedeo 303/305 ☎06.446.4980. Metro A Vittorio or Bus #70, 71, 105 or Tram #5, 14. Daily 11am–3.30pm & 7.30–11.30pm. Wonderful Indian food in a medieval Italian setting. Delicious chicken tikka, courgette curry and palak paneer along with set menus for vegetarians and carnivores. Between Piazza Vittorio and Termini.

Monti D.O.C. Via G. Lanza 93 ☎06.487.2696. Metro A Vittorio or Bus #16, 75, 84, 360, 649. Tues–Fri 1pm–3.30pm & 7pm–1am, Sat & Sun 7pm–1am. Comfortable Santa Maria Maggiore neighbourhood wine bar, with a good wine list and some nice food: cold cuts and cheese, soups, quiches, salads and pastas, including some good veggie dishes.

Il Podista Via Tiburtina 224 ☎06.4470.0967. Bus #71, 492 or Tram #3, 19. Mon–Sat 6.30–midnight. Literally owned and run by marathon-runners — hence, perhaps, the quickly served pizzas and fried food, along with typically Roman fare. Family atmosphere.

Pommidoro Piazza dei Sanniti 44 ☎06.445.2692. Bus #71, 492 or Tram #3, 19. Mon–Sat noon–3pm & 7.30–midnight. A typical, family-run Roman trattoria that's been around forever and was apparently the favoured haunt of Pasolini. It has a breezy open verandah in summer and a fireplace in winter. Try the tasty *pappardelle al cinghiale* (large fettuccine with a wild-boar sauce), *cicoria ripassata* if you like vegetables, and *abbacchio* (lamb) *scottadito*, always perfectly grilled.

Tram Tram Via dei Reti 44–46 ☎06.490.416. Bus #71, 492 or Tram #3, 19. Tues–Sun noon–3pm & 7.30–midnight. Trendy, animated and smoky San Lorenzo restaurant, serving some fine Pugliese pasta dishes, notably seafood lasagne, and unusual salads. Reservations are recommended. There's also a bar if you want to carry on drinking after dinner.

Trattoria Monti Via di San Vito 13a, Bus #16, 71, 714 ☎06.446.6573. Closed Mon. Small, family-run restaurant that specializes in the cuisine of the Marche region, which means hearty food from a short menu – great pasta and interesting cabbage-wrapped *torte* as starters, and mainly meat *secondi*, with beef, lamb and rabbit predominating. Close by Santa Maria Maggiore, this is close enough to the Termini hotel district to be convenient, but is as homely and friendly a restaurant as you could want – something places in this neighbourhood often aren't.

Trastevere and Testaccio

See maps pp.140–141 and pp.86–87

Acqua e Farina? Piazza O. Giustiniani 2 ☎06.574.1382. Bus #23, 30, 75, 95, 170, 280, 716, 781 or Tram #3. Daily noon–3pm & 8pm–midnight. Very reasonable Testaccio restaurant serving dishes that are unique: everything, from starters to desserts, is a variation on the theme of pastry creations – hence the name, "Water & Flour?" Ideal for a light meal, lunch or dinner, for as little as

€10 a head. A very busy place in the middle of an area bustling with streetlife, especially in summer.

Antico Arco Piazzale Aurelio 7 ☎06.581.5274. Bus #44, 75, 710, 870. Mon–Sat 7.30pm–midnight. One of Rome's finest restaurants – a truly wonderful dining experience. Superb dishes exquisitely presented, plus an enormous fine wine list. Located above Trastevere, next to the Janiculum Hill. Reservations definitely required.

ATM Sushi Bar Via della Penitenza 7 ☎06.6830.7053. Bus #23, 75, 280, 630, 780, H or Tram #8. Tues–Sun 7pm–midnight. Tucked away in Trastevere, this cool yet cosy place comes as a real – and affordable – surprise, serving delicious sushi and sashimi, as well as lacy, perfect *tempura*. The sashimi salad is very special. Start off with a flawless miso soup and finish with home-made green tea ice cream, and a lime cocktail. There's a great wine list, too.

Da Augusto Piazza de Renzi 15 ☎06.580.3798. Bus #23, 75, 280, 630, 780, H or Tram #8. Mon–Sat noon–3pm & 8–11pm. Diner-style Trastevere stand-by serving Roman basics in an unpretentious, bustling atmosphere. Good pasta and soup starters, and daily meat and fish specials – not haute cuisine, but decent, hearty Roman cooking.

Augustarello Via G. Branca 98 & ☎06.574.6585. Bus #23, 30, 75, 95, 170, 280, 716, 781 or Tram #3. Mon–Sat noon–3.30pm & 7.30–11.30pm. Moderately priced Testaccio standard serving genuine Roman cuisine in an old-fashioned atmosphere. A good place to come if you appreciate oxtail and sweetbreads, although, as with all Italian restaurants, even strict vegetarians can find good choices.

Bibli Via dei Fienaroli 28 ☎06.588.4097. Bus #23, 75, 280, 630, 780, H or Tram #8. Tues–Sun 11am–midnight; Mon 5.30pm–midnight. After a morning of shopping at Porta Portese flea market, try this multipurpose complex for Sunday brunch. The restaurant offers everything the homesick American might want: some nine different dishes including real American-style pancakes fresh from the griddle, for €16, between 12.30 and 3.30pm. There's also a mini-brunch served on Saturday and a buffet starting at 7pm daily, €15 and €14 respectively. *Bibli* is also a huge bookstore, art centre and Internet access provider. See p.241 overleaf.

Casetta de' Trastevere Piazza de' Renzi 31a/32 ☎06.580.0158. Bus #23, 75, 280, 630,

780, H or Tram #8. Tues–Sun noon–3.30pm & 7pm–1am. A traditional Trastevere eatery in every way. Beautiful setting, good food, low prices. Delicious *spaghetti alle vongole*.

Charro Café Via Monte Testaccio 73 ☎06.578.3064. Bus #23, 30, 75, 95, 170, 280, 716, 781 or Tram #3. Tues–Sun 8.30–2am. Right in Testaccio's busiest stretch (look for the red-pepper-coloured lights in the tree to find it), this has a Tex-Mex menu with everything on it. Prices are higher than average, as with all establishments along this side of Monte Testaccio. But the lively, party atmosphere more than compensates, as does the salsa music.

Checchino dal 1887 Via Monte Testaccio 30 ☎06.574.6318. Bus #23, 30, 75, 95, 170, 280, 716, 781 or Tram #3. Tues–Sat noon–3pm & 8–11.30pm. A historic symbol of Testaccio cookery, with an excellent wine cellar, too. Go to the end of Via Galvani to find the road that circles Monte Testaccio, lined with restaurants and nightspots. Expensive.

Ci-Lin Via Fonte d'Olio 6 ☎06.581.3930. Bus #23, 75, 280, 630, 780, H or Tram #8. Daily 11.30am–3.30pm & 7.30–11.30pm. Excellent Cantonese cooking in a warm and friendly atmosphere – at very friendly prices, too. Handily located right off Trastevere's main piazza.

Felice Via Mastro Giorgio 29 ☎06.574.6800. Bus #23, 30, 75, 95, 170, 280, 716, 781 or Tram #3. Mon–Sat 12.30–2.45pm & 8–10.30pm. Don't be put off by the "riservato" signs on the tables — the owner likes to "select" his customers. Smile and make Felice understand that you're hungry and fond of Roman cooking. Try *bucatini cacio e pepe*, or lamb, and, in winter, artichokes.

Ferrara Via del Moro 1/A ☎06.580.3769. Bus #23, 75, 280, 630, 780, H or Tram #8. Daily 7.30pm–1am. Trastevere's most original spot, with an exciting, if pricey, regional menu, a *sommelier* who really knows the perfect wine for every course, and an inviting series of rooms elegantly stripped back to their medieval walls. The vegetarian antipasto selection is a great choice, and different every time, depending on the season and the chef's inspiration. The Sardinian *ravioloni* are napkin-sized creations using such ingredients as cinnamon, saffron and red peppercorns. Reservations are a must. Expect to spend about €50 a head, including wine.

Ivo Via di San Francesco a Ripa 158 ☎06.581.7082. Bus #23, 75, 280, 630, 780, H or Tram #8. Wed–Mon 7.30pm–1am. *The* Trastevere pizzeria, almost in danger of becoming a caricature, but still good and very reasonable. A nice assortment of desserts, too — try the *monte bianco* for the ultimate chestnut cream and meringue confection. Arrive early to avoid a chaotic queue.

Ketumbar Via Galvani 24 ☎06.5730.5338. Metro B Piramide or Bus #23, 30, 75, 95, 280, 716, 719 or Tram #3. Daily 8–11.30pm; bar open till 2am; closed Aug. One of Rome's handful of fusion restaurants, where Mediterranean tradition meets Oriental pizzazz. The decor of the ultracool Testaccio venue is just as fused, with a most intriguing mix of world music to go with it, and very attitude-free service, despite its chic allure. Convenient to all the district's nightspots.

Da Lucia Vicolo del Mettonate 2 ☎06.580.3601. Bus #23, 75, 280, 630, 780, H or Tram #8. Tues–Sun noon–3pm & 7.30–11.30pm. Outdoor Trastevere dining in summer is at its traditional peak at this wonderful old Roman trattoria. *Spaghetti cacio e pepe* is the great speciality here – get there early for a table outside.

Ai Marmi Viale Trastevere 53/59 ☎06.580.0919. Bus #23, 75, 280, 630, 780, H or Tram #8. Thurs–Tues 6.30pm–2.30am. Nicknamed "the mortuary" because of its stark interior and marble tables, this place serves unique "*suppli al telefono*" (so named because of the string of mozzarella it forms when you take a bite), fresh *baccalà* and the best pizza in Trastevere. Nice house red wine, too. Rapid service, despite the crowds. A lively, inexpensive feel of the real Rome.

Da Olindo Via della Scala 8 ☎06.581.8835. Bus #23, 75, 280, 630, 780, H or Tram #8. Mon–Sat noon–3pm & 8–11pm. Great, family-run Trastevere trattoria with traditional Roman fare. Menu varies daily, depending on what's freshest and on the signora's inspiration.

Da Paris Piazza San Callisto 7a ☎06.581.5378. Bus #23, 75, 280, 630, 780, H or Tram #8. Tues–Sat noon–3pm & 8–11.30pm, Sun noon–3pm. Fine Roman Jewish cookery in one of Trastevere's most atmospheric piazzas. Also offers other traditional dishes. Moderate prices.

Pizzeria da Remo Piazza Santa Maria Liberatrice 44 ☎06.574.6270. Bus #23, 30, 75, 95, 170, 280, 716, 781 or Tram #3. Mon–Sat 7.30–1am. *Remo* is the best kind of pizzeria: usually crowded with locals, very basic, and serving the thinnest, crispiest Roman pizza you'll find. Try also the heavenly *bruschetta* and other snacks like *suppli* and *fior di zucca*. Almost worth travelling out to Testaccio for – and very cheap.

Pizzeria San Callisto Piazza di San Callisto 9a ☏06.581.8256. Bus #23, 75, 280, 630, 780, H or Tram #8. Tues–Sun 7.30–1am. Large pizzas at small prices. Friendly, fast service and a vibrant, welcoming atmosphere.

Dar Poeta Vicolo del Bologna 45 ☏06.588.0516. Bus #23, 75, 280, 630, 780, H or Tram #8. Tues–Sun 7.30pm–1am. Without any doubts, one of the top-ten pizzerias in Rome. Don't expect the typical crusty Roman pizza here; the margherita (ask for it *con basilico* — with basil) comes out of the oven soft and with plenty of good mozzarella on top. They have good imported *birra rossa* — a rarity outside a pub — and there's even a non-smoking room.

Romolo Via Porta Settimiana 8 ☏06581.3873. Bus #23, 75, 280, 630, 780, H or Tram #8. Tues–Sun noon–3pm & 7–11pm. A Trastevere institution, apparently located in the very building where Raphael's lover, "La Fornarina", lived. Great garden setting in fine weather. Traditional, moderately priced Roman menu and nice house wines. Try the *bombolotto al carciofo*. The kiwi ice cream with *Vecchia Romagna* liqueur is great, too. Menus are decorated with sketches by famous artists who have dined here.

Saperi e Sapori Via di Monte Testaccio 34b ☏06.574.3167. Bus #23, 30, 75, 95, 170, 280, 716, 781 or Tram #3. Tues–Sun 8pm–1am. Big pizzas, big salads, all in an area rich with nightlife, especially in the warm months.

La Scala Piazza della Scala 60 ☏06.580.3763. Bus #23, 75, 280, 630, 780, H or Tram #8. Daily 7pm–2am. This place was originally just a *birreria* and gradually expanded its offerings, at reasonable prices, including – usually indigestible – live music. It now has a very broad menu, including really good vegetarian chilli. Almost always packed, so go early or you'll have to wait. See also p.222.

Tuttifrutti Via Luca della Robbia 3a ☏06.575.7902. Metro B Piramide or Bus #23, 30, 75, 95, 170, 280, 716, 781 or Tram #3. Tues–Sun 7.30–11.55pm. Something special in Testaccio – gourmet recipes, different every day, many based on traditional Roman cookery but with highly original *nouvelle* twists. Freshness and quality to the very highest standards. Friday is fish day.

See map pp.150–151

La Grotta Azzurra Via Cicerone 62a ☏06.323.4490. Metro A Lepanto or Bus #30, 70, 280, 913. Fri–Wed noon–3.30pm & 7.30pm–midnight. Moderate, quiet, relaxing refuge after a day at the Vatican. Fish specialities and impeccable service at moderate prices.

Les Étoiles Via dei Bastioni 1 ☏06.687.3233. Metro A Ottaviano or Bus #23, 32, 34, 40, 49, 62, 81, 280, 492, 590, 982 or Tram #19. Daily noon–3.30pm & 7.30pm–midnight. A ravishing roof-garden restaurant with magnificent views of Rome, perfect if you have something to celebrate. Truly sublime food and friendly and courteous staff make this an unforgettable (though very expensive) experience.

L'Insalatiera 2 Via Trionfale 94 ☏06.3974.2975. Metro A Ottaviano or bus #70. Mon–Sat 1–4pm & 8pm–midnight. Moderate vegetarian restaurant specializing in regional Italian cuisine, located right across from Rome's flower market. Try their *tagliolini alle noci* or *gnocchi al radicchio e gorgonzola*. For seconds go for the *rotolo di verdura al cartoccio*, the *focaccia napoletano* (with olives, pine nuts and raisins) or the *involtini di radicchio*. Everything is home-made, including the wonderful desserts, such as chocolate and ricotta pie. No smoking.

Osteria dell'Angelo Via G. Bettolo 24 ☏06.372.9470. Metro A Ottaviano or Bus #23, 32, 34, 40, 49, 62, 81, 280, 492, 590, 982 or Tram #19. Mon–Sat 8–11.15pm; plus Tues & Fri 12.45–2.30pm. Above-average traditional Roman food, in a highly popular restaurant run by an ex-rugby player. Booking advisable. Moderate prices.

Dal Toscano Via Germanico 58/60 ☏06.3972.5717. Metro A Ottaviano or Bus #23, 32, 34, 40, 49, 62, 81, 280, 492, 590, 982 or Tram #19. Tues–Sun 12.30–3pm & 8–11pm. Don't come here for a salad. This restaurant specializes in *fiorentine* (the famous thick Tuscan T-bone steaks), perfectly grilled on charcoal, and delicious *pici* (thick home-made spaghetti) or *ribollita* (veg and bread soup) – all at honest prices. Tremendously popular with Roman families, so reservations recommended for dinner. Near the Piazza del Risorgimento end of Via Germanico.

14

EATING | Restaurants and pizzerias

Drinking

rinking is not something Romans do a lot of, at least almost never to drunken excess. Despite that, you'll find plenty of bars in Rome, although, as with the rest of Italy, most are functional daytime haunts and not at all the kinds of places you'd want to spend an evening. However, due to the considerable presence of Anglo-Americans, there are plenty of bars and pubs conducive to an evening's drinking; indeed, there's now an Irish pub practically on every corner in central Rome. Many drinking spots are slick and expensive excuses for people to sit and pose, but most have the advantage of late opening hours – sometimes until 4am in summer, and almost always until around 1am. One of the perennially favourite types of drinking establishments is the **wine bar**, known as an *enoteca* or *vineria*. The old ones have gained new cachet and newer ones, with wine lists the size of unabridged dictionaries, are weighing in, too, often with gourmet menus to go with the superb wines they offer. There's also been a recent proliferation of wine-tastings (*degustazioni*), which offer a chance to sample some interesting vintages, often at no cost. Those *enoteche* that also feature great food have been listed in Chapter 14. Those that still concentrate on the fruit of the vine, however, are many in number and we've listed the best here. Remember there is sometimes considerable **crossover** between Rome's bars, restaurants and clubs. For the most part, the places listed in this chapter are drinking spots, but you can **eat**, sometimes quite substantially, at many of them, and several could be classed just as easily as nightclubs, with loud music and occasionally even an entrance charge.

Although we've, again, divided these listings into **neighbourhoods**, the truth is that there are plenty of drinking venues all over Rome. However, the areas around Campo de' Fiori and the Pantheon, plus, of course, Trastevere and Testaccio, are the densest and most happening. **Internet cafés** are listed on p.223.

Centro Storico, Campo de' Fiori and the Ghetto

See maps p.37 and pp.52–53

Anima Via Santa Maria dell' Anima 57 ☎06.6889.2806. Bus #30, 40, 46, 62, 64, 70, 81, 116, 492, 628, 916.Tues–Sun 10pm–3am. At present one of the most popular spots in town, tricked out in post-modern-meets-

Baroque and offering an assortment of elegant snacks to go with your cocktails. Music tends towards chill-out, lounge, and softer soul stuff.

Le Bain Art Gallery Via delle Botteghe Oscure 32a/33 ☎06.686.5673. Bus #23, 30, 40, 46, 62, 63, 64, 81, 87, 280, 492, 628, 630, 780, H or Tram #8. Tues–Sun 8pm–2am. Popular with the chic set and just off Largo Argentina; it includes three spaces featuring art

---

Opening hours have been given for all bars and cafés; note, however, that many places are closed during August.

Bar essentials

It's important to be aware of the procedure when you enter an Italian **bar**. It's cheapest to drink standing at the counter (there's often nowhere to sit anyway), in which case you pay first at the cash desk (*la cassa*), present your receipt (*scontrino*) to the barperson and give your order. It's customary to leave an extra €0.10 or €0.20 coin on the counter for the barperson, although no one will object if you don't. If there's waiter service, just sit where you like, though bear in mind that this will cost perhaps twice as much, especially if you sit outside (*fuori*) – the difference is usually shown on the price list as *tavola* (table) or *terrazzo* (any outside seating area).

Coffee and soft drinks

Coffee is always excellent, drunk small and black (*espresso*, or just *caffè*), which costs 80c to €1 a cup, or as a cappuccino (about €1.50). If you want your espresso watered down ask for a *caffè americano* or *caffè lungo*. Coffee with a shot of alcohol is *caffè corretto*; with a drop of milk it's *caffè macchiato*. Many places also now sell decaffeinated coffee (ask for "Hag", even when it isn't), while in summer you might want to have your coffee cold (*caffè freddo*). For a real treat ask for *caffè granitá* – cold coffee with crushed ice, usually topped with cream. In summer you can drink **iced tea** (*tè freddo*) – excellent for taking the heat off; **hot tea** (*tè caldo*) comes with lemon (*con limone*) unless you ask for milk (*con latte*). **Milk** itself is drunk hot as often as cold, or you can get it with a dash of coffee (*latte macchiato* or *caffè latte*) and sometimes as milk shakes – *frappe* or *frullati*.

Among **soft drinks**, a *spremuta* is a fresh fruit juice, squeezed at the bar, usually orange, lemon or grapefruit. There are also crushed-ice granitas, offered in several flavours, and available with or without whipped cream (*panna*) on top. Otherwise there's the usual range of fizzy drinks and concentrated juices. Coke is as prevalent as it is everywhere; the home-grown Italian version, *Chinotto*, is less sweet – good with a slice of lemon. Tap water (*acqua semplice*) is quite drinkable, and you won't pay for it in a bar. Mineral water (*acqua minerale*) is a more common choice, either still (*senza gas* or *naturale*) or sparkling (*con gas* or *frizzante*) – about €0.50 a glass.

Alchohol

Beer (*birra*) is always a lager-type brew which usually comes in one-third or two-third litre bottles, or on draught (*alla spina*), measure for measure more expensive than the bottled variety. A small beer is a *píccola* (20cl or 25cl), a larger one (usually 40cl) a *media* (pronounced "maydia"). If you want Italian beer, ask for *birra chiara*. You may also come across darker beers (*birra nera* or *birra rossa*). Prices start from about €3 for a *media*, but anywhere really fancy won't charge any less than €5.

All the usual **spirits** are on sale and known mostly by their generic names. There are also Italian brands of the main varieties: the best Italian brandies are *Stock* and *Vecchia Romagna*. A generous shot of these costs about €3, imported stuff much more. The home-grown Italian firewater is *grappa*, available just about everywhere. It's made from the leftovers from the winemaking process (skins, stalks and the like) and is something of an acquired taste; should you acquire it, it's probably the cheapest way of getting plastered. You'll also find **fortified wines** such as Campari; ask for a Campari-soda and you'll get a ready-mixed version from a bottle; a slice of lemon is a *spicchio di limone*, ice is *ghiaccio*. You might also try *Cynar* – believe it or not, an artichoke-based sherry often drunk as an aperitif. There's also a daunting selection of **liqueurs**. *Amaro* is a bitter after-dinner drink: it has a base of pure alcohol in which various herbs are steeped, according to various family traditions. It's highly regarded as a digestive aid to cap a substantial meal. *Amaretto* is much sweeter with a strong taste of almond; *Sambuca* a sticky-sweet aniseed concoction, traditionally served with a coffee bean in it and set on fire (though, increasingly, this is something put on to impress tourists); *Strega* – yellow, herb-and-saffron-based stuff in tall, elongated bottles – is about as sweet as it looks but not unpleasant.

DRINKING

exhibitions, a cocktail bar and cool music. A minimalist but not oppressive decor. No entrance fee.

Bar del Fico Piazza del Fico 26/28 ☎06.686.5205. Bus #30, 40, 46, 62, 64, 70, 81, 116, 492, 628. Daily 8am–2am. One of several long-standing hotspots in the area — just around the corner from *Bar della Pace*, and slightly cheaper. Outdoor heating in winter.

Bar della Pace Via della Pace 5 ☎06.686.1216. Bus #30, 40, 46, 62, 64, 70, 81, 116, 492, 628. Daily 10am–2am. Just off Piazza Navona, this is *the* summer bar, with outside tables full of Rome's self-consciously beautiful people. Quietest during the day, when you can enjoy the nine-teenth-century interior – marble, mirrors, mahogany and plants – in peace, although the prices and rather snooty staff may put you off altogether.

Bartaruga Piazza Mattei 7 ☎06.689.2299. Bus #30, 40, 46, 62, 63, 64, 70, 81, 87, 492, 628, 630, 780, H or Tram #8. Daily 3pm–2am. This very theatrical bar attracts members of the city's entertainment demimonde, and even provides costumes for clients who feel like a change of persona. The setting is wonderfully camp, eclectically furnished with all sorts of eighteenth-century bits and pieces; nothing really matches and the feel is sumptuously comfy.

Bevitoria Navona Piazza Navona 72 ☎06.6880.1022. Bus #30, 40, 46, 62, 64, 70, 81, 87, 116, 492, 628. Daily 11am–midnight, till 1am in summer. Right by the Fountain of Neptune, a wine-tasters' tradition. Regulars swear it's the only place in Rome to *really* drink Italian wine, though as with everywhere on this renowned piazza it's grown hyper-touristy over the years.

Black & White Piazza della Pollarola 32 ☎348.364.8808. Bus #30, 40, 46, 62, 64, 70, 81, 87, 116, 492, 628. Daily 6pm–2am. Nestled in a small piazza between Corso Vittorio and the Campo, this fairly spacious pub draws a good mix of Americans and Romans, who come for the soul sounds and the €1 shots. Often stays open well after hours, in keeping with the party zone it inhabits.

Bloom Via del Teatro Pace 29 ☎06.6880.2029. Bus #30, 40, 46, 62, 64, 70, 81, 116, 492, 628. Daily 8pm–2am. Closed Sun. Perhaps the coolest bar in the centre of Rome, at least at the moment, from its leather *banquettes* to its curvy zinc counter. It serves food, too, but you'd do better to fill up elsewhere and come on here afterwards, saving your money for one of Bloom's overpriced cocktails.

Caffè Farnese Piazza Farnese 106 ☎06.6880.2125. Bus #30, 40, 46, 62, 64, 70, 81, 87, 116, 492, 628. Daily 7am–2am. Popular with business types and beautiful young things, but actually not expensive, and a pleasant place to come for breakfast or lunch as well as evening drinks. Good cappuccino and *cornetti*, and excellent pizza and sandwiches. Free seating at the window bar, but you might want to pay to sit outside on a warm evening for the view of Palazzo Farnese.

Le Coppelle Piazza delle Coppelle 52 ☎06.683.2410. Metro A Spagna or Bus #52, 53, 61, 71, 80, 85, 95, 116, 119, 160, 850. Mon–Sat 6pm–2am. This discobar is going for the new-found "design" fashion in the Eternal City. The venue is outdoors during the warm months, with a nice array of sofas and pillows when the time comes to retreat indoors. The music tends toward chill-out lounge sounds.

Cul de Sac Piazza Pasquino 73 ☎06.6880.1094. Daily noon–4pm & 7pm–12.30am. Busy, long-running wine bar with an excellent wine list, a great city-centre location with outside seating, and decent wine-bar food – cold meats, cheeses, salads and soups. One of the best centro storico locations for a snack.

La Curia di Bacco Via del Biscione 79 ☎06.689.3893. Bus #30, 40, 46, 62, 64, 70, 81, 87, 116, 492, 628. Daily 4pm–2am. This bustling place was hollowed out of the ruins of the ancient Teatro di Pompeii, near Campo de' Fiori. A very young crowd, some good wines and interesting snacks.

The Drunken Ship Campo de' Fiori 20–21 ☎06.6830.0535. Bus #30, 40, 46, 62, 64, 70, 81, 87, 116, 492, 628. Daily 11am–2am. A lively meeting-point, with great music, always tremendously popular with young Romans and foreign students. Happy Hour 7–8pm, brunch at weekends.

Il Goccetto Via dei Banchi Vecchi 14 ☎06.686.4268. Bus #30, 40, 46, 62, 64, 70, 81, 87, 116, 492, 628. Mon–Sat 11am–2pm & 4pm–10pm; closed Aug. Probably the most complete and carefully selected wine list in Rome – the proprietor Sergio Ceccarelli is an expert. You can try some of his over 500 labels "*alla mescita*" (by the glass).

'Gusto Piazza Augusto Imperatore 9
☏06.322.6273. Metro A Flaminia. Daily 12.30–3pm & 7.30pm–2am. This stylish modern bar is part of the 'Gusto foodie empire that occupies this corner and serves drinks, sandwiches and Catalan one-bite tapas to the discerning chattering classes of Rome. Entrance to the bar is around the corner on Via della Frezza.

Jazz Café Via Zanardelli 10–12
☏06.6821.0119. Bus #30, 40, 46, 62, 64, 70, 81, 87, 116, 492, 628. Mon–Sat 8.30am–2am. The sophisticated heir to *Jeff Blynn's*, which has moved even further upmarket into the exclusive Parioli district, far from the tourist hordes. Subdued lighting and a few touches of sleek, post-modern decor set the tone for judicious sipping and murmured conversation set to jazzy background music, veering towards hip-hop as the night wears on. A full (American) menu is served, too. And there's live music on Wed.

Jonathan's Angels Via della Fossa 18
☏06.689.3426. Bus #30, 40, 46, 62, 64, 70, 81, 87, 116, 492, 628. Daily 1pm–2am. This quirky bar, just behind Piazza Navona, certainly wins the "most decorated" award. Every inch (even the toilet, which is worth a visit on its own) is plastered, painted or tricked out in outlandish style by the artist/proprietor.

Mad Jack's Via Arenula 20 ☏06.6880.8223. Bus #63, 630, 780, H or Tram #8. Daily 11am–2am. One of many Irish pubs, but one of the nicest and most authentic, as well as one of the easiest to find, right across from Piazza Cairoli. Guinness is a speciality, and there are light snacks available, too, to go with the warm welcome. Frequented by Italians as well as tourists and expats.

Miscellanea Via delle Paste 110a. No phone. Bus #30, 40, 46, 62, 64, 70, 81, 87, 116, 492, 628. Daily 12.30pm–3am. Located halfway between Via del Corso and the Pantheon, this place was the first American-style bar in Rome, a boozy hangout of US students, and inevitably packed at night. Reasonable prices and the best-value sandwiches in town — jaw-breaking doorstops weighing in at about €3. Also open Christmas Eve and other holidays for lonesome expats.

O'Conner's Via dei Cartari 7 ☏06.6830.7161. Bus #30, 40, 46, 62, 64, 70, 81, 87, 116, 492, 628. Daily 9pm–2.30am, later at weekends. Irish pub with live music, cosy atmosphere — and Guinness. Situated off Corso Vittorio Emanuele, just across from Chiesa Nuova.

Riccioli Piazza della Coppelle 10
☏06.6821.0313. Daily 6pm–2am. Swish modern bar that does a good live in oyster and sushi.

Rock Castle Café Via B. Cenci 8
☏06.6880.7999. Bus #63, 630, 780, H or Tram #8. Daily 9pm–3am. In the Jewish Ghetto, just across from Trastevere, a student hangout consisting of six medieval-style rooms, all for dancing and mingling. See also p.229.

Simposio di Piero Costantini Piazza Cavour 16
☏06.321.1502. Bus #23, 280, 492. Mon–Fri 11.30am–3pm & 6.30pm–1am, Sat 6.30pm–1am. Not actually in the centro storico, but close enough, just across the Tiber, a few minutes' walk from Piazza Navona, this place has a fine and authentic Art Nouveau feel. Look for the wrought-iron grapes on the doors and windows. Good food, too.

Taverna del Campo Campo de' Fiori 16
☏06.687.4402. Bus #30, 40, 46, 62, 64, 70, 81, 87, 116, 492, 628. Tues–Sun 8am–2am. Trendy wine bar with a wide range of fancy foods, too. One of the many overflowing spots all lined up around this piazza, where you will certainly have to contend for an outside table.

La Trinchetta Via dei Banchi Nuovi 4
☏06.6830.0133. Bus #30, 40, 46, 62, 64, 70, 81, 87, 116, 492, 628. Mon–Sat 8pm–2am. This wine bar is tucked away in the warren of streets between Piazza Navona and the Tiber and is well worth seeking out. There's not only a great selection of wines, but also what may be Rome's most extensive list of *grappa* labels.

Trinity College Via del Collegio Romano 6
☏06.678.6472. Bus #30, 40, 46, 62, 64, 70, 81, 87, 116, 492, 628. Daily noon–3am. A warm and inviting establishment offering international beers and food. Its two levels can get quite loud and crowded. Food includes complete meals (vegetarian tacos, Greek salad, chicken supreme and much more) until 1am, and a special brunch menu for around €12.

Vin Antico Via del Pellegrino 79–80
☏06.687.7058. Bus #30, 40, 46, 62, 64, 70, 81, 87, 116, 492, 628. Daily 11am–2am. Very stylish and elegant, yet inviting enough, offering a very fine selection of international wines and equally select cheeses and

other snacks to complement them. Brunch at 1pm.

Vineria Campo de' Fiori 15 ☎06.6880.3268. Bus #30, 40, 46, 62, 64, 70, 81, 87, 116, 492, 628. Mon–Sat 9am–1am, Sun 5pm–1am. Long-established bar/wine shop right on the Campo, patronized by devoted regulars, while more recently making some concessions to comfort as well and offering light meals. Much cheaper inside.

Tridente, Quirinale, Via Veneto

See maps p.61 and pp.102–103

Canova Piazza del Popolo 16 ☎06.361.2231. Metro A Flaminio or Bus #88, 95, 117, 119, 495, 628, 926 or Tram #2. Daily 8am–midnight. Once the haunt of the monied classes, but not really the place it was. Still it does all sorts of cocktails and reasonable food, and is a fine place to sit and take the air and watch the world go by on Piazza del Popolo. Politically, Canova's clientele was traditionally a right-wing one, while dyed-in-the-wool lefties patronised *Rosati* across the square (see below).

L'Enoteca Antica Via della Croce 76b ☎06.679.0896. Metro A Spagna or Bus #52, 53, 61, 71, 80, 85, 95, 116, 119, 160, 850. Daily 11am–1am. An old Spanish Steps-area wine bar with a selection of hot and cold dishes, including soups and attractive desserts. Intriguing trompe l'oeil decorations inside, majolica-topped tables outside.

Lowenhaus Via della Fontanella 16d ☎06.323.0410. Metro A Spagna or Bus #52, 53, 61, 71, 80, 85, 95, 116, 119, 160, 850. Daily 11am–2am. Just off Piazza del Popolo, a Bavarian-style drinking establishment with beer and snacks to match. Live jazz from 10pm onwards on Fridays.

New Orleans Via xx Settembre 52, ☎06.4201.4785 More or less a regular Italian bar by day, but a loud pub at night, with American food, good German beer and live music.

Rosati Piazza del Popolo 5 ☎06.322.5859. Metro A Flaminio or Bus #88, 95, 117, 119, 495, 628, 926 or Tram #2. Daily 8am–midnight. This was the bar that hosted left-wingers, bohemians and writers in years gone by, and although that's no longer really the case its cocktails and food still draw the crowds.

Rose Garden Palace Via Boncompagni 19 ☎06.421.741. Metro A Spagna or Bus #52, 53,

63, 80, 95, 116, 119, 630. Daily 7–9pm. This classy Via Veneto hotel lounge offers an unusual place to celebrate your Happy Hour. It's elegant and understated and the Jazz Cats do their very best to bring back the Swing Era, featuring all the standards from the 1940s.

Victoria House Via Gesù e Maria 18 ☎06.320.1698. Metro A Spagna or Bus #52, 53, 61, 71, 80, 85, 95, 116, 119, 160, 850. Daily 6pm–12.30am, Fri & Sat 5.30pm–1am, Sun 5pm–12.30am. Decor imported from Sheffield, along with the beer and the recipes, just a stone's throw from Piazza di Spagna. There's a non-smoking room, and a Happy Hour from 6pm to 9pm.

Termini and around

See map pp.114–115

Al Vino al Vino Via dei Serpenti 19 ☎06.485.803. Metro B Cavour or Bus #40, 64, 70, 117, 170, H. Daily 11.30am–1.30pm & 5pm–12.30am. The Monti district's most happening street offers this seriously good wine bar with a choice of over 500 labels, many by the glass. Snacks are generally Sicilian specialities.

Club Machiavelli Via Machiavelli 49 ☎06.700.1757. Metro A Vittorio or Bus #70, 71, 105 or Tram #5, 14. Mon–Sat 8pm–1am. Located in an historic palace, which accounts for the beautiful vaulted ceilings, this place is in the very much up-and-coming Piazza Vittorio district next to Termini. Wines, cocktails and home-made desserts and other treats. Piano bar-style evenings, with occasional live combos and other cultural events.

The Druid's Den Via San Martino ai Monti 28 ☎06.4890.4781. Metro A Vittorio or B Cavour, Bus #16, 75, 84, 360, 649. Mon–Thurs & Sun 6pm–1.30am, Fri & Sat 6pm–3am. Appealing Irish pub near Santa Maria Maggiore with a genuine Celtic feel (and owners). It has a mixed expat/Italian clientele, and is not just for the homesick. Cheap and lively, with occasional impromptu Celtic music.

Fiddler's Elbow Via dell'Olmata 43 ☎06.487.2110. Metro A Vittorio or B Cavour or Bus #16, 75, 84, 360, 649. Mon–Sat 5pm–1.15am, Sun 3pm–1.30am. One of the two original Irish bars in Rome, one block closer to Santa Maria Maggiore than its rival, *The Druid's*, and roomier, with a decidedly more Latin feel.

The Flann O'Brien Via Napoli 29–34 & Via Nazionale 17 ☎06.488.0418. Metro A Repubblica or Bus #40, 64, 70, 117, 170, H. Daily 7pm–2am. This huge venue has three maxi-screens that you can bet will draw the fans for every football match of any significance. Brews and snacks mollify the crowds, mostly foreigners given the ideal location for tourists. Brunch on Sundays.

Rive Gauche 2 Via dei Sabelli 43 ☎06.445.6722. Bus #71, 492 or Tram #3, 19. Daily 7pm–3am. The San Lorenzo district's smoky, noisy, cavernous evocation of intellectual Left Bank Paris – more or less. Lots of Irish beer choices and snacks to sustain your night of drinking. Happy Hour till 9pm.

Il Sigillo Via del Cardello 13 ☎06.7696.7946. Metro B Cavour or Bus #40, 64, 70, 117, 170, H. Daily 8pm–3am. Opens at 5pm on Sun. Bar with music in which pop hits from the 1970s and 1980s dominate, plus there's a drag show on Sunday evenings, with a mixed gay and gay-friendly crowd.

Trimani Via Goito 20 ☎06.446.9661. Mon–Sat 11am–midnight. Metro Repubblica or Bus #36, 38, 40, 60, 61, 62, 64, 75, 84, 90, 92, 105, 170, 175, 217, 310, 492, 714, 910, H. This fine *enoteca* has a truly vast wine list and has also lately been gleaning accolades for its interesting dining options. Mediterranean specialities such as octopus salad and black rice are hits, as well as some unusual cheeses.

Zest-Es Hotel Via Turati 171 ☎06.444.841. Metro B Cavour or Bus #40, 64, 70, 117, 170, H. Daily 10am–1.30am. Rome's newest designer hotel also sports the city's most elegant new cocktail bar. Poolside drinks give top-floor views over the very much up-and-coming Esquiline district.

Trastevere and Testaccio

See maps pp.140–141 and pp.86–87

Mount Gay Music Bar Via Galvani 54 ☎06.574.6013. Bus #23, 30, 75, 95, 170, 280, 716, 781 or Tram #3. Tues–Sat 8pm–4am, Sun 7pm–2am. Laid-back Testaccio cocktail bar, named after the famous Caribbean rum. Around the corner from the nightspots of Via di Monte Testaccio, it has 250 wines to choose from, and red earth-coloured ethnic decor on two levels, with large, inviting rooms. Occasional live music.

Il Cantiniere di Santa Dorotea Via di Santa Dorotea 9 ☎06.581.9025. Bus #23, 280, 630, 780, H or Tram #8. Wed–Mon 7pm–2am. In the heart of Trastevere, near Piazza Trilussa, this place has some great wines and a range of delicious snacks – don't miss the cheesecake. The cosy decor is part Parisian, part Roman, with tables outside, too. The proprietor, Alberto Costantini, really knows his wines and will be delighted to help you choose the perfect one.

Clamur Piazza del'Emporio 1 ☎06.575.4532 or Bus #23, 30, 75, 95, 170, 280, 716, 781 or Tram #3. Daily 8.30pm–2am. A large, newly redecorated Irish pub, on the Testaccio side of the Porta Portese (Trastevere) bridge, offering the usual beers plus snacks.

Fidelio Via degli Stefaneschi 3/7 ☎06.9784.1585. Bus #23, 75, 280, 630, 780, H or Tram #8. Daily 6pm–3am. Just behind Piazza Sonino in Trastevere, a creakingly old *vineria* that does good traditional food, too. See also p.202.

Fiestaloca Via degli Orti di Cesare 7 ☎06.5833.3494. Bus #23, 75, 280, 780, H or Tram #8. Tues–Sun 8.30pm–3am. Mexico-by-the-Tiber-in-Trastevere with very mixed music and very Tex-Mex menu. You have to pay to get in at weekends – €5, drink included, on Friday, €7, drink included, on Saturday.

Four XXXX Pub Via Galvani 29/29a ☎06.575.7296. Bus #23, 30, 75, 95, 170, 280, 716, 781 or Tram #3.Tues–Sun 7pm–2am. English-style Testaccio pub spread over two floors, with South American-inspired food and snacks. Video, live music, art and photographic exhibitions are frequently arranged.

Gianicolo Piazzale Aurelia 5 ☎06.580.6275. Bus #710, 870. Closed Mon. A cool hangout for Italian media stars, writers and academics from the nearby Spanish and American academies.

Enoteca Malafemmina Via San Crisogono 31 ☎06.580.6941. Bus #23, 75, 280, 630, 780, H or Tram #8. Thurs–Tues 5.30pm–1.30am. This Trastevere wine bar is one of the friendliest places in town. Some amazing wines and delicious light snacks ordered fresh from the first-class restaurant next door.

Il Giardino dei Ciliegi Via dei Fienaroli 4 ☎06.580.3423. Bus #23, 75, 280, 630, 780, H or Tram #8.Daily 6pm–2am, Sat & Sun 5pm–2am. Closed in July & Aug. A cosy, if rather expensive, tearoom in an out-of-the-way corner of Trastevere. Open late, with a selection of 140 teas, BIG salads and other light choices.

Mr Brown Vicolo del Cinque 29 ☏ 06.581.2913. Bus #23, 280, 630, 780, H or Tram #8. Mon–Sat 8pm–3am. This popular night-time hangout is one of Trastevere's best detours. A young, fun-loving crowd, Happy Hour from 9pm to 10pm daily, with beers going for €2.20 instead of the usual €4.20, and an assortment of salads, sandwiches and crêpes, plus chilli and fondue.

Oasi della Birra Piazza Testaccio 41 ☏ 06.574.6122. Bus #23, 30, 75, 95, 170, 280, 716, 781 or Tram #3. Mon–Sat 7.30pm–1am. Unassumingly situated under an *enoteca* on Piazza Testaccio – you wouldn't know this was there. But the cosy basement rooms here house an international selection of beers that rivals anywhere in the world – 500 in all, and plenty of wine to choose from as well. Food is generously assembled plates of cheese and salami, and a great selection of *bruschetta* and polenta dishes. It's not particularly Roman, but it's a very alluring place to get hammered and eat good food nonetheless.

Oxygen Vicolo del Bologna 63 ☏ 338.235.1699. Bus #23, 75, 280, 630, 780, H or Tram #8. Daily 7.30pm–2am. Located on the quiet street between overrun Vicolo del Cinque and Via della Scala, this is a good choice for trying one of over seventy cocktails, as well as the cult microbrew produced by Menabrea.

Picasso Via di Monte Testaccio 63 ☏ 06.574.2975. Bus #23, 30, 75, 95, 170, 280, 716, 781 or Tram #3. Tues–Sat 10.30pm–3am. A cool but not too pretentious Testaccio bar hosting the occasional art exhibition and performance arts event, as well as playing an interesting and eclectic mix of music. Perch on a bar-stool rather than taking a table to avoid paying extra for service. It's also a pizzeria.

San Callisto Piazza San Callisto 4 ☏ 06.583.5869. Bus #23, 75, 280, 630, 780, H or Tram #8. Mon–Sat 6am–1.30am. An old-guard Trastevere dive bar with a smoky side-room full of card-playing old men and their dogs, which attracts a huge crowd of just about everybody on late summer nights. It's a great place to drink: the booze is cheap, and you can sit at outside tables for no extra cost. Things are slightly less demi-monde-ish during the day, when it's simply a great spot to sip a cappuccino, read and

take the sun; and it's perfectly OK to bring your own sandwich or pizza slice. Don't miss the *gelato*.

La Scala Piazza della Scala 60 ☏ 06.580.3763. Bus #23, 75, 280, 630, 780, H or Tram #8. Daily noon–2am, later Sat. Perhaps the most popular Trastevere *birreria* — big, bustling and crowded, with a Texan ranch-meets-McDonald's decor. Food, too, and occasional (dire) music. See also p.215.

Stardust Vicolo de' Renzi 4 ☏ 06.5832.0875. Bus #23, 75, 280, 630, 780, H or Tram #8. Mon–Sat 3.30pm–2am, Sun noon–2am. One of Trastevere's most authentic haunts, with good food as well as drink, including a buffet brunch on weekends between noon and 4.30pm. Just the place, too, for all-night partying – see p.228.

Enoteca Trastevere Via della Lungaretta 86 ☏ 06.588.5659. Bus #23, 75, 280, 630, 780, H or Tram #8. Mon, Tues, Thurs–Sat 5pm–2am, Sun 11am–1am. The district's largest *enoteca* is also a local favourite. Lots of mostly Italian wines to choose from, including some organic labels. Good choices, too, if you're into *grappa* and *amaro*.

Prati and the Vatican

See map pp.150–151

Blue Knight Via delle Fornaci 8–10 ☏ 06.630.011. Metro A Ottaviano or Bus #32, 34, 49, 81, 492, 590, 982 or Tram #19. Daily 7am–3am. Street level is a bar and popular *gelateria*, as well, while live music holds forth downstairs several evenings a week. See p.226 for concert details.

Fonclea Via Crescenzio 82a ☏ 06.689.6302. Metro A Ottaviano or Bus #23, 32, 34, 49, 81, 492, 590, 982 or Tram #19. Daily 7pm–2am. This historic joint is loaded with devoted regulars and those who have happily dis-covered that there is life in the Vatican's somewhat somnolent Borgo area. Live music adds to the excitement (see p.227 for more info).

Four Green Fields Via C. Morin 42 ☏ 06.372.5091. Metro A Ottaviano or Bus #23, 32, 34, 49, 81, 492, 590, 982 or Tram #19. Daily 2pm–2am. This large Irish pub, decked out in wood and terracotta, stretches over two floors, with live music downstairs every evening. Draft Guinness and Kilkenny complement the scene, along with OK pub grub. See p.227 for more about the music.

Internet cafés

The following places offer access to the Internet, although by the time you read this the number is almost certain to have grown.

Art Café Friends Piazza Trilussa 34 ℡06.581.6111. Bus #23, 280, 630, 780, H or Tram #8. Mon–Sat 6am–2am, Sun 5pm–2am. Fashionable Trastevere bar with Internet access for €4 for half an hour.

Bibli Via dei Fienaroli 28 ℡06.588.4097. Bus #23, 75, 280, 630, 780, H or Tram #8. Tues–Sun 11am–midnight, Mon 5.30pm–midnight. A large, multipurpose bookstore, offering snacks, concerts, presentations, performances and Internet access. Half an hour costs €4, an hour €6. See also p.213.

Easyinternet Café Via Barberini 2 ℡06.4290.3388. Metro A Barberini or Bus #52, 53, 61, 62, 63, 80 or Express, 95, 116, 119, 175, 204, 492, 590, 630. Part of the giant Easy Group, this place has three floors and hundreds of terminals, plus loads of other services, and a café. Rates vary according to demand, from €0.50–3 per hour. Also In Piazza In Piscinula 15, Trastevere. Bus #23, 280, 630, 780, H or Tram #8.

Internet Café Via Cavour 213 ℡06.4782.3051. Metro B Cavour or Bus #16, 75, 84, 360, 649. Daily 9am–1am. Efficiently run, this spacious, pleasant environment offers Internet access, scanning and printing. Ten minutes online goes for €1, or, with the "Internet Café Card", you get an hour for €3. Soft drinks and coffee and tea.

Netgate Piazza Firenze 25. Internet access for €4 an hour at this city-wide chain with other branches, at Termini station, among others.

Raccolta Multimedia Vicolo del Cinque 58 ℡06.5833.2474. Bus #23, 280, 630, 780, H or Tram #8. Mon–Sat 6pm–midnight. Another "polifunzionale" multimedia space, featuring books, art and photography exhibitions, workshops, snacks and a suitably bohemian atmosphere to go with the hi-tech environment. Internet access costs €4 an hour.

Punto Blu Via Cavour 168–170 ℡06.481.7857. Metro B Cavour or Bus #40, 64, 70, 117, 170, H. Daily 8am–10pm. This place also has laundry facilities so you can surf the web while you get your washing done.

Nightlife

oman **nightlife** retains some of the smart ethos satirized in Fellini's film *La Dolce Vita*, and designer-dressing-up is still very much a part of the mainstream scene. Entrance prices to the big **clubs** tend to be high, but there are a few smaller, more alternative nightspots, where your travel-crumpled clothes will be perfectly acceptable. To get around the licensing laws, some of Rome's night haunts are run as private clubs – usually known as "centri culturali" – a device that means you may be stung for a membership fee, particularly where there's music, though as a one-off visitor some places will let you in without formalities; and some places charge no fee at all to be a member. In recent decades these sorts of places have sprung up all over the city, particularly in the suburbs, and are becoming the focus of political activity and the more avant-garde elements of the music and arts scene.

If you're after **live music**, there are regular summer festivals (see box, opposite), with several venues all over town, featuring concerts of every sort, including practically free events in Testaccio. However, the chances of catching major rock and pop acts are virtually non-existent, and getting worse. Rome has been all but abandoned by most big UK and US acts because of its almost complete lack of organization and a suitable venue. Big promoters book the cities up north, especially Milan and Bologna, and leave Rome entirely out of the loop. However, there is a chance you can catch up-and-coming US and UK indie bands playing some of the city's more alternative venues.

If you're heading out after dinner or a snack in a bar, Roman nightlife can be found all over the city, including neighbourhoods on the very edge of town. However, in the central zone the **best areas** tend to be Testaccio (especially in summer), Trastevere, and the centro storico from the Jewish Ghetto to the Pantheon. For what's-on information, there's *Romac'è* (€1, Wednesdays), with its helpful section in English, and, if you understand Italian, *Time Out Roma* (€2, Thursdays, publication suspended during summer months). Otherwise the main Rome newspaper, *Il Messaggero*, lists major musical events, and "TrovaRoma" in the Thursday edition of *La Repubblica* is another handy guide to current offerings.

Live music

Rome's **rock** scene is a relatively limp affair, especially compared to the cities of the north, focusing mainly on imported product and the big venues.

See the next chapter, "Culture and entertainment", for details of Rome's ticket services.

Live-music festivals

Rome hosts a variety of music festivals especially during the summer. For **jazz**, the *Dolce Vita Jazz Festival* from May to July, features at least a few superstars and ranges from early jazz to edgy experimentation; check out ⓦwww.dvjazzfestival.com. Throughout the summer, don't miss the relaxed fun and fine dining at *Jazz & Image*, held amongst the umbrella pines in the Villa Celimontana park, and thoroughly international in scope (☎06.589.7807, ⓦwww.romajazz.com). In October and November each year you'll also find the *Roma Jazz Festival*, with an international cast of fairly big names. There's a big **Latin music** scene, too, particularly Brazilian, including a *Festival Latino Americano* in summer, from the end of July to the end of August, held out at the Ippodromo delle Capannelle on the Via Appia Nuova; tickets are available only on site. Other summer live-music offerings include *Testaccio Village*, the *Festa dell'Unità*, the *Festa dell'Indipendenza* and similar events sponsored by political parties of the Left, often held in and around the old slaughterhouse in Testaccio. These events tend to charge no admission and include live music, dancing and an array of other entertainments, as well as ethnic eateries. *Testaccio Village* offers a different group every night during the warm months, followed by three outdoor discos, all for free on production of a very low-priced weekly pass – available at the ticket booth near the entrance. Again, check *Romac'è* or *Time Out* for details.

Note that the old slaughterhouse, which has been home to so many alternative activities, is slated to be taken over by the University of Rome, probably forcing the *Villaggio Globale* (see p.226) and other grass-roots undertakings to seek new venues.

Summer sees local bands giving occasional free concerts in the piazzas, but the city is much more in its element with **jazz**, with lots of venues and a wide choice of styles performed by a healthy array of local talent.

Rome's big arenas

For information about events at either of these two venues – really the city's only options for big, internationally renowned visiting bands and solo acts – call the Orbis agency (details in Chapter 17).

Palacisalfa Viale del Oceano Atlantico ☎06.5728.8024. Metro B EUR Palasport or Bus #72, 77, 703, 706, 707, 779. A giant tent-like structure 400m from Palaeur, one of two sports arenas where major acts tend to end up. It's inadequate, but holds about 3500 people and has served up everything from sporting events to clubbing nights.

Palaeur Piazzale dello Sport. No phone. Metro B EUR Palasport or Bus #30, 671, 714, 780, 791. Holding over 9000 people, this circular hall has recently undergone a total overhaul, including work on its terrible acoustics. It remains to be seen if this will finally give Rome the venue it needs to attract major acts.

Rock and pop

Accademia Vicolo della Renella 90 ☎06.589.6321. Bus #23, 75, 280, 630, 780, H or Tram #8. Daily noon–3pm & 6pm–2am. A popular Trastevere eatery and party spot for a youngish crowd. Live rock Mon & Wed evenings, otherwise a DJ. It's huge – on four floors – but this joint jumps, so it's a good idea to make a reservation if you want a table.

Akab/Cave Via Monte Testaccio 69 ☎06.578.2390. Metro B Piramide or bus #23, 30, 75, 95, 280, 716, 719 or Tram #3. Thurs–Sun 11pm–4.30am. Two venues in one. *Akab* is at ground level and usually plays house music. The *Cave* is below ground and features R&B. Concerts are generally once or twice a week. €10–20, including a drink.

Alpheus Via del Commercio 36 ☎06.574.7826. Metro B Piramide or bus #23, 769, 770. Tues–Sun 10pm–4.30am. Housed in an ex-factory off Via Ostiense, a little way beyond Testaccio, the *Alpheus* has space for three simultaneous events — generally a disco, concert and exhibition or piece of theatre. Entrance €5–20, depending on events, free on Wednesdays for students.

Bluecheese Factory Via Caio Cestio 5b ℡06.5728.7631. Metro B Piramide or Bus #23, 30, 75, 95, 280, 716, 719 or Tram #3. Fri & Sat 11pm–5am. The top choice in town for more cutting-edge creativity, combining electronic music experimentation and media performance work. Admission €3.50–4.

Blue Knight Via delle Fornaci 8–10 ℡06.630.011. Metro A Ottaviano or Bus #32, 34, 49, 81, 492, 590, 982 or Tram #19. Daily 7am–3am. Right near St Peter's, the main floor here is a bar and *gelateria*, while downstairs there are concerts – almost always acoustic music, ranging from rock to blues to pop, featuring some of Rome's best musicians and occasional imports. Concerts take place Thurs–Sat, usually starting at 10.30pm. No admission charge.

Caffè de Oriente Via Monte Testaccio 36 ℡06.574.5019. Metro B Piramide or Bus #23, 30, 75, 95, 170, 280, 716, 781 or Tram #3. Tues–Sun 10pm–3am. Three rooms and a roof terrace for the warm months host Latin music most of the week, with soul, R&B and live cover groups at times. Admission €6–10.

Caffè Latino Via Monte Testaccio 96 ℡06.5728.8556. Metro B Piramide or Bus #23, 30, 75, 95, 170, 280, 716, 781 or Tram #3. Tues–Sun 10pm–3am. Multi-event Testaccio club with varied live music almost every night, as well as cartoons, films, and cabaret. There's also a disco playing a selection of funky, acid jazz and R&B music. Best at weekends when it gets more crowded. Admission €6–10.

Circolo degli Artisti Via Casilina Vecchia 42 ℡06.7030.5684. Metro A Re di Roma or San Giovanni or Bus #105. Tues–Sun 7.30pm–4am. A very large venue, newly remodelled – 800 square metres inside plus 5000 outside in the summer, located beyond Porta Maggiore. A good range of bands, with frequent discos and theme nights – hip-hop, electronic, house, ska, revival, etc. €3 for a three-month membership. Friday is gay-friendly "Omogenic" night.

Circolo Vizioso Via dei Reti 25 ℡0347.814.6544. Bus #71, 492 or Tram #3, 19. Tues–Sun 9pm–2am. Multi-room multi-venue in the San Lorenzo district, featuring live rock, reggae and jazz, plus performance art, theatre and cabaret in the main hall.

Elsewhere you can dine and chat. €5.50 with yearly membership.

I Giardini di Adone Via dei Reti 38a ℡06.445.4382. Bus #71, 492 or Tram #3, 19. Tues–Sun 8pm–3am. A San Lorenzo venue with rock acts every night, plus theme nights from time to time. Also food, cocktails and beer. €5 entrance.

The Groove Vicolo Savelli 10 ℡06.6872.2427. Cool bar with live music that draws both a tourist and a local crowd. Nice atmosphere.

Il Locale Vicolo del Fico 3 ℡06.687.9075. Bus #30, 40, 46, 62, 64, 70, 81, 97, 189, 304, 492, 628, 916. Tues–Sun 10.30pm–2.30am. Centrally located close to Piazza Navona, this trendy joint enjoys a lively, not to say chaotic, atmosphere, and up-to-the-minute musical awareness, featuring English and American alternative bands and Italian folk-rock. €5.20 membership to get in.

Radio Londra Via di Monte Testaccio 67 ℡06.575.0044. Bus #23, 30, 75, 95, 170, 280, 716, 781 or Tram #3. Wed–Mon 9pm–3am, till 4am on Sat. Air force theme rock and new wave live music venue (with food) in Testaccio. One of the stalwart perennials on the scene. Entrance €5–10.

RipArte Café Via Orti di Trastevere 7 ℡06.586.1852. Bus #23, 75, 280, 630, 780, H or Tram #8. Mon–Sat 8pm–1am. Live music at 11pm every evening in an elegantly modern environment, where you can also eat. A current favourite with many, so reserve ahead. €15 and up.

Villaggio Globale Lungotevere Testaccio ℡06.5730.0329. Bus #95, 170, 719, 781. Winter months only; opening hours depend on events. Situated in the old slaughterhouse along the river, the "global village" is an alternative, left-wing meeting space with a multi-ethnic, campus feel. Lectures, concerts, disco, performances and exhibitions make up its busy schedule; there's something on almost every night. Entrance is €3.50 to €5, depending on event.

Jazz and Latin

Alexanderplatz Via Ostia 9 ℡06.3974.2171. Metro A Ottaviano or Bus #32, 34, 49, 81, 492, 590, 982 or Tram #19. Mon–Sat 9pm–2.30am. Rome's top live jazz club/restaurant with reasonable membership and free entry, except when there's star-billing. Reservations recommended. Monthly membership €6.50, annual €26.

Beba Do Samba Piazza dei Campani 12
☎ 339.878.5214. Bus #71, 492 or Tram #3, 19.
Daily 9pm–2.30am. Each night the stage
near the bar highlights a new group, with
the focus often on Brazilian sounds, while
the chill-out room is replete with comfortable cushions and divans.
Berimbau Via dei Fienaroli 30b ☎ 06.581.3249.
Bus #23, 75, 280, 630, 780, H or Tram #8.
Wed–Sun 10.30pm–3am. Plenty of live samba
and strong Brazilian drinks and food in the
heart of Trastevere. €7–10, drink included.
Big Mama Vicolo San Francesco a Ripa 18
☎ 06.581.2551. Bus #23, 44, 75, 280, 630, 780,
H or Tram #3, 8. Opening hours depend on
concerts, generally 9.30pm–1.30am; closed
July–Oct. Trastevere-based jazz/blues club
of long standing, hosting nightly acts.
Membership €6 a month, €13 a year, extra
for star attractions. Fri & Sat concerts only
for those with yearly memberships. Get
tickets ahead of time for important names.
Caruso Via di Monte Testaccio 36
☎ 06.574.5019. Bus #23, 30, 75, 95, 170, 280,
716, 781 or Tram #3. Tues–Sun 8pm–late.
Tropical rhythms in Testaccio. Live concerts
about twice a week. Brazilian bands shake
up the cocktail bar, while varied music –
hip-hop, Latin, rock – pumps you up in the
disco. €8 monthly membership.
Central Do Brasil Via Rosazza 56
☎ 347.534.4357. Bus #170, 781, H or Tram #3,
8. Tues–Sun 6pm–3am. This venue could
pass for Rome's Brazilian cultural centre –
it's a discobar, but above all a temple to
samba, often with live music. Cocktails
include the signature caipirinha, as well as
non-alcoholic fruit creations.
Charity Café Via Panisperna 68
☎ 06.4782.5881. Bus #40, 64, 70, 75, 117, 170,
H. Daily 6pm–3am. The Monti district is full of
interesting venues these days and this is one
of the best. Wines and a tasty assortment of
cheeses and sausages in a relaxed setting,
with live blues. Happy Hour 6–10pm.
Escopazzo Via d'Aracoeli 41 ☎ 06.6920.0422.
Bus #23, 30, 40, 46, 62, 63, 64, 81, 87, 280,
492, 628, 630, 780, H or Tram #8. Daily
8.30pm–2.30am. Halfway between Piazza
Venezia and Largo Argentina, this friendly
bar attracts a crowd of thirty-somethings
and offers food and wine along with live
concerts or jam sessions most nights.
Free entrance.
Fonclea Via Crescenzio 82a ☎ 06.689.6302.
Metro A Ottaviano or Bus #23, 32, 34, 49, 81,

492, 590, 982 or Tram #19. Daily 7pm–2am.
Happy Hour 7–8pm. Concerts begin at 9.30pm.
Located near the Vatican, this 20-year-old
jazz/soul, funk and rock venue is fitted out
like a British pub and has live music most
nights. Free Mon–Fri and Sun, €6 on Sat.
Non-smoking section up near the stage.
Four Green Fields Via C. Morin 42
☎ 06.372.5091. Metro A Ottaviano or Bus #23,
32, 34, 49, 81, 492, 590, 982 or Tram #19. Daily
2pm–2am. Mixed crowds visit this long-
running, versatile Vatican area pub, which
also has a cocktail bar. They call their
Happy Hour "Power Hour" and it happens
every Tues 10–11pm. Live music in the
basement every night starting at 9.30pm.
Free admission.
Four XXXX Pub Via Galvani 29 ☎ 06.575.7296.
Bus #23, 30, 75, 95, 170, 280, 716, 781 or Tram
#3. Tues–Sun 7.30pm–2.30am. Testaccio pub
spread over two floors, with South
American-inspired food and snacks, live
jazz and Latin music. Entrance €3–5 when
there's a gig on. See also p.221.
Gregory's Via Gregoriana 54d ☎ 06.679.6386.
Metro A Spagna or Bus #52, 53, 61, 71, 80, 85,
95, 116, 119, 160, 850. Tues–Sun 5.30pm–3am.
Just up the Spanish Steps and to the right,
an elegant nightspot featuring live jazz impro-
vised by Roman and international musicians.
Always crowded. Snacks on offer, too.
'Gusto Piazza Augusto Imperatore 9 & Via della
Frezza 23 ☎ 06.322.6273. Bus #81, 117, 119,
628, 913, 926. Tues & Thurs 8pm–3am. The
first of Rome's designer restaurants and
determined to remain first with fresh ideas.
The latest is to offer free concerts twice a
week, featuring jazz, swing, soul, ethnic
music (Brazilian and flamenco) and more,
never veering far from the coolly sophisticated. See also p.208 and p.247.
New Mississippi Jazz Club Borgo Angelico
18a ☎ 06.6880.6348. Metro A Ottaviano or Bus
#23, 32, 34, 49, 81, 492, 590, 982 or Tram #19.
Wed–Sat 9pm–3am. Sun noon–4pm. Historic
Vatican area jazz venue which also runs a
music school. They serve cold buffet dinners, and concerts start at 10pm. Annual
membership €8. Look out, too, for their
Sunday live "Jazz Brunch".
No Stress Brazil Via degli Stradivari 35
☎ 06.5833.5015. Bus #170, 781, H or Tram #3, 8.
Mon–Sat 8.30pm–3am. Live Brazilian musicians and dancers every night, with DJs
filling in until all hours. Full Brazilian meals
also served. €10 Fri & Sat, including drink.

The Place Via Alberico II 27 ☎06.6830.7137. Bus #23, 34, 40, 62, 280. Tues–Sun 7.30pm–1am. Live fusion music here to go with the interesting fusion cuisine. Expect everything from jazz to funk, to Latin to R&B performers.

Stardust Vicolo de' Renzi 4 ☎06.5832.0875. Bus #23, 75, 280, 630, 780, H or Tram #8. Mon–Sat 3.30pm–2am, Sun noon–2am. Sometimes much later. One of Trastevere's most authentic haunts, this tiny jazz venue stays open as long as there's somebody there and organizes all-night jam sessions in the basement whenever the mood strikes – or the regulars demand (see also p.222).

Clubs

Rome's **clubs** run the gamut. There are vast glitter palaces with stunning lights and sound systems, predictable dance music and an over-dressed, over-made-up clientele — good if you can afford it and just want to dance (and observe a good proportion of Romans in their natural Saturday-night element). But there are also places that are not much more than ritzy **bars** with music, and other, more down-to-earth places to dance, playing a more interesting selection of music to a younger, more cautious-spending crowd (we've listed some of these in Chapter 15, "Drinking", as well). There is also a small group of clubs catering specifically to **gay or lesbian** customers (see Chapter 18 for details of these). Whichever you prefer, all tend to open and close late, and some charge a heavy entrance fee – as much as €20, which usually includes a drink. During the hot summer months, many clubs close down or move to outdoor locations.

Alien Via Velletri 13/19 ☎06.841.2212. Bus #63. Tues–Sun 11pm–4am. Newly redecorated, the two halls here now feature starkly contrasting decor, one redolent of maharaja plushness, the other all done up in modernistic black and white. Music is a mix of house, tech-house and revival, mostly depending on the night and which room you choose to frequent. It also has a summer venue, *Alien 2 Mare*, in Fregene at Piazzale Fregene 5, ☎06.6656.4761. Entrance fee variable.

Art Café Via del Galoppatoio 33 ☎06.3600.6578. Housed in the underground car park at Villa Borghese, this is one of Romes trendiest clubs. Expect to queue.

Associazione Culturale Vecchio Mattatoio Via di Monte Testaccio 23 ☎06.5823.8321. Bus #23, 30, 75, 95, 170, 280, 716, 781 or Tram #3. Thurs–Sat 11pm–5am. This indoor-outdoor venue is actually several scenes in one, and they change constantly. The most consistent is called "Black Planet", which showcases soul, R&B, reggae, and hip-hop. Full meals are also available until the wee hours. Admission €8.

Blackout Rockclub Via Saturnia 18 ☎06.7049.6791. Metro A San Giovanni or Re di Roma or Bus #85. Thurs–Sat 11pm–4am. Punk, heavy-metal and Gothic music, with occasional gigs by US and UK bands make this industrial space one of the city's most frequented spots. Located out by San Giovanni in Laterano. €5 to get in. Closed in summer.

Gilda Via Mario de' Fiori 97 ☎06.678.4838. Metro A Spagna or Bus #52, 53, 61, 71, 80, 85, 95, 116, 119, 160, 850. Tues–Sun 11.30pm–5am, and Sun 4.30–7.30pm. A few blocks from the Spanish Steps, this slick and expensive club (€20 entry weekends), is the focus for the city's minor (and would-be) celebs though mainly of the middle-aged variety. Dress smart to get in. Their summer venue, *Gilda-on-the-Beach*, is in Fregene, at Lungomare di Ponente 11 (Tues–Sun 10.30pm–4am; ☎06.6656.0649).

Goa Via Libetta 13 ☎06.574.8277. Metro B Garbatella or Bus #29, 769, 770. Tues & Thurs–Sat 11pm–5am. Opened by famous local DJ Giancarlino, this, as you might expect from the name, has an ethnic feel – a shop sells handmade items, there's incense burning – and the music is techno, house, and trance. There are couches to help you recover after high-energy dancing;

the decor changes every few weeks. Located near St Paul's Fuori le Mura Entrance €10–20, including drink.

Jackie O' Via Boncompagni 11 ☎06.4288.5457. **Bus #52, 53, 61, 62, 63, 80, 95, 116, 119, 175, 492. Daily 1.30pm–4.30am. Closed Mon in winter.** Amazingly, this 1960s Via Veneto jet-set glitter palace is still going strong, even attracting its share of celebs from time to time. Long on attitude, it can actually be fun if you enjoy its rather retro notion of a night out, including a preponderance of mainstream pop. €20 entrance, including drink; each additional drink €10.

La Maison Vicolo da Granari 4 ☎06.683.3312. Ritzy club whose chandelier and glossy decor attract Rome's gilded youth and minor celebs. Sunday – gay night – is the one to go for though you'll need to book a table if you want to sit down.

Piper Via Tagliamento 9 ☎06.855.5398. **Bus #63, 86, 92, 217, 360 or Tram #3, 19. Tues–Sun 11pm–4am, Sat & Sun also 4–8pm for youngsters.** Established in the Seventies by cult singer Patty Pravo, the *Piper* has survived by undergoing a reincarnation every season. There are different nightly events (fashion shows, screenings, parties, gigs and the like), a smart-but-casual mixed-aged crowd, and a heavy pick-up scene. It's hard to predict the kind of music you'll hear; it varies hugely, depending on the night. Entrance is €7–15, also depending on the night. Its summer venue, from the end of May to the beginning of September, is by the sea at the *AcquaPiper di Guidonia*, Via Maremmana, before the 23.9km marker (☎0774.326.538).

Qube Via di Portonaccio 212 ☎06.438.5445. **Metro B Tiburtina or Bus #409. Thurs–Sat**

10.30pm–4am. One of the biggest and most frequented clubs in town, with rock and revival featured, including live bands. Currently it plays host to the Mucca Assassina ("Killer Cow") gay night every Friday. Free Thurs, €13 Friday, €8 Sat.

Rock Castle Café Via B. Cenci 8 ☎06.6880.7999. **Bus #23, 63, 280, 630, 780, H or Tram #8. Daily 9pm–3am.** A fun foreign students' hangout playing rock and nothing but. Entrance is €5 Saturdays, including a drink, otherwise free. See also p.219.

Il Sigillo Via del Cardello 13 ☎06.6994.2419. **Metro B Cavour or Bus #40, 64, 70, 117, 170, H. Thurs–Sun 11pm–4am.** Formerly *Jam Session*, this place, just off Via Cavour, hosts a young crowd dancing to 1970s & 1980s disco tunes they couldn't possibly have heard first time around. The €5 entrance fee includes a drink. Sunday is gay and transgender night; see p.221.

La Suite Via degli Orti di Trastevere 1 ☎06.586.1888. **Bus #701, H or Tram #3, 8. Wed–Sat midnight–4am.** More evidence that Rome is coming into its own with designer hotels and clubs. In this case, the effect is a bit too self-conscious, perhaps, but the setting is certainly chic and attracts a clientele who appreciate the pop standards they play. Admission €15.

Zoobar Via di Monte Testaccio 22 ☎06.537.3017. **Bus #23, 30, 75, 95, 170, 280, 716, 781 or Tram #3. Thurs–Sat 11pm–3.30am.** This Testaccio venue is one of the most reliable of late for a good time. Ample indoor and outdoor spaces and music that keeps you interested and the crowd moving. The two main rooms feature oldies, funk, R&B, ska, and much more. Annual membership €3, Fri €2.50, Sat €4.

Culture and entertainment

L et's face it: Rome is a bit of a backwater for the **performing arts**. Northern Italy is where creativity in theatre and dance – and, of course, opera – flourishes, and very few international-class performers put in an appearance here. Nevertheless, there is cultural entertainment available, and the quality is sometimes better than you might expect. In any case, what the arts here may lack in professionalism, they often make up for in the charm of the setting. Rome's **summer festival**, for example, organized by "Estate Romana" (Wwww.estateromana.comune.roma.it), means that there's a good range of classical music, opera, theatre and cinema running throughout the warm months, often in picturesque locations – amidst ancient ruins with soaring columns, or perched on hills with brilliant panoramas of Rome by night – although obviously some of what's on is of little interest if you don't speak Italian. During the winter season, you'll find a regular programme of **classical music** mounted by the Accademia Nazionale di Santa Cecilia (see below), and other sporadic musical offerings of mixed quality, sometimes in beautiful churches or palatial halls, and on occasions free. **Opera** is well established in Rome and now and again approaches world-class levels, but not

Information and ticket agencies

For current **information** about what's on where in English, consult the English section at the back of *Romac'è* (€1, Wed) or *Wanted in Rome*, the English-language bi-weekly (€0.75, every other Wed), which you can pick up at almost any newsstand in the centre. Otherwise, in Italian, *Time Out Roma* (€2, Thurs, publication suspended during summer months) is your best bet. There's also the "TrovaRoma" insert in *La Repubblica*'s Thursday edition.

Ticket agencies
Rome's ticket agencies have recently burgeoned; the following are worth a try:
Orbis Piazza Esquilino 37 (Santa Maria Maggiore), ☎06.482.7403, ☎06.474.4776
Messaggerie Musicali Via del Corso 472, ☎06.684.401
Helló Ticket Desk #6 Stazione Termini, Via Giolitti 16, ☎06.4782.5710
Box Office Ricordi Via del Corso 506, ☎06.320.2790; Viale Giulio Cesare 88 (Prati), ☎06.3750.0375
Interclub Service Piazza Ippolito Nievo 3–5 (Trastevere), ☎06.589.5431, ☎06.580.6090

often enough. Good **dance** is a rarity in Rome, although international companies do show up from time to time, usually at the Teatro Olimpico and the Teatro Argentina (see below). Finally, **cinema-lovers** will find an increasing number of films in the original language, as Italy gradually breaks away from its nationalistic dubbing mania.

Classical music

Under new directors, Rome's own **orchestras** of late are approaching international standards, and although the city attracts far fewer prestigious artists than you might expect of a capital, it is becoming more and more a magnet for contemporary works. The sea-change has been inspired by the completion – far behind schedule – of the new **Parco della Musica** (see below). Critics say that beauty has been entirely sacrificed for acoustics here, but the three halls of various sizes certainly do deliver on sound quality, while the outdoor space can be used for anything from rock to opera. Otherwise, check the listings and keep a look-out for posters advertising little-known **concerts** – a wide range of choral, chamber and organ recitals – in churches or other often spectacular venues, sometimes including the private halls in Renaissance or Baroque palaces. The city's main classical player is the **Accademia Nazionale di Santa Cecilia** (see below), and we've listed a number of other places where the city's other orchestras and musical associations perform. Otherwise, the many national academies and cultural institutes (Belgian, Austrian, Hungarian, British, American, French, et al) frequently offer free concerts as well, along with the *Auditorium Cavour* (℡06.721.9771). In the summer, concerts are staged in cloisters, in the Villa Giulia and Teatro di Marcello, just off Piazza Venezia, and in the ancient Roman theatre at Ostia Antica. In addition there are sponsored Sunday-morning concert cycles, such as the *Telecom Italia* one at the *Teatro Sistina*, Via Sistina 129 (℡06.482.6841), between November and April. It may be that you'll just stumble across a concert-in-progress while out on an evening stroll, passing by some ancient church with all its lights on (a rarity not to be missed); Rome is a city where such magical musical moments can still happen.

Accademia Filarmonica Romana Teatro Olimpico, Piazza Gentile da Fabriano 17 ℡06.320.1752, ☻www.filarmonicaromana.org. Bus #53, 280, 910 or Tram #2, 19. A programme of classical standards, chamber music, ancient music, ballet, and chamber opera, as well as occasional contemporary works. Performances are on Thursdays and run from October to early May. Tickets range from €15 to €30.

Accademia Nazionale di Santa Cecilia Via della Conciliazione 4. Box office ℡06.6880.1044; Information ℡06.361.1064; ☻www.santacecilia.it. Bus #64. One of the world's oldest music institutions, formalized by Pope Sixtus V in 1585 and still the focus of Rome's classical music scene. Santa Cecilia stages concerts throughout the year by its own orchestra (Rome's best) and by visiting orchestras and artists. Orchestral

concerts outside the main season are held at the auditorium, just down the road from St Peter's. Most of the tickets are pre sold by season pass, but for certain special events tickets can go for as little as €8.

Teatro Ghione Via delle Fornaci 37 ℡06.637.2294, ☻www.ghione.it. Bus #34, 46, 64, 916. Box office hours daily 10am–1pm & 4–7.30pm. This traditional little theatre offers chamber music and recitals, often by well-known musical lights, some of whom are legends in their own lifetimes.

Gonfalone Oratorio del Gonfalone, Via del Gonfalone 32a ℡06.687.5952. Bus #64. The season here runs from November to early June, offering performances of chamber music, with an emphasis on the Baroque, every Thursday at 9pm. Tickets cost €15 and you can reserve by phone. Reservations are strongly recommended.

For those wishing to visit the Oratorio, or to pick up tickets in advance, the entrance is at Vicolo della Scimia 1b, during office hours.

Parco della Musica Via P. de Coubertin 15 ☎06.808.2058. ⓦwww.musicaperroma.it. Bus #53, 280, 910 or Tram #2, 19. Daily 10am–6pm to visit; guided tours available €10. Box office hours Mon, Tues, Thurs–Sun 11am–6pm, summer Mon–Fri. A brand-new concert venue, Rome's first for many years; the Accademia Nazionale di Santa Cecilia now uses the largest hall here for its winter season. The smaller halls are used for chamber, choral, recital and experimental works.

Istituzione Universitaria dei Concerti Aula Magna dell' Università la Sapienza Piazzale Aldo Moro 5 ☎06.361.0051, ⓦwww .concertiiuc.it. Bus #61, 490, 495 or Tram #3, 19 or Metro B Policlinico. Musical offerings ranging from Mozart to Miles Davis, and from Ravel to Kurt Weill. Tickets cost €10 to €25. The season runs from October to April, and performances are usually held on Tuesday evenings and weekends.

Opera

Rome's **opera** scene has long been overshadowed by that of Milan, Parma, and even Naples, grand opera's acknowledged birthplace – but it is improving. In summer, opera moves outdoors and ticket prices come down. Summer performances are now once again held in the stunning setting at the ancient **Baths of Caracalla**, as well as in the courtyard of San Clemente basilica and in other churches and venues all around Rome, in the context of the various summer music festivals which have multiplied remarkably in recent years.

Accademia d'Opera Italiana Chiostro del Sacro Cuore, Trinità dei Monti ☎06.784.2702. ⓦwww.accademiadoperaitaliana.it. Metro A Spagna or Bus #52, 53, 61, 62, 71, 80, 85, 95, 116, 117, 119, 160, 850. Held in the beautiful cloister of the imposing church at the top of the Spanish Steps, performances generally include popular standards such as *La Traviata*, *Tosca* and *Il Barbiere di Siviglia*, as well as the Mozart *Requiem* and *Carmina Burana*. Throughout July. Tickets €30.

Festival EuroMediterraneo Villa Adriana, via di Villa Adriana (Tivoli) ☎06.6880.9107, ⓦwww.medfestival.com; COTRAL bus from Ponte Mammolo (Metro B). Seeing an opera amidst the monumental remains of Hadrian's Villa in Tivoli (see p.176) is an unforgettable evening out. July–Aug.

New Operafestival di Roma Piazza San Clemente 1 ☎06.561.1519, ⓦwww .newoperafestivaldiroma.com. Metro B Colosseo or Bus #60, 85, 87, 117, 810, 850 or Tram #3. This festival brings talented opera students from the US and around Italy to mount full productions, recitals and the like. June–Aug.

Teatro dell' Opera di Roma Piazza Beniamino Gigli 1 ☎800.016.665, ⓦwww.operaroma.it; Metro A Repubblica or Bus #40, 60, 64, 70, 117, 170. Nov–May, box office daily 9am–4.30pm; English spoken; summer season July–Aug. Nobody compares it to *La Scala*, but cheap tickets are a lot easier to come by at Rome's opera house, and important singers do sometimes perform here. Expect to pay at least €8, and up to €119. If you buy the very cheapest tickets, bring some high-powered binoculars, as you'll need them in order to see anything at all.

Theatre and dance

There is a great deal of **theatre** in Rome, but it's virtually all in Italian, or even dialect. Very occasional English-language musicals, usually put together by some travelling American company, come to town during the winter season. The venue for such rare events is almost always either the Teatro Olimpico or the Teatro Sistina, sometimes Teatro Argentina of late. There is one English-language theatre group, who perform current American one-acts, mostly off-the-wall comedies, on Friday evenings from October to June. The English Theatre of Rome performs at the L'Arte del Teatro, Via Urbana 107. Map 4, D8. Metro B Cavour or Bus #40, 64, 70, 71, 75, 84, 117, 170, H. Call impresario Gaby Ford on ℡06.444.1375 for current information, or keep an eye out for posters in some of the Anglo-American hangouts – bookshops, cinemas, pubs, etc. Incidentally, virtually all Roman theatres close on Mondays. Again, check the usual sources for your options. As for **dance**, apart from the very occasional international company, home-grown Roman and Italian troupes do their thing on the city's stages, and it is rarely an inspiring sight. Though the origins of ballet can be traced back to eighteenth-century Italy, there are at present few Italian companies that rise above amateurish levels.

English-language theatres

Teatro di Argentina Largo Argentina 52 ℡06.6880.4601. Bus #30, 40, 46, 62, 63, 64, 70, 81, 87, 492, 628, 810, 916 or Tram #8. One of the city's most important theatres for dramatic works in Italian, as well as the occasional production in English, and for dance. Quality varies widely. Tickets go for €10 and up.

Teatro Greco Via Ruggero Leoncavallo 12 ℡06.860.7513. Bus #63, 135, 342, 630. Located well out of the centre, on the far side of Villa Ada, this theatre generally offers some of the best Italian dance and even has its own company, with tickets starting at €8. In October the Italian National Dance competition is often held here.

Teatro Olimpico Piazza Gentile da Fabriano 17 ℡06.326.5991. Bus #53, 200, 910 or Tram #2, 19. Located well beyond Piazza del Popolo, this theatre tends to get Rome's best international dance and sometimes some important alternative performers. Tickets generally cost €20 and up. There's a decent snack bar, where you can sometimes spy the performers taking a break during the interval.

Teatro Sistina Via Sistina 129 ℡06.482.6841. Metro A Spagna or Barberini or Bus #52, 53, 61, 63, 71, 80, 95, 116, 119, 160, 175, 492, 630, 850. Every now and then an English-language (American, very off-Broadway) musical revue blows into town and it generally ends up here, just up from Piazza di Spagna. Expect to pay about €20 for a decent seat. Gershwin seems to be a perennial favourite, along with other jazzy-bluesy musical confections.

Teatro Valle Via del Teatro Valle 23a ℡06.6880.3794. Bus #30, 40, 46, 62, 63, 64, 70, 81, 87, 492, 628, 810, 916 or Tram #8. Between Piazza Navona and the Pantheon, this theatre sometimes offers special works

in English by visiting actors and companies. Tickets start at €8.

Teatro Vittoria Piazza Santa Maria Liberatrice 8 ℡06.574.0598. Bus #23, 30, 75, 95, 170, 280, 716, 781 or Tram #3. In Testaccio's main square, this large theatre sometimes books cabaret-like acts or dance-theatre companies that need no translation. Tickets start at about €10.

Other theatres

Teatro Agorà Via della Penitenza 33 ℡06.687.4167. Bus #23, 280. Once upon a time this Trastevere theatre sometimes produced English-language plays and other entertainments, and it could always happen again. Tickets start at €8.

Teatro Ambra Jovinelli Via G. Pepe 41–45 ℡06.4434.0262. Metro A Vittorio or Bus #70, 71, 105, 360, 649 or Tram #5, 14. Recently saved from terminal decay, this bastion of Rome's comic theatre tradition is now thriving, as is this entire once-blighted neighbourhood. Concerts as well as theatrical works.

Teatro Brancaccio Via Merulana 244 ℡06.4782.4893. Bus #16, 71. Musicals and comedies, sometimes featuring major Italian players, are generally the focus here. Not a top choice for good acoustics, so your Italian has to be excellent to follow the action, if not to enjoy the songs.

Teatro Colosseo Via Capo d'Africa 7 ℡06.700.4932. Metro B Colosseo or Bus #75, 81, 85, 87, 117, 810, 850 or Tram #3. Just up from the Colosseum, this theatre presents new, usually vaguely underground plays by contemporary Italian playwrights or translations. They have also been known to offer English-language one-acts in their small theatre downstairs. Tickets start at €6.

Teatro Eliseo Via Nazionale 183e ℡06.488.2114. Bus #40, 60, 64, 70, 71, 170.

One of Rome's main theatres, hosting plays by Italian playwrights, and adaptations into Italian of foreign works, and featuring some of the top dramatic talent Italy has to offer. Tickets start at €8.

Teatro Prati Via degli Scipione 98 ⊤06.3974.0503. Metro A Ottaviano or Bus #32, 34, 49, 81, 492, 590, 982 or Tram #19. A few blocks away from St Peter's, another small space that often features Italian comic classics. Tickets start at €10.

Teatro Romano di Ostia Antica Ostia Antica. Information ⊤06.6880.4601; box office daily 10am–2pm & 3–6pm. Ostia train from Piramide. Metro B Piramide or Bus #23, 30, 75, 95, 170, 280, 716, 781 or Tram #3. In July and August specially scheduled performances of all kinds are offered in the restored ancient Roman theatre – a spectacular, unforgettable setting,

even if you don't speak Italian. Performances begin at 8.45pm. Go early for a chance to visit the ruins. Tickets cost €8–10. It's a twenty-minute train ride to Ostia Antica, then a short walk over the footbridge into the ruins. A great Roman summer experience.

Teatro Rossini Piazza Santa Chiara 14 ⊤06.6880.2770. Bus #30, 40, 46, 62, 63, 64, 70, 81, 87, 492, 628, 810, 916 or Tram #8. Traditional Roman-dialect productions are one of the main focuses in this atmospheric old theatre.

Salone Margherita Via Due Macelli 75 ⊤06.679.1439. Metro A Spagna or Barberini or Bus #52, 53, 61, 63, 71, 80, 95, 116, 119, 160, 175, 492, 630, 850. Traditional Roman political satire and cabaret – worth it for the atmosphere, even if you don't understand the admittedly difficult verbal sallies.

Film

There tends to be more and more **English-language cinema** on offer in Rome these days, partly due to foreign demand, but also because Italians are finally beginning to realize that they've been at a disadvantage culturally, linguistically and economically by being spoon-fed a steady diet of dubbed movies. If you can manage with Italian, you'll naturally also find current Italian productions available all over town. Apart from summer outdoor **cinefests**, entirely reruns of mainstream hits, there is really no Roman film festival as such, although each year some of the new films – sometimes even the most significant ones – from Cannes and Venice are given special viewings at city theatres a week or two after the festivals.

You'll find usually accurate **listings** in the English-language section of *Romac'è* and in all the newspapers, which also include a section on "film clubs" or "cinema d'essai", a euphemism for stifling rooms where two or three aficionados sit on hard wooden chairs in front of a tiny, blurred screen watching films in their original language. Also, the "Italy Daily" supplement to the *International Herald Tribune* lists current English-language films; and if you speak Italian there's also *Time Out Roma*.

Alcazar Via Merry del Val 14 ⊤06.588.0099. Bus #75, 780, H or Tram #3, 8. Trastevere cinema featuring mainstream American and English films, with the occasional weird one slipping in. Ticket €7.

Metropolitan Via del Corso 7 ⊤06.3260.0500. Metro A Flaminio or Bus #88, 95, 117, 119, 495, 628, 926 or Tram #2. Lots of mainstream and the occasional quirky choice, with at least one of the four screens showing the undubbed version. Tickets €7.

Nuovo Olimpia Via in Lucina 16 ⊤06.686.1068. Bus #63, 492. Very central, just off Via del Corso, with two screens; tickets here cost €6. They sometimes

feature at least one foreign film in the original language.

Nuovo Sacher Largo Ascianghi 1 ⊤06.581.8116. Bus #44, 75, 780, H or Tram #3, 8. Again in Trastevere, this film theatre shows their current film in its original version, often in French, on Mondays. Tickets are €7. Their choices tend toward independent, Left-leaning works from Eastern Europe, France and Asia.

Pasquino Piazza Sant'Egidio 10 ⊤06.580.3622. Bus #23, 75, 280, 780, H or Tram #8. Long-established in Trastevere as Rome's premier English-language cinema, with three screens showing recent general releases and the odd indie from Sundance, etc. The programme changes every Friday, and they also mount their own mini-festivals from time to time. Tickets cost €6.20. A word of warning: avoid screen three unless you're really dying to see the film – the screen is terrible, the sound worse.

Quattro Fontane Via Quattro Fontane 23 ℡06.474.1515. Bus #40, 60, 64, 70, 170. Lots of mainstream and the occasional quirky choice, with at least one of the four screens showing the undubbed version. Tickets are €7.

Quirinale Via Nazionale 190a ℡06.488.2653. Bus #40, 60, 64, 70, 170. They always have films in the original language, nearly all first-run mainstream American fare with subtitles and the occasional artier choice. Tickets here go for €6.

Warner Village Moderno Piazza della Repubblica 45–46 ℡06.4777.9202. Metro A Repubblica or Bus #40, 60, 61, 62, 64, 90, 170, 175, 492, 910, H. This American-style multiplex occasionally shows a Hollywood blockbuster in the original undubbed version on one of its five screens.

Gay and lesbian Rome

Ever since "World Pride 2000" broke down the closet door, **gay and lesbian Rome** seems to have come into its own. The most startling sign is the tremendously successful **Gay Village** (Ⓦwww.gayvillage.it; €15 weekly admission) which holds events throughout the summer in an open-air venue in Testaccio. Italy has never had any laws prohibiting same-sex couplings, but until recently the overwhelming pressure was enough to keep everyone suitably zipped up. These days there are not just generic gay clubs, but specialist bars, restaurants and hotels; and all sorts of regular clubs are organizing **gay nights** to cater for the growing scene. Still, discretion is important in the community at large – remember that Rome remains a city where a man walking around in the historic centre without a shirt on will almost certainly be stopped by the police and told to cover up. As yet there is no particularly gay part of town; clubs and bars are spread far and wide. Also, choices exclusively for women remain very few, although most places welcome both gay men and lesbians.

Contacts and information

ARCI-Gay Ora Via Goito 35b ☏06.687.9939, Ⓦwww.arcigay.it/roma. Rome branch of the nationwide Italian gay organization. Political gatherings every Wed 8.30–10.30pm. Social gatherings every Sun 5–8pm. Membership is useful for getting into clubs, saunas, etc, and costs €14.
ARCI-Lesbica Roma Viale G. Stefanini 15 ☏06.418.0211, Ⓦwww.arcilesbicaroma.org. The local branch of the national lesbian activist group. Social-political gatherings every Thurs 8.30–10.30pm.
Circolo Mario Mieli di Cultura Omosessuale Via Efeso 2a ☏06.541.3985, Ⓦwww.mariomieli .org. Rome's most important gay activist

organization offers a broad range of social and health services, including counselling. Weekly welcome group, political group and volunteer group meetings; call for details.

Magazines

Aut Published by the Circolo Mario Mieli, this magazine features interesting articles, as well as listings. Free at many gay spots.
Babilonia Probably Italy's best gay monthly, keeping readers abreast of the latest political and cultural developments, as well as providing listings for all of Italy. €5.16 in any newsstand.

Bars and clubs

Alcatraz Via Aureliana 38 ☏ 06.4201.3286. **Metro Termini or Bus #36, 60. Thurs–Sat 10pm–3am, Sun 5pm–2am.** Very near Termini Station, this video bar on three floors features music, big screens, a discotheque and a dark room. It has special theme evenings, too, such as "Army Night" on Thursdays, and there's a Sunday Tea Dance starting at 5pm.

L'Alibi Via Monte Testaccio 44 ☏ 06.574.3448. **Metro B Piramide or Bus #23, 75, 95, 716 or Tram #3.Tues–Sun 11.30pm–5am.** Predominantly – but by no means exclusively – male venue that's one of Rome's oldest and best gay clubs. Downstairs there's a multi-room cellar disco and upstairs an open-air bar. There's a big terrace to enjoy in the warm months. Situated in the middle of the lively Testaccio neighbourhood, with lots of fun restaurants and a plethora of activities in the summer. Free admission Tues–Thurs. Fri €10, Sat €15, including drink.

Apeiron Via dei Quattro Cantoni 5 ☏ 06.482.8820. **Metro Termini or Metro B Cavour or Bus #36, 60, 75, 84. Most nights 10.30pm–2am, later on Fri and Sat.** A big-screen video bar upstairs, erotic videos and dark room downstairs. Located in the Termini area, near the Basilica of Santa Maria Maggiore. One-drink minimum for €3.

La Buca di Bacco Via San Francesco a Ripa 165 ☏ 348.764.7388. **Bus #75, 780, H or Tram #3, 8. Mon–Sat 5pm–2.30am.** This cocktail bar, wine bar and tearoom is one of the new breed of openly gay establishments, carrying out its business in full view on this busy Trastevere street. Happy Hour Mon–Thurs 5–9pm, cocktails €3; Sat there's "Aperitivo Trandy," featuring a buffet and a drink for €5.

Caffè Latino Via Monte Testaccio 96 ☏ 06.5728.8556. **Metro B Piramide or Bus #23, 30, 75, 95, 170, 280, 716, 781 or Tram #3. Sun 10pm–3am.** One of the latest to start sponsoring a night aimed at the rainbow crowd – in this case a bisexual night every Sunday. See p.226 for more on this Testaccio club.

Circolo degli Artisti Via Casilina Vecchia 42 ☏ 06.7030.5684. **Metro A Re di Roma or San Giovanni or Bus #105. Fri 7.30pm–4am.** Friday is gay-friendly "Omogenic" night. See p.226 for more on this very successful music venue.

Coming Out Via San Giovanni in Laterano 8 ☏ 06.700.9871. **Metro B Colosseo or Bus #85, 850. Daily 5pm–5am.** If any area is developing as Rome's gay zone, it may be the stretch between the Colosseum and Piazza Vittorio. This little pub is the newest addition to the scene, frequented mostly by a younger clientele.

Garbo Vicolo di Santa Margherita 1/a ☏ 06.5832.0782. **Bus #75, 780, H or Tram #3, 8. Wed–Mon 10pm–2am.** A friendly Trastevere bar, with a relaxed atmosphere and a nice setting, just behind the main piazza. A good mix of Italians and foreigners, presided over by Tom, the Irish proprietor. No admission charge. Drinks start at €2.50.

Gender Via Faleria 9 ☏ 06.7049.7638. **Metro A Re di Roma. Mon–Sat 11pm–3am.** A bit out from the city centre, this multi-gender fetish club specializes in theme nights, covering everything from erotic cartoons to drag lessons to sexy couple contests – taboos of all kinds cheerfuly broken. Entrance €7.75, reduced for couples and transgender guests.

Goa Via Libetta 13 ☏ 339.772.5619. **Metro B Garbatella or Bus #29, 769, 770.** One Friday per month 10.30pm–late. *Venus Rising* is a women-only event, sometimes featuring erotic performances, at this popular disco.

L'Hangar Via in Selci 29 ☏ 06.488.1397. **Metro B Cavour or Metro A Vittorio or Bus #75, 84. Wed–Mon 10.30pm–2.30am.** About halfway between Termini and the Roman Forum, just off Via Cavour, this is one of Rome's oldest and least expensive gay spots, always crammed with young people. Monday night features gay videos, and Saturday night it's almost impossible to get in the door it's so jammed. There's no charge to get in with your ARCI Uno Club card, without a card, you have to pay for at least one drink, whether you had one or not.

Max's Bar Via A. Grandi 7a ☏ 06.7030.1599. **Metro A Monzoni or Tram #3, 5, 14, 19. Mon, Tues, Thurs & Sun 10.30pm–3.30am, Fri & Sat 10.30pm–5am.** A very friendly bar with dancefloor, popular with a nice cross-section of gay Romans. Mon free, €8 Tues, Thurs & Sun, €10 Fri, €11 Sat, including drink.

Piper Via Tagliamento 9 ☏ 06.855.5398. **Bus #63, 86, 92, 217, 360 or Tram #3, 19. Tues–Sun 11pm–4am, Sat & Sun also 4–8pm for youngsters.** Saturday nights are gay nights at this eclectic club. See p.229 for more details.

Qube **Via di Portonaccio 212** ☎06.438.5445. **Metro B Tiburtina or Bus #409. Thurs–Sat 10.30pm–4am.** This plays host to the extremely successful Mucca Assassina ("Killer Cow") gay night every Friday. Free Thurs, €13 Friday, €8 Sat.

Shelter **Via dei Vascellari 35. No phone. Bus #23, 280, H or Tram #8. Daily 9pm–3am.** Bar located on a street with lots of great restaurants, so it's perfect for either pre- or post-dinner cocktails or dessert. More a place to meet with friends to hang out and converse than to check out the newest talent in town.

Il Sigillo **Via del Cardello 13/a** ☎06.6994.2419. **Metro B Cavour or Bus #40, 64, 70, 117, 170, H. Thurs–Sun 11pm–4am.** Sunday is gay and transgender night at this fun club; see p.229

Skyline Club **Via degli Aurunci 26–28** ☎06.444.1417. **Bus #71 or Tram #3, 19. Tues–Thurs & Sun 10.30pm–3am, Fri & Sat 10.30pm–5am.** Gay male strippers, dark zones, and the decidedly macho decor make this place a magnet for various creatures of the night, possibly drawn by the heavy cruising along the balcony.

Restaurants

Asinocotto **Via dei Vascellari 48** ☎06.589.8985. **Bus #23, 280, H or Tram #8. Tues–Sun 7pm–12.30am.** One of the first restaurants to hang the rainbow flag above its door, this *nouvelle*-style Roman restaurant is run by a gay couple and has earned a reputation for consistently good – if overpriced – food.

Baronato Quattro Bellezze **Via di Panico 23** ☎06.687.2865. **Bus #30, 40, 46, 62, 64, 70, 81, 116, 492, 628. Tues–Sun 8pm–2am.** Definitely one-of-a-kind, this place is owned and run by the inimitable Dominot, life-long drag chanteuse, formerly of Paris, who performs Piaf here on Thursday evenings. There's nothing else like it, at least not in Rome. Dominot is Tunisian by birth and the fare here is accordingly couscous, made by himself, including one for vegetarians. The decor is a charming hodge-podge of memorabilia

from his glittering career, including a gaily lit carousel pony that floats above the bar.

La Taverna di Edoardo II **Vicolo Margana 14** ☎06.6994.2419. **Bus #23, 30, 44, 63, 81, 95, 160, 170, 280, 628, 630, 715, 716, 780, 781, 916, H or Tram #8. Wed–Mon 7pm–12.30am.** Right in the middle of the old Jewish Ghetto, just off Piazza Venezia, this place used to be a medieval torture chamber theme bar, and was named after the infamously gay English king. It's now a gay restaurant and still attracts the same young and cruisy crowd. Membership is required, but it's free.

Le Sorellastre **Via San Francesco di Sales 1b** ☎349.762.2845. **Bus #23, 280. Tues–Sat 7pm–midnight.** This Trastevere bar and restaurant, serving Italian and international cuisine, is the only *exclusively* lesbian place in town.

Shops and services

Energie **Via del Corso 486,** ☎06.687.1258. **Metro A Spagna or Bus #52, 53, 61, 62, 71, 80, 85, 95, 116, 117, 119, 160, 850. Mon–Sat 10am–8pm, Sun 10am–1.30pm & 3.30–8pm.** Clothing store with trendy young styles and friendly young assistants, plus a 15 percent discount if you flash your ARCI-Gay membership card.

Libreria Babele **Via dei Banchi Vecchi 116,** ☎06.687.6628. **Bus #40, 46, 62, 64, 916. Tues–Sat 10am–2pm 3.30am–7.30pm, Mon 3.30am–7.30pm.** Rome's gay and lesbian bookshop, with lots of gay-themed books, some in English, plus gadgets, posters,

videos, guides and postcards. Towards the river from Campo de' Fiori, just off Corso Vittorio Emanuele.

Libreria delle Donne: Al Tempo Ritrovato, **Via dei Fienaroli 31d** ☎06.581.7724. **Bus #23, 75, 280, 630, 780, H or Tram #8. Tues–Sat 10am–1pm 3.30am–8pm, Mon 3.30am–7.30pm.** Devoted to women's studies, this bookshop has a good selection of lesbian-related works, with some in English. Events of various kinds are sometimes in the offing, as well.

Internetpoint **Via Cavour 213** ☎06.4782.3051. **Metro B Cavour or Bus #40, 64, 70, 71, 75, 84,**

117, 170, H. Daily 9am–1am. This Internet café is decidedly gay-friendly, as well as lively and inviting, offering a range of other services, including drinks and snacks. Around €3 for 1 hour.

Trevinet Pl@ce Via in Arcione 103 ⊕ 06.6992.2320, ⊛ www.trevinet.com. Bus #62, 63, 81, 85, 95, 117, 119, 160, 175, 492, 628, 630, 850. **Mon–Sat 11am–11pm, Sun 4.30pm–11pm.** This centralissimo

Internet spot offers a 15 percent discount to all gay or lesbian customers – 1 hour costs €3.

Zipper Via Castelfidardo 18 ⊕ 06.488.2730, ⊛ www.zippertravel.it. Metro A Repubblica or Metro B Castro Pretorio or Bus #75. **Mon–Fri 9.30am–6pm.** Gay travel agent, located near Termini, brokering round-the-world or round-Italy travel for gay and lesbian groups and individuals.

Saunas

Europa Multiclub Via Aureliana 40 ⊕ 06.482.3650. Metro Termini or Bus #36, 60. **Sun 2pm–midnight, Mon–Thurs 3pm–midnight, Fri & Sat 2pm–6am.** Near Termini, this has pleasantly stylish, clean facilities, and a snack bar. €13 per visit, €11 after 11pm Fri & Sat, plus €14 for ARCI-Gay membership.

Mediterraneo Via Pasquale Villari 3 ⊕ 06.7720.5934. Metro A Vittorio or Manzoni or Bus #85, 87 or Tram #3. **Daily 2pm–midnight.** Also in the Termini area, near Piazza Vittorio, this is a sauna on three levels, with all the usual choices, including a snack bar. Notably clean and attracts all ages. €12 Mon–Fri, €13 Sat & Sun, plus €14 for ARCI-Gay membership.

Accommodation

Scalinata di Spagna Hotel Piazza Trinità dei Monti 17 ⊕ 06.679.3006, ⊛ www.hotelscalinata.com. Metro A Spagna or Bus #52, 53, 61, 63, 71, 80, 95, 116, 119, 160, 175, 492, 630, 850. Gays and lesbians are welcome at this elegant, centrally located hotel, at the top of the Spanish Steps. Doubles start at €250, singles €230. Everything you would expect at this price, plus a terrace for breakfast. See p.191 for more.

Seiler Hotel Via Firenze 48 ⊕ 06.485.550 or 06.488.0204, ⊕ 06.488.0688. Metro A Repubblica or Bus #40, 60, 61, 62, 64, 90, 170, 175, 492, 910, H. Another gay-friendly accommodation option, and quite a bit cheaper than the *Scalinata di Spagna* – just down from Piazza della Repubblica, across Via Nazionale from the Teatro dell' Opera. Singles here go for €90, doubles €130. Breakfast included.

Shops and markets

A t first glance, you may wonder where to start when it comes to **shopping** in a big, chaotic city like Rome. In fact the city is a more appealing shopping experience than you might think, abounding with pleasant shopping streets and colourful markets, most of which are in the city centre. Many shopping areas have been pedestrianized, and, perhaps best of all, the city hasn't yet been entirely overrun by department stores and shopping malls, or by the international chain stores that characterize most European city centres. One-stop shopping opportunities are rare, but you will find corners of the city that have been colonized by stores featuring the same sort of merchandise – fashion, antiques, food – making it easy for you to check out the competition's products and prices. You will also find true artisans in Rome, who take great pride in their crafts.

You can find the best of Italy in Rome. **Fashion** straight from the catwalk is well represented on the fashionable streets close to the Spanish Steps – Via Condotti, Via Borgognona, and Via Frattina – where you'll find chic boutiques such as *Gucci*, *Prada* and *Valentino* (see box, p.243). If you want to do more than window-shop, head to Via del Tritone, Via Nazionale, below Piazza della Repubblica, or Via Cola di Rienzo, near the Vatican, for more middle-range and affordable fashion. The stores on and around Via del Corso are a mixture, selling mainstream, and fairly youth-orientated, fashions, while Via Veneto, off Piazza Barberini, caters to those who were youthful when Fellini's *La Dolce Vita* opened, and are now the fashionably well-off patrons of the street's expensive leather shops and boutiques. **Antiques** shops – a huge selection – line Via dei Coronari and neighbouring Via dell' Orso and Via dei Soldati, just north of Piazza Navona; Via Giulia, southwest of Campo de' Fiori, and Via del Babuino and Via Margutta, between Piazza del Popolo and the Spanish Steps, are also good sources of art and antiques. As for **food**, if you want to take home a bottle of extra virgin olive oil or some vacuum-packed porcini mushrooms, end your day visiting the food shops and markets around Campo de' Fiori or Via Cola di Rienzo across the river. The city's many **markets** offer a change of pace from Rome's busy shopping streets. Many of these are bustling local food

Opening hours

These days some shops in the centre of Rome stay **open** all day. However, many still observe the city's traditional hours: Monday 3.30–7.30pm, Tuesday–Saturday 9.30am–1.30pm & 3.30–7.30pm, and closed on Sunday. Food shops are also often closed on Thursday afternoon in the winter and Saturday afternoon during the summer; and most shops close for at least two weeks in summer, usually in August. Most places accept all major credit cards.

markets, and, even in the centre, are still very much part of Roman life. The Campo de' Fiori market is probably the most central of these. Otherwise there's Trastevere's **Porta Portese** flea market, a venue for antiques, clothing, books, and indeed virtually anything else, every Sunday morning.

Shops

Antiques

Antichità Via del Babuino 83 ☎06.320.7585. Mon–Sat 9.30am–7.30pm. One of the several fine antiques stores in the area, with a large collection of stunning Italian furnishings from the 1700s. There is also an entrance on Via Margutta.

Antichità Archeologia Largo Fontanella Borghese 76 ☎06.687.6656. Mon 3.30–7pm, Tues–Sat 9am–1pm & 3.30–7.30pm. If you want to take home your own piece of ancient Rome, this is the place for you. Genuine, certified Greek, Etruscan and Roman antiquities, such as terracotta oil lamps, figurines and incised jewels, start at about €100.

Antiquetrade Via del Boschetto 4 ☎06.4782.5539. Mon 3.30–7pm, Tues–Sat 9am–1pm & 3.30–7.30pm. Antiques of all kinds and eras can turn up here. However, the speciality is fine old prints. A satisfying place to browse through Rome's history.

Arabesco Via del Panico 14 ☎06.686.9659. Mon–Sat 9.30am–8pm. One of a couple of such stores on this street, around the corner from Via dei Coronari, this has old Turkish carpets and kilims, oriental glassware and other bits and pieces from the East.

La Bottega del Principino Via Margutta 59b ☎06.320.7979. Mon–Sat 9.30am–7.30pm. An interesting little shop, quite different from the fancy antiques shops that surround it, offering quite an eclectic array of bric-a-brac – everything from eighteenth-century farm equipment to crystal chandeliers from the 1940s.

Devi Via della Lupa 9 ☎06.686.9295. Mon 3.30pm–7.30pm, Tues–Sat 9am–1pm & 3.30pm–7.30pm. Fine Italian antiques of all kinds fill this small shop, but the owners' primary interest is in statuary, from medieval to Baroque. Oriental pieces, as well, from some of Rome's aristocratic houses.

Hendy Piazza di Pietra 42 ☎06.678.5804, ⓦ www.hendy-gioieantiche.com. Mon 3.30pm–7pm, Tues–Sat 10am–7pm. Located

in a peaceful piazza near the Pantheon, this place specializes in *gioie antiche* or antique jewellery. You will find a unique selection of Italian rings, necklaces, bracelets, mostly from 1900–40, although there are some pieces that date back as far as 1870.

Libreria Giuliana di Cave Via dei Pastini 23 ☎06.678.0297. Mon–Sat 2.30pm–8pm. Antique book and print shop run by a friendly mother and son. All the material here is Italian, with books dating from the sixteenth century and prints from the late seventeenth century. They also sell inexpensive print reproductions.

Papadato Antichità Roma Piazza di Pietra 41 ☎06.679.6931. Mon 3.30pm–7pm, Tues–Sat 10.30am–7pm. Friendly store that has both Italian and English antiques. The store is mostly known for its large selection of European fans from the sixteenth and seventeenth centuries.

Polvedra Via della Scrofa 46 ☎06.687.3259. Mon 3.30pm–7pm, Tues–Sat 10.30am–7pm. An eclectic, unique assortment of fine collectables and antiques, both European and Oriental, from major pieces of furniture to fine *objets* for setting around the parlour.

Valerio Turchi Via Margutta, 91a ☎06.323.5047, ⓕ06.323.3209. Mon 3.30pm–7pm, Tues–Sat 10.30am–7pm. A bit different from the other antiques shops on Via Margutta, with exquisite pieces from Rome's past – various pieces of Roman statues and sarcophagi dating from as early as 300 AD.

Books

Anglo-American Via delle Vite 102 ☎06.679.5222. Mon 3.30–7.30pm, Tues–Sat 9am–1pm & 3.30–7.30pm. Large selection of new English books on every subject, including textbooks for university students.

Bibli Via dei Fienaroli 28 ☎06.588.4097. ⓦ www.bibli.it. Mon 5.30pm–midnight, Tues–Sun 11am–midnight. Bookstore, cultural centre and café that has only a small selection of English books, but they do have Internet access, and a helpful bulletin board with many ads in English for those looking for work, apartments, etc.

The Almost Corner Bookshop Via del Moro 45 ☏06.583.6942. Mon–Sat 10am–1.30pm & 3.30pm–8pm, Sun 11am–1.30pm & 3.30pm–8pm. Closed Sun in Aug. Under new ownership and also shifted to a larger space a few doors away from the corner, this shop, of all Rome's English bookshops, is perhaps the best bet for almost certainly having the very latest titles on your list of must-reads.

Economy Bookstore and Video Centre Via Torino 136 ☏06.474.6877. Mon–Sat 9am–8pm. This bookstore has been supplying Rome with both new and used English titles for the past thirty years. They also rent and sell videos in English.

Feltrinelli International Via Emanuele Orlando 84 ☏06.482.7878. Mon–Sat 9am–8pm, Sun 10am–1.30pm & 4–7.30pm. This branch of the Italian chain stocks books in German, French, Spanish, Portuguese – and, downstairs, in English. There are other branches at Via del Babuino 49 (☏06.3600.1842) and at Largo Argentina 5 (☏06.6880.32480).

Libreria la Strada Via V. Veneto 42 ☏06.482.4151. Daily 9.30am–12.30am. Excellent bookshop that boasts a fine stock of books about Rome – in English and Italian – in the pavilion outside: everything from tourist guides to well-selected fiction in English.

Lion Bookshop Via dei Greci 33 ☏06.3265.4007.Mon 3.30–7.30pm, Tues–Sat 10am–7.30pm. The comfortable location of this veteran English bookshop has a lounge area where you can take a break from browsing and enjoy a coffee or tea. A great store, and one of Rome's longest-established outlets for books in English.

Mel Bookstore Via Nazionale 252–255 ☏06.488.5405, ⊛www.melbookstore.it. Mon 9am–Sat 7.30pm, Sun 10am–1pm & 4–8pm. One of Rome's largest, this pleasant bookstore is one of a chain of megastores throughout Italy. It not only carries a good selection of travel-related books in English, as well as CDs and DVDs, but also has an inviting café on one of the upper floors.

Open Door Bookshop Via della Lungaretta 23 ☏06.589.6478. ⊛www.books-in-italy.com. Mon 4.30–8.30pm,Tues–Fri 10.30am–8.30pm, Sat 10.30am–midnight, Sun noon–6pm. Summer hours – afternoons and evenings only. Although they do have some new titles, especially those having to do with Rome and Roman history, used books dominate the shelves at this friendly Trastevere bookshop, where you never know what treasures you might turn up. They also have a selection of books in Italian, German, French and Spanish.

Remainders Piazza San Silvestro 27–28 ☏06.679.2824. Mon 3.30–7.30pm, Tues–Sat 10am–1pm and 3.30–7.30pm. Thousands of remaindered books turn up here at a fraction of their original cost, most of them having something to do with art, so it's a wonderful to shop for gifts, or to flesh out your library with beautiful tomes.

Rizzoli International Largo Chigi 15 ☏06.679.6641. Mon–Sat 9am–7.25pm, Sun 10.30am–7.55pm. Central Rome branch of the Italian chain, with a great stock of books on Italy, and a middling stock of books in English.

TCI (Touring Club Italiano) Bookstore Via del Babuino 19–20 ☏06.3600.5281. Perhaps the city's best travel bookstore, with a great selection of guides – in Italian and in English – and excellent maps on Rome and Italy.

Clothing and accessories

Davide Cenci Via di Campo Marzio 1/7 ☏06.699.0681. Mon 3.30–7.30pm, Tues–Fri 9.30am–1.30pm & 3.30pm–7.30pm, Sat 10am–7.30pm. An exclusive clothing shop that has been offering conservative high-quality fashion to men, women and children for the past 75 years.

La Cravatta su Misura Via Seminario 93 ☏06.6994.2199. Mon 3.30–7.30pm, Tues–Sat 10am–7.30pm. Ezio Pellicano sells only one thing: ties, made by Ezio himself or his daughter. You can buy any of the hundreds of ties you see on display, or you can choose from one of the hundreds of rolls of material and have your own made up in about a week.

Diesel Via del Corso 186 ☏06.678.3933. Mon–Sat 9.30am–7.30pm. Well-known now around the world, this Italian manufacturer of very trendy styles for posy, disaffected youth sports a major outlet in the heart of Rome, where the window displays can always be depended upon to make a statement.

Donèl Piazza Cola di Rienzo 75 ☏06.321.4744. Mon 3.30–7.30pm, Tues–Sat 9.30am–7.30pm.

All the current trendy shoe styles for men and women at below average prices.

Dress Agency Donna Via del Vantaggio 1b ☏06.321.0898.Mon 4–7.30pm, Tues–Sat 10am–1pm & 4pm–7.30pm. Used women's clothing and accessories from Versace, Armani and all the big-name Italian designers. Not as cheap as you might expect, but still worth a rummage.

Esse Tre Group Via del Seminario 111 ☏06.678.7661. Daily 10am–7.30pm. New and used clothing piled high, in this huge, eclectic shop just steps away from the Pantheon. Used leather jackets, American T-shirts, and fake Levis mingled with new business suits and casual wear.

Energie Via del Corso 486 ☏06.322.7046, energie@iol.it. Mon–Sun 10am–8pm. One of the city's most popular clothing stores, mainly aimed at teenagers, with expensive trendy clothes, loud music and an omnipresent group of kids hanging out around the entrance. Definitely the place to be seen if you're loaded and under 21.

Gigoló Via Nazionale 181a ☏06.481.4380. Mon 3.30–7.30pm, Tues–Sat 10am–7.30pm. The focus here, as the name makes clear, is on making men look as sexy as possible – everything from designer swimwear to Lycra and spandex briefs.

Giorgio Sermoneta Gloves Via Frattina 58 ☏06.679.6924. Mon 3.30–7.30pm, Tues–Sat 10am–7.30pm. A glove specialist, with a large collection of Italian gloves in every price range; has catered to celebrities, politicians and tourists for 35 years.

Leo Calzature Via del Portico d'Ottavia 57. No phone. Mon–Fri & Sun 9am–7.30pm. A bargain hunter's delight, hidden away in the Jewish

Ghetto, and selling a large variety of new shoes and occasional leftovers from past fashion shows at a price you can't beat: all shoes are under €15 a pair.

LP Via dei Prefetti 6 ☏06.687.3646. Mon 4–7.30pm, Tues–Sat 10am–1pm & 4–7.30pm. Traditional tailors who make shirts to measure, at least with regard to sleeve length and type of collar and cuff you prefer. Popular with Roman aristocrats, as well as with the politicians who frequent the nearby halls of government.

Salinas Sport Piazza Sonnino 43–45 ☏06.581.2322.Mon 4–7.30pm, Tues–Sat 10am–1pm & 4pm–7.30pm. This is Trastevere's best shop for sporting goods and gear of all sorts, from running shoes to rucksacks.

Ugo Celli Via Arenula 86 ☏06.880.355. Mon–Sat 9am–8pm. Popular shop, filled with high-quality, high-priced shoes from all over Italy.

Vestiti Usati Cinzia Via del Governo Vecchio 45 ☏06.686.1791. Mon 3.30–7.30pm, Tues–Sat 10am–2pm & 3.30–7.30pm. The best of the several used clothing shops along this street, where you can find anything from an elegant raincoat to black leather biker jeans, and much more.

Jewellery, hair and toiletries

Bozart Via Bocca di Leone 4 ☏06.678.1026. Mon 4–8pm Tues–Sat 9.30am–8pm. These fakes are truly fabulous, each necklace or bracelet making its own rich statement. Semiprecious stones, as well as Swarovski crystal pieces and resin and wooden elements are freely used to create dazzlingly alluring costume jewellery, ranging in price from €25 to €300.

Designer stores

Giorgio Armani Via Condotti 77 ☏06.699.1460.
Roberto Cavalli Via Borgognona 7/a. ☏06.693.80130.
Dolce & Gabbana Via Condotti 51–52 ☏06.6992.4999.
Fendi Via Borgognona 36–40 ☏06.696.661.
Ferre Via Borgognona 6 ☏06.679.7445.
Gucci Via Condotti 8 ☏06.678.9340.
Krizia Piazza di Spagna 87 ☏06.679.3772.
Missoni Piazza di Spagna 78 ☏06.679.2555.
Moschino Via Belsiana 53–57 ☏06.6920.0415.
Prada Via Condotti 92–95 ☏06.679.0897.
Salvatore Ferragamo Via Condotti 63 ☏06.679.1565.
Valentino Via Condotti 13 ☏06.679.5862.
Gianni Versace Via Borgognona 24–26 ☏06.679.5037.

ElleEffe Via di San Calisto 6–6a
⌖06.5833.3875 or 06.5834.3483. **Mon–Sat 9.30am–8pm.** If you want the perfect new haircut to go with your fresh Roman fashions, let Fabio, one of Rome's top hair stylists, take care of you. His English is as perfect as his taste and his cutting skills. All the usual salon services, as well.

Fabio Piccioni Via del Boschetto 148
⌖06.474.1697. **Mon–Sat 10.30am–8pm, except closed Mon morning.** Original Art Nouveau and especially Art Deco pieces are impressively displayed here, as are exquisite reproductions and inspired one-of-a-kind adornments made by this workshop.

Lefevre Via Colonna Antonina 50
⌖06.678.3885. **Mon 4–8pm Tues–Sat 9.30am–1.30pm & 4–8pm.** Exclusive designs here include seed pearl ropes hung with cut crystals of ruby, emerald and sapphire matrix, for under €100. Silver frames are also featured, as well as fine porcelains.

Roma-Store Via della Lungaretta 63
⌖06.581.8789. **Mon 4–8pm Tues–Sat 9.30am–1.30pm & 4–8pm.** Scented soaps, lotions and candles plus sophisticated eaux de toilette, this genteel shop has it all. Only the very finest from Italy, France, and England.

Siragusa Via delle Carrozze 64 ⌖06.679.7085. **Mon 4–8pm Tues–Sat 9.30am–1.30pm & 4–8pm.** As much a museum and antiques gallery as it is a jewellery shop; the gems set into rings and things here are almost all ancient sardonyxes, carnelians and other carved semiprecious and precious stones. Also sells ancient coins.

Department stores

COIN Via Cola di Rienzo 173 ⌖06.3600.4298; Piazza Appio 7 ⌖06.708.0020; Via Mantova 1b ⌖06.841.6279. **Mon 3.30–8pm, Tues–Sat 9.30am–1.30pm & 3.30–8pm.** Inexpensive clothes, accessories, and a great place to find stylish kitchenware at bargain prices.

La Rinascente Largo Chigi 20 ⌖06.679.7691. **Mon–Sat 9am–9pm, Sun 10.30am–8pm.** Part of a national chain, this is the closest Rome gets to an upscale department store, with several floors of high-quality merchandise displayed in an architecturally interesting setting.

M.A.S. Piazza Vittorio Emanuele 138
⌖06.446.8078. **Mon–Sat 9am–1pm & 3.45–7.45pm.** It doesn't get any cheaper than this. The *"Magazzini allo Statuto"*

(Statutory Warehouses) are like one vast, multilevel rummage sale, but take your time and you'll find something you want. There's everything from clothing to housewares.

UPIM Via Nazionale 211 ⌖06.484.502; Piazza Santa Maria Maggiore ⌖06.446.5579; Via Tritone 172 ⌖06.678.3336. **Mon noon–8pm, Tues–Sat 9am–8pm.** The most inexpensive of the chain stores, good for cheap clothes and household goods, as well as basic toiletries and other necessities for travellers. There's a handy branch on Termini station too.

Food and wine

Buccone Via di Ripetta 19 ⌖06.361.2154. **Mon–Thurs 9am–8.30pm, Fri & Sat 9am–midnight, Sun 10am–5pm.** Every alcoholic beverage you could dream of, with a large selection of wines from all over the world, spirits, even ten-litre bottles of *grappa*.

Castroni Via Cola di Rienzo 196 ⌖06.687.4383. **Mon–Sat 8am–8pm.** Huge international food store with a large selection of Italian treats including chocolates, pastas, sauces, and olive oils, as well as hard-to-find international favourites such as plum pudding and Mexican specialities.

Centro Macrobiotico Italiano Via della Vite 14 &06.679.2509. **Mon–Fri noon–4pm, Mon–Sat 7–11pm.** If you love authentic Italian food but are also a devotee of natural foods, this is Rome's most central option for stocking up on wholegrain pastas and other *integrali* products from Italy's rich countryside.

Del Frate Via degli Scipioni 118/128a
⌖06.321.1612. **Mon–Sat 8am–8pm.** This large wine and spirits shop is located on a quiet street near the Vatican, and has all the Barolos and Chiantis you could want, alongside shelves full of *grappa* in all shapes and sizes.

Panella Via Merulana 54 ⌖06.487.2435, ⌖06.487.2344. **Mon–Fri 8am–1.30pm & 5–8pm, Sat 8am–1.30pm and 4.30–8pm, Sun 8.30am–1.30pm.** The art of bread-making is the speciality here, as well as pasta, like colourful *sombrerini* (hats), packaged to take home.

Quetzalcoatl Via delle Carrozze 26
⌖06.6920.2191, ⌖06.6929.1932. **Mon–Sat 10am–7.30pm.** Rome's most sublime chocolates, presented as if they were art. Once you taste them, you'll probably feel that they are. All sizes of gifts boxes available.

△ Energie, Via del Corso

Roscioli Via dei Giubbonari 21–23
℡06.687.5287. **Daily 8.30am–8pm.** Cheeses,
salamis and a very good selection of wine.
Plus food is served at lunch and early
evening.

Shaki Piazza di Spagna 65 ℡06.678.6605
Mon–Sat 9am–8pm, Sun 10am–7pm. Located
right in Piazza di Spagna to make it easy
for visitors to stock up on the entire range
of canned sauces and delectables Italy has
to offer. A unique selection of Italian pottery
and other handicrafts, as well.

Teichner Piazza San Lorenzo in Lucina 17
℡06.679.0612. **Daily 7.30am–9pm.** Good all-
round foodstore and deli that has stocks of
all those Italian goodies you want to take
home with you. Also with a branch outside
the city centre at Porta San Giovanni.

Trimani Via Goito 20 ℡06.446.9661. **Mon–Sat**
11am–midnight. One of the city's best wine
shops, and handily close to Termini if you
want to stock up before heading off to the
airport.

Volpetti Via Marmorata 47 ℡06.574.2352.
Mon–Sat 8am–2pm & 5–8pm. It's worth
seeking out this Testaccio deli, which is
truly one of Rome's very best. If you're
lucky, one of the staff will give you samples
of their truly incredible *mozzarella di bufala*.
There's another, city-centre branch at Via
della Scrofa 31–2 ℡06.686.1940, open the
same hours, but the original is probably
friendlier and more atmospheric – plus has
its own eatery round the corner; see p.202.

Gifts and crafts

Artigianato in Cuoio Via dei Chiavari 39
℡06.6830.7297. **Mon 3.30–7.30pm, Tues–Sat**
9.30am–1.30pm & 3.30–7.30pm. On a quiet
street near Campo de' Fiori, this leather
shop is filled with beautifully hand-crafted
products – belts, luggage, handbags,
etc – all made in their workshop a few
doors down.

Bazar Bolivar Via Silla 93–95 ℡06.324.2845.
Mon 3.30–7.30pm, Tues–Sat 9.30am–1.30pm &
3.30–7.30pm. If you can't make it to Porta
Portese flea market, this is Rome's best
alternative. Curiosities, crafts, art and *objets*
from all over the world, including some
wonderfully kitsch Italian collectables,
along with semiprecious stones and tribal
jewellery of virtually all cultures.

La Bottega del Marmoraro Via Margutta 53b
℡06.320.7660. **Mon–Sat 9am–1pm and**

3.30–7.30pm. Enrico and Sandro Fiorentini,
a father-and-son team, are skilled artisans,
creating personalized marble plaques for
every occasion, as well as statuary, both
ancient and modern repros.

Campo Marzio Penne Via Campo Marzio 41
℡06.6880.7877. **Mon 3.30–7.30pm, Tues–Sat**
9.30am–1pm & 3.30pm–7.30pm. Small shop
dedicated to exquisite pens and writing
accessories.

Canova Via della Conciliazione 4f
℡06.6880.6373, ℻06.689.3507. **Daily**
9am–7pm. One of the nicer gift shops
leading up to St Peter's, with its fair share
of religious souvenirs, and some delicately
hand-crafted chess sets.

Carmignani Via della Colonna Antonina 42–43
℡06.679.5449. **Tues–Sat 10am–2pm and**
3pm–7.30pm. Even if you don't smoke, you
will appreciate the beauty of the handmade
pipes, shiny silver cigar holders and cutters,
and poker sets, in this small shop a few
minutes from the Pantheon.

Cesare Diomedi Piazza San Bernardo 99
℡06.488.4822. **Mon–Sat 9am–7.30pm.** A few
minutes' walk from Piazza della Repubblica,
two floors filled with Versace clocks, Cartier
wallets, and all sorts of other fancy gifts for
every occasion.

Fratelli Alinari Via Alibert 16a ℡06.679.2923,
℻06.6994.1998. **Mon–Sat 3.30–7.30pm.** If you
want to know what Rome's piazzas looked
like before McDonald's came to town,
come here for a fine selection of black-and-
white photographs of Rome from at least
100 years ago.

Frette Piazza di Spagna 10 ℡06.679.0673,
℻06.6994.1843, ℮nromad@frette.it. **Mon**
3.30–7.30pm, Tues–Sat 9.30am–1.30pm &
3.30–7.30pm. A luxurious linen shop, located
among all the designer shops in Piazza di
Spagna. They are happy to fill custom orders
and will ship their products anywhere.

Il Gancio Via del Seminario 82/83
℡06.679.6646. **Mon 3.30–7.30pm, Tues–Sat**
10am–1pm and 3.30–7.30pm. High-quality
leather bags, purses, shoes all made right
here, in the workshop on the premises.

Il Giardino di Domenico Persiani Via Torino
92 ℡06.488.3886. **Mon 3.30–7.30pm, Tues–Sat**
10am–1pm and 3.30–7.30pm. An experience
not to be missed – a quiet garden setting
filled to the brim with all sorts of creations
of the ceramicist's art. Everything from
glazed tiles to full-sized copies of famous
statuary. Pieces made to order.

Horvath Via V.E. Orlando 91 ☎06.474.1607.
Mon–Sat 9am–9pm, Sun 11am–9pm. Unusual
collection of replica ancient Roman armour,
swords and daggers.

Ai Monasteri Piazza Cinque Lune
☎06.6880.2783. Mon 3.30–7.30pm, Tues–Sat
10am–1.30pm & 3.30–7.30pm. Cakes, spirits,
toiletries and other items made by monks in
monasteries.

Nostalgica Via dello Statuto 32, no phone. Old-
fashioned Italian football shirts from around
€70 – ironically enough, made in England.

Pineider Via Due Macelli 68 ☎06.239.344,
🖷06.239.447. Mon 3.30–7.30pm, Tues–Sat
10am–1.30pm & 3.30–7.30pm. This exclusive
store has been selling beautiful handmade
paper, invitations, and writing materials for
Roman society since 1774.

Polvere di Tempo Via del Moro 59
☎06.5880.0704. Mon 3.30–8pm, Tues–Sat
10am–1pm & 4–8pm. For that astrolabe
you've always dreamed of, as well as a huge
array of ancient and medieval devices for
telling time, stop by this arcane little shop.
Also, alchemists' rings that double as sun-
dials and loads of oddities and curiosities.

Vacanze Romane Via dei Pastini 18a
☎06.6992.5056. Mon 3.30–7pm, Tues–Sat
10.30am–7pm. Upscale gift shop with fun
and often tacky "art" souvenirs – suitcases
decorated with Raphael's angels,
Michelangelo lampshades and suchlike.

Household goods

Art'e Piazza Rondanini 32 ☎06.683.3907. Mon
1–7.30pm, Tues–Sat 9.30am–7.30pm. Ultra-
modern kitchenware and home furnishings,
including lamps, clocks and kitchen utensils
and appliances in flashy neon colours and
shiny stainless steel. The perfect stylish gift
to yourself from Italy.

Azi Via San Francesco a Ripa 170
☎06.588.3303 & Via Manara 7 ☎06.581.8699.
Mon 3.30–7.30pm, Tues–Sat 9.30am–1.30pm
& 3.30–7.30pm. Anything curiously or
cunningly designed for the home is likely to
be found here. The owners comb the earth

for trendy, generally high-tech treasures,
and the result is a truly unique shop – in
two locations, around the corner from each
other in Trastevere.

C.U.C.I.N.A. Via Mario de' Fiori 65
☎06.679.1275. Mon 3.30–7.30pm, Tues–Sat
10am–7.30pm. A shop filled with modern
kitchen appliances, including a large selection of Italian *caffetterie*.

'Gusto Piazza Augusto Imperatore 7
☎06.323.6363. Daily 10.30am–2am. Everything
for the aspirant gourmet: wines, decanters,
glasses, and all the top-of-the-line kitchen
gadgets you could ever hope to find. Also a
large selection of cookbooks in English.

Spazio Sette Via dei Barbieri 7 ☎06.6880.4261.
Mon 3.30–7pm, Tues–Sat 10.30am–7pm.
Designer housewares of all sorts are the
speciality here, for decades the shop of
choice for Romans who want something
chic and stylish for their home or as a gift.

Music

Disfunzioni Musicali Via degli Etruschi 4–14
☎06.446.1984. Mon 3.30–7.30pm, Tues–Sat
10.30am–8pm. Supplying nearby college
students with a huge collection of both new
and used music. A large selection of underground, rare and bootlegged recordings.

Messagerie Musicali Via del Corso 472
☎06.684.401. Mon–Sat 10am–11pm, Sun
10am–8.30. One of the city's best mainstream collections of CDs, plus a wide array
of foreign magazines and books.

Metropoli Rock Via Cavour 72 ☎06.488.0443.
Mon–Sat 9am–1pm & 4–8pm. The place to
come if you are looking for old and out-of-
print recordings, whether it's classical, rock,
or jazz. Two floors stocked floor-to-ceiling
with vinyl, 33rpm and 45rpm, as well as
new and used CDs.

Ricordi Via Cesare Battisti 120 ☎06.679.8022.
Mon–Sat 9am–7.30pm, Sun 3.30pm–8pm.
Rome's largest and most complete music
store, with a good array of CDs, plus books
on music, scores, musical instruments, DVDs,
sound equipment – and concert tickets.

Markets

L'Antico in Terrazza Peroni Via Mantova 24.
Third Sun of every month 10am–8pm; entrance
€1.50. Located in the underground parking
garage of the former Peroni brewery, this is

basically a regular car-boot sale.

Borghetto Flaminio Piazza della Marina 32.
Sept to mid-June Sun 10am–7pm; mid-June to
mid-July 5pm–midnight; entrance €1.60. A

Food markets

Rome's **food markets** are a perfect place to stop to pick up a snack or picnic provisions. The one on Piazza di Campo de' Fiori is the city's most famous and picturesque, and has been around for the last four hundred years. Other central options include the Quattro Coronati market, near the Colosseum, the one between Termini and Piazza Vittorio Emanuele, on Via Lamarmora, and Piazza San Cosimato, in Trastevere. Most are open Mon–Sat 6am–2pm.

partly covered flea market with plenty of knick-knacks, designer clothing and antiques. Rummage alongside Rome's upper classes and celebrities.

Fontanella Borghese Piazza Fontanella Borghese. Mon–Sat 8am–sunset. A small print market off Via del Corso, where you can find expensive antique prints and etchings along with inexpensive reproductions.

Galleria delle Stimmate Largo delle Stimmate 1. Sept–April last Sun of the month 10am–7.30pm. Mostly household goods, and some jewellery, with some great finds like antique lace, silver serving dishes, and old cutlery.

Porta Portese Off Viale Trastevere, enter at Piazza Ippolito Nievo, across from the *Café Arabo*. Sun 5am–2pm. By far, Rome's most famous and largest market, with hundreds of stalls selling myriad goods, including antiques, oriental artefacts, clothing, carpets, art, tools, appliances, fake

brand-name jeans, linens, and even puppies.

La Soffitta Sotto I Portici Piazza Augusto Imperatore ☎06.3600.5345. Sept–June third Sun of every month 10am–sunset. Flea market selling a diverse mix of clothing, household items and antiques.

Underground Via Francesco Crispi 96. Oct–June first Sun of each month and the Sat before; Sat 10am–8pm, Sun 10.30am–7.30pm. Located in an underground parking garage near Piazza di Spagna, and selling all the usual flea market finds, but with a special section for children's goods.

Via Sannio Via Sannio. May–Oct Mon–Fri 10am–1.30pm, Sat 10am–2pm; Nov–Apr Mon–Fri 10am–1.30pm, Sat 10am–6pm. Centrally located market selling mostly new (with lots of fake brand names) and used clothing. To get to the extensive secondhand section, go past all the stalls selling new things.

SHOPS AND MARKETS | Markets

Sports and outdoor activities

S
pectator sports are popular in Italy, although the hallowed *calcio*, or football, is far and away the most popular, and tends to overshadow everything else and Rome, with two clubs in the top division (Serie A), is no exception. As for participation in sport, there isn't quite the same compulsion to hit the hell out of a squash ball or sweat your way through an aerobics class after work as there is, say, in Britain or the US. However, the notion of keeping fit and being active is becoming as fashionable here as it is in most European countries, especially when it offers the opportunity to wear the latest designer gear.

Cycling

The month of May sees the *Giro d'Italia* (Italy's national race) spin through Rome's cobbled lanes, but for most visitors **cycling**, is far too daunting to be enjoyable. However, the Appia Antica is ideal for a ride, especially on Sundays when it's (theoretically) closed to automobile traffic. See the Directory (p.258) for places you can rent bikes.

Football

Rome's two principal **football teams**, Roma and Lazio, both play at the Stadio Olimpico, on Via del Foro Italico, on alternate Sundays from September to May, reachable by bus #32, 280, or Tram #2. Unsurprisingly, feelings run high between the two teams, and derby games are big – and sometimes violent – occasions. **Roma**, traditionally the team of the inner-city urban working-class, was, until recently, perennially the better of the two sides, while traditionally right-wing Lazio trailed. However, in 2000 **Lazio** won the championship, only to have Roma then bounce back in 2001 to take its third *scudetto*. Needless to say, it's a breathless rivalry that can go either way, despite Lazio's recent financial ills. We've given ticket details below, but bear in mind that the Stadio Olimpico is an enormous stadium, capacity 100,000, and at most games, except perhaps Roma-Lazio clashes, you should be able to get a ticket for all but the cheapest seats on the night.

If you want more information about the Italian football season in general, the Federazione Italiana Giuoco Calcio (®www.figc.it) has information (in English) about all the season's games. Or, if your Italian is good enough, get hold of one of the Italian sports newspapers, which are published daily. The Rome paper is the *Corriere dello Sport* and will have details of any upcoming games.

Lazio ®www.sslazio.it. To book ahead, try *Lazio Point*, Via Farini 34 (Mon–Sat 9am–7pm; ⊤06.482.6768), the Lazio ticket office ⊤06.323.7333, or the stadium itself. Lazio supporters traditionally occupy the Curva Nord end of the ground (colours blue and white, symbol, the eagle), where you can get seats for around €15; seats in the *distinti*, or corners of the ground, or the *tribuna*, along the sides, are more expensive; reckon on paying as much as €85 for a reasonable *tribuna* ticket.

Roma ®www.asromacalcio.it. The *As Roma Store* sells tickets, as well as fan supplies (Piazza Colonna 360 ⊤06.678.6514), or go to Orbis at Piazza Esquilino 37 (Mon–Sat 9.30am–1pm & 4–7.30pm; ⊤06.482.7403, no credit cards). Fans of Roma (symbol, the wolf, colours red and yellow) occupy the Curva Sud, which is usually completely sold out to season-ticket holders, making a visit to a Roma game a slightly more expensive business, since the cheapest seat you'll find will be in the *distinti*, at about €20.

Golf

If you simply can't go a week or two without hitting a ball, it's worth knowing that **golf** is slowly becoming a popular sport in Italy. Most clubs welcome non-members but you must be able to produce a membership card from your hometown club. For more information, call the *Federazione Italiana Golf*, Viale Tiziano 74 (⊤06.323.1825). All of the following offer an eighteen-hole course and a driving range:

Circolo del Golf di Roma Via Appia Nuova 716a ⊤06.780.3407, ⊕06.7834.6219; closed Mon. **Golf Club Parco de' Medici** Viale Parco de' Medici 22 ⊤06.655.3477, ⊕06.655.3344; closed Tues).

Country Club Castel Gandolfo Via Santo Spirito 13, Castel Gandolfo ⊤06.931.2301, ⊕06.931.2244; daily.

Gyms

If you're in the habit of a regular workout and want to keep it up even while you're checking Rome's sights off your list, here are a few handily located facilities:

Farnese Fitness Vicolo delle Grotte 35 ⊤06.687.6931; Mon–Thurs 9am–10pm, Fri 9am–9pm, Sat 11am–6pm, Sun 10am–1pm, closed 3 wks in Aug. Aerobics classes included in the daily fee. €10 per day. **Fitness First** Via Giolitti 44 ⊤06.4782.6300 Mon–Fri 8am–11pm, Sat & Sun 9am–7pm. A variety of classes, such as yoga, spinning and Thai kickboxing, on offer in this

spanking clean establishment. €15 per day. **Moves** Via dei Coronari 46 ⊤06.686.4989 or 06.686.5248; Mon–Fri 9am–9pm, Sat 10am–4pm, closed Aug. Choice of one class included in the fee, including yoga and Pilates. €16 per day. **Roman Sports Center** Viale del Galoppatoio 33 ⊤06.320.1667, 06.321.8096 or 06.322.3665; Mon–Sat 9am–10pm, Sun 9am–3pm, closed

Sun Jun–Aug. Rome's largest, oldest and most prestigious, with a host of offerings, including Olympic-sized pools and hydro-massage. €26 per day.

Jogging

Except for the third Sunday in March, when the Rome Marathon circles around the city's most famous monuments, crazy drivers and crowds of people make it impossible, and sometimes even dangerous, to **jog** in Rome. Luckily, though, there are plenty of green parks where you can escape the traffic. The most popular is Villa Borghese, where there are plenty of places to jog, including the Piazza di Siena, a grass horsetrack in the centre of the park. Other good options include the Villa Ada, a lush and vast green space some kilometres north of the city centre, which has a running track, and the Villa Doria Pamphilj above Trastevere, which offers nice paths with exercise stations along the way. For more central – and public – jogging, the Circo Massimo is the perfect size, and shape, although it gets busy with tourists early on. For more information about the Rome Marathon call the Italia Marathon Club (☎06.406.5064, ⓦ www.italiamarathonclub.it).

Riding

There are not very many options for those who are looking to go horse riding in Rome. The only place really is *Il Galoppatoio*, Via del Galoppatoio (☎06.322.6797), a posh riding club that offers expensive lessons in an idyllic atmosphere deep in the heart of Villa Borghese.

Swimming

If you feel like cooling off from a hot summer day, a dip in a **pool** may be the perfect cure. Unfortunately, most of Rome's pools are privately run and can be quite expensive, though there are a couple of affordable public pools (see also "Gyms", opposite). If you fancy a spot of real pampering it's worth booking a day at a hotel spa.

Public pools

The following will set you back only around €10 for a swim.
Oasi della Pace Via degli Eugenii 2
☎06.718.4550; June–Sept daily 9.30am–6pm. The "Oasis of Peace" is just off the Via Appia – an atmospheric place to take a dip.
La Piscina delle Rose Viale America 20
☎06.592.6717; June–Sept daily 9am–7pm. Rome's largest public pool, offers a weekly pass for €45.

Hotel pools

These hotels let the public use their facilities for around €50 per day.
Cavalieri Hilton Via Cadloro 101
☎06.3509.2950, ⓦ www.cavalieri-hilton.it. Luxury outside and indoor pools – the outdoor pool is Olympic size.
Es Hotel Via F. Turati 171 ☎06.444.841, ⓦ www.eshotel.it. Rome's trendiest pool at its trendiest hotel.
Parco dei Principi Via Frescobaldi 5
☎06.854.421, ⓦ www.parcodeiprincipi.com. Outdoor pool set in its own gardens.

Tennis

The massive **Foro Italico** sports complex (see p.138) hosts the Italian Open, one of Rome's major sporting events, each May. For more information contact the Federazione Italiana Tennis, Via Eustachio 9 (☎06.855.894, Ⓦ www .federtennis.it), or the Foro Italico itself (☎06.3685.8218). If you want to hire courts to play, the Foro Italico also has public courts, or there's the Circolo della Stampa, Piazza Mancini 19 (☎06.323.2452) and Tennis Belle Arte, Via Flaminia 158 (☎06.360.0602).

Kids' Rome

talians love children. Don't be surprised by how much attention people pay yours here: peeking into buggies and cheek-pinching are quite normal, as is help lugging pushchairs up steps and giving up a seat for you and your child on public transport. That said, Rome has a surprisingly limited number of activities specifically geared towards children, though there have been significant improvements of late. Luckily, touring the sights of Rome is something that children can enjoy if it's approached in the right way – especially Castel Sant'Angelo with its park and playground, the Colosseum (where there are usually Roman soldiers dressed up in full costume), and of course throwing coins into the Trevi Fountain and sticking your hand in the so-called Bocca della Verità and daring to tell a fib. There is also a handful of relatively new attractions, aimed directly at children, notably the Time Elevator, Explora – Museo dei Bambini di Roma, and the refurbished Bioparco. Of Rome's parks, the Villa Borghese is the most convenient, and has a lot to offer kids – rowboats, a little train, pony rides, bikes, and a newly enhanced zoo. If all else fails, there's always LUNEUR Park, a large, old-fashioned amusement park in EUR. Roman food often appeals to kids: remember you can always head to the nearest *gelato* stand, or grab a slice of juicy pizza to keep them quiet. For more information, *Romaè's* English section often has details of what's on for children that week.

Babysitting services

If you simply have to have a break from the kids one day or for an evening, English-speaking babysitters are available through a firm called *Angels*, Via dei Fienili 98 ☎06.678.2877 or 338.667.9718, ℗06.678.9246.

Day trips

If it's hot and you're having a hellish time in the city, it might just be best to call it a day and get out for a day, either for a picnic or an energy-releasing romp. **Day-trips** kids might enjoy include Ostia Antica (see p.177), Villa d'Este and Villa Adriana in Tivoli (see p.176), and, farther afield, certainly the Parco dei Mostri (Park of Monsters) at Bomarzo (☎0761.325.989, ℗www.bomarzo.net, daily 7am–sunset; €7.75), 93km north of Rome – basically a garden, but with crazy sculptures, weird buildings and surreal conceits that make it one of Lazio's top tourist attractions. You can get to Bomarzo by bus from Viterbo, which in turn is easily reached by train from either Rome San Pietro or the Laziale platform at Termini.

Books and maps

Pick up the English version of *ConosciRoma*, available free from any tourist kiosk; it's a children's map of the centre with interesting facts about sights, daily life of ancient Rome, and stickers. The "then and now" books of ancient sites with overlay transparencies can also work wonders to bring piles of weathered stones to life; they're available at most city-centre bookstores.

Parks and outdoor activities

Bioparco Via del Giardino Zooliogico, Villa Borghese ☎06.360.8211, ⊛www.bioparco.it; daily 9.30am–5pm; €8 adults, €6 4- to 12-year-olds. Rome's zoo in the Villa Borghese (see below) was once a pretty depressing place but it is now much improved, renaming itself "Bioparco" and focusing on conservation and education yet still providing the usual animals kids are after. It now also has a museum next door – see below – and often face-painting at weekends.

Gianicolo This park, high up on Janiculum Hill, is a good place to keep kids amused, with pony rides, bumper cars, puppet shows and other games, while adults enjoy a great view of the city below. The puppet shows (see box, p.256), are top-notch and kids can choose to take their favourite character home with them from the colourful selection on sale.

LUNEUR Park Via delle Tre Fontane ☎06.592.5933, ⊛www.luneur.it. Mon–Fri 4pm–midnight, Sat 4pm–1am, Sun 4pm–midnight; free entrance, rides cost €1–3. This amusement park in the EUR district is the only place in Rome that you'll find big-scale amusements – a rollercoaster, haunted house, Ferris wheel and the like. It's a bit dated, but is still very popular with families, and lately they've added loads of diversions aimed at pint-sized clients.

Villa Ada Beautiful grounds just north of the city with plenty to keep youngsters amused, including a roller-skating rink, bike paths, two playgrounds, and ponds.

Villa Borghese As well as the Bioparco (see above), this huge park offers plenty of entertainment for young ones. Enter at the Viale delle Belle Arti entrance to find pony rides, a children's train, swings and paddleboats. You can also take a fifteen-minute ride in a tethered hot-air balloon during certain months (☎06.321.1511).

Museums

Explora – Museo dei Bambini di Roma Via Flaminia 82 ☎06.361.3776, ⊛www.mdbr.it. Guided tours last 1hr 45min (see website for exact times); adults €6, 3- to 12-year-olds €7, under-3s free; advance booking recommended. Geared towards children under 12, this new learn-as-you-play centre has a variety of hands-on activities, teaching youngsters about all aspects of themselves and the world beyond; there's also plenty of purely fun stuff, such as a puppet theatre and a playground.

Museo di Zoologia Via Aldovrandi 18 ☎06.6710.9270. Tues–Sun 9am–5pm; €4, kids under 18 free. Located next to the Bioparco, this museum is getting a facelift. A new permanent exhibit, *Animals and their Habitats*, is on display in a new wing, while a variety of stuffed animals fill the older part of the museum, and the "bear cave" is always a scary treat.

Museo della Civiltà Romana Piazza Agnelli 10 ☎06.592.6041. Tues–Sat 9am–7pm, Sun 9am–1pm; €4.13, kids under 12 free. On your way to LUNEUR Park, stop by this Roman Civilization museum, where you can see replicas of Rome's famous statues and buildings, as well as interesting models of imperial and ancient Rome.

Time Elevator Via dei Santissimi Apostoli 20 ☎06.699.0053, ⊛www.time-elevator.it. Daily 10am–midnight; €11, under-12s €9.20. Flight-simulator seats and headphones set the stage for a virtual tour of three

△ Bioparco, Villa Borghese

Rome's puppet theatres

Puppetry has been delighting Italian children for hundreds of years, and Rome has a few venues for viewing true puppeteers in action. Sometimes you can find a show in English, but the storyline is visually explanatory and kids don't seem to care whether they understand the words or not.

The **outdoor theatres** on the Janiculum Hill (see p.254), and in EUR on Largo K. Ataturk, are said to be the only places to view the true puppeteers left in Rome. Both are free, although a small donation is expected. You can also see shows near the Janiculum at Teatro Verde, Circonvallazione Gianicolense 10 (☎06.588.2034, ⓦwww.teatroverde.it), a children's theatre where they also put on musicals and marionette shows (€6.80). Most puppet shows run from around 4pm till 7pm on weekdays and from10.30am until 1pm at weekends. *The Puppet Theatre*, Piazza dei Satiri (☎06.589.6201), puts on familiar fairy tales at 5pm on Sunday afternoons, while Testaccio's Teatro Vittoria (see p.233) has been known to mount variety shows that children can easily enjoy.

thousand years of Roman history; an excellent way to prime the kids for the sights they will be seeing, not to mention their parents. Not, however, very appealing to children under 5.

Shops: toys and clothing

Benetton Via Cesare Battisti 129 ☎06.6992.4010. Mon 3.30–7.30pm, Tues–Sat 9.30am–1pm & 3.30–7.30pm. Just one of the several locations of this famous Italian chain store that sells fairly expensive clothes for children and adults. This one conveniently has a children's hairdresser on the second floor.

Bertè Piazza Navona 108 ☎06.687.5011. Mon 3.30–7.30pm, Tues–Sat 9.30am–1pm & 3.30–7.30pm. One of Rome's oldest toy stores at the other end of the piazza from *Al Sogno* (see below), that has a complete range of toys for children of all ages.

La Bottega di Marinella Via Margutta 34 ☎06.324.4793, ⓕ 06.361.4143. Mon 3.30–7.30pm, Tues–Sat 9.30am–7.30pm. Adorable children's store on swanky Via Margutta, selling their own designs of infant and young children's clothes, plus fabrics to brighten up any child's bedroom.

La Cicogna Via Frattina 138 ☎06.679.1912; Via Cola di Rienzo 268 ☎06.689.6557. Mon 3.30–7.30pm, Tues–Sat 9.30am–1pm & 3.30–7.30pm. From newborns to adolescents, these outlets of the national chain

La Befana

There are many stories about **La Befana**, always depicted as an ugly old woman who flies along on a broom draped in black. The most recognized version is that she was outside sweeping when the three kings walked by; she stopped them and asked where they were going. The kings responded that they were following a star, in search of a newborn baby. They invited her to come along, but she declined, saying she had too much sweeping and cleaning to do. When she found out who it was the kings were off to find, her regret for not having joined them was so great that she has spent eternity rewarding good children with presents and sweets and bad children with pieces of coal on the day of Epiphany, January 6. Each year, from early December until January 6, Piazza Navona sets up the Befana toy fair, where endless stalls tempt children with every sort of sticky sweet and even chunks of black sugar made to look like coal. There are also toy stands and several manger scenes where children sometimes leave letters for La Befana, asking her for specific presents and toys.

("The Stork") carry everything for kids, and maternity wear for expectant mothers, too.

Città del Sole Via della Scrofa 66 ☎06.6880.3805. **Mon 3.30–7.30pm, Tues–Sat 11am–1.30pm.** Toys, games and books for kids in a great central location.

IANA Via Cola di Rienzo 182 ☎06.6889.2668. **Mon 3.30–7.30pm, Tues–Sat 10am–1.30pm & 3.30pm-7.30pm.** Popular Italian chain store offering moderately priced kids' clothes.

Marina Menasci Via del Lavatore 87 ☎06.678.1981. **Mon 3.30–7.30pm, Tues–Sat 9.30am–1pm & 3.30–7.30pm.** Toy store that sells exclusively wooden toys, in a great location a few steps from the Trevi Fountain.

Al Sogno Piazza Navona 53 ☎06.686.4198. **Mon 3.30–7.30pm, Tues–Sat 9.30am–1pm & 3.30–7.30pm.** Perfectly located at the north end of Piazza Navona, two floors of stuffed animals, handmade dolls, board games, and replicas of Roman soldiers.

21

KIDS' ROME | Shops: toys and clothing

Directory

Airlines Most of the big airline offices are located in the Via Bissolati/Piazza Barberini area. Air Canada ☎06.655.1112; Alitalia domestic ☎06.65.641, international ☎06.65.642, general ☎06.65.643; American Airlines ☎06.6595.8074; British Airways ☎199.712.266; Continental ☎06.6605.3030; Delta ☎800.477.999; easyJet ☎848.887.766; Ryanair ☎899.88.99.73; 06.7949.4225.

Airport enquiries ⓦwww.adr.it. Fiumicino ☎06.6595.3640 or 06.6595.4455; Ciampino ☎06.794.941.

American Express Piazza di Spagna 38 (Mon–Fri 9am–5.30pm, Sat 9am–12.30pm; longer hours in the summer; ☎06.6764.2413). Travel office, poste restante, exchange facilities.

Car rental All the usual suspects have desks at Fiumicino, Termini and elsewhere in the city. Avis ☎06.419.941, 06.65011531; Europcar ☎06.488.2854, 800.014.410; Hertz ☎06.474.0389, 06199.112211; Maggiore ☎06.4880049, 06.6501.0678.

Car repair Call ☎116 for emergency breakdown service. Otherwise, consult the *Yellow Pages* under "Autoriparazioni" for specialized repair shops.

Dentist The Ospedale di Odontoiatria George Eastman, Viale Regina Elena 287b, has a 24hr emergency service (☎06.8448.3232). If you're an EU citizen be sure to take your E111 form, which entitles you to buy a "ticket" for a consultation – around €20.

Disabled travellers Although changes are in the works, Rome can be quite a challenge for those with disabilities. Contact the Consorzio Cooperative Integrate-COIN, Via Enrico Giglioli 54a (☎06.2326.7504, toll-free in Italy ☎800.271.027), who have

English-speaking 24hr information on their phone line, and produce a guide, *Roma Accessible*, which contains information on accessibility to major sites, museums, hotels and restaurants. Also, their website ⓦwww.coinsociale.it/tourism has additional information.

Electricity 220 volts. If coming from the US buy an adaptor before you come as they are more expensive once you get here.

Embassies Australia, Corso Trieste 25 ☎06.852.721 or for emergencies toll-free at ☎800.877.790; Britain, Via XX Settembre 80a ☎06.4220.0001; Canada, Via Zara 30 ☎06.445.981; Ireland, Piazza Campitelli 3 ☎06.697.9121; New Zealand, Via Zara 28 ☎06.441.7171; USA, Via Veneto 119a ☎06.46.741.

Emergencies Police ☎113; Carabinieri ☎112, Fire ☎115, Ambulance ☎118.

Exchange American Express (see above); Thomas Cook, Piazza Barberini 21a (Mon–Sat 9am–8pm, Sun 9.30am–5pm), and Via della Conciliazione 23 (Mon–Sat 9am–8pm, Sun 9.30am–5pm). Post offices will exchange American Express traveller's cheques and cash commission free. The last resort should be any of the many Ufficio Cambio, almost always offering the worst rates (despite "no commission" signs).

Hospital In case of emergency ☎113 or ☎118. Otherwise the most central hospitals are the Policlinico Umberto I, Viale del Policlinico 155 (☎06.49.971), and the Santo Spirito, Lungotevere in Sassia 1 (☎06.68.351), near the Vatican. The Rome American Hospital, Via E. Longoni 81 (☎06.22.551) is a private multi-speciality hospital with bilingual staff.

Laundry Onda Blu, Via Vespasiano 50, near the Vatican (daily 8am–10pm); Wash and Dry, Via della Pelliccia 35; Via della Chiesa

Nuova 15/16 (both daily 8am–10pm). All offer a wash including soap and tumble-drying for €7–10 for a 6kg (15lb) load.

Libraries The British Council, Via delle Quattro Fontane 20 (Mon–Tues & Thurs–Fri 10am–1pm, Wed 2–5pm; closed Aug & Christmas; ☎06.478.141), has a small video library, but the best library is at the American church of Santa Susanna, Via XX Settembre 14 (☎06.482.7510), which costs around €18 a year, and which also has a good noticeboard for finding work, accommodation and so on, and at the American Studies Center, Via M. Caetani 32 (☎06.6880.1613), though this last is for reference only.

Lost property For property lost on a train call ☎06.4730.6682 (daily 7am–11pm); on a bus ☎06.581.6040 (Mon & Fri 8.30am–1pm, Tues–Thurs 2.30–6pm); on the metro ☎06.487.4309.

Medical assistance ☎06.488.2371, 06.884.0113 (24hr), 06.808.0995 (English-speaking).

Newspapers English newspapers are available the same day of publication later in the afternoon at newsstands in Termini, Piazza Colonna and Via Veneto. *The International Herald Tribune*, available at most newsstands, is printed in Italy and includes an Italian news supplement.

Pharmacies Farmacia Internazionale, Piazza Barberini ☎06.679.4680; Piram, Via Nazionale 228 ☎06.488.0754; Farmacia della Stazione, Piazza dei Cinquecento 49–50 ☎06.488.0019, are all open 24hr, year-round.

Police ☎113. Both the Police and the Carabinieri have offices in Termini. Otherwise the most central Police Station is off Via del Corso in Piazza del Collegio Romano 3 (☎06.46.86), and there is a Carabinieri office in Piazza Venezia to the right of Via del Corso.

Radio *Radio Centro Suono* (101.3 FM), plays more interesting music than most of the local radio stations; otherwise try *Radio Rock* (106.6). *Radio Città Futura* (97.7) plays a variety of alternative sounds, and at 10.30am daily has information on what's on in Rome.

Study American Academy, Via Angelo Masina 5, 00153 Rome ☎06.58.461 ＠www.aarome.org; British School at Rome, Via Gramsxi 61, 00197 Rome ☎06.326.4939 ＠www.bsr.ac.uk.

Time Rome is one hour ahead of GMT, six hours ahead of Eastern Standard Time, and nine hours ahead of Pacific Standard Time.

Train enquiries Termini ☎06.488.1726. Tiburtina ☎06.473.0184. Fiumicino ☎06.6501.1821. For general enquiries about schedules and prices ☎1478.88.088 (daily 7am–9pm).

Travel agents For discount tickets try the CTS offices at Via Genova 16 ☎06.462.0431 and Corso Vittorio Emanuele II 297 ☎06.687.2672, both open on Saturday mornings, when all the other travel agents are closed. Other good places to try are Viaggiare, Via San Nicola da Tolentino 15 ☎06.421.171, who have some English-speaking staff, and Elsy Viaggi, Via di Torre Argentina 80 ☎06.689.6460.

Contexts

Contexts

History

The history of Rome is almost the history of the western world, and as such is hard to encapsulate in a potted guidebook form. Inevitably the best we can do here is provide the basic framework. However, knowing at least some Roman history is crucial to an understanding of the city – its sights and monuments are often interconnected and will mean much more if you have a basic grasp of the continuum of events and their relationships to each other. We've tried to contextualize as much of the information in the guide as possible, but we recommend you take a look at some of the historical texts we list in "Books", p.287 – Edward Gibbon or Tom Holland on ancient Rome and the Empire, and perhaps the novels of Robert Graves of Allan Massie for a dramatized take on the same. For a general and very readable overview, Christopher Hibbert's "biography" of the city is excellent. Rough Guides' *History of Italy* also gives a good chronological account of key events on Italian history and how they shaped and affected the capital.

Beginnings

No one knows precisely when Rome was founded. But excavations on the Palatine Hill have revealed the traces of an **Iron Age** village dating back to the ninth or eighth century BC. However it wasn't until 616 BC, when **Tarquinius Priscus** – an Etruscan – became the first king of Rome, that the city was truly developed, with the first buildings of the forum being raised and the rudiments of the city's sewage and water system – the *Cloaca Maxima* – being put in place.

The **legends** relating to Rome's earliest history tell it slightly differently. Rea Silvia, a vestal virgin and daughter of a local king, Numitor, had twin sons – the product, she alleged, of a rape by Mars. They were supposed to be sacrificed to the god but the ritual wasn't carried out, and the two boys were abandoned and found by a wolf, who nursed them until their adoption by a shepherd, who named them **Romulus and Remus**. Later they laid out the boundaries of the city on the Palatine Hill (Remus chose the Aventine Hill and Romulus the Palatine Hill, and the latter won), but it soon became apparent that there was only room for one ruler, and, unable to agree on the signs given to them by the gods, they quarrelled, Romulus killing Remus and becoming in 753 BC the city's first ruler. Whatever the truth of this, there's no doubt that Rome was an obvious spot to build a city: the Palatine and Capitoline hills provided security, and there was, of course, the river Tiber, which could be easily crossed here by way of the Isola Tiberina, making this a key location on the trade routes between Etruria and Campania.

The Roman Republic

Rome as a kingdom lasted until about 509 BC, when the people rose up against the last, tyrannical Etruscan monarch, **Tarquinius Superbus**. Tarquinius was a brutal, unpopular ruler, but the crunch came when his son

Sextus raped a Roman noblewoman, Lucretia. She committed suicide shortly after, and her husband, along with one Lucius Junius Brutus, helped to lead an uprising that led eventually to the establishment of a **Republic** – a reaction, basically, against the autocratic rule of the Etruscan monarchs. The Roman Republic was to last nearly five hundred years, and was a surprisingly modern, and democratic, form of government, based on the acknowledged fact that the fate of the Roman people and its patrician classes were inextricably bound up together (the words SPQR, which you still see everywhere, stand for "Senatus Populesque Romani" or "The Roman Senate and People"). The **Senate** represented the patrician families, and elected two consuls from their number to lead Rome – in itself a forward-thinking act after years of absolute rule – while the people were allowed to elect two tribunes to represent their interests, even vetoing the appointment of senators they disagreed with. The city prospered under the Republic, growing greatly in size and subduing the various tribes of the surrounding areas – the Volsci and Etruscans to the north, the Sabines to the east, the Samnites to the south. The Etruscans were subdued in 474 BC, at the battle of Cumae, and the Volsci and Sabines soon after. Rome later drew up its first set of laws, in 451 BC, inscribing them on bronze tablets and displaying them prominently in the Forum – by now the city's most important central space.

Despite a heavy defeat by the **Gauls** in 390 BC, when they took the entire city except for the Capitoline Hill (a night assault was reputedly foiled by the cackling of sacred geese kept on the hill which woke the besieged soldiers), by the following century the city had begun to extend its influence beyond the boundaries of what is now mainland Italy, pushing south into Sicily and across the ocean to Africa and Carthage. In the meantime Rome was also trying to subdue the **Samnites**, who occupied most of the land in the southern part of what is now Italy, waging wars on and off between 343 BC and 304 BC that led eventually to the Romans occupying most of the region that is now Campania, south of Rome. Beyond mainland Italy, the next hundred years or so were taken up by the **Punic Wars**, against **Carthage**, the other dominant force in the Mediterranean at the time, and really the only thing standing between Rome and total dominance of the region. The First Punic War, fought over Sicily, began in 264 BC, and continued for around twenty years until Carthage surrendered all rights to the island of Sicily, while the Second Punic War was famously started in 218 BC by Hannibal's march across the Alps by elephant, and ended, after years of skirmishes in southern Italy, in 202 BC. By the time Rome had fought and won the Third Punic War, in 146 BC, it had become the dominant power in the Mediterranean, subsequently taking control of present-day Greece and the Middle East, and expanding north, also, into what is now France, Germany and Britain.

Domestically, the Romans built **roads** – notably the Via Appia, which dates back to 312 BC – and developed their civic structure, with new laws and far-sighted political reforms, one of which cannily brought all of the Republic's vanquished enemies into the fold as **Roman citizens**. However, the history of the Republic was also one of internal strife, marked by factional fighting among the patrician ruling classes, as everyone tried to grab a slice of the riches that were pouring into the city from its plundering expeditions abroad – and the ordinary people, or plebeians, enjoying little more justice than they had under the Roman monarchs. In 87 BC, one of the consuls, Lucius Cornelius Sulla, went off to subdue a rebellion in Asia Minor, while his counterpart, Gaius Marius, stayed behind and took sole control of the city, leading to a civil war in which Sulla, in 82 BC, eventually emerged as the sole

leader of Rome, initiating a terrifying revenge against his opponents and introducing laws which greatly reduced the powers of the city's elected and
appointed officials. Gaius Marius's nephew, **Julius Caesar**, later emerged as a
powerful military leader, conquering Gaul and Britain, and returned to fight
another civil war against his rival Pompey, which he won. He was proclaimed
"dictator of Rome". It was the last straw for those eager to restore some
semblance of the republican vision, and Caesar was murdered in the Theatre
of Pompey on March 15, 44 BC, by conspirators concerned at the growing
concentration of power into one man's hands.

However, rather than returning Rome to the glorious days of the Republic,
the murder of Caesar in fact threw it back into turmoil. After his death, Julius
Caesar's deputy, Mark Antony, briefly took control, joining forces with Lepidus
and Caesar's adopted son, Octavian, in a **triumvirate** that marshalled armies
that fought and won against those controlled by Caesar's assassins, Brutus and
Cassius, in a famous battle at Philippi, in modern-day Greece, in 42 BC. Their
alliance was further cemented by Antony's marriage to Octavian's sister,
Octavia, in 40 AD, but in spite of this a brief period of turmoil followed, in
which Antony, unable to put his political ambitions before his emotional
alliance with the queen of Egypt, Cleopatra, was defeated by Octavian at
the battle of Actium in 31 BC – escaping to Alexandria, where he committed
suicide, with his lover, the queen.

The Imperial era

A triumph for the new democrats over the old guard, **Augustus** (27 BC–14
AD) – as Octavian became known – was the first true Roman emperor, in
firm control of Rome and its dominions; indeed "Augustus" became the name
by which all future Roman emperors were known. Responsible more than
anyone for heaving Rome into the Imperial era, Augustus was determined to
turn the city – as he claimed – from one of stone to one of marble, building
arches, theatres and monuments of a magnificence suited to the capital of an
expanding empire. Perhaps the best and certainly the most politically canny of
Rome's many emperors, Augustus reigned for forty years.

Augustus was succeeded by his stepson, **Tiberius** (14–37), who ruled from
the island of Capri for the last years of his reign, and he in turn by **Caligula**
(37–41), a poor and possibly insane ruler who was assassinated after just four
years in power. **Claudius** (41–54), his uncle, followed, at first reluctantly, and
proved to be a wise ruler, only to be succeeded by his stepson, **Nero** (54–68),
whose reign became more notorious for its excess than its prudence, and led
to a brief period of warring and infighting after his murder in 68 AD, with
Vitellius, Galba and Vespasian all vying for the position of emperor.

Vespasian (69–79) was eventually proclaimed emperor, thus starting a
dynasty – the **Flavian** – which was to restore some stability to Rome and its
empire. Vespasian started as he meant to go on, doing his best to obliterate all
traces of Nero, not least with an enormous amphitheatre in the grounds of
Nero's palace, later know as the Colosseum. Vespasian was succeeded by his son,
Titus (79–81), and soon after by his other son – Titus' brother – **Domitian**
(81–96), who reverted to imperial type, becoming an ever more paranoid and
despotic ruler until his murder in 96 AD, when all his decrees were declared
void. **Nerva** was declared emperor (96–98), but was soon succeeded by his
adopted son, **Trajan** (98–117), whose enlightened leadership once again

allowed Rome and its colonies to settle to some sort of stability. Trajan also expanded the empire greatly, conquering the lands to the east – Turkey and modern-day Romania – and it was under his rule that the empire reached its maximum limits. Trajan died in 117 AD, giving way to his cousin, **Hadrian** (117–38), who continued the grand and expansionist agenda of his predecessor, and arguably provided the empire's greatest years. The city swelled to a population of a million or more, its people housed in cramped apartment blocks or insulae; crime in the city was rife, and the traffic problem apparently on a par with today's, leading one contemporary writer to complain that the din on the streets made it impossible to get a good night's sleep. But it was a time of peace and prosperity, the Roman upper classes living a life of indolent luxury, in sumptuous residences with proper plumbing and central heating, and the empire's borders being ever more extended. Hadrian's successor, **Antoninus Pius** (138–61), and then **Marcus Aurelius** (161–80), ruled over a largely peaceful and economically successful empire, until 180 AD, when Marcus Aurelius' son, **Commodus** (180–92), assumed the throne but wasn't up to the task, and Rome entered a more fragile phase. Predictably, Commodus was murdered, and eventually replaced by **Septimus Severus** (193–211), thus initiating the Severan dynasty – again a time of relative calm, although the political and miltary skills of Severus unfortunately weren't matched by those of his sons, Galba and Caracalla. **Caracalla** (211–17) murdered his brother before assuming power for himself in 211 AD.

The **decline of Rome** is hard to date precisely, but it could be said to have started with the emperor **Diocletian** (284–305), an army officer from present-day Croatia who assumed power in 284 and in an attempt to consolidate the empire divided it into two parts, east and west, each of which was divided into four territories. Known also for his relentless persecution of Christians, Diocletian abdicated in 305, retiring to the vast palace he had built for himself in what is now Split, on the Dalmatian coast, giving rise to a power struggle that concluded with the battle of the Ponte Milvio in Rome, in which Constantine defeated his rival, Maxentius, at the same time as converting to Christianity due to a vision of a cross in the sky he saw during the battle. The first Christian emperor, **Constantine** (312–37), ended Diocletian's persecution of the Faith, and shifted the seat of power to Byzantium in 325, renaming it Constantinople. Rome's heady period as capital of the world was over, and the wealthier members of the population moved east. A series of invasions by Goths in 410 and Vandals about forty years later only served to quicken the city's ruin. By the sixth century the city was a devastated and infection-ridden shadow of its former self, with a population of just 20,000.

The rise of the papacy

It was the papacy, under Pope **Gregory I** ("the Great"; 590–604) in 590, that rescued Rome from its demise. In an eerie echo of the empire, Gregory sent missions all over Europe to spread the word of the Church and publicize its holy relics, so drawing pilgrims, and their money, back to the city, and in time making the papacy the natural authority in Rome. The pope took the name "Pontifex Maximus" after the title of the high priest of classical times (literally "the keeper of the bridges", which were vital to the city's well-being). Four of the city's great basilicas were built during this time, along with a great many other early Christian churches, underlining the city's phoenix-like resurrection under the popes, who as well as building their own new structures converted those Roman buildings that were still standing – for example fortifying the Castel Sant'Angelo to repel invaders. The crowning a couple of centuries later of Charlemagne as Holy Roman Emperor, with dominions spread Europe-wide but answerable to the pope, intensified the city's revival, and the pope and city became recognized as head of the Christian world.

There were times over the next few hundred years when the power of Rome and the papacy was weakened: Robert Guiscard, the Norman king, sacked the city in 1084; a century later, a dispute between the city and the papacy led to a series of popes relocating in Viterbo; and in 1308 the French-born Pope **Clemente V** (1305–16) transferred his court to Avignon. In the mid-fourteenth century, Cola di Rienzo seized power, setting himself up as the people's saviour from the decadent ways of the city's rulers and forming a new Roman republic. But the increasingly autocratic ways of the new ruler soon lost popularity; Cola di Rienzo was deposed, and in 1376 Pope **Gregory XI** (1370–78) returned to Rome.

The Renaissance and Counter-Reformation

As time went on, power gradually became concentrated in a handful of **families**, who swapped the top jobs, including the papacy itself, between them. Under the burgeoning power of the pope, the city began to take on a new aspect: churches were built, the city's pagan monuments rediscovered and preserved, and artists began to arrive in Rome to work on commissions for the latest pope, who would invariably try to outdo his predecessor's efforts with ever more glorious self-aggrandizing buildings and works of art.

This process reached a head during the **Renaissance**; Bramante, Raphael and Michelangelo all worked in the city, on and off, throughout their careers. The reigns of Pope **Julius II** (1503–13), and his successor the Medici pope, **Leo X** (1513–22), were something of a golden age: the city was at the centre of Italian cultural and artistic life and site of the creation of great works of art like Michelangelo's frescoes in the Sistine Chapel, Raphael's Stanze in the Vatican Palace and fine buildings like the Villa Farnesina, Palazzo Farnese and Palazzo Spada, not to mention the commissioning of a new St Peter's as well as any number of other churches. The city was once again at the centre of things, and its population had increased to 100,000. However, in 1527 all this was brought abruptly to an end, when the armies of the Habsburg monarch, Charles V, swept into the city, occupying it – and wreaking havoc – for a year, while Pope **Clement VII** (1523–34) cowered in the Castel Sant'Angelo.

The ensuing years were ones of yet more restoration, and perhaps because of this it's the **seventeenth century** that has left the most tangible impression on Rome today, the vigour of the **Counter-Reformation** throwing up huge sensational monuments like the Gesù church that were designed to confound the scepticism of the new Protestant thinking, and again using pagan artefacts (like obelisks), not to mention the ready supply of building materials provided by the city's ruins, in ever more extravagant displays of wealth. The Farnese pope, **Paul III** (1534–50), was perhaps the most efficient at quashing anti-Catholic feeling, while, later, Pope **Sixtus V** (1585–90) was perhaps the most determined to mould the city in his own image, ploughing roads through the centre and laying out bold new squares at their intersections. This period also saw the completion of St Peter's under **Paul V** (1605–21), and the ascendancy of Gian Lorenzo Bernini as the city's principal architect and sculptor under the Barberini pope, **Urban VIII** (1623–44) – a patronage that was extended under the Pamphilj pope, **Innocent X** (1644–55).

The eighteenth and nineteenth centuries

The **eighteenth century** saw the decline of the papacy as a political force, a phenomenon marked by the occupation of the city in 1798 by Napoleon; **Pius VI** (1775–1800) was unceremoniously sent off to France as a prisoner, and Napoleon declared another Roman republic, with himself at its head, which lasted until 1815, when papal rule was restored under **Pius VII** (1800–23). The years that followed were relatively quiet in Rome, if not in the rest of Italy, where the relatively despotic rules of the various city-states and fiefdoms that made up what we now know as Italy were at odds with the new ideas of centralization and modernization of the **reunification movement**, led by Giuseppe Mazzini. The revolutionary year of 1848, when popular revolts were sparked all over Europe, led to widespread unrest in Italy. In 1849 a pro-Unification caucus under **Mazzini** declared the city a republic but was soon chased out; and there was further fighting all over Italy in 1859 and 1860. Giuseppe **Garibaldi** had defended Rome with Mazzini in 1849 and later waged an effective guerrilla campaign in Sicily and southern Italy which ceded the territories to King Victor Emmanuel (Florence became capital of the new kingdom in 1864). Garibaldi made repeated attempts to capture Rome – occupied by Pope Pius IX and protected by the French – but he was arrested and sidelined by the new regime, embarrassed by his growing power and charisma. In 1870 French troops were withdrawn from Rome to fight the Franco-Prussian war allowing Italian forces to storm the walls at Porta Pia and retake the city. Rome was declared the capital of the kingdom under Victor Emmanuel I (who moved into the Quirinale Palace), and confined the by now quite powerless pontiff, **Pius IX** (1846–78), in the Vatican until agreement was reached on a way to coexist. The initial **Law of Guarantees** drawn up by the new government defined the relationship of the state to the papacy, and acknowledged the pope as sovereign within the Vatican but no further; it was rejected by the pope, leaving the status of the Vatican in limbo for years to come. In the meantime **Agostino Depretis** became the first prime minister of the new Italian state, and one of its greatest politicians, remaining in power until 1887, and seeing the new country through the difficult early years.

Modern times

As capital of a modern European country, Rome was (some would say still is) totally ill-equipped, and the **Piemontese rulers** of the new kingdom set about building a city fit to govern from, cutting new streets through Rome's central core (Via Nazionale, Via del Tritone) and constructing grandiose buildings like the Altar of the Nation. **Mussolini** took up residence in Rome in 1922, and in 1929 signed the **Lateran Pact** with Pope **Pius XI** (1922–39), a compromise which finally forced the Vatican to accept the new Italian state and in return recognized the Vatican City as sovereign territory, together with the key basilicas and papal palaces in Rome, which remain technically independent of Italy to this day. Mussolini's motivations weren't dissimilar to those of the pope, however, when he bulldozed his way through the Roman Forum and began work on the futuristic, self-publicizing planned extension to the city known as EUR. Rome was declared an "open city" during **World War II**, and as such emerged from the war relatively unscathed. However, after Mussolini's death, and the end of the war, the Italian king, Vittorio Emanuele III, was forced to abdicate and Italy was declared a republic – still, however, with its capital in Rome.

After the war Italy became renowned as a country which changes its government, if not its politicians, every few months, and for the rest of Italy Rome has come to symbolize the inertia of their nation's government – at odds with both the slick, efficient North, and the poor, corrupt South. Despite this, the city's growth was phenomenal in the post-war years, its population soaring to close on four million and its centre becoming ever more choked by traffic. Rome was internationally famous for fifteen minutes during the **Sixties**, when it was the (cinematic) home of Fellini's *Dolce Vita* and Italy's bright young things. However, in the **Seventies**, when the so-called Anni Piombi or "years of lead" arrived, Rome became a focus for the polarization and terrorism that was going on nationwide in Italian politics – a period when there were troops on the streets and the country often seemed on the brink of civil disruption. Since then, beginning with the "mani puliti" or "clean hands" enquiries of the **early 1990s**, the landscape of Italian politics has changed massively; and Rome in particular saw a period of stable government under the Green party mayor, Franceso Rutelli. Great efforts were made to prepare the city for the arrival of the **Millennium**, and the millions of visitors who came to celebrate the Jubilee (Holy Year) declared by the pope: buildings and monuments that had been closed for decades were reopened, restoration was completed, and as a result the city is looking better than ever. Nonetheless, in many ways Rome hasn't altered a bit. It's still clogged with traffic and, even by Italian standards, remains a relatively provincial place, and one which is in some ways still trying to lug itself into the twenty-first century. It will do so – eventually; and the city is changing fast in lots of obvious ways, with rundown neighbourhoods like Ostiense becoming gentrified, rents and other prices shooting up with the advent of the euro, and long-closed galleries and attractions becoming ever more accessible. But, perhaps uniquely among European capitals, it retains a feel in its central districts that is still peculiarly local – and defiantly Roman. Visit now while it still exists.

Writing on Rome

There has been so much written about Rome over the years that picking out something that encapsulates the city in a few words is a hard if not impossible task. There's nothing, however, quite like the reaction that Rome induces in first-time visitors. However much they may have read, and no matter how well travelled they are, no one is ever quite prepared for the exuberant confusion of the city. The three pieces we have chosen are all about coming to Rome for the first or second time; all were written in the modern era, and as such are still highly relevant to what you see today; but they were written long enough ago also to be enjoyed as history.

Elizabeth Bowen

A novelist and travel writer, Elizabeth Bowen was born in Dublin in 1899. Her book, *A Time in Rome*, from which the following extract was taken, was first published in 1960.

The Confusion

Too much time in too little space, I thought, sitting on the edge of my bed at the end of the train journey from Paris. Never have I heard Rome so quiet before or since I had asked for a quiet room, this was it. It was on the fourth floor, at the back. The bed was low, the window was set high up, one half of it framing neutral sky, the other a shabby projection of the building. Colour seemed, like sound, to be drained away. The hour was half-past four, the day Tuesday, the month February. I knew myself to be not far from the Spanish Steps, which had flashed past the taxi like a postcard. These anti-climactic first minutes became eternal. My bedroom's old-fashioned double room, with key in the lock and the tab dangling, had been shut behind him by the outgoing porter; stacked on trestles at the foot of the bed here was my luggage for three months. Through a smaller doorway showed the tiles of a bathroom wanly reflecting electric light. I was alone with my tired senses.

The hotel, from what I had seen of it, was estimable and dignified, nothing gimcrack. The corridor, dark and extremely long, had been lined with noble old-fashioned furniture, and in here was more of it, on top of me, Close to my pillows was the telephone, sharing the marble top of a commode with a lamp with the Campidoglio on its shade. After my one thought I felt unequal to any others and lay down flat. The bedhead was in a corner, so I switched on the lamp and tipped up the shade, to continue my reading of a detective story – interrupted just at the crucial point by my train's arrival at Rome station.

When I emerged from the story, darkness had fallen and I was hungry. Taking with me the *Walks of Rome* of Augustus Hare, I left the hotel to look for dinner. In these surrounding little streets, lit up like aquariums and tonight anonymous, saunterers passed me in vague shoals. Restaurant after restaurant was empty; blue-white electricity, hatless hatstands, as chalky and void as the tables' napery. Here and there a waiter posed like a waxwork. Spying through glass doors or over blinds, I began to fear something had gone wrong – actually all that had happened was, I was ahead of the Roman dinner-hour. So I ended in yellow-brocaded Ranieri's, where they showed a polished lack of surprise, among foreigners other than myself. Great gilt candelabra were on the chimney-piece, and for each of us a little vase of anenomes. But here I was afflicted by something else: it seemed uncouth to read while dinner was served. Stealing a glance now and then at Augustus Hare, I never succeeded in getting further than Dr Arnold's 1840 letter to his wife: "Again this date of Rome; the most solemn and interesting that my hand can write, and even now more interesting than when I saw it last." This was not my first visit to Rome either.

Next day, I changed my room for an outside corner one, a floor higher. This, with the freshness following on what seemed more absolute than a mere night's sleep, altered the feeling of everything like magic. I found myself up in a universe, my own, of sun-coloured tiled floor, sunny starchy curtains. Noise, like the morning, rushed in at the open windows, to be contained by the room in its gay tranquillity. Roses, bleached by seasons of light, rambled over the cretonne coverings of the two beds. The idea of Rome, yesterday so like lead, this noonday lay on me lighter than a feather. Life at this level had a society of its own: windows across the way, their shutters clamped back, looked pensively, speakingly in at mine.

The quarter in which the Hotel Inghilterra stands is early nineteenth-century. It fills the slight declivity, shallow as the hollow of a hand, between the Pincio and the Corso, and is bisected by the *de luxe* Via Condotti, apart from which the quarter is unassuming. It has acoustics of its own, echoes and refractions of steps and voices, now and then of the throb of a car in low gear nosing its way among the pedestrians. Every narrow street in this network is one-way; the system is dementing to motorists, who do not embroil themselves in it willingly. Radio jazz, a fervent young singer at her exercises, a sewing-machine tearing along, and the frenetic song of a small-caged bird, hooked to my sill, were my sound-neighbours. From top-but-one storey windows I beheld one crinkled continuous tawny roofline: all the buildings fitted into this quarter, like segments of a finally solved jigsaw, are one in height as they are in age. They are ochre, which was giving off a kind of August glow on to the mild spring-winter morning: on throughout the chilliest time of year smoulders the afterglow of Rome's summers. And my streets, on a grid plan, sunken deep between buildings, also are all alike: sunless, down there, for the greater part of the day, they stretch so far that they fade away at the ends. Small shops, work-shops, bars and restaurants line them, with apartments or offices above. Banal, affable, ripe to become familiar, this was the ideal Rome to be installed in: everything seemed to brim with associations, if not (so far) any of my own. I began to attach myself by so much as looking. Here I was, centred. I dared to hope that all else might prove as simple. It did not.

One trouble is that Rome's north-south axis, Via del Corso, does not run due north, due south. It slants, thereby throwing one's sense of direction, insofar as one has one, out of the true. The Piazza Venezia, at one end, is east of Piazza del Popolo at the other. Then, there are the exaggerated S-curvings of the Tiber; one minute the river is at one's elbow, the next lost. A stroll along the embankment is one of the least enjoyable in Rome; the dustiest, baldest, most unrewarding. (To stand on a bridge is another thing.) The Tiber is not intended to be followed; only trams do so, and those in very great numbers. They grind by unceasingly, and one does well to take one.

Then again, there are far more than seven hills: how is one to be clear which the seven are? This seems to be one of the primal facts which guidebooks are obstinate in withholding. Viewed from above, from the Janiculum lighthouse or a terrace of the Pincio gardens, Rome as a whole appears absolutely flat, or, if anything, sunken in the middle like a golden-brown pudding or cake which has failed to rise. Down again in the city, you register gradients in aching foot muscles – this does establish that Rome is hilly. Knowledge of Rome must be physical, sweated into the system, worked up into the brain through the tinning shoe-leather. Substantiality comes through touch and smell, and taste, the tastes of different dusts. When it comes to knowing, the senses are more honest than the intelligence. Nothing is more real than the first wall you lean up against sobbing with exhaustion. Rome no more than beheld (that is, taken in through the eyes only) could still be a masterpiece in cardboard – the eye I suppose being of all the organs the most easily infatuated and then jaded and so tricked. Seeing is pleasure, but not knowledge.

In shape the Capitoline and the Palatine are hills unmistakably; so is the Aventine, at the other side of the trough of the Circo Massimo. But the Caelian, Esquiline, Viminal and Quirinal are ambiguously webbed together by ridges. On the whole I have come to suppose that these *are* the Seven – but if so, what of the Pincian, "hill of gardens" and Janiculum, bastion across the river? I asked a number of friends, but no two gave me the same answer; some did not want to be pinned down, others put forward their own candidates. That I should be set on compiling a definitive list of the Seven Hills, eager to check on all, to locate each, was, I can see, disillusioning to people who had hoped I might show more advanced tastes. So, given the equal unwillingness of guide-books to disgorge anything like a list, I left Rome, when the end of my time came, no more certain as to the Seven Hills.

An excerpt from *A Time in Rome*, reprinted with the kind permission of
Curtis Brown Ltd on behalf of Elizabeth Bowen. ©Elizabeth Bowen

William Weaver

William Weaver served as an ambulance driver during World War II and first visited Rome a few years later. He became the most sought-after translator of Italian literature of the second half of the twentieth century, translating most of the modern Italian literary greats at one time or another. The following extract, part of his introduction to Steerforth Press's anthology of modern Roman literature, details his first impressions of the city, and his relationships with some of the writers he later came to work with.

Open City

It was raining when we arrived, and the rickety bus finally emptied us – me and my Neapolitan friend Raffaele – into a small, dark square near the Borsa. This was Rome? True, there were some scarred ancient columns along a street-front, but they were grimy with soot. I had imagined a city of snowy white, elegant classical forms, resembling perhaps the columned Citizens National Bank in Front Royal, Virginia, my childhood paragon of fine architecture. Rome, I saw, in shock, was different from the black-and-white Alinari photographs of art history courses; it was orange, yellow; rust-color; there were even a few neon signs blinking on baroque facades in the early winter dusk.

From the Piazza di Pietra we went to our pensione. Again, with reminiscences of E.M. Forster in my head, I imagined a place of relaxed conversation and, of course, a room with a view. The Pensione Sieben had once been a solid, spacious, middle-class apartment. Now the Siebens (he was an elderly German, a retired translator) lived in the kitchen and in a crammed bedroom next to it. An old lady, Herr Sieben's mother, occupied the next bedroom. In the front of the apartment, my friends Peppino and Mario shared the former salon, a once-splendid room now almost empty save for two cots, a desk, and a wood-burning stove, jutting from what was a formerly decorative fireplace.

Across the vestibule was a much smaller room, where I was to sleep. It also contained two cots, but the few square meters could not accommodate even a small desk. The cot farther from the door was occupied by Achille, another Neapolitan friend, an actor just getting his first small roles in a repertory company specializing in new Italian plays (they were not usually very good, so the bill changed often; Achille was building a large, useless repertory). Until the previous week, my cot had been occupied by yet another Neapolitan, Francesco Rosi, an aspiring film-maker; now he had landed an enviable job, as assistant to Luchino Visconti, and had just gone off to Sicily to join the director in working on what was to prove an enduring masterpiece, *La terra trema*. The room's single window gave on an air-shaft and a blank wall.

Achille was a trying roommate. Unless he had a rehearsal, he slept until midday (so I had to dress in the dark). Afternoons, he received his lovely and long-suffering girl-friend, and I was expected to go out for an extended walk – it was a rainy winter – and stay out until dark. He was a hypochondriac, and when he discovered my super-giant family-size bottle of aspirin – calculated to last me for my whole Italian stay – he began happily popping pills; the aspirin level in the big jar descended at an alarming rate. He was also fascinated by my clothes, ordinary as they were, and constantly borrowed them, with or without asking me first. He particularly liked to wear them on stage; so I became used to seeing my Princeton sweatshirt or my favorite striped pyjamas turn up on a set representing an Italian living room.

After a few days in Rome, I dutifully made my way to the University, planning to enroll in some courses, to justify and, presumably, enrich my Italian stay. My first real tangle with Italian bureaucracy ensued: a nightmare of waiting in the wrong line, lacking this or that document, failing to understand angry, shouted directions from the grouchy staff behind the windows or the confusing attempts at help from equally beleaguered Italian students.

I gave up (two years later, thanks to a Fulbright, I actually enrolled at the University and attended a few classes), and determined to dedicate myself to my other Roman project: the novel I expected to write. Having published two stories in national magazines (*Harper's Bazaar* and *Mademoiselle*, which had published stories of Truman Capote and other rising stars), I – and my friends – assumed that a novel was the next step. There was just one difficulty: I had nothing I particularly wanted to write about. But I didn't let that stop me. Mornings, when Peppino had gone off to his job at the Rai, the Italian State Radio, and Mario to his classes at the Accademia di arte drammatica, I moved into the former salon, sat at their desk, opened my copious notebooks (a Gide fan, I could not contemplate writing a novel without keeping journals, cahiers), and tried to work. I had never been successfully self-critical. But even permissive me soon had to concede that the novel was a dud.

If the rain let up, I soon found an excuse to go out. The excuse was always the same: my determination to get to know Rome. It was not a matter of visiting churches, studying frescoes, deciphering inscriptions. I wanted to gulp down real Roman coffee in the morning, eat real Roman pasta at lunch, drink all the real Roman wine I could afford. I wanted to read the newspapers, see the movies and the plays, hear the music.

I was perfectly situated. Dreary as the Pensione Sieben looked at first, it turned out to be a hive of cultural, and social activity; a center of fun. The big salon of Peppino and Mario served as a gathering-place for a host of young people from the Accademia, writers from the rai, and other newly-arrived Neapolitans aiming to break into film or journalism.

And I had a trump-card of my own. I was an American, and to the Italians – whatever their ages or degree of fame – that nationality inspired endless curiosity. For many I was the first American they had encountered, except perhaps for a stray GI a few years earlier. And so I was consulted as the expert on everything American: my opinion on William Wyler was seriously pondered. I was asked whether I would place Gershwin in the mainstream of white jazz or in the area of classical music (the question, for me, was unanswerable, as I knew far more about Puccini than about my popular compatriot). I was invited to contribute to nascent literary magazines, some of them born only to die after the first issue, which perhaps included my little piece on Karl Shapiro or John O'Hara.

Through a visiting American I met the Italian painter and writer Dario Cecchi, a few years my senior, scion of an Italian literary/artistic family with ramifications extending into every area of Italy's cultural life. Dario's father was the eminent and powerful critic Emilio Cecchi; his sister was Suso Cecchi d'Amico, the script-writer of Visconti and others, and her husband, Fedele d'Amico, was a brilliant, polemical music critic and polymath, eventually to become a treasured friend and colleague.

The chain of acquaintances grew, link by link, creating degrees not of separation but of connection. And some of these connections soon became hubs, branching off in one direction after another. It was Dario who took me first to meet Princess Marguerite Caetani. He told me little about her beyond the fact that she was American-born (a Chapin from Connecticut), a patron of the arts who had lived for many years in France, but had returned to Italy with her musician husband before the second world war and had remained in Rome. In Palazzo Caetani she edited an international literary review, *Botteghe Oscure*, after the name of the street where the Palazzo had stood for many centuries. The fact that Communist Party Headquarters now stood in that same street, making its name a synonym for the pci, was a minor nuisance that the Principessa airily dismissed.

We stepped into the dark courtyard of the great, grim palace, took an elevator to the piano nobile, and were shown into a huge, high-ceilinged hall, hung with dusty portraits (I looked around for Boniface VIII, the Caetani pope pilloried by Dante, but I couldn't identify him): then Dario, who knew his way around the palace, led me to a modern corkscrew staircase in a corner of the room. We climbed it and, passing through a plain little door at its top, stepped into a large, but cozy, New England living room: sofas covered in beige monkscloth, low tables, a fire in the fireplace, French windows revealing a broad terrace beyond. A large tea-pot stood on one table, and plates of sand-wiches circulated.

The Principessa, in heather tweeds, only a few wisps of her gray hair out of place (to hint at her artistic side?), welcomed me warmly. And the welcome was equally warm from other guests, all clearly frequenters of the house. They were not many, and I remember almost all of them, as they all became friends of mine very soon: Elena Croce, the daughter of the philosopher but with a lively mind of her own; Umberto Morra, an aristocratic anti-Fascist and old friend of Bernard Berenson; Ignazio Silone – whose works I had read in translation – with his beautiful, ebullient Irish wife Darina, whom I had already met for a fleeting moment. And Giorgio Bassani, titular editor of *Botteghe Oscure*, though Marguerite clearly made all the operative decisions, while encouraging Bassani to propose new writers, especially for the Italian section of the magazine. At that time, Bassani was known, if he was known at all, as a poet; he had just published the first of what were to become the now classic *Five Stories of Ferrara*.

After that first visit, I returned to Palazzo Caetani countless times, and each visit was memorable, especially those when I was alone with Marguerite, who soon discovered – and exploited – my boarding-school experience as a proof-reader. The Italian printers, excellent artisans, inevitably made gibberish of some of the magazine's English and French texts, and complaining authors drove Marguerite to despair ("Alfred Chester called me this morning from Paris, he cried all last night because of the mistakes in his story.") My work was unpaid – and I put in long hours – but I had ample occasion to appreciate Marguerite's real generosity. Not only did she soon publish my work: she also invited me to any number of meals. Food at the Caetani table was plain, but as I lived from day to day, a steak gained was a steak earned.

And the company! For foreign literary visitors of a certain level, Palazzo Caetani was an obligatory stop. One week there would be a tea-party for "Cousin Tom" (known to me as T.S. Eliot), in Rome to give a reading at the British Council, but also to enjoy a honeymoon with his new wife Valerie. The great poet's radiant happiness was evident, irrepressible. For much of the party he and his wife sat side-by-side on one of Marguerite's comfortable low sofas, and he could not refrain from touching her, patting her hand, pressing her arm, like an enamored schoolboy. Standing not far away, I pointed out Eliot's enraptured behavior to Alberto Moravia. "Senile sexuality," the novelist commented tartly. I remembered this remark some decades later when Moravia himself, by then close to eighty, married Carmen Llera, forty-odd years his junior.

Between the world wars, Marguerite had lived much of the time in Paris, where her house just outside the city was also an intellectual gathering place (Berenson's letters tell of visits there from the Armistice meetings, which he was attending). So the Palazzo in Rome welcomed many French visitors, among them René Char, Francis Ponge, Henri Sauguet. And there were also musicians, partly because of Prince Roffredo's background as a composer (he was Liszt's godson and had known the Wagners); in the Caetani salon I first heard Gian Carlo Menotti and Tommy Schippers discuss a festival they were beginning to think about, a place for young artists in some Umbrian town, perhaps Todi, or perhaps Spoleto.

Umberto Morra, a Piedmontese count, whose family had been close to the royal family (Umberto's father, a general, had served as the Savoys' ambassador to the court of the Czar), lived in a single room in Rome, in the apartment of some old friends. But he led an intense social life, and he particularly enjoyed entertaining new arrivals to Rome, arranging introductions. Often he would invite a new acquaintance, with perhaps one or at most two old friends, to tea at Babington's tea rooms in Piazza di Spagna. The atmosphere at Babington's certainly belonged to another world, but what world was it? I suppose the unpretentious setting was meant to evoke pre-war England (pre-first war, that is), and the motherly old ladies with their starched frilly caps who brought the tea and scones and cake looked like Margaret Rutherford stand-ins, imported directly from some Staffordshire village. But then you realized they spoke little English, and that smattering came out with a thick Italian accent.

In any case, the tea was authentic and delicious, the scones came with home-made jams; and the company was always stimulating. Whether at Babington or, for grander luncheons, at the Stanze dell'Eliseo, a quirkish private club, with Morra you were always sure to meet someone who was not just interesting but was actually a person you were eager to know: Jimmy Merrill was a Morra gift to me, and so – in Florence – was Bernard Berenson. Later, when Morra headed the Italian Institute in London, he introduced me to the great Maurice Bowra, to the equally legendary Judge Learned Hand. His was a mobile salon. When you came to know him really well, he would invite you for a weekend at his comfortable, slightly shabby villa in Tuscany (Moravia "stole" the villa to use as the setting of his novel Conjugal Love). Again the house party was always varied, relaxed, unexpected. Even the occasional bore – the garrulous widow of a distinguished anti-fascist friend, for example – was, somehow, a bore you were glad to meet.

Morra seemed to be a friend of every Italian I encountered. But I soon realized he was unusual, if not unique in his pan-amicability. By some of my new literary acquaintances, the Cecchi family was considered tainted. For, while never an aggressive Fascist, Cecchi had been something of a social and political opportunist, not above putting his pen to the regime's service, while not compromising his high literary standards or marring the beauty of his jeweled prose. Still, his name appeared on the scenario of the absurdly, blatantly racist film *Harlem*, and his biased book *America amara* was virtually a gift to the anti-USA dictatorship. So at the Cecchis', while you might meet important writers, including the art historian Cesare Brandi or the once-notorious, feminist poet Sibilla Aleramo, you would not find Silone or Moravia. Hence my young Neapolitan friends, and their Roman acquaintances, looked somewhat askance at my association with the Cecchis, though my friendship was with the Cecchi son and daughter rather than the writer himself.

When I first arrived in Italy, in the fall of 1943, I knew the name of only one living Italian writer: Ignazio Silone, and that name was one I had learned only a few months earlier. For my generation – I was born in July 1923 – my knowledge of Italian culture was, I should think, typical. Though a couple of Alberto Moravia's books had been translated before the war, they had not attracted much attention, had not established him as the literary leader he had long been in Italy. A few Americans perhaps knew of the poems of Montale and Ungaretti, but I was not one of them.

I had discovered Silone's works in the Western Desert, in Libya. Isolated with the other thirty-odd members of my company, idle, I spent all my time reading. But books were scarce, and so there was a constant trading. I even read *Winnie the Pooh* for the first time (my father's stern literary standards would not allow the coy Milne in our house, and, after reading him, I agreed with my father). Then a fellow-driver – I forget who it was – lent me the Penguin edition of *Fontamara*, the stark title printed on a white band between two orange ones; when I had read that, the same friend handed me the Harper first US edition of *Bread and Wine*. When I came across a copy of that same edition recently in the Bard College library, it was like running into a long-lost wartime buddy; I could almost feel grains of Libyan sand between the pages.

Silone represented much more than simply my introduction to contemporary Italian fiction; those first two novels of his served also as a political primer. Though I was involved in a great war against Fascism, I had only a vague notion of what the word meant. Silone's fiction led me beyond the headlines, newsreel parades and balcony histrionics to the human facts, the meaning of Fascism in terms of daily bread and loss of freedom.

In Rome, three years later, shortly before I met Silone at Palazzo Caetani, I met – for an unforgettable instant – his beautiful, captivating Irish wife Darina.

I had had a drink at the Caffè Greco with Stephen Spender (whom I had met in New York through Chester Kallman and Auden – another of the radial paths of my cultural landscape). He was on his way to a dinner party at the nearby Palazzo Torlonia, at the residence of the Irish ambassador, the elegant poet Denis Devlin. I walked Stephen to the door of the Palazzo; as we were saying good night, a taxi squealed to a stop, and from it, in breathless haste, a tall, blonde Viking of a woman descended, her face half-covered by a light veil. I was introduced, and I heard her soft, melodious accent for the first of many times.

Of course, I was envious. I wished with all my heart that I had been invited to Denis Devlin's party, and I imagined all sorts of beautiful and brilliant guests, as I saw Stephen and Darina disappear inside the massive portal. A moment later, when I was alone in the Via Bocca di Leone, I grasped the irony of seeing a Silone enter the palace of the Torlonia family, the landlords of southern Italy, who are the ultimate villains of Silone's peasant world.

I met Darina soon again at Marguerite's, and at the same time I met Silone. At a first encounter, he was a forbidding presence, taciturn and – this was my impression – disapproving. This impression persisted after I had been invited to several dinners and parties at the Silone apartment, in an anonymous, outlying part of the city near Piazza Bologna. The foreign visitors who gravitated there were often different from the Botteghe Oscure salon. At the Silones, in addition to a small group of left-wing dissidents, among them Nicola Chiaramonte and his delightful American wife Miriam, you might encounter *Partisan Review* people, Philip Rahv, William Phillips or Dwight Macdonald, or (separately) Edmund Wilson or Mary McCarthy.

One day, after I had been there several times, never exchanging more than a few formal remarks with my host, Darina called with another dinner invitation. Unfortunately I was already engaged for that evening, and so expressed my regrets. "What a pity!" Darina exclaimed. "Silone always enjoys himself so much when you're here."

I was dumbfounded. True, at the Silones', as elsewhere, I liked to talk (and also listen): I told stories, asked questions, ventured opinions, sometimes shaky ones. And then, more often than not, the next morning, if I didn't have an out-and-out hangover, I had the nagging suspicion that I had talked too much and maybe even made a fool of myself. Remembered, Silone's stern silence took on an accusatory quality. But now I could slough off those qualms, and speak to the admired writer more easily. At about this time I made another parallel discovery. Reading a book about anti-Fascists in exile, I found a reference to Silone's humor, which kept his companions' spirits up, making the table in some humble Swiss beer-hall rock with laughter.

Incredulous, I asked Morra about this Silone, so different from the one I knew. "Oh, yes," Umberto confirmed. "Silone has a wonderful, quick wit. He can be very funny indeed."

Eventually, I came to appreciate this side of him (I should have sensed it also from his novels, rich in sly irony). After some years of our acquaintance, he asked me to translate a book of his, an old work, *The School for Dictators*, written in exile and first published in 1938, in German. Darina, herself a first-rate translator, had been responsible for some English versions of his works; but for personal reasons about which she remained vague, she preferred to pass the assignment on to me.

I set to work happily, although the text – a Platonic dialogue on the subject of power, rule, authority – was not the sort of thing I had translated thus far. But both Darina and Silone were separately helpful. I went a number of times to the Piazza Bologna apartment and, over tea, discussed my problems. When I had almost finished a last revision, Darina had to go off to London, and I began to see Silone alone.

Often between a translator and the author a kind of subtle conflict can grow up. (In some cases, as with Italo Calvino, it was not all that subtle.) That competitiveness did not develop with Silone, but, all the same, I was a bit pleased with myself when I uncovered a couple of minor factual errors in the Italian text (Hitler's birthplace was given as Brunau, which I corrected to Braunau). I was also smugly amused to discover that a book by Napoleon III, which Silone referred to as *Rêveries poetiques*, was, in reality, entitled *Rêveries politiques*, a more plausible but less entertaining title. I pointed out Silone's mistake tactfully; he thanked me for the information and, in an apologetic tone, he murmured. "You see, I didn't have any libraries at hand." Ashamed of myself, I realized he had written the book in exile, perhaps in the Davos sanatorium or even in prison, under conditions that other writers would consider heroic.

But that same evening, as we went out to dinner, I had a glimpse of Silone's humorous side; in fact, I provoked it, insisting that he be my guest. To convince him to accept my invitation, I used a Jesuitical argument, explaining that paying the bill would be an excellent spiritual exercise for me. In the past, I had always considered myself poor, but recently I had been awarded a Fulbright fellowship, so I should stop thinking of myself as needy. And anyway I wanted to repay – or, at least, make a gesture of gratitude – after months of Silone's hospitality.

"Ah, but paying would be a splendid spiritual exercise for me, too," Silone, said, immediately picking up the spirit of the discussion. And, as he really had been educated by Jesuits (I, by mere Franciscans), his arguments were much more dazzling and elaborate – and funny – than mine. And, to cap them, as we finished the meal, he added: "And besides, this is an Abruzzese restaurant; they'd never let a guest pay." Actually, I'm not even sure they let him pay. I didn't see a bill.

When I settled into the Pensione Sieben where I stayed most of the winter of '47–'48, Alberto Moravia and Elsa Morante had only recently moved nearby, into the apartment that was to be their home for the rest of their marriage (and Elsa's chief residence, after the separation, almost until her death). It was in Via dell'Oca, an oddly broad, but short street, running the two or three blocks from Piazza del Popolo to the embankment at the Tiber. Though they had been married for over five years (and had been together for some time before the marriage), Alberto and Elsa had never had a proper house of their own. Now thanks to Alberto's foreign royalties and the film work he continued to do, they were able to fit out the house comfortably, with many sofas and easy chairs in white or cream slipcovers, with paintings on the walls (at this time largely by Moravia's sister Adriana Pincherle, later by Elsa's tragic infatuation Bill Morrow), and with a varying number of Siamese cats, long ruled over by the imperious Gatto Tit.

For Elsa, who had grown up in grimly respectable poverty, the Via dell'Oca house represented luxury; and, to crown this elegance, she engaged a cook. Thus – probably for the first time in her life – she gave dinner parties. For the rest, Alberto and Elsa almost never ate alone, even in earlier times, when they went every evening to some trattoria. Then, if you called up during the day to ask Alberto for supper, his characteristic reply was "come by around eight and we'll go out somewhere."

Sometimes – but very rarely – I'd be able to go out to dinner with just Alberto and Elsa. More often, I would find other friends with them, or indeed I would find strangers, anybody who had called either him or her in the course of the day to ask what they were doing for dinner. When that evening's group had collected, there would be a discussion, sometimes heated, about where to go. La Campana? Too crowded. Trastevere? Too noisy. Another trattoria was regularly rejected because, according to Elsa, the proprietor treated his cat badly. Sometimes we would end up at La Carbonara, in Campo de' Fiori, not because anyone was particularly fond of the place, but because there was always room. I remember those big impromptu dinners with mixed emotions. Moravia's circle of acquaintance included a few inevitable hangers-on, whom he treated, I felt, with more consideration than they deserved, especially since some of them – trying to assert a factitious independence – openly criticized him and belittled him. One particularly aggressive Communist art critic I found insufferable, and ill-luck sometimes placed me beside or opposite him at the long table, with Elsa and Moravia at separate, unbreachable distance from me.

But once in a while it would be just the three of us. Still, these more intimate nights were also fraught with risk. Speaking of Elsa once, some time after her death, Moravia – who continued to refer to her with affection and understanding long after their separation – said, "Elsa was profoundly ingiusta." "Unfair" is too mild a translation, and "unjust" sounds too juridical. What Moravia meant, I think, was "Elsa liked to deal low blows." And I have to agree with him. She could also be impulsive, and the blows could hit the innocent.

To make matters worse, Elsa – at least, in certain frequent moods – loved to quarrel, and to cast blame, almost always on Alberto: if the chosen restaurant happened to be closed, or the service was poor, or if a special dish was absent from that night's menu, the fault was somehow Alberto's. Elsa had a piercing voice that could cut, knife-like, through normal restaurant hum. Whether or not the deafness that later affected Alberto was already incipient in those days, he also tended to speak in a louder voice in restaurants. So their debates were, willy-nilly, overheard by fellow diners.

There is one restaurant in Rome – *Romolo* at Porta Settimiana – that I still enter with hesitation, though the embarrassing argument must have taken place fifty years ago. Unlikely as it now seems, the argument, as I recall, was about motherhood or perhaps about Southern Italian peasants. What I indelibly remember is Elsa's culminating retort: "Don't talk nonsense, Alberto, in the south peasant mothers masturbate their children to put them to sleep at night." The crucial verb was uttered in a shrill, loud cry, which seemed to echo interminably beneath the low vaults of the restaurant ceiling. The other diners had long since suspended their conversations in order to listen to ours. We ate the rest of our meal surrounded by silence and by the total attention of everyone in the place, customer or waiter or host. Only Elsa remained supremely unaffected.

Often I saw Alberto and Elsa separately, as did all their friends (for that matter, each also had separate friends, whom they saw on their own). It was easy to run into Alberto on the street, not only because Rome was small in those days and we lived in the same neighborhood, but also because Alberto was an indefatigable walker, his lame, rollicking gait recognizable blocks off. For a long period, when he was suffering from some form of sciatica, he took long, therapeutic walks for hours every afternoon on doctor's orders. When you encountered him, he would invariably ask you to accompany him for a while, as walking seemed to stimulate his conversation (not that it needed stimulation: it flowed naturally, with fascinating shifts and turns, unexpected aperçus).

In those immediate post-war years, Rome was a walker's paradise. There was barely any traffic, and the cluttering crowds of tourists were yet to return. At that time, American tourists were still afraid of drinking the water or of running out of toilet-paper. Often, in the course of that first winter, when I went to see the Sistine ceiling or the Caravaggios in San Luigi dei Francesi, I would find myself totally alone.

Taking walks was also a recognized convivial activity. At lunch-time, on a fine day, a friend might call up and suggest a walk later in the afternoon, as he or she might invite you for tea or a cocktail. One particularly enjoyable walking companion was Elena Croce, whose quirkish conversation (never a received idea) and irreverent opinions made the walks such fun that often I remained unaware of the streets we passed, the monuments, the genre scenes that are still an integral part of Roman outdoor life.

For one season, while she was at the American Academy, I went on walks with Eleanor Clark. Either I would take a bus up to the Janiculum and we would stroll among Risorgimento memories, the places where Bixio and Manara fought, perhaps where Jessie White or Margaret Fuller tended the wounded. Or we would walk downhill, to follow the curving alleys of Trastevere. But these walks were never aimless, and our attention never flagged: Eleanor had a list of things to be seen that day, and she ticked off the palazzo or the church or the historic spot. Later, when I first read Rome and a Villa, I recognized some of the ticked-off places, now caught in a double light: the illumination of Eleanor's recorded perceptions and the warm recollection of sharing with her the external experience if not necessarily also her intellectual epiphany.

I don't remember ever sight-seeing with Elsa, though any reader of her novel History will realize that she knew her native city stone by stone. But, in the early years of our friendship, I remember many occasions where I saw her alone – or, rather, without Moravia. For a time, around 1950, I was lent an elegant apartment near Piazza di Spagna, and there I also could do some entertaining at last.

I quickly learned the protocol to adopt in inviting Elsa. The important thing NOT to do was issue a double invitation. You were never to say, "Could you and Alberto come – ?" Even the use of the plural voi was a grave infraction of Elsa's personal rules. Sometimes Elsa's reply would be a simple no. More often she would say curtly, "Ah, you want Alberto? Call him at –" And she would supply the number of his studio.

The proper course was to invite Elsa: Can you – tu – come for dinner on Thursday? Almost invariably Elsa would accept, and set a time. In later years, she would perhaps inform you of the restrictions of her diet, never the same on successive occasions. Then, when all was agreed, you could venture, in as offhand a tone as possible: "If Alberto's free, tell him to join us." "I'll tell him," she would reply, audibly dubious. But then Alberto never failed to show up; or, if he really couldn't come, he would telephone separately and explain.

Elsa, socially, had a low boredom threshold. One evening, in my elegant borrowed apartment, she discovered a complete run of Connaissance des Arts in a living-room bookcase. For the entire evening, without a word to any of the other guests (or to me), she sat on the floor in a corner and, with almost scholarly attention, went through one number of the review after another, dutifully reading the texts as well as studying the illustrations.

But, on another occasion in the same apartment, when boredom threatened, she reacted in an entirely different way. She took charge of the guests – most of them old friends – and invented a series of guessing games, bouts rimés, the anti-social game of the tower, enjoying herself hugely but also inspiring the others. I had a moment of overweening pride when a verse of mine won her praise. There was this childish side of Elsa, rarely allowed to shine forth, yet irresistible when given free rein.

The child-Elsa could also be naughty; and like other naughty children, she liked to cause discomfiture. For this the tower game was ideal: the game consisted simply of obliging the player to imagine him (or her) self on a high tower with two people one of whom he had to push off. Elsa would insist on dreadful choices (herself? or Alberto?), always among people present at the table; and she would become truly angry at any waffling on the part of her victim.

At one of her dinners, she had invited Marco Visconti, a younger cousin of Luchino's, with his fiancée, the only other woman present, who was meeting Elsa for the first time. Wilfully, Elsa directed the conversation to sex and, specifically, to Lesbianism.

"I know, I know," she said, "some people say that I'm attracted to members of my own sex. Absolutely false. I do not like women. What's more, I don't like men who like women."

The three or four male guests exchanged impassive looks and tried hard not to glance at Moravia, the most impassive of all.

Elsa answered the unasked question. "Yes, even Alberto. Though I know he hasn't had any such experience... still he would have a strong tendency."

Moravia's blank astonishment made all of us laugh, and enabled someone to change the subject.

An excerpt from *Open City: Seven Writers in Postwar Rome,* edited by William Weaver, published by Steerforth Press of Hanover, NH. ©William Weaver.

William Murray

William Murray wrote regularly on Italy for the *New Yorker.* The following piece – one of many from his now out-of-print collection of Italian writings, *Italy. The Fatal Gift,* records his early years living in the city at the start of the 1950s – in particular a Campo de' Fiori that perhaps no longer exists but is still eminently recognizable today.

Voices

I don't think I began to understand Rome, and my own involvement in Italian life, until I moved to the apartment on the fourth floor of a run-down Renaissance palazzo at one end of a piazza called the Campo de' Fiori. The piazza is in the middle of the old papal city, surrounded by narrow, twisting little streets that thread their way among blocks of ancient houses dating back, many of them, to the fourteenth century. The rooms of my apartment were huge, with beamed and frescoed ceilings, thick walls, and tiled floors, and there was a terrace, awash in flowers and trellised ivy. I slept, or tried to, in a front room with a large window looking out over the piazza. At first, I was startled by the noise. There were lulls, but never long periods of uninterrupted silence. In the very early morning hours, I would sometimes be wakened by the explosive buzzing of a motor scooter, the rumbling of cart wheels over the cobblestones, the crash of some unbelievably heavy objects onto the pavement. Mostly, however, even at night, the sounds consisted of voices, individual and concerted, blending into and succeeding each other in a never ending choral composition of pure cacophony. It was astonishing.

Actually the sheer volume of sound at certain periods of the day didn't surprise me. I had known all along that the Campo de' Fiori was the site, six days a week, of a large open-air market. I would get up in the morning and open my shutters to look down over a sea of gray canvas umbrellas sheltering perhaps as many as two hundred stands. A great crowd of shoppers ambled and pushed down narrow aisles between rows of heaped edibles of all kinds. Directly beneath my window alone, at the northwestern end, of the piazza, I counted thirteen vendors of vegetables and several selling preserves, cheeses, and sausages. On my way across the piazza to a café where I often had breakfast and read the morning paper, I would pass pushcarts of fresh vegetables piled into great green mounds, tables buried under soft white and brown mushrooms, pyramids of cherries, apples, oranges sliced to reveal their dripping interiors, pears, apricots, bunches of white and green asparagus, enormous beets and onions, tiny round potatoes, huge heads of fresh lettuce, green and red peppers, artichokes, tomatoes, carrots and wild strawberries. Along one whole side of the piazza stretched a seemingly endless line of butcher stands, behind which the butchers themselves, in soiled white smocks, wielded their cleavers and large flat knives under the plucked bodies of chickens and the bloody carcasses of of lambs and kids hanging in rows from steel hooks. There were also bunches of pigs' feet, chunks of tripe, chains of plump sausages. At the far end of the piazza, the fishmongers presided over damp boxes and basket's of the day's catch – fish of all shapes, flaming red, blue, and silver, soft masses of squid and small octopuses, mountains of white-and-gray minnows with tiny, dead bright-button eyes, dozens of small, dark-red clawless Mediterranean lobsters. And scattered along the periphery of these crowded rows of comestibles were still other stands, selling pots and pans, dishes, glassware, cheap toys, shoes, and clothing. The stone face of the piazza, roughly rectangular and roughly the same size as football field, diappeared every morning of the week but Sundays and holidays under umbrellas, the tons of merchandise, the shuffling feet of thousands of shoppers.

Many other voices besides those of the market invaded my room. The most insistent and violent one belonged, I guessed, to a woman in her thirties. She lived in one of the apartments near the corner of Via dei Cappellari, somewhere behind the lines of laundry that hung, dripping relentlessly, across the street. Her voice was shrill and hard and piercing: it would come soaring across the piazza from behind the wall of laundry like a battle cry from the ranks of an army advancing behind flapping pennants. "Ah Massimo-o-o" it would scream. "Massimo-o-o, where the hell are you, you dirty onkey? Get the hell up here right this minute! Massimo-o-o! If you aren't home in two minutes, you little bastard, I'll break you head! Massimo-o-o imbecile! You hear me? Get right up here now before I come down and break your arm! Ah Massimo-o-o! Massino-o-o! Cretino! Imbecille! A' vie' qua-a-a!" These tirades often became so vituperative, menacing and foul-mouthed that I'd find myself wondering how the woman could keep it up. I'd go to the window and gaze down into the piazza, hoping to spot Massimo among the hordes of children swarming through the market or, on Sunday, around the base of Bruno's statue. The voice would scream on, threatening mayhem and the vengeance of heaven on the object of its wrath, but no little boy would separate himself from his fellows and go running across the cobblestones. At least, I never noticed him.

Massimo apparently did hear, however, and eventually he would come home. The voice would cease its screaming imprecations and remain silent for some time. After a while, though, I'd hear it again – usually around two o'clock in the afternoon, when the market had closed up and the commercial uproar had abated somewhat. The intensity and depth of emotion would still be evident in the voice, but the tone had altered dramatically. "Massimo! Massimo!" I would hear it shout. "Treasure of my heart, flower of my life, why don't you eat? Eat, eat! You want to die of hunger? You want your mother to perish of grief? You want your papa to die of shame, to tell me I don't cook like I used to? My love, my sweet, my angel, have another tomato, eat your bread, drink your milk. Eat, eat, love of my life! Here, Mama will give you a big hug and a kiss! You eat now! Massimo-o-o! Tesoro! Amore! Mangia, che ti fa bene! Cocco! Angelo!"

I tried often to imagine what Massimo looked like. I saw a small boy of seven or eight with dirty knees and scuffed shoes, black hair and red eyes, red cheeks, and sturdy shoulders, but too fat for his age. I'd see him climb the stairs to the sounds of threats and fury, bursting in to be met by a hug and a light cuff and a mound of steaming spaghetti. Who, anywhere around the Campo, would not have heard of him? At the newsstand, I once idly enquired about him, but the young man who sold me my newspaper couldn't identify him, either. "Ah, Signore, it could be any one of them," he said, indicating with a flick of his hand a crowd of urchins then engaged in kicking a soccer ball around the piazza. "Masimo? A common enough name. And here everyone shouts from the windows all the time. Do you not notice?"

This young man's name was Remo. He and his family had been tending their stand, on the corner of Via dei Baullari, for thirty-five years. They would take turns sitting like benevolent gnomes inside a very small wooden booth festrooned with magazines and newspapers. Nothing escaped their vigilant attention. Remo rarely smiled, and he thought that life in the piazza had deteriorated a good deal since he first began to observe its goings-on. "Ah Signore," he said to me one day, "you like this market? It is not what it was. No indeed it isn't. On Saturdays you had to fight your way into the piazza, that's what I remember. Now – ". He shrugged. "Now, it's nothing. People are moving out. The ones who were brought up in this quarter, they do not like the old palazzi. When they have money, they move away. The rich and the foreigners are moving into the buildings now, but they don't buy in the market. They go to the supermarkets in the Parioli – drive all the way out there rather than buy in the piazza. No, it's not what it was." He was unhappy, too, about the crime in the area. "Dirty people," he said. "Gentaccia, that's what they are. The quarter is full of them. Every thief in town lives here. Do you have a car?" I told him I didn't.

"That's lucky for you," he said. "It would be stolen. Don't trust anyone you meet in the piazza. Anyone can see you're an American." At the time, I had seen no evidence of crime in the piazza, and I paid no attention to Remo's advice.

One night at about 2am I was awakened by the sound of loud masculine laughter and conversation outside my window. I looked down and saw a group of men directly below. They were talking and joking, making no effort to keep from disturbing the neighbourhood. I shouted down at them to keep quiet. One of them looked up briefly, but otherwise paid no attention. Their hoarse, merry voices continued to resound in the night air. After about ten minutes more of this, I went to the kitchen and cam back with a large pot full of water. I asked them one more time to keep quiet, but I was ignored. I then leaned out of the window and poured cold water on their heads. Bellowing and cursing, they quickly scattered out and regrouped beyond the fountain, out in the piazza and well out of range. Through the slats in my shutterd I saw them conferring angrily and occasionally pointing up toward my window. Slightly uneasy, I went back to bed.

The next morning, when I stepped out into the piazza, I was greeted by a young tough in wrinkled slacks and a torn jersey. He was unshaven, with close-set eyes and a snarl of oily-looking curls, and he had evidently been lounging against the wall of my building, waiting for me. "Hey you," he said hoarsely. "Hey, are you the one who threw water on us last night?"

The market was in full swing and the piazza crowded with people. I made up my mind not to be intimidated. "Yes," I said. "You woke me up."

The youth shook his head gravely. "That was a very stupid thing to do."

"Listen," I said. "I have some rights. I asked you twice to keep quiet and you paid no attention. You have no right to wake everybody up."

"And you have no right to throw water on people."

This seemed a rather weak rejoinder to me, so I pressed my luck a little. "I could have called the police, you know."

The tough smiled, revealing a bright row of gold teeth. "No, no," he said, shaking his head. "You would not do that. No one in this quarter would do such a stupid thing. You have to live here – no?"

"I don't live here all the time," I said. "Besides, I don't like to be threatened."

The tough smiled again and spread his hands out wide. "Threatening you? Who is threatening you, Signore? I? I merely wish to protest against being doused with water in the middle of the night, that's all. That's not unreasonable, is it?"

"Mario, introduce me to the gentleman," I heard someone say.

I turned, and was confronted by a short, stocky, bald roman in a rumpled but well-tailored brown suit. He had a round, affable face with large brown eyes and a strong, prominent, straight nose. He was smiling broadly. "Mario does not know my name," I said, and I introduced myself.

"Of course he does," the new arrival declared. "You are the American who lives on the fourth floor. Everyone knows who you are. I myself have often seen you in the piazza. Pleased to meet you. My name is Domenico. My friends call me Memmo."

"Were you also in the piazza last night?" I asked.

Memmo laughed. "Alas, yes," he admitted, "Luckily, you missed me. Mario, here, was soaked. That probably accounts for his sour face." He turned to Mario and clapped him roughly on the shoulder. "Hey Mario, cheer up! The bath did you good, eh? The first one you've had in weeks."

Mario made an effort to smile, but it did not seem entirely genuine. I concentrated on Memmo. "I'm sorry about it," I said. "But I was tired and wanted to get some sleep. You were directly under my window, and I asked you all several times to be quiet."

"Right," said Memmo. "Quite right. I think we will not chat there again. However, caro Signore" – he took my arm confidentially and pulled me a few feet off to one side – "don't do such a thing again. For your own good, Signore. No one would harm you, of course – Dio Mio, an American! But Mario and his friends can play such tricks, Signore! The apartment is so full of beautiful things. I have not seen it, but I know that it is. Apartments can be broken into, Signore, and even the most beautiful object can be made to disappear. What is the sense in playing tricks on people like Mario, eh?"

I looked back at Mario, who was still standing by the entrance to the building and regarding me sourly. "And you?" I asked. "What about you?"

"I?" he said. "Oh, I'm a friend of Mario's. He runs little errands for me. I have a shop here, just around the corner. You've passed it many times. Electrical equipment – radios, iceboxes, toasters, things like that. You've seen my shop, haven't you?"

I said that I had passed it often.

"Well, of course you have," Memmo said. "It's a very well-known store.

Everyone in the neighbourhood knows me. Ask anyone."

"It's very kind of you to warn me," I said.

Memmo looked astonished. "Warn you?" he said. "Signore, I would not think of presuming to warn you. Still, it is important that you know how things are here on the piazza, eh?"

"Yes, I understand," I said. "Thanks very much."

"Forget it," Memmo said. "Forget the whole thing. And don't worry about Mario. Nothing will happen. Come and see me in the shop. Drop in any time – right there, just around the corner." He shook my hand and departed in the direction of his store. As he went, I saw him nod almost imperceptibly to Mario, who went off with him, not casting so much as a backward glance in my direction.

A couple of days later, I did drop in on Memmo. From the outside, the store looked like any other small shop dealing in electrical housewares, but since my encounter with Mario and Memmo and our oblique conversation, I had become curious about it. When I stepped inside the door, I discovered that the place was all but empty of merchandise. The window display featured a cheap washing machine and a secondhand refrigerator, but except for a couple of toasters and a small radio or two the store looked cleaned out. Mario and a couple of other shady-looking men lounged against the walls, smoking American cigarettes, while Memmo sat behind a small wooden desk. He had been talking into the telephone, but he hung up immediately when I came in. "Ah, buon giorno, buon giorno," he said, coming out from behind his desk and rubbing his hands briskly together. "How nice to see you! Thanks for dropping in."

"Business seems to be a little slow," I said.

"On the contrary," Memmo answered, smiling broadly. "Business could not be better."

"You've sold everything in the shop, then?"

"Well, not quite," Memmo said. "Come back here."

Memmo led me back to his desk, opened a top drawer, and pulled out a large, flat box full of Swiss wristwatches. "Look at this," he said, holding one up by the strap. "Fifty thousand lire, this watch costs. I sell it for thirty. Would you like it?"

I told Memmo that I already had a watch.

He put the watch back in the drawer and closed it. "Well, then, how about this?" he opened another drawer and showed me a pile of cigarette lighters. "Or these?" He produced boxes of cufflinks, tie clasps, studs, men's and women's bracelets, earrings, electric razors, razor blades, small bottles of cheap cologne, key rings, charms. Finally, with an elaborate little flourish of one hand, he opened still another drawer and took out a long, thin, expensive-looking case. "Perhaps there is a lady in your life?" He opened the box to reveal a handsome pearly necklace. "For you," he said, "for my friend the American, only a hundred thousand lire, eh?"

"No, thanks," I said. "I can't afford it."

Memmo sighed, cheerfully stuffed the box back into the drawer, and closed it.

"You seem to be selling everything here," I said.

Memmo smiled and shrugged. "Well, Signore, I believe in floating with the traffic, eh?" What you Americans call, I believe, the laws of supply and demand."

"How can you afford to sell these things so cheaply?" I asked.

"Signore, we have our own direct sources of supply," Memmo said. "We eliminate the middleman, as you would say. We import everything directly. You understand?"

"I think so," I said.

After that, I became increasingly aware of Memmo and his boys. Mario and half a dozen other young toughs strolled in and out of the shop, and several times I noticed them peddling objects through the marketplace. Once, I found Mario and a friend presiding at the corner of Via dei Baullari over a large stack of shoeboxes. They were selling sandals for five hundred lire a pair – a ridiculously low price. Occasionally, they would operate out of the back of a panel truck, selling everything from shirts to hardware. I never saw Memmo anywhere except inside his store, usually on the phone or in deep conversation with one of his young men.

One day, at the newsstand, I asked Remo about Memmo and his friends. Remo glanced sharply at me, then looked around to see if we were alone. "Stay away from them, Signore," he said in an undertone. "They are no good, that bunch. I let everything I hear go in one ear and out the other. It is better that way. But I tell you this Signore – the police drop in there from time to time, and it is not to pass the hours chatting, Memmo wasn't around for a long time last year, and that Mafrio – you know him?"

I said that I did.

"A bad one," Remo said. "He was a carpenter. Then he killed a man one day just because the fellow clapped him too hard on the back, or something. He did three and a half years. A hood, *un vero teppista*. Don't have anything to do with them."

"But who are they? Are they from around here?"

"All from this quarter, Signore, every one of them," Remo said sadly. "They give it a bad name. All over Rome, people say the Campo de' Fiori is a den of thieves. Memmo and his crowd – they're responsible for that. It's really too bad."

An excerpt from *Italy: The Fatal Gift*, reprinted with the kind permission of the author. ©William Murray.

Books

There have been an enormous number of books published about Rome over the years, both in English, and of course in Italian, and the list below is inevitably extremely selective, concentrating on the odd travelogue, key texts on history and art, and on works of fiction that might be instructive – or fun – to read while you're in Rome. Particular favourites are marked with the ⊡ symbol. To help find the books, we've listed the publisher, with the British publisher first, and the US publisher second, except when the publisher is the same in both territories, when we've only mentioned it once; where a book is published in only one territory, we've said so.

History, art and architecture

Jerome Carcopino *Daily Life in Ancient Rome* (Yale, US). Originally published in 1941, and consistently in print since, Carcopino's book is a classic, bringing to life the beliefs, social life and customs of ordinary Romans during the first two centuries AD, at the height of the Roman Empire.

Amanda Claridge *Oxford Archeological Guides: Rome.* (OUP). A well-conceived and excellently written concise guide to the archeology of the ancient city – a good investment if this is your particular area of interest.

Christopher Duggan *A Concise History of Italy* (CUP). The best all-round history of the Italian nation that you can buy, concise and well-written, covering everything from the fall of the Roman empire to Unification and beyond. For a more accessible, though less portable, alternative, there is also Oxford's *Illustrated History of Italy* edited by George Holmes.

⊡ **Edward Gibbon** *The History of the Decline and Fall of the Roman Empire* (Penguin). If you can't manage all six volumes, this abridged version is your best chance to read this classic text, covering the period from the second century AD to the fall of Constantinople in 1453, which was conceived amidst the ruins of the Roman Forum in the latter part of the eighteenth century. If the shortened version isn't enough

for you, then check out Everyman which publishes the whole thing in three volumes.

⊡ **Christopher Hibbert** *Rome: The Bio-graphy of a City* (Penguin). Simply put, the most entertaining and accessible historical introduction to Rome that you can buy – which is perhaps no more than you would expect from this most prolific of popular historians.

⊡ **Tom Holland** *Rubicon* (Abacus/Anchor). Tom Holland's readable book pinpoints a specific but crucial period of Roman history, beginning with the Roman republic at the height of its greatness and charting its decline, starting in around 140 BC and ending with the death of Augustus in AD 14. Good narrative history, documenting a fascinating era.

Ingrid D. Rowland *The Culture of the High Renaissance: Ancients and Moderns in Sixteenth-Century Rome* (CUP). A relatively expensive but highly regarded and scholarly evocation of the high Renaissance in Rome – looking not only at the art and architecture of the period, but also at its economics, culture and sociology.

Charles L. Stinger *The Renaissance in Rome* (Indiana UP). The best-value book to focus exclusively on the Renaissance period in Rome, documenting the rehabilitation of the city under the papacy.

Giorgio Vasari *The Lives of the Artists* (OUP). There is no better background work on the artists of the Renaissance, written by a contemporary and correspondent of his subjects, who include Raphael, Michelangelo, and others less relevant to Rome. Available in a very readable English translation.

★ **Margaret Visser** *The Geometry of Love* (Penguin/North Point Press). This book is basically an extended tour of the church of Sant'Agnese fuori le Mura, and is an absorbing study not just of the building and its history but also of the iconography and architecture of all Christian churches. Visser looks at things that are often taken for granted when looking at churches, and gets deep into the meaning of why they are as they are, as well as digging back into the history of Sant'Agnese specifically and the ancient times that created it.

Travel and impressions

Elizabeth Bowen *A Time in Rome* (Vintage). Though written in the 1960s, Bowen's book endures because it is so engaging, and because it summarizes so well the longevity and continuity of Rome.

★ **Tobias Jones** *The Dark Heart of Italy*. (Faber/North Point Press). Jones's book is immediately different from other books on Italy because it's about how Italians live now – not what happened centuries ago. As such, it's a good book to take with you on any Italian trip, focusing as it does on football, politics, terrorism, religion – all the things that surround you when in Rome or indeed any other Italian city. A refreshing guide to the sleaze, corruption and dysfunctionality that make up the contemporary nation.

H.V. Morton *A Traveller in Rome*. Like all Morton's books, this is a marvellously personal stroll around the sights, reflecting on history, architecture and culture. Rather dated, and currently out of print, but it should be relatively easy to get hold of.

William Murray *Italy: The Fatal Gift*. Out of print, but worth trying to get hold of for its perceptive essays on history and contemporary Italian life and culture, especially with regard to Rome, where Murray lived for many years – first as a child, then as an aspiring opera singer and later as a writer and journalist, filing regular pieces for the *New Yorker*. He writes with flair and enthusiasm, and, best of all, knows the city intimately. Try also *City of the Soul* (Crown Journeys, US), Murray's latest slim volume of essays, walks and musings on the city.

Literature

Lyndsey Davies *Shadows in Bronze* (Arrow/Ballantine). Davies's second novel is perhaps the best introduction to the ancient Roman thrillers in which she specializes, following the doings of her ancient Roman sleuth, Marcus Didius Falco, during the period of the emperor Vespasian. Like later volumes, it has pace and humour, and is creditably well researched and nicely written. In the UK, *Falco on his Metal* (Arrow) incorporates three Falco novels, and as such makes for a good sample of Davies's work.

★ **Robert Graves** *I Claudius; Claudius the God* (Penguin /Vintage). Graves's two-volume pseudo-autobiography is perhaps the definitive dramatized account of Rome in the early years of its decline – and deservedly so: both books are a thumping good read.

Conn Iggulden *The Gates of Rome* (HarperCollins/Dell). A tub-thumping historical romp that documents the rites of passage of the young Julius Caesar to a backdrop of the turmoil of the last decades of the Republic – notably the wars with Mithridates and the civil war that led to Sulla's rise to power.

Allan Massie *Augustus; Tiberius; Caesar, Caligula* (Sceptre/Carroll & Graff). Massie's series of novels aspires to re-create the Roman empire at its height through the imagined memoirs of its key figures. Massie takes himself rather seriously, and sometimes his characters don't quite come to life; but his research is impeccable, and these novels offer a wonderfully palatable way into the minutiae of the era.

Alberto Moravia *A Woman of Rome* (Steerforth Press, US). Probably the most pre-eminent post-war Roman novelist, Moravia uses the Rome of the Mussolini era as a delicate backdrop for this detached yet compassionate tale of a Roman model and prostitute. See also *Roman Tales* (OUP), a varied collection of short stories that has the lives of ordinary Romans of the 1950s as its thread.

Margaret Mazzantini *Don't Move* (Chatto & Windus). This intense psychological novel of mid-life crisis, sex and obsession in Rome was a massive best-seller in Italy. The city and its outskirts form a bleak, rain-soaked backdrop.

Iain Pears *The Raphael Affair; The Bernini Bust; The Titian Committee* (HarperCollins/Berkeley). Pears writes thrillers with an art historical theme, of which these, primarily Rome-based examples, make great holiday reading. Plenty of local colour, not to mention fast-paced art-world intrigue concerning robbery, forgery and general skullduggery.

Stephen Saylor *The House of the Vestal; Arms of Nemesis; A Mist of Prophecies; The Judgement of Caesar;* (Constable & Robinson/St Martin's Press). Light, occasionally amusing detective yarns set in the days of the Roman republic, in which Saylor's fictional detective, Giordanius the Finder, solves mysteries with consummate ease.

John Varriano (ed.) *A Literary Companion to Rome* (John Murray/St Martin's Press). Arranged as a series of walking tours, this picks out the best of the many observations made about the city over the years. Entertaining in itself, but also a taster for many other writers and books on Rome that you may not have yet come across.

William Weaver (ed.) *Open City: Seven Writers in Postwar Rome* (Steerforth Press, US). An anthology of pieces by some of the best modern Italian novelists – Bassani, Silone, Moravia, Ginzburg, among others – selected and with an introduction by one of the most eminent post-war Italian translators.

Marguerite Yourcenar *Memoirs of Hadrian* (Penguin/FSG). Yourcenar's slow-moving, reflective narrative, most of it in the form of letters to his nephew, Marcus Aurelius, details the main events of the emperor Hadrian's rule, documenting at once the Roman Empire at its height and the very human anxieties of perhaps its wisest and most accomplished leader. See also Yourcenar's conceptual Roman novel, *A Coin in Nine Hands* (Harvill, UK).

Language

Language

Italian

The ability to speak English confers prestige in Italy, and there's often no shortage of people willing to show off their knowledge, especially in Rome. But using at least some Italian, however tentatively, can mark you out from the masses in a city used to hordes of tourists, and having a little more can open up the city no end. The words and phrases below should help you master the basics. If you want a decent phrasebook, look no further than the *Rough Guide Italian Phrasebook*, which packs a huge amount of phrases and vocabulary into a handy dictionary format. There are lots of good pocket dictionaries – the Collins range represents probably the best all-round choice, with their Gem or Pocket formats perfect for travelling purposes.

Pronunciation

Italian is one of the easiest European languages to learn, especially if you already have a smattering of French or Spanish. Easiest of all is the **pronunciation**, since every word is spoken exactly as it's written, and usually enunciated with exaggerated, open-mouthed clarity. All Italian words are stressed on the penultimate syllable unless an accent (´ or `) denotes otherwise. The only difficulties you're likely to encounter are the few consonants that are different from English:

c before e or i is pronounced as in church, while **ch** before the same vowels is hard, as in **cat**.

sci or **sce** are pronounced as in **sh**eet and **sh**elter respectively.

The same goes with **g** – soft before e or i, as in **g**eranium; hard before h, as in **g**arlic.

gn has the ni sound of onion.

gl in Italian is softened to something like li in English, as in stallion.

h is not aspirated, as in **h**onour.

When **speaking** to strangers, the third person is the polite form (ie lei instead of tu for "you"); using the second person is a mark of disrespect or stupidity. It's also worth remembering that Italians don't use "please" and "thank you" half as much as we do: it's all implied in the tone, though, if in doubt, err on the polite side.

Words and phrases

Basics

Good morning	**Buon giorno**	Hello/goodbye	**Ciao** (informal;
Good afternoon			to strangers use
/evening	**Buona sera**		phrases above)
Good night	**Buona notte**	Goodbye	**Arrivederci**

Yes	Si	Let's go!	Andiamo!
No	No	In the morning	Di mattina
Please	Per favore	In the afternoon	Nel pomeriggio
Thank you (very much)	Grázie (molte/mille grazie)	In the evening	Di sera
		Here/There	Qui/La
You're welcome	Prego	Good/Bad	Buono/Cattivo
All right/that's OK	Va bene	Big/Small	Grande/Píccolo
How are you? (informal/formal)	Come stai/sta?	Cheap/Expensive	Económico/Caro
		Early/Late	Presto/Ritardo
I'm fine	Bene	Hot/Cold	Caldo/Freddo
Do you speak English?	Parla inglese?	Near/Far	Vicino/Lontano
I don't understand	Non ho capito	Quickly/Slowly	Velocemente /Lentamente
I don't know	Non lo so		
Excuse me	Mi scusi/Prego	With/Without	Con/Senza
Excuse me	Permesso (in a crowd)	More/Less	Più/Meno
		Enough, no more	Basta
I'm sorry	Mi dispiace	Mr/Mrs/Miss	Signor/Signora/ Signorina
I'm here on holiday	Sono qui in vacanza		
I'm British/Irish	Sono britannico /irlandese	Entrance/Exit	Entrata/Uscita
		Free entrance	Ingresso líbero
American	americana	Gentlemen/Ladies	Signori/Signore
Australian	australiana	No smoking	Vietato fumare
a New Zealander	neozelandese	WC/Bathroom	Gabinetto/Il bagno
Today	Oggi	Open/Closed	Aperto/Chiuso
Tomorrow	Domani	Closed for restoration	Chiuso per restauro
Day after tomorrow	Dopodomani	Closed for holidays	Chiuso per ferie
Yesterday	Ieri	Pull/Push	Tirare/Spingere
Now	Adesso	Cash desk	Cassa
Later	Più tardi	Go, walk	Avanti
Wait a minute!	Aspetta!	Stop, halt	Alt

Accommodation

Hotel	Albergo	hot/cold water	acqua calda/freddo
Is there a hotel nearby?	C'è un albergo qui vicino?	How much is it?	Quanto costa?
		It's expensive	È caro
Do you have a room ...	Ha una cámera ...	Is breakfast included?	È compresa la prima colazione?
for one/two/three person/people	per una/due/tre persona/e	Do you have anything cheaper?	Ha niente che costa di meno?
for one/two/three night/s	per una/due/tre notte	Full/half board	Pensione completa /mezza pensione
for one/two week/s	per una/due settimana/e	Can I see the room?	Posso vedere la cámera?
with a double bed	con un letto matrimoniale	I'll take it	La prendo
with a shower/bath	con una doccia /un bagno	I'd like to book a room	Vorrei prenotare una cámera
with a balcony	con una terrazza	I have a booking	Ho una prenotazione

Questions and directions

Where?	Dove?	How far is it to … ?	Cuant'è lontano a …?
(Where is/where are … ?)	(Dov'è/Dove sono … ?)	Can you tell me when to get off?	Mi può dire scendere alla fermata giusta?
When?	Quando?		
What? (What is it?)	Cosa? (Cos'è?)	What time does it open?	A che ora apre?
How much/many?	Quanto/Quanti?	What time does it close?	A che ora chiude?
Why?	Perché?	How much does it cost	Quanto costa?
It is/there is (Is it/is there … ?)	C'e … ?	(… do they cost?)	(… Quanto cóstano?)
What time is it?	Che ora è/Che ore sono?	What's it called in Italian?	Come si chiama in italiano?
How do I get to … ?	Come arrivo a … ?		

Numbers

1	uno	20	venti
2	due	21	ventuno
3	tre	22	ventidue
4	quattro	30	trenta
5	cinque	40	quaranta
6	sei	50	cinquanta
7	sette	60	sessanta
8	otto	70	settanta
9	nove	80	ottanta
10	dieci	90	novanta
11	undici	100	cento
12	dodici	101	centuno
13	tredici	110	centodieci
14	quattordici	200	duecento
15	quindici	500	cinquecento
16	sedici	1,000	mille
17	diciassette	5,000	cinquemila
18	diciotto	10,000	diecimila
19	diciannove	50,000	cinquantamila

Menu reader

Basics and snacks

Aceto	Vinegar	Cioccolato	Chocolate
Aglio	Garlic	Formaggio	Cheese
Biscotti	Biscuits	Frittata	Omelette
Burro	Butter	Marmellata	Jam
Caramelle	Sweets	Olio	Oil

Olive	Olives	**Uova**	Eggs
Pane	Bread	**Yogurt**	Yoghurt
Pepe	Pepper	**Zúcchero**	Sugar
Riso	Rice	**Zuppa**	Soup
Sale	Salt		

The first course (*il primo*)

Brodo	Clear broth	**Pastina in brodo**	Pasta pieces in clear broth
Farfalle	Butterfly-shaped pasta		
Fettuccine	Narrow pasta ribbons	**Penne**	Smaller version of rigatoni
Gnocchi	Small potato and dough dumplings	**Rigatoni**	Large, grooved tubular pasta
Maccheroni	Macaroni (tubular pasta)	**Risotto**	Cooked rice dish, with sauce
Minestrina	Clear broth with small pasta shapes	**Stracciatella**	Broth with egg
Minestrone	Thick vegetable soup	**Tagliatelle**	Pasta ribbons, another word for fettucine
Pasta al forno	Pasta baked with minced meat, eggs, tomato and cheese	**Tortellini**	Rings of pasta, stuffed with meat or cheese
Pasta e fagioli	Pasta with beans	**Vermicelli**	Thin spaghetti ("little worms")

... and pasta sauce (*salsa*)

Amatriciana	Cubed bacon and tomato sauce	**Peperoncino**	Olive oil, garlic and fresh chillies
Arrabbiata	Spicy tomato sauce, with chillies ("Angry")	**Pesto**	Sauce with ground basil, garlic and pine nuts
Bolognese	Meat sauce	**Pomodoro**	Tomato sauce
Burro	Butter	**Puttanesca**	Tomato, anchovy, olive oil and oregano ("Whorish")
Carbonara	Cream, ham and beaten egg		
Funghi	Mushroom	**Ragù**	Meat sauce
Panna	Cream	**Vóngole**	Sauce with clams
Parmigiano	Parmesan cheese		

The second course (*il secondo*): meat (*carne*) ...

Agnello	Lamb	**Coniglio**	Rabbit
Bistecca	Steak	**Costolette**	Cutlet, chop
Carpaccio	Slices of raw beef	**Fégato**	Liver
Cervella	Brain, usually calves'	**Maiale**	Pork
Cinghiale	Wild boar	**Manzo**	Beef

Ossobuco	Shin of veal	Salsiccia	Sausage
Pancetta	Bacon	Saltimbocca	Veal with ham
Pollo	Chicken	Spezzatino	Stew
Polpette	Meatballs	Trippa	Tripe
Rognoni	Kidneys	Vitello	Veal

... fish (*pesce*) and shellfish (*crostacei*)

Acciughe	Anchovies	Merluzzo	Cod
Anguilla	Eel	Ostriche	Oysters
Aragosta	Lobster	Pesce spada	Swordfish
Baccalà	Dried salted cod	Polpo	Octopus
Calamari	Squid	Rospo	Monkfish
Céfalo	Grey mullet	Sampiero	John Dory
Cozze	Mussels	Sarde	Sardines
Déntice	Sea bream	Sógliola	Sole
Gamberetti	Shrimps	Tonno	Tuna
Gámberi	Prawns	Trota	Trout
Granchio	Crab	Vóngole	Clams

Vegetables (*contorni*), herbs (*erbe aromatice*) and salad (*insalata*)

Asparagi	Asparagus	Insalata verde/mista	Green salad/mixed salad
Carciofi	Artichokes		
Carciofini	Artichoke hearts	Lenticchie	Lentils
Cavolfiori	Cauliflower	Melanzane	Aubergine
Cávolo	Cabbage	Patate	Potatoes
Cipolla	Onion	Peperoni	Peppers
Fagioli	Beans	Piselli	Peas
Fagiolini	Green beans	Pomodori	Tomatoes
Finocchio	Fennel	Radicchio	Red salad leaves
Funghi	Mushrooms	Spinaci	Spinach

Some terms and useful words

Arrosto	Roast	Alla griglia	Grilled
Ben cotto	Well done	Alla milanese	Fried in egg and breadcrumbs
Bollito/lesso	Boiled		
Alla brace	Barbecued	Pizzaiola	Cooked with tomato sauce
Cotto	Cooked (not raw)		
Crudo	Raw	Ripieno	Stuffed
Al dente	Firm, not overcooked	Al sangue	Rare
Al ferri	Grilled without oil	Allo spiedo	On the spit
Al forno	Baked	Stracotto	Braised, stewed
Fritto	Fried	In umido	Stewed

Cheese (*formaggi*)

Dolcelatte	Creamy blue cheese	Pecorino	Strong, hard sheep's cheese
Fontina	Northern Italian cheese, often used in cooking	Provola/Provolone	Smooth, round mild cheese, made from buffalo or sheep's milk; sometimes smoked
Gorgonzola	Soft, strong, blue-veined cheese		
Mozzarella	Soft white cheese, traditionally made from buffalo's milk	Ricotta	Soft, white sheep's cheese

Sweets (*dolci*), fruit (*frutta*) and nuts (*noci*)

Amaretti	Macaroons	Mándorle	Almonds
Ananas	Pineapple	Mele	Apples
Anguria/Coccómero	Watermelon	Melone	Melon
Arance	Oranges	Pere	Pears
Banane	Bananas	Pesche	Peaches
Cacchi	Persimmons	Pignoli	Pine nuts
Ciliegie	Cherries	Pistacchio	Pistachio nut
Fichi	Figs	Torta	Cake, tart
Fichi d'India	Prickly pears	Uva	Grapes
Frágole	Strawberries	Zabaglione	Dessert made with eggs, sugar and marsala wine
Gelato	Ice cream		
Limone	Lemon		
Macedonia	Fruit salad	Zuppa Inglese	Trifle

Drinks

Acqua minerale	Mineral water	Succo	Concentrated fruit juice with sugar
Aranciata	Orangeade		
Bicchiere	Glass	Tè	Tea
Birra	Beer	Tónica	Tonic water
Bottiglia	Bottle	Vino	Wine
Caffè	Coffee	Rosso	Red
Cioccolata calda	Hot chocolate	Bianco	White
Ghiaccio	Ice	Rosato	Rosé
Granita	Iced drink, with coffee or fruit	Secco	Dry
		Dolce	Sweet
Latte	Milk	Litro	Litre
Limonata	Lemonade	Mezzo	Half
Selz	Soda water	Quarto	Quarter
Spremuta	Fresh fruit juice	Caraffa	Carafe
Spumante	Sparkling wine	Salute!	Cheers!

Rough Guides

advertiser

...music & reference

Also! More than 120 Rough Guide music CDs are available from all good book
and record stores. Listen in at www.worldmusic.net

Don't bury your head in the sand!

Take cover!

with Rough Guide Travel Insurance

Worldwide cover, for Rough Guide readers worldwide

UK Freefone **0800 015 09 06**
Worldwide **(+44) 1392 314 665**
Check the web at
www.roughguides.com/insurance

ROUGH GUIDES

Insurance organized by Torribles Insurance Brokers Ltd, 21 Prince Street, Bristol, BS1 4PH, England

small print and

Index

A Rough Guide to Rough Guides

In the summer of 1981, Mark Ellingham, a recent graduate from Bristol University, was travelling round Greece and couldn't find a guidebook that really met his needs. On the one hand there were the student guides, insistent on saving every last cent, and on the other the heavyweight cultural tomes whose authors seemed to have spent more time in a research library than lounging away the afternoon at a taverna or on the beach.

In a bid to avoid getting a job, Mark and a small group of writers set about creating their own guidebook. It was a guide to Greece that aimed to combine a journalistic approach to description with a thoroughly practical approach to travellers' needs – a guide that would incorporate culture, history and contemporary insights with a critical edge, together with up-to-date, value-for-money listings. Back in London, Mark and the team finished their Rough Guide, as they called it, and talked Routledge into publishing the book.

That first *Rough Guide to Greece*, published in 1982, was a student scheme that became a publishing phenomenon. The immediate success of the book – with numerous reprints and a Thomas Cook prize shortlisting – spawned a series that rapidly covered dozens of destinations. Rough Guides had a ready market among low-budget backpackers, but soon also acquired a much broader and older readership that relished Rough Guides' wit and inquisitiveness as much as their enthusiastic, critical approach. Everyone wants value for money, but not at any price.

Rough Guides soon began supplementing the "rougher" information about hostels and low-budget listings with the kind of detail on restaurants and quality hotels that independent-minded visitors on any budget might expect, whether on business in New York or trekking in Thailand.

These days the guides – distributed worldwide by the Penguin group – offer recommendations from shoestring to luxury and cover more than 200 destinations around the globe, including almost every country in the Americas and Europe, more than half of Africa and most of Asia and Australasia. Our ever-growing team of authors and photographers is spread all over the world, particularly in Europe, the USA and Australia.

In 1994, we published the *Rough Guide to World Music* and the *Rough Guide to Classical Music*, and a year later the *Rough Guide to the Internet*. All three books have become benchmark titles in their fields – which encouraged us to expand into other areas of publishing, mainly around popular culture. Rough Guides now publish:

- Travel guides to more than 200 worldwide destinations
- Dictionary phrasebooks to 22 major languages
- History guides ranging from Ireland to Islam
- Maps printed on rip-proof and waterproof Polyart™ paper
- Music guides running the gamut from Opera to Elvis
- Restaurant guides to London, New York and San Francisco
- Reference books on topics as diverse as the Weather and Shakespeare
- Sports guides from Formula 1 to Man Utd
- Pop culture books from *Lord of the Rings* to Cult TV
- World Music CDs in association with World Music Network

Visit **www.roughguides.com** to see our latest publications.

Rough Guide credits

Text editor: Andy Turner
Layout: Jessica Subramanian, Ajay Verma
Cartography: Jai Prakash Mishra,
Rajesh Mishra
Picture research: Mark Thomas
Proofreader: Carole Mansur
Editorial: **London** Martin Dunford, Kate
Berens, Helena Smith, Claire Saunders, Geoff
Howard, Gavin Thomas, Ruth Blackmore,
Polly Thomas, Richard Lim, Lucy Ratcliffe,
Clifton Wilkinson, Alison Murchie, Fran
Sandham, Sally Schafer, Alexander Mark
Rogers, Karoline Densley, Andy Turner, Ella
O'Donnell, Keith Drew, Andrew Lockett, Joe
Staines, Duncan Clark, Peter Buckley,
Matthew Milton; **New York** Andrew
Rosenberg, Richard Koss, Hunter Slaton,
Chris Barsanti, Steven Horak
Design & Pictures: **London** Simon Bracken,
Dan May, Diana Jarvis, Mark Thomas, Jj
Luck, Harriet Mills; **Delhi** Madhulita
Mohapatra, Umesh Aggarwal, Ajay Verma,
Jessica Subramanian

Production: Julia Bovis, John McKay,
Sophie Hewat
Cartography: **London** Maxine Repath, Ed
Wright, Katie Lloyd-Jones, Miles Irving; **Delhi**
Manish Chandra, Rajesh Chhibber, Jai
Prakash Mishra, Ashutosh Bharti, Rajesh
Mishra, Animesh Pathak, Jasbir Sandhu,
Karobi Gogoi
Cover art direction: Louise Boulton
Online: **New York** Jennifer Gold, Cree
Lawson, Suzanne Welles, Benjamin Ross;
Delhi Manik Chauhan, Narender Kumar,
Shekhar Jha, Rakesh Kumar
Marketing & Publicity: **London** Richard
Trillo, Niki Smith, David Wearn, Chloë
Roberts, Demelza Dallow, Kristina Pentland;
New York Geoff Colquitt, Megan Kennedy
Finance: Gary Singh
Manager Delhi: Punita Singh
Series editor: Mark Ellingham
PA to Managing Director: Julie Sanderson
Managing Director: Kevin Fitzgerald

Publishing information

This second edition published January 2005 by
Rough Guides Ltd,
80 Strand, London WC2R 0RL.
345 Hudson St, 4th Floor,
New York, NY 10014, USA.
Distributed by the Penguin Group
Penguin Books Ltd,
80 Strand, London WC2R 0RL
Penguin Putnam, Inc.
375 Hudson Street, NY 10014, USA
Penguin Books Australia Ltd,
487 Maroondah Highway, PO Box 257,
Ringwood, Victoria 3134, Australia
Penguin Books Canada Ltd,
10 Alcorn Avenue, Toronto, Ontario,
Canada M4V 1E4
Penguin Books (NZ) Ltd,
182–190 Wairau Road, Auckland 10,
New Zealand
Typeset in Bembo and Helvetica to an original
design by Henry Iles.

Printed in Italy by LegoPrint S.p.A

© Martin Dunford 2005

320pp includes index
A catalogue record for this book is available from
the British Library

ISBN 1-85828-901-7

The publishers and authors have done their best
to ensure the accuracy and currency of all the
information in **The Rough Guide to Rome**;
however, they can accept no responsibility for any
loss, injury, or inconvenience sustained by any
traveller as a result of information or advice
contained in the guide.

1   3   5   7   9   8   6   4   2

Help us update

We've gone to a lot of effort to ensure that the
second edition of **The Rough Guide to Rome**
is accurate and up to date. However, things
change – places get "discovered", opening
hours are notoriously fickle, restaurants and
rooms raise prices or lower standards. If you
feel we've got it wrong or left something out,
we'd like to know, and if you can remember
the address, the price, the time, the phone
number, so much the better.

We'll credit all contributions, and send a
copy of the next edition (or any other Rough

Guide if you prefer) for the best letters.
Everyone who writes to us and isn't already a
subscriber will receive a copy of our full-
colour, thrice-yearly newsletter. Please mark
letters: **"Rough Guide Rome Update"** and
send to: Rough Guides, 80 Strand, London
WC2R 0RL, or Rough Guides, 4th Floor, 345
Hudson St, New York, NY 10014. Or send an
email to **mail@roughguides.com**
Have your questions answered and tell
others about your trip at
www.roughguides.atinfopop.com

Acknowledgements

Martin would like to thank Norm and Jeffrey for their usual, excellent contributions; Andy Turner, whose careful attention to detail has made this into a much better guide; James McConnachie for taking some great photos, and Mark Thomas for helping to choose them and additional photo research; Philippa Hopkins for a great index; and finally Caroline and Daisy for past, present and future days in Rome.

The editor would also like to thank Ajay Verma and Jessica Subramanian for skillful layout; Jai Prakash Mishra and Rajesh Mishra for the new maps; Carole Mansur for careful proofreading and Karoline Densley for unflappable editorial assistance.

Readers' letters

Thanks to all those readers who wrote in with updates to the first edition: Richard Fearn, Eric Vellend, Hans Jorgen, Monica Shelley, Sophie Gee, Sally James and Gerry Hill, Jennifer Colbert, Kath Dance, David Macdonald, Lorna Harper, Philip Livingstone, Larry Jackson, David Hollingsworth and Ian Bullock.

Photo credits

All images ©Rough Guides except the following:

Cover
Main picture car number plate
  ©Neil Setchfield
Small front top picture Colosseum
  ©Robert Harding
Small front lower picture Cator, Capitoline Hill
  ©Neil Setchfield
Back top picture Parthenon
  ©Robert Harding
Back lower picture Piazza Navona
  ©Neil Setchfield

Things not to miss
02 Francesco Totti, Roma ©EMPICS/Studio Buzzi
04 Bust of Hadrian, Museo Nazionale Romano (Palazzo Massimo alle Terme) ©Foto Scala, Firenze – su concessione Ministero Beni e Attività Culturali
10 Relief of flute player on the Ludovici throne, Museo Nazionale Romano (Palazzo Altemps) Roma ©Foto Scala

16 *The Fall of Man* by Michelangelo (1475–1564), Sistine Chapel ceiling ©Vatican Museums and Galleries, Vatican City, Italy/Bridgeman Art Library
18 *Lady with Unicorn* by Raphael (1483–1520), Galleria Borghese ©Foto Scala, Firenze – su concessione Ministero Beni e Attività Culturali
21 The Colosseum ©Nick Hanmer
22 Hand of Constantine, fragment of colossal statue, Capitoline Museums ©Foto Scala
26 *School of Athens* from the Stanza della Segnatura by Raphael (1483–1520) ©Vatican Museums and Galleries, Vatican City, Italy/Bridgeman Art Library Giraudon/Bridgeman Art Library
32 *Portrait of Pope Innocent X* by Diego Rodriguez de Silva y Velasquez (1599–1660) ©Galleria Doria Pamphilj, Rome, Italy/Bridgeman Art Library

SMALL PRINT

Index

Map entries are in **colour**

INDEX

INDEX

P

Map symbols

maps are listed in the full index using coloured text

– – –	Chapter boundary	🅃	Toilets
▬▬▬	Motorway	ⓘ	Information office
═══	Major road	∴	Ruin
═══	Minor road	✈	Airport
▬▬	Pedestrianized road	Ⓜ	Metro station
�咖啡	Steps	✡	Synagogue
- - - -	Path	⊠	Post office
━─━	Railway	⊞	Hospital
────	River	🅿	Parking
────	Wall	▬	Building
‿‿	Bridge	⊞	Church
⚠	Campsite	⬭	Stadium
◆	Place of interest	⁺₊⁺	Christian cemetery
⚑	Fountain	▨	Park

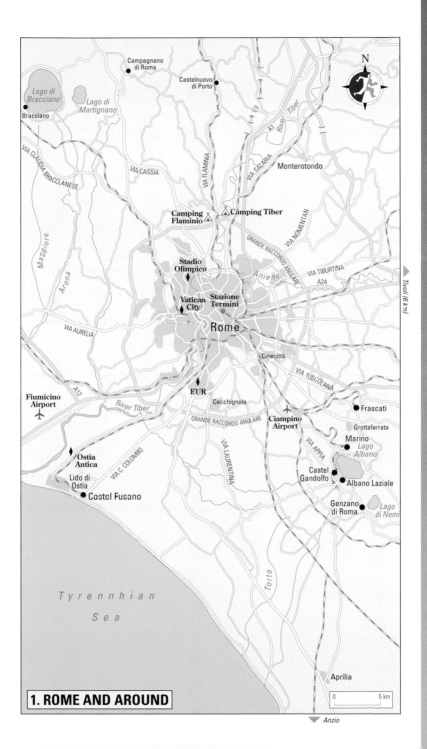

1. ROME AND AROUND

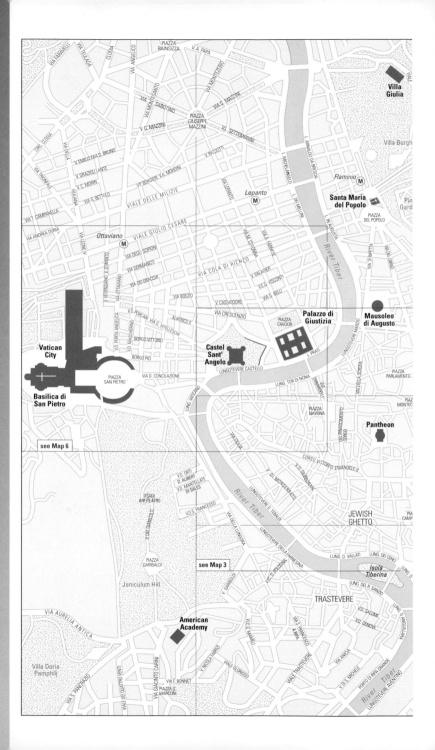

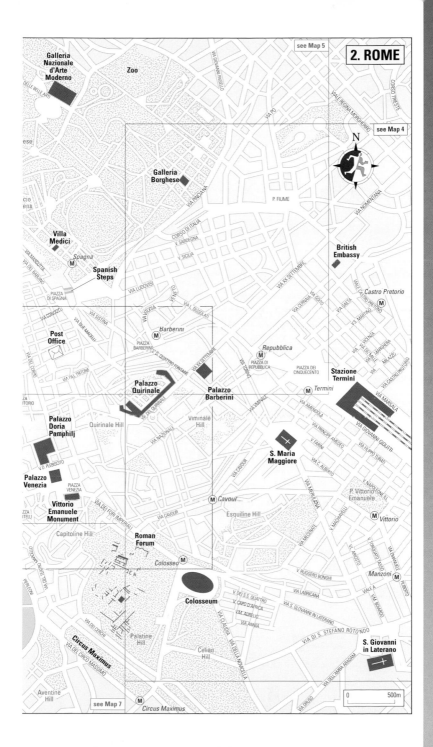

Galleria
Nazionale
d'Arte
Moderno

Zoo

N

Galleria
Borghese

P. FIUME

Villa
Medici

Spagna Ⓜ

Spanish
Steps

PIAZZA
DI SPAGNA

British
Embassy

Castro Pretorio Ⓜ

Post
Office

Barberini Ⓜ

PIAZZA
BARBERINI

Repubblica

Ⓜ

PIAZZA DI
REPUBBLICA

PIAZZA DEI
CINQUECENTO

Stazione
Termini

Palazzo
Quirinale

Palazzo
Barberini

Ⓜ Termini

Palazzo
Doria
Pamphilj

Quirinale Hill

Viminale
Hill

Palazzo
Venezia

PIAZZA
VENEZIA

S. Maria
Maggiore

P. Vittorio II
Emanuele

Vittorio Ⓜ

Vittorio
Emanuele
Monument

Ⓜ Cavour

Esquiline Hill

Capitoline Hill

Roman
Forum

Colosseo Ⓜ

Manzoni Ⓜ

Colosseum

S. Giovanni
in Laterano

Circus Maximus

Palatine
Hill

Celian
Hill

Aventine
Hill

see Map 7

Ⓜ

Circus Maximus

0   500m

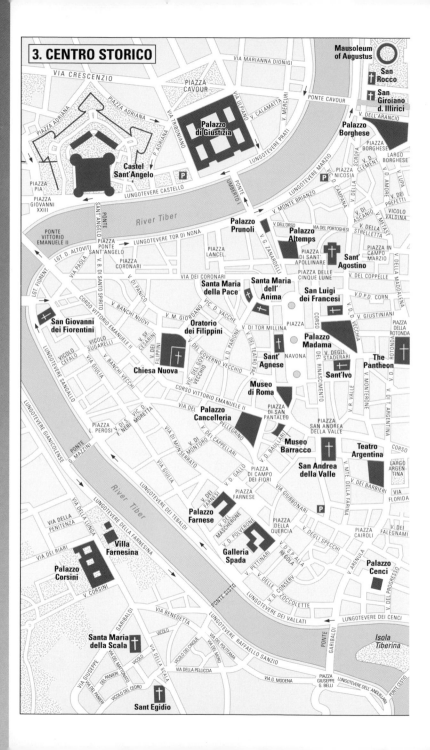

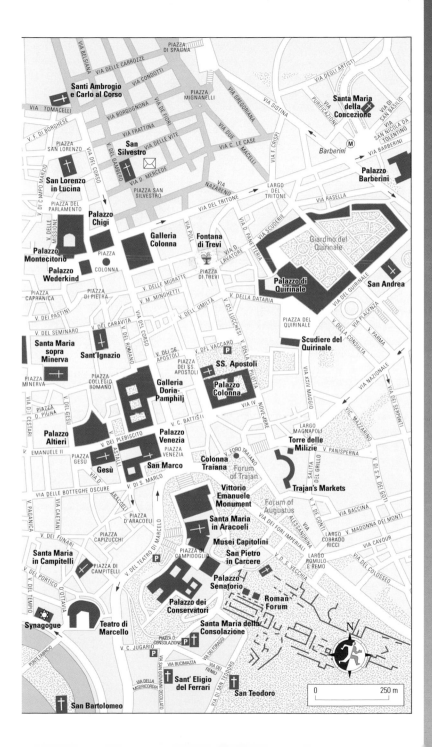

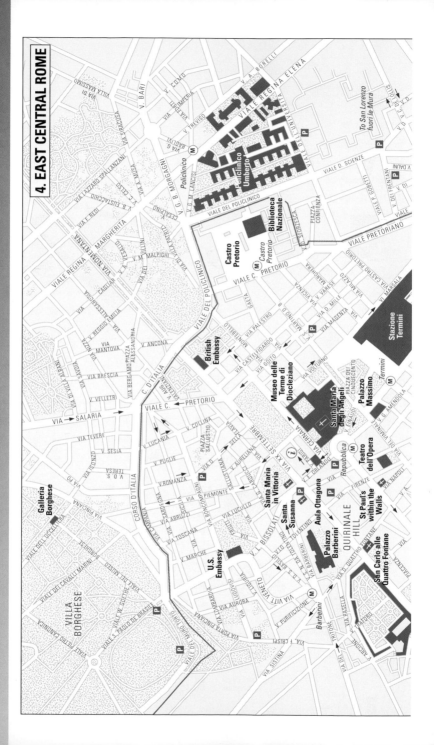

4. EAST CENTRAL ROME

VILLA BORGHESE

Galleria Borghese

U.S. Embassy

British Embassy

Museo delle Terme di Diocleziano

Santa Maria in Vittoria

Santa Susanna

Aula Ottagona

Palazzo Barberini

QUIRINALE HILL

St Paul's within the Walls

Teatro dell'Opera

San Carlo alle Quattro Fontane

Castro Pretorio

Biblioteca Nazionale

Policlinico Umberto

Santa Maria degli Angeli

Palazzo Massimo

Stazione Termini

To San Lorenzo fuori le Mura

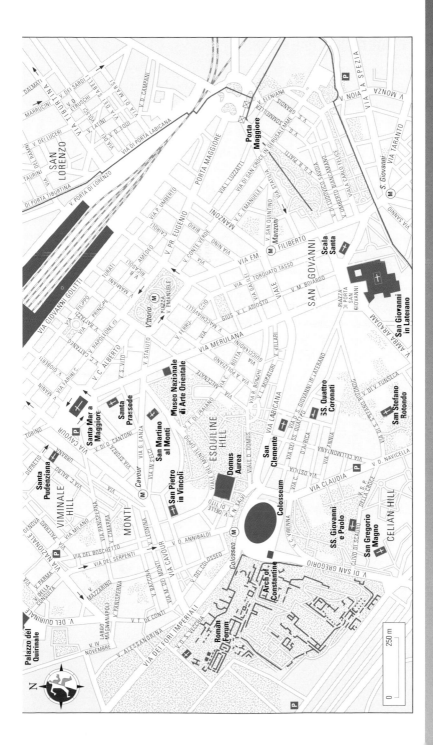

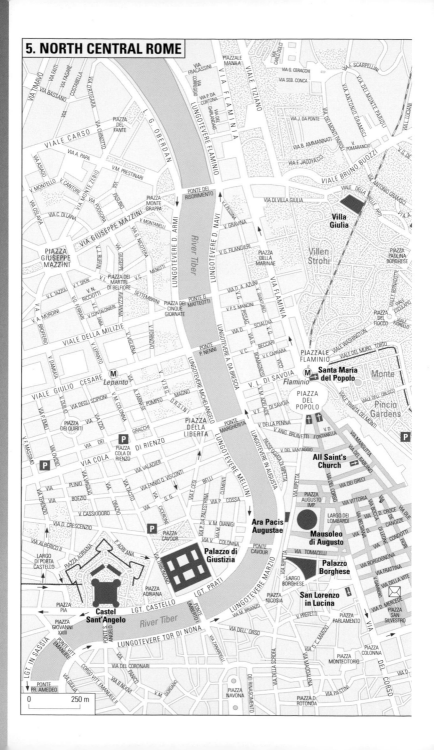

5. NORTH CENTRAL ROME

VIA FAITI
VIA FAGARE
COSTABELLA
VIA TIMAVIO
VIA BASSANO
VIA ORTIGARA
VIA CHINOTTO
VIALE CARSO
VIA A. PAPA
V.M. PRESTINARI
PIAZZA DEL FANTE
VIA ASAGO
V. MONTELLO
V. CANTORE
VIA MONTE ZEBIO
VIA PODGORA
VIA C. DI LANA
VIA OSLAVIA
VIALE GIUSEPPE MAZZINI
V.E. TAZZOLI
V.T. SPERI
V. N. RICCIOTTI
V. GIUSEPPE
VIA NICOTERA
VIA G. GIUSEPPE
VIA BIXIO
V.G. BUFFINI
PIAZZA DEI MARTIRI DI BELFIORE
V.C.
MENOTTI

PIAZZA GIUSEPPE MAZZINI
VIG. FERRARI
V.E. CONTALDONER
SETTEMBRINI
ATTEZZANNA
PIAZZA DEI CINQUE GIORNATE
V.A. MORDINI
BROFFERIO
VIALE DELLA MILIZIE
V.F. CORIOLANO
V.VIGLIENA
V.F. CAVALOTTI
V.E. LEPANTO

PIAZZALE MANILA
VIA FRACASSINI
VIA CORRIDORI
VIA P. DA CORTONA
VIA DEL GIANICOLO
VIALE TIZIANO
VIA G. CERACCHI
VIA SEB. CONCA
VIA ANTONIO DEL MONTE PARIOLI
VIA J. DA PONTE
VIA DEL MONTE PARIOLI
V. POMARANCIO
VIA F. JACOVACCI
VIALE BRUNO BUOZZI
VIA ANTONIO GRAMSCI

PONTE DEI RISORIMENTO
PIAZZA MONTE GRAPPA
V. MONTANELLI
PIAZZALE FLAMINIO
VIA FLAMINIA
V. GRAVINA
V.G. FILANGIERI
PIAZZA DELLA MARINAE
VIA DI VILLA GIULIA

Villa Giulia

Villen Strohi

PIAZZA PAOLINA BORGHESE

River Tiber
LUNGOTEVERE FLAMINIO
LUNGOTEVERE D. ARMI
LUNGOTEVERE D. NAVI
V. VESSINA
PONTE G. MATTEOTTI
PIAZZA DEI CINQUE GIORNATE
VIA D. A. AZUNI
VIA FLAMINIA
V.P.S. MANCINI
SCIALOIA
VIA D.
V.C.
BECCARI
V.E. FARRARA
V.C. ROMAGNOSI
PIAZZALE FLAMINIO
VIALE WASHINGTON
VIALE DEL MURO TORTO

PONTE P. NENNI
LUNGOTEVERE A. DA BRESCIA
VIA D.
V.L. DI SAVOIA
Flaminio M Santa Maria del Popolo
Monte

VIALE GIULIO CESARE
VIA DEGLI SCIPIONI
V.M. COLONNA
FARNESE POMPEO
O.R.S.I.N.I
MAGNO
PIAZZA DELLA LIBERTA
PONTE MARGHERITA
V.L. DI SAVOIA
V.F. ADELE
PIAZZA DEL POPOLO
VIA DELL'OBELISCO
Pincia Gardens
VIALE TRINITÀ DEI MONTI

PIAZZA DEI QUIRITI
VIA P. EMILI
VIA EZIO
VIA DEI GRACCHI
PIAZZA COLA DI RIENZO
VIA COLA
VIA DI RIENZO
V.F. DELLA PENNA
V.ANG. BRUNETTI FONTANELLA
V. D.
VIA MARGUTTA
VIA DEL BABUINO
VIA DEI GRECI
VIA VITTORIA
VIA DELLE CROCE
VIA DELLE CANOZZE
VIA DELLE CONDOTTI

V.E. MASSIMO
VIA OVIDIO
PLINIO
VIA VIRGILIO
V. TACITO
VIA VALADIER
VIA ENNIO Q. VISCONTI
G.G.
VIA P. COSSA
VIA DEL VANTAGGIO
LUNGOTEVERE IN AUGUSTA

All Saint's Church

VIA BOEZIO
V. CASSIODORO
VIA CICERONE
V.M. DIANIGI
V.M. COLONNA
PONTE CAVOUR
Ara Pacis Augustae
PIAZZA AUGUSTO IMP.
LARGO DEI LOMBARDI
Mausoleo di Augusto
VIA TOMACELLI
Palazzo Borghese
VIA BORGOGNONA
VIA FRATTINA
VIA DELLA VITE

VIA ALBERICO II
VIA D. CRESCENZIO
PIAZZA CAVOUR
Palazzo di Giustizia
LUNGOTEVERE MARZIO
LARGO BORGHESE
PIAZZA NICOSIA
San Lorenzo in Lucina
PIAZZA SAN SILVESTRO
VIA D. MERCEDE

LARGO DI PORTA CASTELLO
PIAZZA ADRIANA
P. ADRIANA
PIAZZA ADRIANA
LGT. PRATI
PONTE UMBERTO I
VIA M. BRIANZO
V. PREFETTI
PIAZZA PARLAMENTO

PIAZZA PIA
Castel Sant'Angelo
LGT. CASTELLO
River Tiber
VIA DELL'ORSO
PIAZZA MONTECITORIO
PIAZZA COLONNA

PIAZZA GIOVANNI XXIII
PONTE VITT. EMANUELE
LUNGOTEVERE TOR DI NONA
VIA DEL CORONARI
VIA DELLA SCROFA
VIA C.S. MAGGIO
VIA MADDALENA
PIAZZA D.

LGT. IN SASSIA
PONTE PR. AMEDEO
CORSO VITT. EMANUELE II
V.B. NUOVA
V.M.
PIAZZA NAVONA
PIAZZA DI RINASCIMENTO
PIAZZA D. ROTONDA

0   250 m

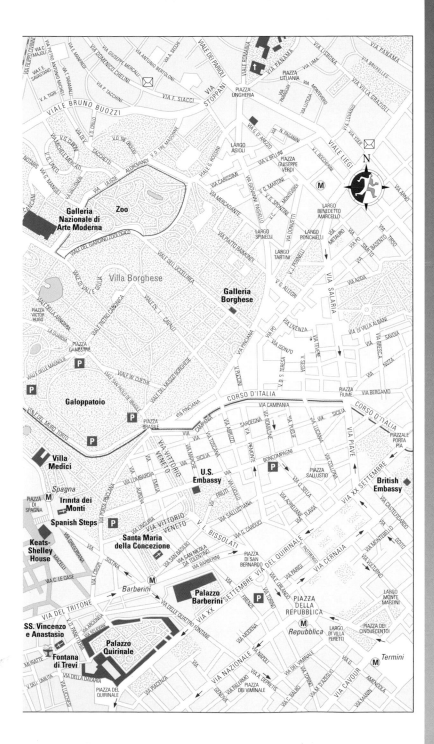

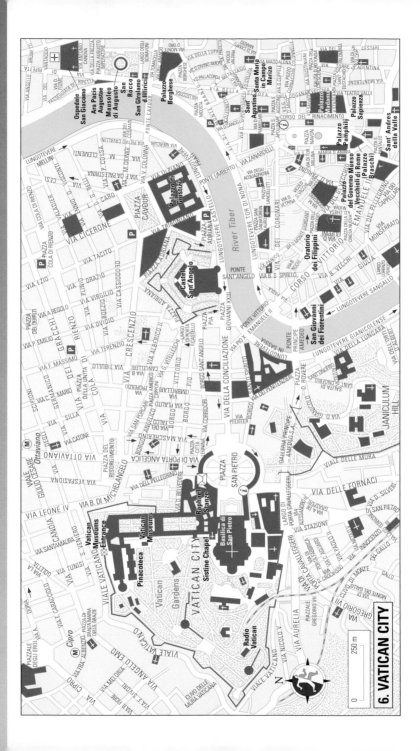

6. VATICAN CITY

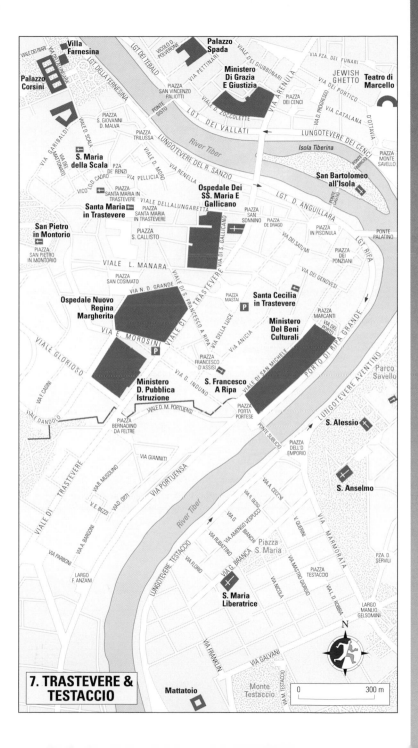

7. TRASTEVERE & TESTACCIO

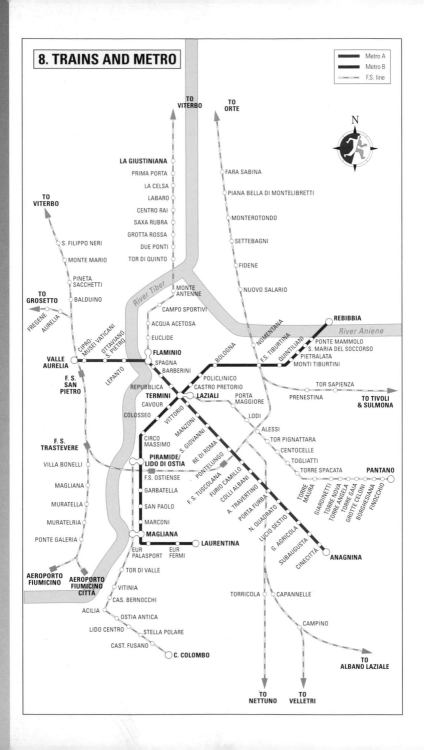

8. TRAINS AND METRO

Metro A
Metro B
F.S. line

N

TO
VITERBO

TO
ORTE

LA GIUSTINIANA
PRIMA PORTA
LA CELSA
LABARO
CENTRO RAI
SAXA RUBRA
GROTTA ROSSA
DUE PONTI
TOR DI QUINTO

FARA SABINA
PIANA BELLA DI MONTELIBRETTI
MONTEROTONDO
SETTEBAGNI
FIDENE
NUOVO SALARIO

TO
VITERBO

S. FILIPPO NERI
MONTE MARIO
PINETA
SACCHETTI
BALDUINO

TO
GROSETTO

FREGENE
AURELIA

River Tiber

MONTE
ANTENNE

CAMPO SPORTIVI

ACQUA ACETOSA

EUCLIDE

FLAMINIO
SPAGNA
BARBERINI

BOLOGNA

NOMENTANA
F.S. TIBURTINA
QUINTILIANI

REBIBBIA
River Aniene
PONTE MAMMOLO
S. MARIA DEL SOCCORSO
PIETRALATA
MONTI TIBURTINI

VALLE
AURELIA

F. S.
SAN
PIETRO

CIPRO-
MUSEI VATICANI
OTTAVIANO
S. PIETRO
LEPANTO

REPUBBLICA
TERMINI
CAVOUR
COLOSSEO

VITTORIO

LAZIALI

POLICLINICO
CASTRO PRETORIO

PORTA
MAGGIORE

LODI

TOR SAPIENZA
PRENESTINA

TO TIVOLI
& SULMONA

F. S.
TRASTEVERE

VILLA BONELLI
MAGLIANA
MURATELLA
MURATELRIA
PONTE GALERIA

CIRCO
MASSIMO

PIRAMIDE/
LIDO DI OSTIA
F.S. OSTIENSE
GARBATELLA
SAN PAOLO
MARCONI
MAGLIANA

MANZONI
S. GIOVANNI
RE DI ROMA
PONTELUNGO
F.S. TUSCOLANA
FURIO CAMILLO
COLLI ALBANI
A. TRAVERTINO
PORTA FURBA
N. QUADRATO
LUCIO SESTIO
G. AGRICOLA
SUBAUGUSTA
CINECITTÀ

ALESSI
TOR PIGNATTARA
CENTOCELLE
TOGLIATTI
TORRE SPACATA

PANTANO

TORRE
MAURA
GIARDINETTI
TORRE NOVA
TORRE ANGELA
TORRE GAIA
GROTTE CELONI
BORGHESIANA
FINOCCHIO

EUR
PALASPORT
EUR
FERMI

LAURENTINA

ANAGNINA

AEROPORTO
FIUMICINO

AEROPORTO
FIUMICINO
CITTÀ

TOR DI VALLE
VITINIA
CAS. BERNOCCHI
ACILIA
OSTIA ANTICA
LIDO CENTRO
STELLA POLARE
CAST. FUSANO

TORRICOLA
CAPANNELLE

CAMPINO

C. COLOMBO

TO
NETTUNO

TO
VELLETRI

TO
ALBANO LAZIALE